France since the 1970s

France since the 1970s

1970s

History, Politics and Memory in an Age of Uncertainty

Edited by Emile Chabal

Bloomsbury Academic
An imprint of Bloomsbury Publishing Plc

BLOOMSBURY

LONDON · NEW DELHI · NEW YORK · SYDNEY

Bloomsbury Academic

An imprint of Bloomsbury Publishing Plc

50 Bedford Square	1385 Broadway
London	New York
WC1B 3DP	NY 10018
UK	USA

www.bloomsbury.com

First published 2015

British Library Cataloguing-in-Publication Data
A catalogue record for this book is available from the British Library.

ISBN: HB: 978-1-4725-0613-9
PB: 978-1-4725-0977-2
ePDF: 978-1-4725-0636-8
ePub: 978-1-4725-0744-0

Library of Congress Cataloging-in-Publication Data
France since the 1970s : history, politics and memory in an age of uncertainty / edited by Emile Chabal.
pages cm
Includes bibliographical references and index.
ISBN 978-1-4725-0977-2 (pbk.) — ISBN 978-1-4725-0613-9 (hardback) —
ISBN 978-1-4725-0636-8 (epdf) — ISBN 978-1-4725-0744-0 (epub)
1. France—Politics and government—1958– 2. France—Politics and government–1974–1981. 3. France—Politics and government—1981–1995. 4. France—Politics and government—1995-2007. I. Chabal, Emile.
DC417.F716 2014
944.083—dc23
2014017403.

Typeset by RefineCatch Limited, Bungay, Suffolk
Printed and bound in India

CONTENTS

LIST OF ILLUSTRATIONS

LIST OF CONTRIBUTORS

Emile Chabal is a Chancellor's Fellow in History at the University of Edinburgh. His research focuses on postwar French political culture, Franco–British relations and local politics in the Languedoc. His first book, *A Divided Republic: Nation, state and citizenship in contemporary France*, will be published by Cambridge University Press in 2015.

Michael C. Behrent is Associate Professor of History at Appalachian State University. He has published articles on religion in nineteenth-century French political thought and on the intellectual legacy of Michel Foucault in *The Journal of Modern History*, *Modern Intellectual History*, and *Journal of the History of Ideas*.

Daniel A. Gordon is Senior Lecturer in European History at Edge Hill University and a member of the editorial board of the journal *Modern and Contemporary France*. His research focuses on the history of social movements, especially the international movements of 1968; intertwined histories of migration, racism and anti-racism in France from the 1930s to the present day; and the history from below of transport users. He is the author of *Immigrants and Intellectuals: May '68 and the rise of anti-racism in France*, published in paperback by Merlin Press in 2012.

Sophie Guérard de Latour is Maître de conférences at the Université Paris 1-Panthéon-Sorbonne, France. She works on multicultural issues related to contemporary theories of justice and of democratic citizenship, with a specific focus on republicanism. She has recently published *Vers la république des différences* (2009), and co-edited (with Peter Balint) *Liberal Multiculturalism and the Fair Terms of Integration* (2013). Her articles have appeared in journals such as *Raison publique*, *Revue philosophique de Louvain*, *Ateliers de l'éthique*, *Diacritica* and *Politics in Central Europe*.

Sudhir Hazareesingh is a Fellow in Politics at Balliol College. His research focuses on modern French political culture. His most recent book was *In the Shadow of the General: Modern France and the myth of de Gaulle* (2012).

Nick Hewlett is Professor of French Studies at the University of Warwick. He has published widely on French politics and political thought. His most recent book is *The Sarkozy Phenomenon*, published by Imprint Academic in 2011, and he is currently writing a book on ethics and political violence.

Isabel Hollis is a research fellow at the Institute for Collaborative Research in the Humanities at Queen's University Belfast. Her research focuses on postcolonial migration and colonial memory between North Africa and France. She has published articles on gender and migration, on French integration, and the literature and film that represents migration. Her first book, *Belonging Together: Narratives of family migration from North Africa to France*, will be published in 2014 by IGRS Books.

Patricia M. E. Lorcin is Professor of History at the University of Minnesota–Twin Cities. Her research focuses on French and Western imperialism. Her published works include *Imperial Identities: Stereotyping, prejudice and race in colonial Algeria* (1995), *Historicizing Colonial Nostalgia: European women's narratives of Algeria and Kenya 1900–present* (2012), several edited volumes, and numerous articles on different aspects of French or Western imperialism.

Pascal Perrineau is Professor of Political Science at Sciences Po (Paris). His research focuses on the rise of national-populism as an electoral force, and on political divisions in France and Europe. His latest book, *La France au Front: Essai sur l'avenir du Front National*, was published by Fayard in 2014.

Christophe Prochasson is a Directeur d'études at the École des hautes études en sciences sociales (EHESS), Paris, and the recteur of the Académie de Caen. He has published widely on French cultural history in the nineteenth and twentieth centuries. He is particularly interested in the history of intellectual engagement in France, the socio-cultural history of the Third Republic, the origins of French socialism, and the First World War. His most recent books include *14–18. Retours d'expériences* (2008), *La Gauche est-elle morale?* (2010), and a major biography of the historian François Furet, *François Furet. Les Chemins de la mélancolie* (2013).

Camille Robcis is Assistant Professor of History at Cornell University. Her research deals with three broad themes: the relationship between intellectuals, ideas, and politics; the historical construction of norms; and the articulation of universalism and difference in modern France. Her first book, *The Law of Kinship: Anthropology, psychoanalysis, and the family in twentieth-century France*, was published by Cornell University Press in 2013.

Yann Scioldo-Zürcher is a Chargé de recherche at the CNRS and a member of the MIGRINTER research group at the Université de Poitiers (UMR 7301). His early work was on the migration of the French *rapatriés* who left

Algeria after independence in 1962. This resulted in a monograph entitled *Devenir métropolitain: Politique d'intégration et parcours de rapatriés d'Algérie en métropole (1954–2005)* (2010). His current work focuses on Jewish postcolonial migrations in France, Canada and Israel.

James Shields is Professor of French Politics and Modern History, and Head of French Studies at Aston University. He specialises in the history and politics of the far right, and is the author of *The Extreme Right in France: From Pétain to Le Pen* (2007). He has published recent articles and special issues in *Parliamentary Affairs*, *Politics*, *French Politics*, and *French Politics, Culture and Society*. He was the inaugural winner in 2007–9 of the American Political Science Association's Stanley Hoffmann Best Article Award. He is a Fellow of the Academy of Social Sciences and a regular media commentator on French politics.

Iain Stewart is a Lecturer in Modern European History at Queen Mary, University of London. He works on twentieth-century French intellectual history, with a particular emphasis on the political thought of Raymond Aron. He has published articles in *History of European Ideas*, *European Review of History*, and *Sartre Studies International*, and is currently working on a monograph about Aron and the French liberal revival.

ACKNOWLEDGEMENTS

The idea for this volume emerged from a workshop entitled 'French politics in an age of uncertainty', which was held at the Maison Française d'Oxford on 15 September 2012. This could not have taken place without the patient encouragement of Sudhir Hazareesingh: my first thanks are to him. I would also like to give a special mention to the wonderful staff at the Maison Française for their help, in particular Claire Stevenson and Anne Simonin. Funding for the event was provided by the John Fell Fund, the Society for the Study of French History, the Society for French Studies, and the Faculty of History, University of Oxford.

The success of any workshop or edited volume rests almost entirely on the shoulders of contributors and I have been very fortunate that so many interesting scholars have been willing to take part in this project. Of those who participated in the original workshop, most have chosen to publish their work in this volume, for which I am very grateful. But I am equally indebted to those who supported me from an early stage and whose work is not represented here, especially Claire Eldridge, Cécile Laborde and Robert Gildea. At Bloomsbury, Frances Arnold, Rhodri Mogford and Emma Goode did an excellent job in approving and preparing the book for publication.

On a more personal note, I would like to thank my wife, Akhila Yechury, and my mother for their love, support and forbearance. This book is dedicated to my father, who died while I was preparing the final manuscript. His deep commitment to academia and his scholarly integrity will always be an inspiration to me.

Introduction

French Politics in an Age of Uncertainty

Emile Chabal

It has now become a cliché to say that France is 'in crisis'. Polling organisations repeatedly claim that the French are the 'most depressed' people in Europe, the most 'hostile' to capitalism of any advanced Western economy, and the most unsure of their 'identity'.[1] This unease is echoed in much of the scholarly literature about contemporary France, which denounces the country's 'pathologies', 'scleroses' and 'contradictions'.[2] In the press and the media, commentators draw unflattering comparisons between a 'French model' and a 'Nordic', 'Anglo-Saxon' or 'Germanic' model.[3] And, although politicians desperately reassure their audiences that they will cure France's many ills, this has not stopped French intellectuals from bemoaning the 'malheur français' and urging a 'morose' population to halt the country's inexorable 'fall'.[4] Even the literary élite have joined the chorus of complaints. After spending more than ten years in Ireland and Spain, the well-known author Michel Houllebecq returned to France in early 2013. When journalists asked about his attitude to his home country, he replied in characteristically grumpy fashion that the French have a 'knack for depression'.[5]

There is plenty of needless polemic amid the talk of decline, but we should not dismiss all of it as mere idle chatter. Quite apart from being an indicator of the deep unease in France about the future of the nation, I have argued elsewhere that this pervasive language of crisis is an expression of France's liberal tradition and serves a vital political function by galvanising recalcitrant groups around the idea of reform and change.[6] Yet it would be equally unwise to take every popular and scholarly assertion about France's crisis at face value. This is especially true with respect to contemporary French politics, which has often been the focal point for criticism from all sides of the political spectrum. For those on the left and extreme-left, French politics has become a dismal spectacle, with different brands of centrism facing off one against the other. This view was succinctly captured in the idea of 'la pensée unique', a term that emerged in the mid-1990s to describe the supposedly hegemonic neo-liberal ideology that was said to have taken hold among France's ruling élites.[7] The paradox is that those very same politicians, senior civil servants and business leaders who are seen as the repository of the 'pensée unique' are themselves deeply dissatisfied with the status quo. In the pages of learned journals like *Commentaire* and *Le Débat*, they deplore French 'immobilism' and the country's inability to undertake 'necessary' structural reforms. Almost four decades since the sociologist Michel Crozier diagnosed France as a 'blocked society', strangled by an ossified bureaucracy and an unwieldy state, nothing much seems to have changed.[8]

The result of these parallel discourses of decline – one from the left and far-left, the other from the liberal centre-left and centre-right – has been to obscure many of the fundamental changes that have taken place in French politics. These include the reconfiguration of political affiliations, the transformation of the extreme-left and extreme-right, and the reshaping of French intellectual life after the evaporation of a post-war Marxist consensus. With rare exceptions, these themes have all tended to be discussed in terms of an overall decline in the 'quality' or 'exceptionalism' of French politics.[9] Other themes – such as France's colonial legacy and the question of immigration – have played a prominent part in public debate and generated a good deal of exciting new scholarly literature, but the general atmosphere of gloom has meant that they have often been analysed in a resolutely negative light. For instance, the struggles over the memory of the Algerian War or the resurgence of a neo-republican rhetoric of integration have been cast as examples of the extent to which a paralysed French political culture has failed to adapt to a brave new world of globalisation, cultural cosmopolitanism and insecurity.[10]

I would argue that this view is both misleading and misguided. In fact, the premise of this book is not so much that France has struggled to adapt to the twenty-first century but that scholars of France have struggled to come up with innovative ways of understanding contemporary French politics. One important reason for this is that, since the 1970s, almost every aspect of French politics has been transformed. Marxism and Communism were pushed out of mainstream politics in the wave of anti-totalitarian thought that swept across the French left in the period from 1975 to 1985.[11] Gaullism struggled to retain its identity after the right's defeat in 1981 and the rise of neo-liberalism in the 1980s.[12] Colonial and post-colonial memories – that had been held in check by economic growth – started to surface as the post-war economic boom came to an end in the late 1970s. Even at a supranational level, a French vision of European integration – so ardently championed by figures such as the former President of the European Commission, Jacques Delors – appeared inadequate to a post-Communist world.[13] As Pascal Perrineau points out in his chapter, these changes have made the political space increasingly difficult to interpret. In France (and elsewhere) traditional ideological faultlines have become blurred, while political parties and politicians no longer seem to know who their core constituencies are or, indeed, should be.

This uncertainty is not simply an issue for political actors; it is also a problem for historians and social scientists trying to analyse contemporary politics. In recent years, some of the most original approaches to the field have addressed this problem directly by imagining novel analytical frameworks that take into account the prevalence of political uncertainty. 'Age of fracture', 'the new spirit of capitalism', 'liquid modernity', 'post-Marxism': in each of these interpretations, there is an awareness that uncertainty is not simply a by-product of contemporary politics, but the very condition of its existence.[14] Mass democracies – of which France is a case in point – draw their strength from the apparent 'fickleness' of the electorate and the plasticity of ideology. The challenge, then, is not to dismiss the blurring of political affiliations as just another example of the 'decline' of politics, but to understand the kinds of debates, ideas, events and narratives around which political identities have tended to cluster and the socio-economic structures that underpin them. This kind of imaginative thinking about the meaning and boundaries of politics has a number of advantages. It helps avoid facile polemic or the temptation of excessive 'presentism'. It tries to elaborate more appropriate categories for understanding how and why people continue to engage with politics in an ever-more crowded ideological market. And, above all, by acknowledging political uncertainty, it works with, rather than against, the dominant concerns of contemporary politics.

This desire to analyse the fluid and uncertain structures of French politics is reflected in the book's structure. Each part is focused on one major theme, with four chapters arranged in broadly chronological order. The last chapter of each part is more explicitly conceptual or normative, thereby building on the insights of preceding chapters through discussions of such concepts as the 'passions', 'nostalgia' and 'solidarity'. Inevitably, there are many subjects that have been left untouched; one thinks especially of environmental politics, social movements and France's relationship with Europe. Nevertheless, the twelve contributions draw on a variety of expertise in different fields – from post-colonial theory and administrative history, to philosophy and political science – and discuss a wide range of different topics. The combination of close-grained historical analysis and normative reflection suggests alternative approaches and makes it possible to explore France's obsession with the past as well as its response to a rapidly-changing contemporary context. Perhaps most importantly, the varied contributions paint a picture of a state and society that have, since the 1970s, tried to adapt to a new political context. As many of the contributors make clear, there is no agreement over whether this adaptation has been a success or a failure – and nor should there be given how recently many of the events discussed below took place. But, if nothing else, France's 'crisis' has given us a unique opportunity to look closely at some of the most pressing political issues of the twenty-first century.

Right and left: The end of an era?

Part One examines a perennial concern in the study of modern politics, namely the usefulness of the right and left divide. This issue has a particular resonance in France since the left–right classification has its origins in the arrangement of *députés* in the Assemblée nationale constituente during the French Revolution.[15] Symbolically at least, it was therefore the French who bequeathed the idea to the rest of the world. But this history did not permanently fix the meaning of right and left in political discourse. Indeed, the proliferation of alternative words to describe French political affiliations – most famously, the idea of a 'party of order' opposed to a 'party of movement' – suggests that there was very little agreement on how political battle lines should be drawn. This was exacerbated by the chronic weakness of French political parties throughout the nineteenth and twentieth centuries: parties decomposed and recomposed, changed their names and transformed themselves with bewildering speed, a tendency that has continued right up to the present day.[16] Thus, in contrast to, say, the United States, the United Kingdom or Germany, there has been no stable institutional repository for left- and right-wing values. Particular political figures and movements were variously associated with the right or the left at specific moments but the country's most emblematic leaders – such as Napoleon or de Gaulle – constantly sought to transcend any such division.

Nevertheless, for all their limitations, the terms 'right' and 'left' remained key markers in France's political vocabulary from the mid-nineteenth century onwards. Not everyone could agree on exactly what the terms meant, but voters and politicians were usually willing to identify themselves as right or left – and they were certainly willing to label their opponents as one or the other. Likewise, historians and political scientists took the left–right divide as a given; they provided two poles around which their analyses of French politics could be structured, even if this meant putting them in the plural ('les droites', 'les gauches').[17] More recently, however, the left–right divide has appeared increasingly unstable. As Perrineau argues in Chapter 1, the 1980s and 1990s saw a fragmentation of voter preferences. Migration and social mobility transformed hitherto stable voting blocs; electoral geographies were durably modified; and voters began to question the utility of the left–right divide. At the same time, abstention rates rose, and the traditional patterns of support for the parties of the left and right collapsed.

This meant, for instance, that the 'culture of the left' which Tony Judt described in his early work on French socialism was scarcely recognisable by the end of the twentieth century.[18] Similarly, since the 1990s, the traditional correlations between voting preferences and religious affiliation or socio-economic class have become increasingly unreliable. Political scientists today struggle to predict accurately which social groups will vote for which parties.

One of the major consequences of this realignment of voter preferences has been a transformation in the political extremes. This is the subject of James Shields (Chapter 2) and Nick Hewlett's (Chapter 3) contributions, both of which take different approaches to the question of radical politics in contemporary France. As Shields reminds us, the greatest beneficiary of the weakening of the left–right bipolarity has undoubtedly been the Front National (FN). In the 1980s, the political élite could dismiss it as a party of protest, only able to score local victories or gain seats because of the one-off change in the legislative electoral system in 1986. But, by the 2000s, the party – and its leader Jean-Marie Le Pen – had become a powerful and persistent force in French politics. Le Pen's spectacular success in the first round of the 2002 presidential election, when he came second and confined the Socialist candidate Lionel Jospin to third, merely confirmed the party's electoral potential. Sarkozy tried to regain far-right support with his hardline rhetoric during the election campaign of 2007 but, a few years later, the FN was once again making the headlines. In the first round of the 2012 presidential election, its new leader, Marine Le Pen (the youngest daughter of Jean-Marie), scored 17.9 per cent. With over 6.4 million votes, she received more votes than any previous FN candidate, including her father who received 5.5 million votes in the second round of the presidential election in 2002. Nor are there any signs that the FN will wither away: with the approval ratings of the Hollande government currently in freefall and the centre-right bitterly divided, there is a high likelihood that the party will continue to grow.

The question, of course, is whether the FN can finally become a 'respectable' party. This is Marine Le Pen's stated aim and she has been working hard to scrub the party's image and loosen its umbilical association with her cantankerous and controversial father. But the two-round French electoral system has traditionally blocked FN candidates from gaining seats in the National Assembly and experiences of FN municipal government in Vitrolles, Orange and Toulon have been resounding failures. Moreover, the current unwillingness of the centre-right to sign any electoral pact with the FN has seriously limited its ability to become a properly institutionalised party. Still, as Shields points out, the FN has profoundly affected the configuration of French politics: in three-way run-offs between candidates, the party can play 'king-maker', and its support base is getting younger and more diverse. The FN's message, too, has become normalised. This has led to what some commentators have called a 'lepénisation' of political discourse, in which candidates from across the political spectrum are forced to harden their attitudes towards immigration, European integration and globalisation in response to the FN.[19] Even on the centre-left – a traditional bastion of anti-FN views – there has been a noticeable rightward drift on certain key issues such as immigration or European integration. Given that the FN currently has only two *députés* in the French parliament, its disproportionate impact on French politics is something of which its leader can justifiably be proud.

Few political groupings are as aware of the success of the FN as the extreme-left, which has been its principal victim. Not only has the main party of the extreme-left – the Parti communiste français (PCF) – experienced a catastrophic loss of support since the 1980s but, to add insult to injury, many former bastions of Communist support in northern and southern France have been penetrated by the FN. So grave was the crisis on the extreme-left that, for the first time since the *programme commun* of 1974, the PCF did not put up its own presidential candidate in 2012, choosing instead to join forces with other extreme-left parties under the banner of the Front de Gauche and its (ex-Socialist) leader Jean-Luc Mélenchon. This union meant that Mélenchon was able to gather 11.1 per cent of the vote, which gave the extreme-left its highest single result in a presidential election since Georges Marchais scored 15.5 per cent in 1981. But this was not enough to hide the weakness of the extreme-left: the Front de Gauche continues to lose seats at a local level, and none of the other non-Communist or former Trotskyist parties (such as the Nouveau parti anticapitaliste) have been able to gain more than a few percentage points in national elections. For those die-hard activists who have not been tempted by the Socialist Party, the picture is bleak.

Yet, as Hewlett observes, the political foundations on which the extreme-left built its support in the twentieth century have not disappeared. While some of the statistics that Perrineau cites in Chapter 1 suggest that income inequality in France has not increased since the 1980s, the overwhelming perception is that the world has become a more unequal place, especially since the financial crisis of 2008. The fear of insurrection, which was so central to French politics in the nineteenth century, may have disappeared, but the profound sense of injustice that nurtured generations of revolutionaries has not entirely dissipated. Hewlett argues strongly that the idea of France as a less divided and more equal society is not simply inaccurate but obscures the lingering strength of horizontal, class-based affiliations. That these classes no longer turn naturally towards the extreme-left or the labour movement does not mean that they are apathetic. On the contrary, they feel excluded from a neo-liberal consensus, which assures them that their situation is improving when it quite clearly is not. Hewlett is particularly critical of the centre-left in the form of the Parti socialiste (PS). In its effort to appeal to the widest possible electoral base, it has wholly accepted the prevailing orthodoxy of France as a classless society and, by extension, detached itself from the values that made it so appealing to voters in the first place.

The difficulties that Hollande and his government have faced since their electoral victory in 2012 suggest that there is a good deal of truth to this interpretation. The accusation that the PS has 'sold out' can be heard almost as vocally now as in 1983, when the last Socialist president, François Mitterrand reversed his 'socialist' policies and imposed economic austerity in an effort to save the French economy.[20] Optimists will argue that, despite such a radical about-turn, Mitterrand was still re-elected for a second term in 1988. It is not at all clear, however, that Hollande can pull off the same trick, especially given the increasing number of floating voters and the haemorrhaging of votes to the FN. Does this mean that the extremes will become the natural home for all those who feel excluded from the current political system? If so, this raises a fundamental question: on what basis will the disaffected cast their vote? Perrineau argues for a multi-causal explanation for voter preference, while Hewlett maintains that class will continue to play a pivotal role. But the final chapter of Part One offers us an alternative vision of political affiliation structured around the historian François Furet's notion of political 'passion'.

As Christophe Prochasson reminds us in Chapter 4, the term 'passion' has a venerable history in French political thought. It featured in the writings of Jean-Jacques Rousseau and, above all, in the work of Alexis Tocqueville, who used the concept of the 'passions' to understand the rise of democracy and egalitarianism in the modern world. The revival of interest in Tocqueville in the late 1970s and 1980s meant that some of his key concepts were rehabilitated. Nowhere was this more apparent than in the writings of Furet, who was one of Tocqueville's keenest disciples.[21] In Furet's view, the hideous violence and ideological polarisation of the twentieth century could only be understood using the deliberately ambiguous term 'passion'. This could come in many forms – 'egalitarian passion', 'revolutionary passion', 'democratic passion' – but only the word 'passion' could capture the blinding intensity of emotion that underpinned the great ideological collision between Communism and Fascism. Even once the dust had settled on the killing fields of the Second World War, the human propensity for utopian and unachievable 'passion' did not die down: it was the unbridled 'passion' for equality that gave strength to the identity politics of the 1960s and 1970s, and destroyed the Communist regimes of Eastern Europe. According to Furet, once the French Revolution had unleashed the 'passions' in the late eighteenth century, there was no way to avoid them: they had been at the heart of politics ever since.

Obviously, such an all-encompassing view of political action is open to many criticisms, not least because of the vagueness of the term 'passion' and its questionable social-psychological implications. But Furet's use of the term nevertheless hints at other ways we might interpret the blurring of political affiliations and growing voter disaffection in France and beyond. Could it be that, rather than personality alone, voters will henceforth be swayed by the extent to which a party or politician can embody their individual 'passion'? Or is it that neo-liberalism and centrism have extinguished the 'passions' once and for all? Furet's pessimism about contemporary politics in his final writings implied the latter, but he never ruled out a (potentially dangerous) resurgence of political 'passion'. Indeed, just as he identified the 'anti-bourgeois passion' as the defining feature of radical politics in the first half of the twentieth century, we might identify the 'anti-immigrant passion' as the new horizon of French politics in the twenty-first century. Seen this way, the FN is not a vessel for political apathy, but rather the vehicle for a destructive new 'passion' – one with which political actors of all persuasions will have to reckon.

The tangled memories of an imperial past

The history of colonial and post-colonial France has been completely rejuvenated in the past two decades and it is only right that some of these new developments should feature prominently in a book devoted to French politics since the 1970s. Scholars have once again begun to take seriously the idea of a 'global France' connected to the rest of the world through imperial networks, and there has been a growing interest in the legacy of the colonial encounter on metropolitan French society.[22] Not since the Algerian War has there been such broad public and scholarly interest in the French empire, a trend that has been encouraged by the growing importance of immigration as a political issue.[23] Yet despite this renewed interest, we still do not know enough about how French politics has adapted to the end of empire and the rise in post-colonial identity politics – two themes that are at the heart of Part Two. The latter is particularly problematic since the French republican tradition prohibits positive discrimination and the gathering of statistics along ethnic grounds. As a result, few empirical studies exist on ethnic minority political activism and French graduate students shy away from the subject because it is so obviously taboo.[24]

The main exception to this is the case of the *pieds-noirs* – French Algerians of European origin who fled at the time of independence in 1962. Their claims on the French state and their sustained activism have attracted a small but significant amount of scholarly attention, which means we now have a much better idea about how they mobilised themselves as a specific community.[25] One of the scholars whose work has done much to shed light on *pied-noir* politics is Yann Scioldo-Zürcher and, in Chapter 5 in this book, he examines the measures that were put in place by the French state to 'reimburse' the lost assets of the one million or so *rapatriés* (the official name given to displaced persons formerly resident in French overseas territories).[26] His main focus is the compensation law of 1970, which provided for a partial reimbursement of the value of certain lost assets. The law itself was controversial and bitterly criticised by *députés* of all political persuasion, but the debates that preceded it give us a remarkable insight into the conflicting memories of French colonialism less than ten years after the end of the

Algerian War. The principal disagreement revolved around the issue of rights and responsibilities. Whereas some argued that the *pieds-noirs* had a 'right' to state compensation as French citizens dispossessed of assets in a former French territory, others maintained that such a measure would, in effect, privilege one community at the expense of the metropolitan French who did not have access to equivalent subsidies. Similarly, opinions differed on whether compensation should be for the full value of lost assets at current prices or simply a percentage of their value at the time of loss. Finally, there were those who believed that, since Algeria had been a part of France, it was the French state that should reimburse the *pieds-noirs*, and others who insisted that the newly-independent Algerian state should be made to pay for the assets it had nationalised or requisitioned.

This violent clash of opinions in parliament did not prevent the law from being passed, but almost everyone saw it as a botched compromise that would require further legislation to put right. The sceptics were subsequently proved right: the French state would spend the next three decades trying to find new ways of fulfilling its 'responsibilities' towards the *pieds-noirs* and expiating its colonial guilt through further compensation packages. More fundamentally, however, the debates over the first compensation law signalled the transition from the politics of decolonisation to the politics of post-colonialism. Whereas the substantial housing, employment and business subsidies provided to the *pieds-noirs* in the years after their arrival in 1962 can be understood as a set of policies put in place to support French citizens displaced by decolonisation, the compensation law of 1970 was the beginning of a battle over memory, identity and 'reparations'. This battle has continued right up until the present-day, most notoriously in the 2005 law that stipulated, among other things, that French schoolchildren should be taught about 'the positive effects of colonisation'. After a public outcry, this particular line of the legislation was repealed by presidential decree, but what is less well-known is that the original title of the law 'recognised the *rapatriés* on behalf of the [French] nation and institut[ed] a national contribution in their favour'.[27] In other words, the 2005 law was not a piece of educational legislation but actually yet another attempt on the part of the French state to put to rest the thorny question of how to compensate the *pieds-noirs*. The difference was that, by the 2000s, the symbolism of compensation was as important as its financial underpinnings. Since the *pied-noir* lobby knew it would not realistically be able to achieve complete compensation, the very least it could do was change the negative perception of the *pied-noir* community as rapacious and racist settlers. Hence the importance of an educational 'injunction' that would rehabilitate a *pied-noir* narrative of benevolent colonisation: without this, the very idea of compensation would be stripped of its historical legitimacy.

The *pieds-noirs* were not the only post-colonial minority within French society to experience the transition from activism to identity politics from the 1970s onwards. Other immigrant populations also tried to find ways of making their voices heard at a time of growing political uncertainty. Many of these immigrant groups were socio-economically marginalised and could only dream of the kind of state assistance that was provided to the *pieds-noirs*, but they nonetheless slowly joined the civic struggle over France's post-colonial memory. One of the most emblematic events in the politicisation of ethnic minority identity was the Marche pour l'égalité et contre le racisme – a two-and-a-half month anti-racist protest march that travelled from Marseille to Paris in late 1983 and brought the plight of first- and second-generation migrants to public attention. Over the next few years, France saw the development of novel forms of identity-based activism (often centred on second-generation young Arabs, known as *beurs*) and an explosion of popular interest in anti-racist movements, of which the most famous was SOS Racisme.[28] The trouble with this new wave of identity politics in the 1980s was that it frequently played down – or ignored altogether – older forms of activism in the 1960s and 1970s. This was largely due to the change in patterns of immigration. Where before immigrants were predominantly young male labour migrants in specific industries, by the 1980s, there were large and varied communities of settled migrants, including women and children. Older forms of immigrant politics, centred around the far-left and the trade union movement, no longer seemed appropriate to young activists who did not always have stable employment and were more interested in celebrating their cultural rather than class identity.

Yet, as Daniel Gordon shows in Chapter 6, there were organisations that straddled these multiple generations.[29] One of these was the magazine *Sans Frontière*, founded in 1979 by a group of former Maoist activists in Paris. It only lasted seven years but its trajectory perfectly exemplified the transition from the *gauchiste*-inspired immigrant politics of the late 1960s to the identity politics of the 1980s. In its pages, a younger generation of activists argued with their elders about Third World politics, their 'cultural' heritage and the prospect for change in France. Especially interesting are the individual interviews conducted by *Sans Frontière* journalists, which reveal the full complexity of the immigrant experience in France and will be a vital resource for future historians. Indeed, the founders of *Sans Frontière* themselves quickly realised that they would be better off working to safeguard immigrant memory rather than producing a magazine. Shortly after *Sans Frontière* closed down, several of them were involved with the founding of Génériques in 1987, an organisation dedicated to 'the history and memory of immigration, and the recuperation, preservation and classification of immigration archives in France and in Europe'. It continues to operate today and has become a major repository for documentary sources about immigration.[30] Just like those *pied-noir* activists who campaigned for their version of history to be enshrined in law, today's immigrant activists recognise that the campaign for history and memory can be as politically potent as a strike or sit-in.

These present-day 'memory wars' are the subject of Chapter 7, in which Isabel Hollis examines two commemorations of the Algerian War in 2012.[31]

Here, too, the main issue was how to interpret and represent the imperial past – in this case, a violent war of decolonisation that, in the words of the historian Todd Shepard, 'remade France'.[32] Since the late 1990s, the Algerian War has become the pre-eminent site of struggle over the meaning of French imperialism: debates have raged in the press and in French historiography about the legitimacy of torture, the treatment of 'native' populations, the colonial state's attitude to Islam and the practices of systemic violence that defined the end of the French empire in North Africa. This has been accompanied by a bewildering array of commemorations, ranging from the plaque inaugurated in Paris in 2001 in honour of the victims of police repression on 17 October 1961, to the Mur des disparus unveiled in Perpignan in 2007 in honour of the thousands of *pieds-noirs* who were killed in North Africa in the 1950s and early 1960s.[33] Each one of these commemorations raised questions about which historical narrative of the war should be prioritised and who has the 'right' to speak on behalf of the war's victims.

These questions were also at the heart of the two contrasting commemorations that Hollis discusses – an exhibition on the Algerian War at the Musée de l'Armée in Paris and a set of street 'installations' by an organisation called Raspouteam. The former represented the most traditional form of commemoration: a museum exhibition that aimed to be both 'objective' and 'accessible'. The displays and captions were designed to set the Algerian War within a longer history of French colonialism, and explain the historical causes of the conflict. By contrast, Raspouteam chose to invest the physical space of the city, by putting up QR codes at specific locations in Paris. These codes could then be scanned by mobile phone users who would be redirected to an accompanying website on the Algerian War, with documents, videos and interviews. Raspouteam had already adopted this approach in a previous project on the Paris Commune and, on both occasions, the goal was to make passers-by engage with the geography of conflict and inscribe it within an urban landscape. Unlike the exhibition at the Musée de l'Armée, which drew tens of thousands of visitors, it is too early to judge whether Raspouteam's initiative has been a success or even whether this form of commemoration can be effective. But creating active engagement with history through technology has the potential to counteract the strong tendency for memorials and commemorative events to freeze memory in time and space.

Of course, the intense desire on the part of different groups to commemorate their distinct memories of the colonial past and the post-colonial present has been driven by a powerful wave of nostalgia. Whether in the form of erstwhile *soixante-huitard* activists reminiscing about their youthful engagement on the barricades, or elderly *pieds-noirs* eagerly recreating their lost Algerian 'homeland', nostalgia has become a constitutive part of French politics since the 1970s.[34] So pronounced is this tendency that one of the major criticisms of contemporary French politics is that it is irrevocably 'stuck in the past', clinging to its old ideals, values and myths without any regard for a rapidly-changing global context. But, as Patricia Lorcin suggests in her analysis of France's nostalgias for empire, the phenomenon of nostalgia is not simply an unthinking escape into the past; it is a way of adapting conflicting memories to the present. In her discussion in Chapter 8, Patricia Lorcin distinguishes between imperial nostalgia, 'which concerns the practices, activities and utterances of politicians and statesmen with an eye on the world stage' and colonial nostalgia, which 'is connected to reminiscences and evocations of a past lifestyle and an idealised vision of the inter-cultural relations within the colony'. Both are intimately connected to France's perception of its colonial past, but they operate at different (and occasionally contradictory) levels.

Crucially, this distinction gives us a framework we can use to interpret different events, processes and commemorative practices related to the French empire. For example, we could read the debates over the 1970 compensation law as a collision between the imperial nostalgia of a French state 'taking responsibility' for the collapse of the French empire, and the colonial nostalgia of the *pieds-noirs* who demanded reimbursement as a form of compensation for the destruction of their 'homeland'. Likewise, we might interpret the exhibition on the Algerian War at the Musée de l'Armée as a form of imperial nostalgia, in contrast to the colonial nostalgia that is implicit in the list of individual names on the Mur des disparus in Perpignan. What is most interesting about Lorcin's theory of imperial and colonial nostalgia is that, like Furet's 'passions', it captures the emotional undercurrent of contemporary politics. We can surely all agree with her claim that a 'sentiment of loss of power or status underpins the nostalgias of both empire and colony', but one could argue that nostalgia is also a way of taking control of an increasingly fragmented political landscape, in which historical grand narratives have come under sustained attack. We might even say that today there is a veritable 'nostalgic passion' in French politics, which expresses itself through an emotional attachment to various imagined histories. Given the omnipresence of France's imperial legacy in its diverse population and its commemorative landscape, it makes sense that these emotions should feature prominently in discussions of the colonial past, where different groups demand attention both on the grounds that the 'emotional' pull of their story is more real and that their version of 'history' is more accurate.

After Marxism? Rebuilding French political thought

The temptation of nostalgia has been just as clearly visible in French intellectual life as it has in post-colonial identity politics. Much of this rests on the perennial view of France as the home of Sartrean engagement, radical politics and critical thinking. But with the collapse of the Marxist – or *marxisant* –

consensus that dominated French intellectual life from the end of the Second World War until the 1970s, this image has been progressively dismantled. France no longer represents the possibility of revolutionary theory and practice that it did in the 1960s and, in the eyes of its harshest critics, its intellectual life has become little more than another neo-liberal validation of the status quo.[35] This has been reflected in a startling lack of interest in contemporary French political thought. Major French thinkers like Pierre Rosanvallon, Claude Lefort and Marcel Gauchet have received far less scholarly attention than comparable thinkers of earlier periods like Claude Lévi-Strauss or Louis Althusser, especially in the Anglo-American world.[36] Critical philosophers such as Michel Foucault and Jacques Derrida continue to exert a strong hold on the fields of literary and cultural studies, but it is not the 'Frenchness' of their thought that is of interest.[37] In the words of Perry Anderson, French culture of recent years appears as little more than a 'fallen landscape'.[38]

But there are a number of problems with this resoundingly negative reading of French intellectual life. First, it seriously overstates the influence of French philosophy on post-war French political life in general. Sartre and Derrida were extraordinarily gifted thinkers and extremely influential outside France, but their impact on French politics was negligible, especially when compared to other, less celebrated, intellectuals like the sociologist Raymond Aron, whose articles and essays were widely read by the political élite. Second, it rests on an unusually élitist view of the French 'intellectual', which has proved increasingly untenable in a more democratic and more open university system.[39] Finally, the focus on radical politics has obscured some of the recent theoretical contributions of French thinkers to the elaboration of theories of the modern state, democracy, human rights, and citizenship. Obviously, it is not possible to fill these gaps and examine all the innovations in contemporary French political thought in the space of four short chapters, but Part Three does tackle two of the most prominent intellectual movements since the 1970s: the revival of interest in liberalism and the elaboration of a new republican theory of citizenship and the state.

Liberalism is a notoriously tricky concept in French politics. This is largely because it has failed to make a major impact on a French political space overpopulated with grand ideologies. In the nineteenth century, the myriad temptations of Jacobinism, republicanism, Bonapartism, ultramontane Catholicism and socialism left liberalism with few supporters.[40] And, in the twentieth century, neither Gaullists nor Communists had much time for a philosophy of compromise, consensus and pluralism. This hostility to liberalism was also a characteristic of French intellectual life. Until the late 1960s, many of those who might have been willing to embrace the ideas and language of liberalism shied away from doing so in public. They were usually afraid of the stigma and unwilling to engage in the lengthy discussions that would be required to defend their position. The overwhelmingly left-wing environment meant that liberalism was deeply unfashionable: in the words of the time, it was 'better to be wrong with Sartre than right with Aron'.

This climate of anti-liberalism began to change in the late 1960s. The protests of 1968 and the sustained attack on hierarchy in French society provided an opening for some technocrats and intellectuals to extol the virtues of individual liberty, free enterprise and liberal democracy. As Michael Behrent reminds us in Chapter 9, one of the few places where it had still been acceptable to call oneself a liberal was among France's powerful post-war technocratic élite. It was among this group that a new, more militant brand of liberalism emerged with the inauguration in 1966 of the Association pour la liberté économique et le progrès social (ALEPS). This group of academics, senior civil servants and business leaders aimed to reintroduce liberal economic thought into public discourse and undermine the statist and collectivist doctrines of the French state. Through a series of conferences and publications, ALEPS members disseminated their own brand of liberalism, which focused heavily on economic reform and a critique of socialism. At certain moments, there were attempts to harness what some saw as the latent liberalism of the 1968 protests, but Behrent makes clear that this was only ever a partial project: for most members, the strongly left-leaning rhetoric of 1968 was far too ideologically suspect. The brand of liberalism that was most appealing to ALEPS was economically liberal but politically conservative.

A study of the early years of ALEPS nevertheless offers a glimpse into the roots of French neo-liberalism. While it is undoubtedly true that liberalism in France has been much less visible than in Britain or the United States, organisations like ALEPS – and, later, the Fondation Saint-Simon – have played a pivotal role in elaborating a specifically French version of neo-liberalism that acknowledges the pivotal role of the state, but also seeks to promote social and economic pluralism. Indeed, the success of Nicolas Sarkozy's avowedly 'liberal' election campaign in 2007 – which featured former members of ALEPS like Hervé Novelli – was a clear indication that a certain kind of authoritarian liberalism could appeal to a French electorate notoriously disinterested in liberal politics. But the activities of a small number of technocrats alone cannot explain the growing attraction of liberalism in France. To understand this change more fully, we need to turn to Chapter 10, in which Iain Stewart discusses the liberal revival in French intellectual life.

In comparison to other trends, there has been a good deal of polemical and scholarly interest in the resurgence of liberalism in French political thought.[41] This is hardly surprising given the scale of the ideological transformation that took place in the period from the mid-1970s to the mid-1980s. The unequivocal 'victory' of anti-totalitarian thought was evident even to informed members of the general public for whom the French publication of Alexander Solzhenitsyn's *The Gulag Archipelago* in 1974 seemed to signal the end of a decades-long Marxist consensus. In recent years, however, intellectual historians have begun to examine this shift more critically, raising questions about its origins and its direction. In his chapter,

Stewart suggests that there were in fact multiple liberal revivals, each with different roots in post-war French political thought. By looking at the development of two journals that were closely associated with Raymond Aron – *Contrepoint* (1970–6) and *Commentaire* (1978–present) – he is able to untangle one particular strand of the French liberal revival. These two journals aimed to provide a forum in which young intellectuals could develop an 'Aronian' liberalism that would combine a critique of radical egalitarianism, an attack on relativist 'anti-humanism', and a defence of intellectual 'responsibility'.

The liberalism to be found in the pages of *Contrepoint* and *Commentaire* did not have its roots in a Solzhenitsyn-inspired anti-totalitarianism but in a critical engagement with 1968. Aron himself had bitterly criticised the student protests in his famous essay *La Révolution introuvable* (1968) and his disciples adopted an equally sceptical stance towards its legacy. Unlike some members of ALEPS who were willing to embrace the 'liberal' potential of 1968, the core group of young intellectuals in charge of both journals saw the late 1960s as the root cause of the 'illiberalism' of French politics. While other branches of the liberal revival in France were driven by a strong anti-Communist element, which expressed itself concretely in a fear of a Socialist and Communist electoral victory in the late 1970s, the intellectual horizon against which the journals' editors were fighting was the far larger legacy of 1968. This meant that, for all the diversity of contributors, the editorial line of both journals consistently emphasised the need for French politics to break free from the shadow of the 'gauchiste' 1960s and embrace the widening liberal horizon of the 1980s and 1990s. The fact that *Commentaire* has long outlived the collapse of the Berlin Wall suggests that this is a battle that has not yet been won.

Stewart's emphasis on an 'anti-68 liberal revival' not only broadens our view of the liberal revival, but also reinforces the centrality of 1968 as a positive and negative reference point in contemporary French politics.[42] For the extreme-left, 1968 was the last cry of revolution; for liberals, 1968 was a reconfirmation of the deeply illiberal character of French politics; and, for the right, 1968 was the celebration of a 'lazy' and 'decadent' France, entirely given over to needless ideological quarrels. But there is one thing about 1968 that almost everyone can agree on: that France has never again experienced a period of such polarised political intensity. The result has either been a lingering nostalgia for the days of 'engagement' and protest, or repeated attempts to do away once and for all with 'la pensée 68'.[43] Nevertheless, since the 1980s, some thinkers and politicians have resisted this general disenchantment with politics. They have done this by launching a spirited defence of the French model of state intervention, citizenship and *laïcité* (secularism). This movement, which draws heavily on the history of French republicanism, has come to be known as neo-republicanism.[44] As with the liberal revival, there have been many variants of neo-republicanism, but the final chapters of Part Three deal with two of its most important characteristics: its relation to liberal theories of human rights and its critique of multiculturalism.

The relationship between neo-republicanism and human rights is complex and, in Chapter 11, Camille Robcis chooses to approach it through Marcel Gauchet's well-known essay 'Human rights are not a politic' (1980). Gauchet argued that the prevalence of a 'human rights discourse' in Western Europe was merely a way of avoiding the more significant social and political issues that had arisen from the collapse of Marxism and the concomitant absence of any collective 'project' for society. Moreover, the individualising tendency of human rights was encouraging the atomisation and fragmentation of society. As Robcis observes, this second argument raised a particular problem since, both in its historical and contemporary incarnations, French republicanism emphasises the importance of the unity of the body politic. So, for Gauchet, it was not simply that human rights promoted individualisation; they also posed a direct threat to the integrity of the French Republic.

As we have seen in the case of *pied-noir* and *beur* activism, these theoretical reflections coincided with the public emergence of identity politics. They therefore provided a strong philosophical justification for intellectuals who were hostile to the recognition of identity-based diversity within French society. Specifically, Robcis discusses the cases of Frédéric Martel and Irène Théry, who opposed the 'gay rights' movement and the Contrat d'union sociale (civil union) respectively. In their public interventions, they both adapted Gauchet's interpretation of human rights in order to support their claim that gay rights and civil unions would run counter to France's republican tradition and contribute to a dangerous fragmentation of society. Anyone familiar with contemporary French politics will know that, since the mid-1980s, this same argument has been used by neo-republicans to protest against numerous other proposals – including the *parité* law to guarantee equal representation of women in parliament, the European Charter for Regional and Minority Languages, and the banning of the Islamic headscarf in state schools. In each case, the justification is that giving special consideration to a particular sexual, cultural, ethnic or linguistic identity will lead to 'communautarisme' and undermine the values of the French Republic.

Not surprisingly, this position has been widely criticised outside France as reactionary and ethno-centric.[45] After all, why should minority groups be asked to relinquish their multiple identities in the name of 'republican citizenship'? Is this not simply another way of imposing a univocal 'Frenchness' on an increasingly plural society? There is much truth to these criticisms, but the problem is that they have a tendency to cast neo-republicanism – and the French republican tradition more generally – as a frozen caricature. Yet, as many scholars have pointed out, French republicanism is an exceptionally malleable ideology that has frequently adapted itself to radically different contexts.[46] This being the case, there is no reason why it should not adapt itself yet again to the uncertain politics of the twenty-first century. If the aim is to contribute actively to the reconstruction of French politics, the focus should be on what kind of philosophical and theoretical innovations are required in order to make republicanism 'work' in contemporary France. This is the subject of the final chapter in Part 3 by the political theorist Sophie Guérard de Latour (Chapter 12), in which she suggests ways in which French republicanism can square its theory of unity and social solidarity with the reality of multicultural diversity.

Using Emile Durkheim as her philosophical guide, Guérard de Latour critically examines three different approaches to solidarity in contemporary French republican philosophy. First, a 'Rousseauist' account that emphasises transcendence, civic virtue and the need for all minorities to relinquish their identities and integrate into the nation. Second, a theory of non-domination in which the republican state seeks to elaborate rules that reduce forms of domination within society, especially where this domination relates to cultural preconceptions inherited from older forms of solidarity (such as ethnic identity). And, finally, a liberal-communitarian form of republicanism that positively recognises ethno-cultural difference, with a view to pluralising national cultures and acknowledging the diversity of the civic community. The latter remains within a republican logic since it emphasises political freedom and maintains that the rights of the individual are inseparable from membership of a political community and its networks of solidarity. It nevertheless allows neo-republicanism to work towards what Guérard de Latour calls 'an intersubjective understanding of citizenship'. The implication is that adapting French republicanism to the realities of cultural diversity does not require either the jettisoning of a republican ideology that has been an integral part of French political culture for almost 150 years or the awkward grafting of Anglo-American liberal multiculturalism on to a distinctly French political tradition. What is needed instead is a more open reading of republicanism that, for Guérard de Latour, can draw its inspiration from the work of Durkheim.

This creative approach seems to be the most fruitful normative way of responding to the neo-republican concern about minorities. At a time when, as we saw in Part One, the traditional frameworks of French politics are falling apart and support for the extreme-right is growing; it is only through this kind of reflection on the relationship between political thought and sociological reality that any positive new synthesis is likely to emerge. The difficulty, of course, is in identifying a possible source for this synthesis. In his brief conclusion, Sudhir Hazareesingh not only questions whether any party or individual can provide adequate answers, but also whether French political culture can accommodate any original thinking at all. It is a gloomy note on which to end, but the early years of the Hollande presidency have given little cause for optimism. The country's economic problems are still plain to see, and the most visible ideological struggle is between a defensive and widely-criticised neo-republicanism and the aggressive ethnic nationalism of the extreme-right. It would seem that, with depoliticisation and unemployment the defining features of contemporary French society, the French have good reason to be depressed. However, the twelve contributions to this book suggest that there is now a growing interest in investigating the historical and philosophical roots of France's current predicament. We can only hope that, by starting a conversation about the changing shape of contemporary French politics, this book will make a modest contribution to the civic renewal of a country that has already suffered its fair share of 'crises'.

Notes

1 For a summary, see Anne Chemin, 'Liberté, égalité, morosité', *Le Monde*, 20 June 2013. See also the IPSOS report 'France 2013: Les nouvelles fractures', http://www.ipsos.fr/ipsos-public-affairs/actualites/2013-01-24-france-2013-nouvelles-fractures and Claudia Senik, 'The French unhappiness puzzle: The cultural dimension of happiness', *Paris School of Economics Working Papers* 34 (November 2013), http://halshs.archives-ouvertes.fr/halshs-00628837

2 For different expressions of this, see Yann Algan, Pierre Cahuc and André Zylberberg, *La Fabrique de la defiance . . . et comment s'en sortir* (Paris: Albin Michel, 2012); Timothy Smith, *France in Crisis: Welfare, inequality and globalization since 1980* (Cambridge: Cambridge University Press, 2004) and the Epilogue ('Confronting the national identity crisis') in Jack Hayward, *Fragmented France: Two centuries of disputed identity* (Oxford: Oxford University Press, 2007).

3 On France and the 'Anglo-Saxon' model, see Emile Chabal, 'The rise of the Anglo-Saxon: French perceptions of the Anglo-American world in the long twentieth century', *French Politics, Culture and Society* 31, 1 (2013): 35–42.

4 Jacques Julliard, *Le Malheur français* (Paris: Flammarion, 2005); Nicolas Baverez, *La France qui tombe* (Paris: Perrin, 2004).

5 Aude Vernuccio, 'Houllebecq: "La France a un don pour la dépression"', *Le Figaro*, 16 April 2013.

6 Emile Chabal, *A Divided Republic: Nation, state and citizenship in contemporary France* (Cambridge: Cambridge University Press, 2015), Ch. 9.

7 The term *pensée unique* was first coined in 1995 in Ignacio Ramonet, 'La pensée unique', *Le Nouvel observateur*, January 1995. The book that did much to cement the idea that 1990' France had become a 'consensual' and 'centrist' country was François Furet, Jacques Julliard and Pierre Rosanvallon, *La République du Centre: La Fin de l'exception française* (Paris: Hachette, 1988). This book has since been widely criticised by left-wing commentators as the first (and perhaps finest) example of the *pensée unique*.

8 Michel Crozier, *La Société bloquée* (Paris: Seuil, 1970).

9 For two different approaches to this question, see Tony Chafer and Emmanuel Godin, eds., *The End of the French Exception? Decline and revival of the 'French model'* (Basingstoke: Palgrave, 2010) and Perry Anderson, *La Pensée tiède: Un Regard critique sur la culture française* (Paris: Seuil, 2005).

10 This discourse of 'backwardness' frequently finds its way into foreign press coverage of France, but it was particularly noticeable around the time of the

2005 riots. See for instance, Jonathan Freedland, 'France is clinging to an ideal that's been pickled into dogma', *The Guardian*, 9 November 2005.

11 Sudhir Hazareesingh, *Intellectuals and the French Communist Party: Disillusion and decline* (Oxford: Clarendon Press, 1991).

12 There is surprisingly little good work on the centre-right under the Fifth Republic although some essays in Jean-François Sirinelli, *Histoires des droites en France*, 3 vols. (Paris: Gallimard, 1992) are useful. On the myth of de Gaulle, see Sudhir Hazareesingh, *In the Shadow of the General* (Oxford: Oxford University Press, 2012).

13 Michael Sutton, *France and the Construction of Europe, 1944–2007: The geopolitical imperative* (Oxford: Berghahn, 2007); George Ross, *Jacques Delors and European Integration* (Cambridge: Polity, 1995); or, for a much more critical reading of France's role in Europe, John Gillingham, *European Integration, 1950-2003: Superstate or new market economy?* (Cambridge: Cambridge University Press, 2003).

14 Daniel Rodgers, *Age of Fracture* (Cambridge, MA: Harvard University Press, 2011); Luc Boltanski and Ève Chiapello, *Le Nouvel esprit du capitalisme* (Paris: Gallimard, 1999); Zygmunt Bauman, *Liquid Modernity* (Cambridge: Polity, 2000); Warren Breckman, *Adventures of the Symbolic: Post-Marxism and radical democracy* (New York: Columbia University Press, 2013).

15 There is an illuminating discussion of this in Jacques Julliard, *Les gauches françaises, 1762–2012: Histoire, politique, imaginaire* (Paris: Flammarion, 2012), 127–38.

16 To pick but one example, the main Gaullist Party was called Rassemblement du people français (RPF) from 1947–1955, Union pour la nouvelle République (UNR) from 1958–1976, Rassemblement de la République (RPR) from 1976–2002 and Union pour un mouvement populaire (UMP) from 2002 until the present day. At the time of writing (November 2013) the UMP still exists, but the party has split because of a bitter leadership struggle between the current leader of the party, Jean-François Copé, and François Fillon, who has founded the dissident Rassemblement UMP (R-UMP), which sits separately from the UMP in the National Assembly.

17 There have been various attempts to write the histories of left and right in modern French politics, including, most famously, René Rémond, *La Droite en France de 1815 à nos jours* (Paris: Aubier, 1954) and, more recently, Julliard, *Les Gauches françaises*. See also Kevin Passmore, *The Right in France from the Third Republic to Vichy* (Oxford: Oxford University Press, 2012) and Jean-Jacques Becker and Gilles Candar, eds., *Histoire des gauches en France* (Paris: La Découverte, 2004).

18 Tony Judt, *Marxism and the French Left: Studies on labour and politics in France* (Oxford: Clarendon Press, 1996).

19 For a wry take on this phenomenon, see Pierre Tévanian and Sylvie Tissot, *Mots à maux: Dictionnaire de la lepénisation des esprits* (Paris: Dagorno, 1998). On the extreme-right more generally, see James Shields, *The Extreme Right in France: From Pétain to Le Pen* (London: Routledge, 2007).

20 On this period, see for example, Mairi Maclean, ed., *The Mitterrand Years: Legacy and evaluation* (Basingstoke: Palgrave, 1998).

21 On the 'Tocqueville revival' in France, see Serge Audier, *Tocqueville retrouvé: Genèse et enjeux du renouveau tocquevillien français* (Paris: Vrin, 2004).

22 There are far too many books and articles to list here but some indicative titles include Alice Conklin, *A Mission to Civilize: The republican idea of empire in France and West Africa, 1895–1930* (London: Stanford University Press, 1997); Carole Paligot, *La République raciale: Paradigme racial et idéologie républicaine (1860–1930)* (Paris: PUF, 2006); Laurent Dubois, 'La République metissee: Citizenship, colonialism, and the borders of French history', *Cultural Studies* 14, 1 (2000): 15–34; Nicolas Bancel, Pascal Blanchard and Françoise Vergès, *La République coloniale: Essai sur une utopie* (Paris: Albin Michel, 2003); and Charles Forsdick and David Murphy, eds., *Francophone Postcolonial Studies: A critical introduction* (London: Arnold, 2003).

23 Different treatments of immigration in contemporary French history include Gérard Noiriel, *The French Melting Pot: Immigration, citizenship and national identity* (Minneapolis, MN: University of Minnesota Press, 1996); Riva Kastoryano, *Negotiating Identities: States and immigrants in France and Germany* (Oxford: Princeton University Press, 2002); Abdelmalek Sayad, *La Double absence: Des Illusions de l'émigré aux souffrances de l'immigré* (Paris: Seuil, 1999).

24 The work that does exist tends to be focused on local case studies, where identity politics is particularly visible. For some examples of a mixed approach, see Beth Epstein, *Collective Terms: Race, culture, and community in a state-planned city in France* (Oxford: Berghahn, 2011); Lydie Fournier, *Le Fait musulman à Montpellier: Entre réalités sociologiques et enjeux politiques* (Paris: Dalloz-Sirey, 2008); and Emile Chabal, 'Managing the postcolony: Minority politics in Montpellier, c.1960–c.2010', *Contemporary European History* 23, 2 (2014): 237–58.

25 Andrea Smith, *Colonial Memory and Postcolonial Europe: Maltese settlers in Algeria and France* (Bloomington, IN: Indiana University Press, 2006); Claire Eldridge, '"We've never had a voice": Memory construction and the children of the harkis (1962–1991)', *French History* 23, 1 (2009): 88–107; Jean-Jacques Jordi, *De L'Exode à l'exil: Rapatriés et pieds-noirs en France* (Paris: L'Harmattan, 1993); Yann Scioldo-Zürcher, *Devenir métropolitain: Politique d'intégration et parcours de rapatriés d'Algérie en métropole (1954–2005)* (Paris: Éditions de l'EHESS, 2010); Emmanuelle Comtat, *Les Pieds-noirs et la politique: Quarante ans après le retour* (Paris: Presses de la Fondation nationale des sciences politiques, 2009).

26 The term *pied-noir* has no legal validity in France. Even though it is widely used, the official term for the *pieds-noirs* and other groups displaced by decolonisation is *rapatrié*.

27 The original law was entitled 'Loi n° 2005–158 du 23 février 2005 portant reconnaissance de la Nation et contribution nationale en faveur des Français rapatriés (1)'. The line relating to the 'positive effects of colonisation' was abrogated by decree in February 2006. For a full analysis of the law, see Claude Liauzu and Gilles Manceron, eds., *La Colonisation, la loi et l'histoire* (Paris: Syllepse, 2006).

28 On SOS Racisme, see Philippe Juhem, 'SOS-Racisme. Histoire d'une mobilisation "apolitique". Contribution à une analyse des transformations des représentations politiques après 1981' (unpublished PhD thesis, Université de Nanterre: Faculté de Sciences Politiques, 1998). On the *beur* phenomenon, see for example, Alec Hargreaves, *Immigration and Identity in Beur Fiction: Voices from the North African immigrant community in France* (Oxford: Berg, 1997).

29 He has dealt with many of these questions in more detail in his book Daniel Gordon, *Immigrants and Intellectuals: May '68 and the rise of anti-racism in France* (Pontypool: Merlin Press, 2012).

30 The organisation describes its activities and its history on its website, http://www.generiques.org

31 Pascal Blanchard and Isabelle Veyrat-Masson, eds., *Les Guerres de mémoires: La France et son histoire* (Paris: La Découverte, 2008).

32 Todd Shepard, *The Invention of Decolonization: The Algerian War and the remaking of France* (London: Cornell University Press, 2006).

33 On the memory of 17 October 1961, see especially, Part 2 of Jim House and Neil Macmaster, *Paris 1961: Algerians, state terror and memory* (Oxford: Oxford University Press, 2006). On the controversy surrounding the Mur des disparus, see José Bueno, 'Le Droit de mémoire enfin respecté pour les disparus', *La Provence*, 27 November 2007 and 'Le "Mur des Disparus" fait polémique à Perpignan', *Nouvel Observateur*, 25 November 2007.

34 On 1968, see for instance, Robert Gildea, James Mark and Anette Warring, eds., *Europe's 1968: Voices of revolt* (Oxford: Oxford University Press, 2013). On *pied-noir* nostalgia – known as 'nostalgérie', see Smith, *Colonial Memory and Postcolonial Europe*, see Note 25.

35 See for example, Daniel Lindenberg, *Le Rappel à l'ordre: Enquête sur les nouveaux réactionnaires* (Paris, 2002).

36 There are some exceptions – notably the work of scholars like Samuel Moyn and Warren Breckman – but, in general, these thinkers have been ignored outside France: for instance, English translations of Pierre Rosanvallon's works have sold poorly.

37 For an interesting approach to Derrida and his relationship to post-war French intellectual life, see Edward Baring, *The Young Derrida and French Philosophy, 1945–1968* (Cambridge: Cambridge University Press, 2011).

38 Perry Anderson, 'Dégringolade', *London Review of Books* 26, 17 (September 2004).

39 On intellectual engagement in France, see among many others, David Drake, *Intellectuals and Politics in Post-War France* (Basingstoke: Palgrave, 2002); Pascal Ory and Jean-François Sirinelli, *Les Intellectuels en France de l'Affaire Dreyfus à nos jours* (Paris: Armand Colin, 1992); Jeremy Jennings, ed., *Intellectuals in Twentieth-Century France: Mandarins and Samurais* (Basingstoke: Palgrave, 1993); Tony Judt, *The Burden of Responsibility: Blum, Camus, Aron and the French Twentieth Century* (London: University of Chicago Press, 1998); Sunil Khilnani, *Arguing Revolution: The intellectual left in post-war France* (London: Yale University Press 1993); Stefan Collini, *Absent Minds: Intellectuals in Britain* (Oxford: Oxford University Press, 2006).

40 For an overview, see Jeremy Jennings, *Revolution and the Republic: A history of political thought in France since the eighteenth century* (Oxford: Oxford University Press, 2011).

41 Mark Lilla, ed., *New French Thought: Political philosophy* (Princeton, NJ: Princeton University Press); Julian Bourg, ed., *From Revolution to Ethics: May 1968 and contemporary French thought* (Montréal, QC: McGill-Queen's University Press, 2007); Michael Scott Christofferson, *French Intellectuals against the Left: The anti-totalitarian moment of the 1970s* (Oxford: Berghahn, 2004).

42 The mixed legacies of 1968 are comprehensively discussed in Serge Audier, *La Pensée anti-68: Essai sur une restauration intellectuelle* (Paris: La Découverte, 2008).

43 Most recently by Sarkozy who, as Stewart reminds us, wanted to 'liquidate' the legacy of 1968.

44 Chabal, *A Divided Republic*, see Note 6.

45 See for example Adrian Favell, *Philosophies of Integration: Immigration and the idea of citizenship in France and Britain* (Basingstoke: Macmillan, 1998); and Joan Wallach Scott, *The Politics of the Veil* (Princeton, NJ: Princeton University Press, 2007).

46 There is now a vast literature on the history of the French Republic, which represents a considerable body of scholarly work. See for instance, Claude Nicolet, *L'Idée républicaine en France: Essai d'histoire critique* (Paris: Seuil, 1982); Serge Berstein and Odile Rudelle, eds., *Le Modèle républicain* (Paris: PUF, 1992); Maurice Agulhon, *République, Tome 1: 1880–1914* (Paris: Hachette, 1990); and Sudhir Hazareesingh, *Political Traditions in Modern France* (Oxford: Clarendon Press, 1994).

PART ONE

French Politics beyond Right and Left

1

The Great Upheaval:

Left and Right in Contemporary French Politics

Pascal Perrineau

Translated from the French by Emile Chabal

Until the mid-1980s, French politics was dominated by a confrontation between left- and right-wing coalitions that together represented a large majority of the vote. But the presidential election of 2002 revealed the extent to which this pattern had broken down. In addition to the political trauma of Jean-Marie Le Pen's surprise presence in the second round, the election laid bare the weakness of the two main government parties that had embodied the left–right divide – the Parti socialiste (PS) and the Rassemblement pour la République (RPR). The two candidates from the PS (Lionel Jospin) and the RPR (Jacques Chirac) only managed to gain 36.1 per cent of the vote. The collision between left and right was subsequently reignited in the presidential elections of 2007 and 2012 when the main candidates on the right (Nicolas Sarkozy) and the left (Ségolène Royal and then François Hollande) gained a clear majority of votes cast: 57 per cent and 55.9 per cent respectively. Yet, despite this apparent return to the status quo, the crisis of political identity on the right and left continues unabated.

Of course, the illusion of bipolarity remains strong. At the start of the twenty-first century, it can seem as if French political culture has not fundamentally changed. Indeed, the second round of the 2012 presidential election was an example of just the kind of left–right confrontation of which the French are especially fond. A left-wing candidate – François Hollande – aspired to the Elysée Palace; a right-wing candidate – Nicolas Sarkozy – wanted to remain in place. Moreover, the traditional contours of left and right, present at the end of the nineteenth century and throughout the twentieth century, appear to have remained intact. The left continues to define itself around the triple imperative of equality, universalism and redistribution, while the right stands for economic liberalism, ethno-centrism and order. The cultures of French Catholicism and the right are still closely connected, as the recent protests against gay marriage in 2013 made clear. Likewise, the public sector remains a bastion of the left that no Socialist government can afford to ignore. Finally, class divisions have not entirely evaporated, even if they have mutated into a public and private sector divide that now forms the basis of two contrasting political worldviews.[1]

The simultaneous impact of a two-round electoral system, party coalitions and the reduced choice in the second round of presidential and legislative elections has fixed the preferences of voters. In their necessary simplification of political choice, election results confirm rather than undermine existing patterns. The left and right continue to exist. But a wide range of surveys suggest that the antagonism between the two has lost much of its meaning. In 2011, 58 per cent of those questioned by the polling agency SOFRES considered ideas of right and left to be 'out of date', while only 35 per cent thought they were 'valid'. In March 1981, the results were 33 per cent and 43 per cent respectively. Today, Socialist Party supporters are the only ones to believe that the left–right divide remains pertinent; voters for all the other main parties – from the centre to the extreme-right – share the same scepticism. Why is it that today a large majority of French people no longer recognise the importance of the left–right divide? One of the main reasons is the consistent difficulty that political actors have faced in reducing complex and multi-faceted social issues to a simple, foundational left–right matrix. Over the past thirty years, two significant processes have blurred the lines of political affiliation and contributed to the restructuring of political culture. First, the growing fragmentation of French society has affected the collective structures that traditionally underpinned political preferences. Second, greater economic, social and political internationalisation has precipitated a re-evaluation of the left–right divide and opened new lines of fracture

The ideological and social fragmentation of French political culture

In 1990, the political theorist Marcel Gauchet observed that society was moving towards 'an individualism of disconnection and disengagement, where the demand for authenticity works against a sense of belonging to the collective'.[2] This process of fragmentation has been particularly noticeable in terms of ideological affiliation and social belonging. With respect to ideological affiliation, it is clear that notions of left and right have lost much of their meaning. While an Opinion Way–CEVIPOF survey from June 2012 found that a majority of French people still use the two terms to position themselves on the political spectrum (34 per cent on the left, 35 per cent on the right), 31 per cent consider themselves to be in the 'centre' or of no political orientation. Moreover, a large majority reject the binary opposition of left and right: in January 2002, 60 per cent of those surveyed (51 per cent on the left, 62 per cent on the right) agreed with the statement that 'notions of right and left are outdated: they no longer provide a useful means by which to judge the stance of individual politicians and political parties'. In 1981, only 33 per cent thought the same way. In a little over twenty years, the proportion of French people who rejected the left–right divide had almost doubled. This change was remarkable for its speed and its depth. For much of the 1980s, the proportions of those who saw the left–right divide as 'valid' and 'outdated' remained relatively stable. After 1989, and in subsequent decades, a large gap opened up between the two groups as the collapse of Communism and Mitterrand's 14-year presidency (1981–1995) acted as veritable catalysts for a change in public opinion. By the mid-1990s, the disintegration of a binary political model was visible among every age group and social class. A system that had defined French politics for two centuries – and formed the basis on which the Fifth Republic was founded – was falling apart.

When the constitution of the Fifth Republic was revised in 1958–1962, the distribution of powers and electoral legislation were predicated on the idea of a binary political system. This was embodied in successive left- and right-wing coalitions as well as a series of elections that explicitly opposed the two competing blocs (in 1965, 1967, 1968, 1973, 1974, 1978 and 1981). In each of these elections, 80–90 per cent of the electorate voted for what the political scientist Maurice Duverger called the 'bipolar quartet' of the Communist Party (PCF), the PS, the Gaullists and the non-Gaullist right.[3] These four parties, grouped into left- and right-wing coalitions, dominated every election until the middle of the 1980s when the political landscape was transformed by the emergence of the Green Party and the Front National (FN). The result was, in the words of another political scientist, a 'cacophonous sextet'.[4] Within a few years, the four major political groupings around which the binary political system of the Fifth Republic had originally been organised represented little more than 60–70 per cent of the votes. To take only the most recent example, in the 2012 legislative election, the parties that represented the four main groups (the Front de Gauche, the PS, the Union pour un movement populaire (UMP) and the now-defunct Union pour la démocratie française (UDF)) received 67.4 per cent of the vote.

It would appear, then, that a left–right divide which has its origins in the French Revolution, crystallised during the early Third Republic and remained prescient during the Fourth and the early Fifth Republic, has been profoundly disrupted. Of course, notions of left and right have not remained fixed throughout this period. Themes such as the nation, ecology and decentralisation have been appropriated by both sides. Pluralism has also been a major feature of French politics, to such an extent that most commentators have preferred to put 'left' and 'right' in the plural – 'les gauches', 'les droites' – in an attempt to capture the diversity of political opinions.[5] Thus, several major issues on which the identities of right and left were constructed are no longer as salient as they once were.

First, the question of institutions. This was the source of violent disagreements between right and left in the nineteenth-century, with partisans of a Republic, a constitutional monarchy and a monarchy of divine right fighting to impose their preferred form of government. More recently, there were echoes of these divisions in the clash between supporters of a parliamentary Republic and advocates of a stronger, presidential Republic in the late 1950s. But, with the left's acceptance of the Fifth Republic and its victory in 1981, the problem of institutional legitimacy has receded.[6]

Second, the question of religion. This, too, was a defining feature of nineteenth-century French politics. Those who defended a clerical vision of society and politics found themselves at odds with those who supported a more secular vision, and this disagreement was mapped on to political preferences. As the historian René Rémond remarked: 'anyone who observed the practices of the Catholic Church was by default classed on the right, while anyone who was seen as anticlerical needed to provide no further proof of his or her democratic credentials and attachment to the Republic'.[7] The Dreyfus Affair, the Affaire des Fiches, and the separation of Church and State in 1905 were highpoints of this confrontation.[8] Yet, despite some momentary revivals (notably on the issue of schooling), the religious question has gradually lost its hold on politics, in large part because of the secularisation of French society, a sharp decline in religious practice and the internal evolution of the Catholic Church.

Finally, the social question. Again, this has its roots in the nineteenth century, with the industrial revolution and the rise of an organised working class that was almost always associated with the left. The Popular Front of 1936, the debates surrounding the welfare state at the time of the Liberation of France in 1944, and the protests of May 1968 were all expressions of a social question that polarised politics along left- and right-wing lines. But an increase in the overall standard of living, the rapid growth of the middle class, and a widespread consensus surrounding the value of the welfare state have contributed to a sense that the social question is no longer a critical factor in the division between right and left.

These long-term historical processes have been complemented by more specific political changes. One of these is increased electoral instability.[9] This has been caused by the emergence of a new type of voter, less defined by his or her environment, and more willing to change his or her political preference in accordance with the immediate context. So, for instance, the difference in votes cast for specific candidates between the presidential elections of 2002 and 2012 shifted markedly: from 16.2 per cent to 28.6 per cent for the Socialist candidate; 19.9 per cent to 27.2 per cent for the UMP candidate; 3.4 per cent to 11.1 per cent for the PCF/Front de Gauche candidate; 6.8 per cent to 9.1 per cent for the centrist UDF candidate; 10.4 per cent to 1.7 per cent for the Trotskyist candidate; and 5.2 per cent to 2.3 per cent for the Green candidate.[10] Voters have become more fickle, while the number of traditionally 'loyal' voters has dropped. At the same time, French political life has become noticeably more centrist and consensual.[11] The left has accepted the market economy, the institutions of the Fifth Republic and nuclear deterrence. The right has accepted the abolition of the death penalty, artificial insemination, contraception and the reduction in the number of working hours. The reality of government means that, once the polemics of each successive electoral campaign have died away, there is little discernible difference between the policies of left- and right-wing governments. This divergence between confrontational political rhetoric and the consensual practice of power has left voters disillusioned, with an ever greater number choosing to cast a protest vote or abstain altogether. Even for the first round of the presidential election in 2012 where commentators were talking of a 're-bipolarisation' of politics around the PS and the UMP, an absolute majority of registered voters (56.5 per cent) chose to abstain, spoil their ballot papers, or vote for candidates at the margins of the political system. The main government parties now represent only a minority of the electorate. A certain modern political configuration, in which voter choice was defined by major ideological divisions embodied in the two main parties on the left and right, appears to be at an end. The ideological fragmentation of the past two or three decades has made political choice more obviously hybrid, unstable and resistant to classification.

Ideological fragmentation has been reinforced by social fragmentation.[12] In the decades following the end of the Second World War, a clear social binary underpinned the opposition between left and right. The 1970s and early 1980s marked the apex of this 'socio-political' clash. For example, in the second round of the 1974 presidential election, 68 per cent of workers voted for Mitterrand, while 66 per cent of senior executives, professionals and industrialists voted for Giscard d'Estaing. The left-wing parties of the time presented themselves, in the language of the PS, as the vanguard of a 'class front' that was supposed to bring together the working class, the salaried middle class and self-employed exploited workers. The PCF, still the dominant party on the left in the 1970s, justified its strategy of cooperation with the PS as one of a 'union of popular forces'. And both parties explicitly cast the right as the handmaidens of the 'ruling classes'. The political struggle between left and right over the social question in this period was seen as a straightforward expression of class struggle. By the early years of the twenty-first century, however, these socio-economic foundations had withered away. In the second round of the presidential election in 2007, 52 per cent of workers and 57 per cent of senior executives and professionals voted for Sarkozy. There was something of a return of social class in 2012 when 59 per cent of workers voted for Hollande and 55 per cent of senior executives and professionals opted for Sarkozy. But, even then, the idea that this was somehow a form of 'class struggle' is unconvincing. Today, the salaried middle class is more likely to be on the left than the working class; indeed, according to a post-election survey conducted by Opinion Way–CEVIPOF in 2012, senior executives and professionals are marginally more likely to describe themselves as 'on the left' (33 per cent) than workers (32 per cent).

The classic model of a social pyramid, with a large working class and a small ruling class, has been undercut by other socio-economic distinctions that cross class boundaries: employed vs. unemployed; single-earning vs. dual-earning households; or access to welfare services vs. limited access to services. These have been accompanied by a sharp growth in the salaried middle classes who, for the first time in the late 1980s, became numerically superior to the working class among the active population. This enormous 'central constellation', to use the terms of the sociologist Henri Mendras, has entailed a veritable 'middle-isation (*moyennisation*)' of French society and a corresponding disappearance of the social distinctions that underpinned political representation.[13] The fundamental question of a 'good society' is now just as likely to create divisions *within* the left and the right as it is to create divisions between them.

Where did this decline in class conflict come from? During France's post-war economic boom from 1945 to 1975 – often known as the 'Trente glorieuses' (Thirty Glorious Years) – strong economic growth minimised class differences, even though many scholars and intellectuals at the time talked about 'a new working class', 'working-class consciousness', 'class alliances' and a wide range of books on social class were available in academic bookstores. Political debate, above all on the left, was weighed down by interminable debates about the working class and its various configurations, the relationship between the 'social majority' and the 'political majority', the importance of a 'class front', the role of the middle class and so on. From the early 1980s onwards, this debate quickly evaporated, among both the intellectual and political élites. Such a trend was all the more paradoxical as this was exactly the moment at which France was entering a period of protracted crisis caused by stagnant economic growth, high unemployment and rising social inequality. But instead of talking more about class at a time when inequality was growing, the debate turned away from the issue. This disjunction clearly demonstrates the extent to which intellectual life can sometimes be out of touch with social reality.

In the past few years, there has been a renewed interest in the social question. A number of books have discussed the profound changes in social structure, the problem of downward social mobility, and the issue of 'social separatism'.[14] Nevertheless, the debate is no longer about the clash between the 'bourgeoisie' and the 'proletariat'. Instead, scholars prefer to talk about the evolution of the salaried classes, the development of a new 'precarious' class, the marginalisation of a disaffected 'underclass' and the breakdown of mechanisms of upward social mobility. This is far from the caricatured image of a working class in frontal collision with an embattled middle class and its vested interests. These strong class identities have now disappeared. Intra- and inter-generational mobility in the 1950s, 1960s and 1970s eroded them; class solidarity, where it existed, has fragmented or vanished altogether. And, of course, the sense of belonging to two diametrically opposed social classes has dissipated. At the start of the 2000s, a majority of French people claimed to have no attachment to a specific class.

To a large extent, the explanation for this change lies in the generalised rise in incomes during the Trente glorieuses, as well as a steep reduction in social inequalities and the vigorous development of the middle- and upper-income brackets. While workers still made up 31.5 per cent of the working population in 1983–4, non-routine manual workers, mid-level employees and senior executives made up 26 per cent, 18.5 per cent and 8.8 per cent respectively of the working population. The three or four decades since 1945 thus saw a noticeable decrease in social stratification. At the same time, the middle classes expanded as a consequence of a burgeoning public sector driven by the development of the welfare state and a strong demand for trained technicians and engineers who could contribute to France's post-war economic recovery.

Some of these trends have continued since the beginning of the 1980s, but new issues have arisen that have changed the ways in which the question of class is perceived. One trend that shows no sign of slowing down is the decline of the working class, which represented 28 per cent of the working population at the start of the 2000s. Today, the proportion of clerical workers (29.9 per cent) is greater than that of workers (27.9 per cent). Likewise, the fragmentation of the working class has continued. A majority of workers are employed in the service sector as opposed to the industrial sector, and they work in small or medium-sized companies. The working class is now also divided along various lines. There are differences between those in stable employment, those in insecure employment and those who are marginalised or unemployed; there are differences between French and 'immigrant' workers; and there are differences between a younger post-industrial generation that works in the service sector and an older industrial working class. In addition, a number of new developments have modified our perception of class. Globalisation, economic crises, and the desire to create a more flexible labour force have all contributed directly to what the French sociologist Robert Castel has called the end of a 'salaried society' that was tied to a strong welfare state and its ability to limit risk.[15] A form of 'social citizenship' that went hand in hand with full employment and social compromise has fallen apart. The working class is no longer the key collective actor that it was during the Trente glorieuses, nor is it at the heart of the Fordist–Keynesian compromise that made post-war social mobility and the welfare state possible. Today, the working class is inaudible. In the words of the sociologists Stéphane Béaud and Michel Pialoux, the working class has 'in a certain sense, made itself invisible in French society'.[16] This has been reinforced by a postmodern tendency to reject large collective organisations in favour of smaller entities that appeal to specific individual micro-identities. In this context, scepticism towards collective social action and the rise of identity politics have undermined ideas of class, with many of today's political conflicts revolving around symbolic, cultural or identity-based issues.

Social class provides an increasingly imperfect guide to political behaviour and orientation. Only 55 per cent of French people in 2002 identified with a particular class (the figure was 61 per cent in 1966), but it is above all the sense of belonging to the middle classes that has changed. In 2002, 42 per cent of people identified with the middle class and 24 per cent with the working class; the figures in 1966 were 21 per cent and 39 per cent respectively. The evidence for a sustained 'middle-isation' of French society becomes even stronger when survey respondents are not offered the option of not identifying with a class. In a 2006 SOFRES survey, 75 per cent of people said they belonged to the middle classes, 8 per cent to the upper classes, and only 16 per cent to the lower classes (classes modestes). This perception is consistent with objective measures of income stratification. In 2010, the French national institute for statistics (INSEE) revealed that the average monthly full-time salary for senior executives and salaried company owners (3,963 Euros) was not even three times greater than the average salary for workers (1,569 Euros). The average standard of living measured in 2010 by means of disposable household income divided by the number of adults and children living at the same address shows a significant if not excessive difference: the ratio between the average standard of living of the top 10 per cent (56,190 Euros) and the bottom 10 per cent (7,940 Euros) is 1 to 7. Obviously, the disparity between the two groups grows if income from assets such as property or investments is taken into account, especially given that the richest 10 per cent controlled almost half of France's assets in 2010.

Nevertheless, the gap between the richest and the poorest is not as large as one might imagine. Despite the dominant sense that income inequality has grown, statistics suggest a more complex picture. INSEE figures show that, between 1996 and 2007, the standard of living rose by 16.7 per cent (with adjustment for inflation) and that the gap between the top and bottom 10 per cent remained stable. In fact, the bottom 10 per cent saw their standard of living rise by 21 per cent, while for the top 10 per cent the rise was only 14.7 per cent. The 2008 financial crisis modified this picture somewhat since it depressed the spending power of more modest households and led to higher unemployment. Since 2008, unemployment has continued to rise. It now stands at over 10 per cent (10.8 per cent in the first quarter of 2013). At the same time, in the period from 2007 to 2012 the active population grew by 2 per cent and the number of jobs reduced by 121,700, especially in the industrial sector. This is undoubtedly the most severe economic contraction France has experienced since the Second World War. Yet, even in these straitened times, the spending power of French households increased by 0.5 per cent a year between 2008 and 2013. France, then, is not reverting to a polarised, class-based society in which an all-powerful bourgeoisie are at loggerheads with a pauperised and insurrectionary proletariat. Rather, French society has undergone irreversible change. The growth of the service sector continues unabated; the overall standard of living continues to increase; and the education system and the media continue to homogenise popular culture and social norms. Indeed, property ownership has now become France's number one aspiration: 58.1 per cent of French households owned their property in 2012, compared to 50.7 per cent in 1984, and the size of the average household has increased by 10 square metres in the same period. In a parallel development, the number of people who own securities and other financial instruments has risen to 24 per cent of the population above the age of 15 (approximately 11 million people). These and other trends strongly suggest that France is no longer a society governed by a binary relationship between classes.

This does not, of course, mean that all forms of social stratification have disappeared. As the sociologist Olivier Schwartz has observed, France is 'both more and less of a [class society today] than at the end of the 1970s'.[17] On the one hand, class has declined in importance for all of the aforementioned reasons; on the other, the boundaries between social groups have, in many cases, hardened. The élites and the middle classes are less open today to the idea of 'social mixing (*mixité sociale*)'; a growing hierarchy of educational qualifications has reinforced the divisions between different groups; the dream of upward social mobility among the working classes has evaporated; and many have been hit by a new wave of income and employment insecurity. Still, the difference between the present situation and the 1960s and 1970s is that these fractures are plural and cannot be reduced to a binary opposition between classes. The idea of a left deeply rooted in the working classes and a right deeply rooted in the élites is anachronistic. In 1974, these associations accurately reflected the distribution of the working-class and élite vote between Giscard d'Estaing and Mitterrand but, thirty years later, the picture is much less clear.

This deep transformation in French society has been reflected in the country's politics. The 2007 presidential election was highly significant in that it demonstrated the extent to which the left has struggled to mobilise the working-class vote in recent years. In 2007, 55 per cent of clerical workers and 52 per cent of workers chose to vote for Sarkozy. Until then, no right-wing candidate under the Fifth Republic had succeeded in gaining the majority of votes among workers. Five years later, in the presidential election of 2012, the financial crisis and the constraints of power had taken their toll and Sarkozy was only able to gain 41 per cent of the vote among workers and 49 per cent among clerical workers. It might seem that the left was again making inroads into a constituency that had hitherto been its sole preserve. But such an analysis is unconvincing. The Socialist Party has seen its working-class support collapse and, even at the time of Hollande's victory in 2012, he was far from the two-thirds support among workers that Mitterrand had enjoyed in the 1980s. Worse still, in an IPSOS/*Le Point* poll at the end of August 2013, a mere 25 per cent of workers and 21 per cent of clerical workers thought positively about Hollande's tenure as President. For now, the only beneficiary of the current crisis of confidence in the government is the FN: in the same poll from August 2013, 48 per cent of workers and 34 per cent of clerical workers thought positively about the FN leader, Marine Le Pen. The political and ideological system elaborated at the end of the nineteenth century in which the working class were represented by the socialist movement has begun to come apart. The changing professional identity of workers and their disillusionment with the left has damaged the privileged relationship between the working class and the left.

This process of detachment has been reinforced by the values that dominate the present-day Socialist Party. In the immediate post-war years, working-class values of order and hierarchy found an outlet in organisations like the Communist Party, which made no secret of its 'vertical' chain-of-command structure. But the left today has taken on many of the values of cultural liberalism and 'post-materialism'. As a consequence, it finds it increasingly difficult to respond to a working class desire for authority and order. In France, as elsewhere, the composition of the left has changed. Like its electorate, it has become more bourgeois. This is evident in the most significant legislation passed under the Jospin government (1997–2002) and Hollande's presidency (since 2012), which has largely reflected the interests and values of the middle class rather than the working class (civil unions (PACS), the 35-hour working week and gay marriage). These measures have strengthened the identity of the Socialists as the party of France's 'bohemian bourgeoisie' and therefore out of touch with the concerns of ordinary working people. From this perspective, the moderate left's flirtation with liberalism and multiculturalism has alienated a working class that shares few, if any, of the same values.

This separation is not simply political; it is also cultural. As a rule, the middle classes are more permissive than the working classes. This is true about topics as varied as education, immigration and the justice system. According to a recent study, 78 per cent of workers believe that 'above all, education should instil a sense of discipline and hard work'; only 48 per cent of senior executives and professionals feel the same way. 55 per cent of workers agree that 'there are too many immigrants in France', compared to only 38 per cent of senior executives and professionals. And 45 per cent of workers support the reintroduction of the death penalty, whereas only 20 per cent of senior executives and professionals agree.[18] At a time when voters are increasingly defined by their 'values', the left (and the Socialist Party in particular) find themselves in a delicate position since the values they choose to promote will have a direct consequence on their ability to mobilise voters among specific social groups.

More generally, the erosion of traditional class affiliations has transformed the left–right dynamic in French politics. Today, the working classes are likely to vote to the right or the extreme-right, as they did in the presidential elections of 2007 and 2012. Meanwhile, the middle classes remain undecided as to their political identity: in 2012, 57 per cent of artisans and shopkeepers voted for Sarkozy while 58 per cent of mid-level employees voted for Hollande. This fractured political landscape, in which political groupings have become unmoored from their sociological base, reflects contemporary French society. The latter has fragmented to the point that no single social division has the power to mobilise and organise large swathes of the electorate. These changes are even visible in the political geography of the country where formerly right-wing regions have switched to the left and vice-versa. For more than a century, left and right each had their own geographies. While this often remains the case, there have been some important reconfigurations due to internal migration and the weakening of local political traditions. Economic changes, urbanisation, the attraction of France's southern regions, the break-up of older territorial units and varied land use patterns are all indicators of a more mobile and fluid society. Specific regions are no longer so closely associated with specific political identities. Today, the Socialists have become a powerful force in the traditionally conservative western regions, the right has succeeded in penetrating republican Provence, and the FN has pushed deep into the former industrial bastions of the left and far-left.

The internationalisation of politics

Another key factor in explaining the transformation of French political culture is the internationalisation of economics, society and politics. This has given rise to a number of issues that do not fit easily into categories of left and right, such as the financial crisis of 2008, European integration, and globalisation. Surveys reveal that there is a strong correlation between educational levels and attitudes towards the wider world. Highly educated groups are consistently more optimistic and open to globalisation. By contrast, less educated groups – who have often been at the sharp end of the economic crisis – are uncomfortable with globalisation and more likely to be hostile to 'outsiders' and European integration. Not surprisingly, this tension has found its expression on both sides of the political spectrum. On the right, there has been an open conflict between a nationalist right (*droite souverainiste*) and a more open, liberal right. And, on the left, there has been a long-standing disagreement between a left open to the outside world and one that urges France to protect itself from globalisation. Today, the electorates that are most likely to reject globalisation can be found among voters for the extreme-left, the PCF, the nationalist right and the FN. What was once a clearly legible distinction between left and right has disintegrated entirely.

This change needs to be understood in the context of a widespread scepticism about the current state of the global economy. A 27-country survey conducted by GlobeScan/PIPA in 2009 confirmed a general French uneasiness with free-market capitalism and globalisation. Three results were especially significant. First, France emerged as the country in which the largest proportion of people believed in the need for an alternative economic system: 43 per cent of French respondents agreed that free-market capitalism 'is wrong and we need another system' – 29 per cent of Italians and Spaniards felt the same way, and only 19 per cent of Britons, 13 per cent of Americans and 9 per cent of Germans. Second, the French were the most enthusiastic about state intervention (after the Brazilians and the Chileans), with 76 per cent of French respondents agreeing on the need for state intervention in the regulation of companies, as opposed to 73 per cent in Spain, 70 per cent in Italy, 56 per cent in the United Kingdom, 45 per cent in Germany and 43 per cent in the United States. Finally, a majority of French respondents argued for greater oversight and regulation of large corporations: 57 per cent, as opposed to 53 per cent in Italy, 45 per cent in Spain, 40 per cent in the United Kingdom, 31 per cent in Germany and 24 per cent in the United States.

This desire for regulation and oversight stems from French pessimism vis-à-vis the financial crisis and globalisation. A Eurobarometer poll found that, in November 2010, 57 per cent of French people (as opposed to 48 per cent across Europe as a whole) believed the 'worst was still to come' with respect to the financial crisis and its impact on the labour market. Another Eurobarometer survey a few months later suggested that, of the major European nations, the French were the most pessimistic about the state of their economy: 79 per cent of French respondents thought the French economy was in 'quite bad' or 'very bad' shape (compared to an average of 68 per cent across the European Union) and 89 per cent thought the employment situation in France was 'quite bad' or 'very bad' (compared to an average of 74 per cent across the European Union). This pessimism has developed alongside a growing uneasiness with globalisation. In a third Eurobarometer poll from May 2011, only 44 per cent of French respondents agreed that 'globalisation is an opportunity for economic growth', as opposed to 50 per cent of Europeans as a whole, 52 per cent of Britons, 62 per cent of Germans and 69 per cent of Dutch. In an IFOP survey from January 2011, a large majority of French people (62 per cent) believed that France is not internationally competitive, whereas only 44 per cent of Britons, 18 per cent of Germans and 17 per cent of Dutch thought the same way.

This perception of the economy has its roots in a negative view of the free-market capitalist system: in a survey from January 2011, 52 per cent of French people agreed that 'the market economy and capitalism is broken, but must be retained because there is no alternative', while 33 per cent thought that the system needed to be changed altogether. Such negative attitudes towards the current global economic configuration are unparalleled elsewhere in the Western world. Contrary to the 1930s, however, this discontent has not expressed itself in destructive forms of political opposition. There are frequent protests, but the demand for change is rarely presented as a direct challenge to the existing political system. There is little evidence that we are seeing the return of the utopian dreams of many inter-war political activists, whose fantasies ended up fanning the flames of totalitarianism across Europe. Moreover, French attitudes towards free-market capitalism and globalisation vary markedly between social groups. An IFOP survey from December 2010 revealed that 61 per cent of those from higher socio-economic groups agreed that 'the development of international commercial exchanges is mostly positive' compared to 49 per cent of those from a lower socio-economic demographic. Different electorates within the right and left were equally divided on this issue: only 31 per cent of Front de Gauche supporters and 42 per cent of FN supporters agreed with the statement that commercial exchanges were positive, as opposed to 57 per cent of Socialist supporters and 75 per cent of UMP supporters.

This strongly suggests that globalisation and the recent financial crisis have precipitated new political splits that do not easily fit into the established politics of left and right. The FN, like many of its extreme-right nationalist European counterparts, has positioned itself at the forefront of the fight against all forms of globalisation. In her nomination speech in January 2011, the FN leader Marine Le Pen put it bluntly: 'Identity-massacring globalisation (*mondialisation identicide*) has transformed itself into an economic nightmare, a social tsunami, a moral Chernobyl!' This is consistent with her proposed policy of rigorous national preference in the labour market and the welfare state. By attacking cosmopolitanism and multiculturalism, Marine Le Pen wants her brand of ethno-cultural nationalism to become the vehicle for France's latent hostility to globalisation. But she faces stiff opposition for this mantle from far-left parties like the Front de Gauche, who share many of the same analyses of capitalism as the FN. The difference is that the far-left parties are much less comfortable with a purely national response. A long-standing tradition of internationalism limits their ability to defend protectionist policies. They are reduced instead to arguing in favour of a global Socialist economic system that would replace the existing capitalist order. Unfortunately for the far-left, the disillusioned working classes prefer the nationalist response of the extreme-right to the brave new world of radical socialism. It is not surprising, therefore, that France has followed the same pattern as many other European countries, where large swathes of the working classes have been seduced by the extreme-right. In the first round of the 2012 presidential election, Marine Le Pen succeeded in obtaining 17.9 per cent of votes cast (36 per cent among the unemployed, 24 per cent among workers and 26 per cent among non-routine manual workers). By contrast, Jean-Luc Mélenchon only managed to obtain 11.1 per cent of votes cast (6 per cent among the unemployed, 14 per cent among workers and 9 per cent among non-routine manual workers).

Of the traditional centre parties, the moderate left in particular has found it difficult to deal with this sustained hostility to globalisation. Since the mid-1980s, the French and European left has struggled with the effects of globalisation and the dismantling of the welfare state. As the political scientist Dominique Reynié argues, the moderate left has been affected by

> the process of globalisation, which exposes workers to acute economic pressures; the exhaustion of the welfare state, which reduces the state's productive and regenerative capacities; an ageing population, which has ideological side-effects such as the increasing importance of the theme of [crime] and 'security'; and demographic changes tied to immigration.[19]

In addition to these structural weaknesses, the left has faced a rising tide of populism among its traditional working-class support base. This has often come from right-wing parties and politicians who argue forcefully that they alone can protect France from the nefarious consequences of globalisation and immigration. Since the moderate left remains committed to internationalism and universalism, it cannot be seen to favour domestic labour over immigrant labour. But this has not prevented a working-class electorate from being drawn to nationalist and protectionist ideas.

As a result, various dissident groups have emerged on the left that have tried to build a 'neo-nationalist' platform. These include the anti-globalisation wing of the Socialist Party, the Nouveau parti anticapitaliste (NPA), the Front de Gauche, some members of the Green Party and the remains of the PCF. Together, they are the standard-bearers of a political discourse that combines visceral anti-liberalism with a glorification of the state and a xenophobic, protectionist nationalism. This resembles what the Socialist leader Léon Blum in the 1930s called 'social-nationalism' and it played a major part in the campaign for the 'no' vote in the referendum on the European constitution in 2005. In the run-up to the referendum, this 'social-nationalist' left succumbed to a nationalist vision that was nourished by hostility towards free-market capitalism, a rejection of the European project, a belief in the value of the state, but also a distinctly xenophobic fear of the 'Polish plumber'. Since 2005, in an attempt to halt the forward march of the extreme-right, left-wing politicians such as Jean-Luc Mélenchon and Arnaud Montebourg have tried to develop this vision further through ideas of 're-localisation' and 'de-globalisation'. But their efforts to reclaim the populist vote have largely failed. The working classes continue to find Marine Le Pen's fusion of cultural and economic nationalism more alluring.

On a number of key issues, then, the working classes have moved to the right, while the more affluent classes have remained attached to universalist and internationalist values. This shift in 'ideological tectonic plates' has led scholars such as Gérard Grunberg and Etienne Schweisguth to argue that French political culture has been durably transformed:

> The wind that is currently sweeping over France's ideological landscape does not seem likely to encourage the re-composition of the French political system around a left, supported by the working class and defending the values of economic anti-liberalism and universalism, and a right, supported by the rich and defending economic liberalism alongside a rejection of universalist values. On the contrary, at a time when the difficulties of European integration have become more than ever a source of political controversy and immigration remains a subject of major debate, there is the real possibility of a new political synthesis that would have on one side partisans of parochial nationalism and, on the other, supporters of some degree of economic liberalism and universalism.[20]

To put it another way: increasing social fragmentation, the breakdown of traditional patterns of collective organisation and greater cultural and economic diversity, the new split that is opening up in French politics is between those who support the idea of an 'open society' and those who prefer a 'closed society'.

Today, the already complex tapestry of French politics has become a veritable palimpsest of divisions, affiliations and identities. This would be perfectly normal were it not for the fact that the latest collision between 'open' and 'closed' visions of society has no clear expression in a political system that was built on and continues to feed off the bipolarity of right and left. And, since this division appears to be increasingly ill-adapted to the underlying trends within French society, the result is an unsettled and fractured political space in which contemporary social, cultural and political disagreements no longer fit inside an old-fashioned binary political system. The challenge now is to elaborate a political system that will take new forms of social conflict into account as well as the reality of a fragmented and disunited society.

Notes

1 François de Singly and Claude Thélot, *Gens du privé, gens du public: La Grande différence* (Paris: Dunod, 1988).

2 Marcel Gauchet, 'Pacification démocratique, désertion civique', *Le Débat* 60 (1990): 77–87.

3 Maurice Duverger, 'Un quadrille bipolaire', *Le Monde*, 15 March 1973.

4 Olivier Duhamel, 'Et après? Sur les conséquences politiques nationales des élections de mars 1992' in Philippe Habert, Pascal Perrineau and Colette Ysmal, eds., *Le Vote éclaté: Les Elections régionales et cantonales des 22 et 29 mars 1992* (Paris: DEP du Figaro et Presses de la FNSP, 1992).

5 René Rémond, *Les Droites aujourd'hui* (Paris: Louis Audibert, 2005); Jean-François Sirinelli, ed., *Histoire des droites*, 3 vols. (Paris: Gallimard, 1992); Jacques Julliard, *Les Gauches françaises. 1792–2012: Histoire, politique, imaginaire* (Paris: Flammarion, 2012).

6 Olivier Duhamel, *La Gauche et la Ve République* (Paris: PUF, 1993).

7 René Rémond, *La Politique n'est plus ce qu'elle était* (Paris: Calmann Lévy, 1993), 26.

8 The Affaire des Fiches was a political scandal that erupted at the same time as the Dreyfus Affair. In an attempt to 'republicanize' the army, a file containing information on the political and religious profiles of those in command in the French army was drawn up by Masonic Lodges belonging to the Grand Orient de France at the initiative of General Louis André who was Minister for War at the time. The scandal came to light in 1904, forcing the minister to resign.

9 Pascal Perrineau, ed., *La Décision électorale en 2012* (Paris: Armand Colin, Collection Recherches, 2012).

10 Pascal Perrineau, ed., *Le Vote normal. Les Elections présidentielle et législatives d'avril–mai–juin 2012* (Paris: Presses de Sciences Po, 2013).

11 François Furet, Jacques Julliard and Pierre Rosanvallon, *La République du Centre. La Fin de l'exception française* (Paris: Calmann-Lévy, 1988).

12 These analyses have been developed in greater depth in Pascal Perrineau, *Le Choix de Marianne. Pourquoi et pour qui votons-nous?* (Paris: Fayard, 2012).

13 Henri Mendras, *La seconde Révolution française: 1965–1984* (Paris: Gallimard, 1994).

14 Camille Peugny, *Le Déclassement* (Paris: Grasset, 2009); Louis Chauvel, *Le Destin des générations: Structure sociale et cohortes en France du XXième siècle aux années 2010* (Paris: PUF, 2010); Eric Maurin, *Le Ghetto français: Enquête sur le séparatisme social* (Paris: Seuil, 2004).

15 Robert Castel, 'Genèse et crise de la société salariale', *Mouvement social* 174 (1996): 7–14.

16 Stéphane Beaud and Michel Pialoux, *Retour sur la condition ouvrière: Enquête aux usines Peugeot de Sochaux-Montbéliard* (Paris, Fayard, 1999).

17 Olivier Schwartz, 'Vivons-nous encore dans une société de classes?, *La Vie des idees* (2009), http://www.laviedesidees.fr/Vivons-nous-encore-dans-une.html

18 Laurent Bouvet, *Le Sens du peuple, la gauche, la démocratie, le populisme* (Paris: Gallimard, 2012).

19 Dominique Reynié, 'Situation de la droite en Europe', *Commentaire* 135 (2011), 648.

20 Gérard Grunberg and Etienne Schweisguth, 'Vers une tripartition de l'espace politique', in Daniel Boy and Nonna Mayer, eds., *L'Électeur a ses raisons* (Paris: Presses de Sciences Po, 1997), 179–218.

2

The Front National since the 1970s:

Electoral Impact and Party System Change

James Shields

In a book about the changing landscape of French politics since the 1970s, no party presses its case for consideration more forcefully than the Front National (FN). Between the National Assembly elections of 1973, which the FN was founded to contest in the name of a unified French nationalist right, and the most recent corresponding elections of 2012, the party increased its national vote share from 0.5 per cent (fewer than 125,000 votes) to 13.6 per cent (over 3.5 million votes). Between the same two elections, by contrast, the once powerful French Communist Party (PCF) saw its vote share collapse from 21.4 per cent in 1973 to a mere portion of the 6.9 per cent polled collectively in 2012 by the far-left alliance, the Front de Gauche (FG). Measured by performance in presidential elections over the same period, the growth of support for the FN is even more spectacular: from 0.7 per cent (fewer than 200,000 votes) in 1974 to 17.9 per cent (over 6.4 million votes) in 2012.[1]

Located close to the perimeters of the FN's lifespan, these elections frame some of the most profound changes in French politics under the Fifth Republic. The long-term rise of the FN and decline of the PCF are part of a wider picture of change that has seen the ever disunited centre-right combine forces (mostly) in the Union pour un Mouvement Populaire (UMP) while the

Socialist Party (PS) has come to exert an unrivalled domination on the left. With the PS (29.3 per cent), the UMP (27.1 per cent) and the FN (13.6 per cent) accounting for fully 70 per cent of the vote in the 2012 National Assembly elections, and with no other party exceeding the 6.9 per cent of the Front de Gauche, the contours of France's political map seem defined today by a clear tripartite structure of centre-left, centre-right and far-right blocs. This three-way concentration of voting was even more pronounced in the 2012 presidential election, where almost three out of four first-round votes (just under 74 per cent) went to the Socialist (28.6 per cent), UMP (27.2 per cent) and FN (17.9 per cent) candidates, leaving barely a quarter of the entire ballot to be shared among the remaining seven contenders.

Yet this apparently simple 'tripolarisation' masks complexities in relation to the FN's current positioning within French political space. In light of the defining structural tensions in post-war French politics between fragmentation and bipolarisation, this chapter examines the role of the FN within the French party system today.[2] It seeks to provide some historical context for understanding the current strength of the FN and how this fits within the evolution of party competition in France over recent decades. It discusses the FN as a force for both fragmentation *and* bipolarisation, considering the positioning and repositioning of other parties vis-à-vis the FN; and it shows the FN to be a party whose reserves of support lie not only on the right but also on the left. The chapter concludes by assessing the prospects opened by the switch from a strategy of systematic opposition under Jean-Marie Le Pen to one of systemic integration under Marine Le Pen.

Fragmentation and bipolarisation in contemporary French politics

For party system analysts, France's political landscape offers a rich and varied topography stretching back to the restoration of democracy following the Vichy regime of the Occupation years. Under the Fourth Republic (1946–58), the most marked feature of the French party system was its fragmentation, with electoral support dispersed across an array of old and new parties competing for power in a National Assembly elected by proportional representation. Geographical specificities, socio-economic cleavages, sectoral interests and divergent policy agendas made for unstable and short-lived coalitions, shifting party alliances, and an average government life expectancy of some six months. Under the Fifth Republic (since 1958), this tendency to fragmentation has been constrained by the powerful countervailing force of a two-ballot majority voting system that exerts a polarising pull towards broad coalitions of right and left.

These polarising constraints have not resulted in any lessening of inter-party competition. French voters continue to select from a wide range of parties, and those parties compete not just for the grand prize of the presidency but also for 577 seats in the National Assembly and 348 in the Senate, 1,880 seats in regional councils, 4,052 seats in departmental councils, 74 seats for France in the European Parliament, and no fewer than 519,417 seats on municipal councils.[3] Competition at all of these electoral levels, however, is tempered by the imperative to preserve tactical alliances, observing what the Socialist and Communist parties have long called 'la discipline républicaine', most evident in second-ballot withdrawal agreements. The resulting 'bipolar multipartism' has ensured that, whatever the proliferation of parties and candidates contesting elections, every government under the Fifth Republic (except for the transitional administration of 1958–62) has been supported by an effectively sound parliamentary majority or coalition of right or left. This prevalence of polarisation over fragmentation has given Fifth Republic politics their structural logic.

The classic expression of this polarisation is a presidential election by universal suffrage where only two candidates can advance to the run-off, each dependent for election on mustering the larger presidential coalition; but the same polarising pull has been a structuring force in all arenas of political competition. It has also led recently to what some analysts have identified as a shift from multiparty to bipartisan polarisation, or the beginnings in France of a predominantly two-party system on the Anglo-Saxon model.[4] Other analysts see pluralist fragmentation as a defining feature still of the French party system, a fragmentation that continues to be artificially masked by institutional curbs and strategic imperatives.[5]

The respective performances of the PCF and the Gaullist Union pour la Nouvelle République (UNR) in 1958 laid bare the mechanics of electoral competition under the Fifth Republic. Having won over a quarter of the vote and over a quarter of National Assembly seats (145) in 1956 under the proportional system of the Fourth Republic, the PCF saw its 18.9 per cent of first-round votes in 1958 translated into just over 2 per cent of seats (10) on the second round. The most powerful party of 1956 was thus reduced to the weakest in 1958 by a two-ballot voting system that nullified a party as strong as the PCF if it could not reach out to wider support through tactical alliances for the crucial run-off ballot. The Gaullist UNR, with a smaller share of the first-round vote (18 per cent), drew sufficient support from conservative, centre-right and even centre-left voters in the second round to win some 40 per cent of the seats (188).[6]

This inauguration of the new electoral rules in 1958 and the early dominance enjoyed by the UNR would compel other parties to reassess their political alliances and to seek wider reserves of second-preference support. This would result in the re-mapping of the political landscape into what Maurice Duverger would call a 'bipolar quartet', a configuration that was to find its most balanced expression in the National Assembly elections of 1978 when the PS, the PCF, the neo-Gaullist Rassemblement pour la République (RPR), and the smaller centre-right parties in and around the Union pour la

Démocratie Française (UDF) each attracted 20–25 per cent of the ballot, accounting between them for close to 90 per cent of the entire vote.[7]

Though the neat symmetry of the 1978 election was to be the exception rather than the rule, the power balance between the opposing left–right coalitions was broadly maintained in the 1980s and 1990s, with a strengthened PS compensating for its declining Communist partner and with the RPR competing with its UDF ally for supremacy on the right. As Pascal Perrineau reminds us in the previous chapter, Jean-Marie Le Pen's qualification for the second round of the presidential election in 2002 put an end to the comfortable assumption that such run-offs were the preserve of centre-right and centre-left. It did not, however, alter the power balance between the dominant forces of French politics. In the subsequent National Assembly elections of 2002, the newly formed centre-right UMP was returned with an emphatic majority – a majority it would retain in 2007 in defiance of a pattern that had seen governing majorities swing from right to left and back again at all National Assembly elections since the victory of the right in 1978: 1981 (left), 1986 (right), 1988 (left), 1993 (right), 1997 (left) and 2002 (right).

This period saw the normalising not only of left–right alternation in government but also of power sharing, with three spells of left–right 'cohabitation' (1986–8, 1993–5, 1997–2002) tightening the hold over power exercised by the 'parties of government'. The same period witnessed the emergence of new political forces (far-right, far-left, green and other) as challengers and/or auxiliaries to the established blocs of right and left. Despite what seemed to be a trend of growing multipartism and increasing fragmentation through the 1990s and early 2000s, the 2007 presidential and National Assembly elections gave all the appearance of a strongly bipolarised system structured not around four main parties now but around two, with the PS consolidating its dominance on the left and the UMP on the centre-right. In the 2007 elections to the National Assembly, the UMP and PS between them won almost 65 per cent of the vote in the first round and almost 90 per cent in the second, securing 499 of the 577 seats and leaving the UMP on an absolute majority with 313. These elections seemed to mark the end of a period of bipolarised multipartism and the beginnings in France of a two-party system in which both UMP and PS had passed a point of critical dominance on right and left respectively.

The Front National within the French party system

Throughout the early electoral history of the Fifth Republic, institutional constraints and the dynamics of the party system effectively barred entry to non-mainstream parties wishing to impose themselves as new and independent players. The founding rationale of the Fifth Republic had been to concentrate power and to exclude outsider parties (like the Poujadists under the Fourth Republic) that might constitute a threat to the political order. Within a presidency-oriented political culture where parties now acted primarily as presidential support groups, the breakthrough of a serious new challenger party looked a remote prospect. The National Assembly elections of 1978 were, we have seen, monopolised by the 'big four' political forces of the PCF, PS, RPR and UDF, each of which would field its heavyweight champion for the presidency in 1981 (the four garnering between them over 87 per cent of the vote in a field of ten contenders).

Within this closed party system, there was no non-Communist far-left alternative of any note, nor any electorally significant environmental party, and no far-right party with even the faintest electoral prospect. In his study of political parties in France in the 1970s, François Borella described far-right and far-left movements alike as mere 'spectators' and 'occasional agitators' on the outer margins of an inaccessibly bipolarised system.[8] In the National Assembly elections of 1981, non-Communist far-left movements mustered 1.4 per cent of the vote, ecologists 1 per cent, and the combined forces of the far-right 0.4 per cent, with less than 0.2 per cent going to the Front National of Jean-Marie Le Pen, who could not secure sufficient support from elected sponsors to stand in the presidential election. In 1981 as in 1978, therefore, the parties of the 'bipolar quartet' occupied the political terrain to the near exclusion of all others. Their combined scores in the National Assembly elections of 1981 came to over 92 per cent, higher even than in 1978. Adding the moderate 'divers droite' and 'divers gauche' scores plus that of the Socialists' long-time centre-left allies, the Left Radicals, brought the figure to over 97 per cent, leaving less than 3 per cent for protest, anti-system, single-issue or other parties.

This four-way monopoly of electoral support was not to last. From the mid-1980s, the emergence of new challengers on right and left, combined with the decline of the PCF, tested the solidity of the established party system. Of the new political players emerging in this period, the FN was by far the most significant and the most durable. While various configurations of greens and fringe movements such as Chasse, Pêche, Nature et Traditions (CPNT) or the sovereignist Rassemblement pour la France (RPF) recorded isolated successes in regional, European or National Assembly elections, the FN established itself as a tenacious challenger at every point in the electoral cycle, for vote share if not for actual seats. Following its breakthrough in the European elections of 1984, the FN went on to attain average first-round scores of over 10 per cent in seven National Assembly elections (1986–2012) and of 15 per cent in five presidential elections (1988–2012).

Although Tables 2.1 and 2.2 chart an electoral challenge sustained over a quarter of a century, the influence of the FN within the French party system has not been constant throughout that period. It can be divided into four phases: electoral consolidation despite continued marginality (1986–94), increasing electoral impact (1995–98), decline (1999–2009), and reinvigoration (since 2010).

TABLE 2.1 *The Front National vote in National Assembly elections (first or single round), 1986–2012*

Year	Votes	%
1986	2,703,442	9.6
1988	2,359,528	9.7
1993	3,159,477	12.4
1997	3,784,018	14.9
2002	2,873,556	11.1
2007	1,116,136	4.3
2012	3,528,663	13.6

TABLE 2.2 *The Le Pen vote in presidential elections, 1988–2012*

Year	Votes	%
1988	4,376,742	14.4
1995	4,571,138	15.0
2002 (1st round)	4,804,713	16.9
2002 (2nd round)	5,525,906	17.8
2007	3,834,530	10.4
2012	6,421,426	17.9

From 1986 to 1994, the FN consolidated its electoral presence and raised its capacity to threaten the political balance, but without any decisive influence on election outcomes (despite winning 35 seats in the National Assembly under an exceptional department-list proportional system in 1986). This changed in 1995, when Jacques Chirac owed his presidential victory against the Socialist Lionel Jospin to vote transfers from Jean-Marie Le Pen (with an estimated 2.3 million first-round Le Pen voters ensuring Chirac's 1.6 million margin of victory in the run-off).[9] This was the first occasion when FN voters brought a decisive, if indirect, impact to bear in a national election, an impact that would be repeated in subsequent presidential elections. In 2002, Le Pen's ousting of Jospin and qualification for the run-off assured Chirac's landslide re-election in a contest the incumbent had been uncertain to win against his Socialist challenger. In 2007, Nicolas Sarkozy's strong appeal to Le Pen supporters in the first round, together with an estimated 2.5 million vote transfers for the second round, provided his margin of victory (2.2 million votes) against the Socialist Ségolène Royal; and, conversely, Sarkozy's inability in 2012 to rally enough Marine Le Pen voters for the second round consigned him to defeat.[10]

A clear impact on election outcomes was also exerted in the municipal elections of 1995, the National Assembly elections of 1997 and the regional elections of 1998. In the 1995 municipal elections, the FN won control of the towns of Toulon, Orange and Marignane in the southern Provence–Alpes–Côte d'Azur region, adding Vitrolles in a by-election in 1997. In the National Assembly elections of 1997, 76 three-way run-offs in legislative constituencies contested by FN candidates split the vote on the right and helped secure 47 seats for the left and the defeat of a number of prominent centre-right candidates. The FN could not claim here to have been the determining factor in the left's 63-seat majority, but it did play a highly influential role. Even in the 445 constituencies where it did not contest the second round, the FN had an influence on some results through the votes cast by its supporters (with an estimated 50 per cent transferring to the RPR–UDF, 21 per cent voting for PS candidates, and 29 per cent abstaining or spoiling their ballot).[11]

In the regional elections of 1998, the FN emerged with 15 per cent and 275 regional councillors as almost the strongest party on the right (ahead of the UDF with 262 councillors and close behind the RPR with 285). In four of France's 22 metropolitan regions (Bourgogne, Languedoc-Roussillon, Picardie, Rhône-Alpes), local centre-right leaders secured governing majorities with the tacit or overt support of FN regional councillors. These elections allowed the FN to increase not just its tactical bargaining power but also its regional administrative role and clientelist influence.

This period of 1995–1998 marked a high point in the pressure exerted by the FN on the RPR and UDF. It gave rise to intense discussions on both sides about the strategic sense of continuing to resist an alliance and thereby splitting the vote on the right. The dilemma was resolved only by the scission of the FN in January 1999 and the departure of much of the party's administrative and elected personnel with former deputy leader Bruno Mégret, who had been more favourable to a deal with the centre-right than the old guard faithful to Jean-Marie Le Pen and wedded to a posture of continued anti-system populism. This damaging split weakened the party and saw membership fall by around half from a peak of some 50,000 in the 1990s.[12] It seemed to presage the end of the FN as a major force in French politics, ushering in a period of declining electoral performance and influence between 1999 and 2009.

Despite Jean-Marie Le Pen's election to the presidential run-off in 2002 and a record score for the FN in the regional elections of 2004, this period saw a sequence of electoral results at different levels (European 1999, 2004, 2009; presidential 2007; legislative 2007; municipal 2008) that returned the FN to levels not seen since the party's breakthrough in the mid-1980s, depriving it of the bargaining power that had so imposed upon elements of the centre-right in the 1998 regional elections. The score of 4.3 per cent in the 2007 National Assembly elections was the FN's poorest since 1981, cutting its annual state funding from 4.6 to 1.8 million euros and landing the party with a bill for the campaign costs of 361 candidates who had failed to win state reimbursement by securing at least 5 per cent of the vote.[13] In the municipal elections of March 2008, the party would plumb further depths, falling below 1 per cent in its national average. The FN seemed a party that had run short of ideas, was facing financial ruin, and whose electoral dynamism was approaching exhaustion.

The fourth phase, that of strong electoral recovery, can be synchronised with Marine Le Pen's emergence as prospective then confirmed successor to her father as FN leader in 2010–11. A partial electoral recovery in the regional elections of March 2010 (11.4 per cent) and an unprecedented score in the first round of cantonal elections in March 2011 (15 per cent) set the party on track for its record result in the 2012 presidential election and near-record performance in the National Assembly elections that followed. Electorally reinvigorated, it also began to recover financially, seeing its annual state funding rise now to 6 million euros on the strength of its 13.6 per cent share of the ballot and the election of two parliamentary deputies in 2012.

The Front National: A force for fragmentation or bipolarisation?

This brief overview of the FN's fluctuating fortunes raises the question of its role as a disruptive element within the bipolarising logic that has so defined Fifth Republic politics. The FN was formed in 1972 to be a fragmenting force upon the Republic, a 'receptacle of all discontent' working to 'bring down the regime'.[14] Although it affected a posture of democratic engagement, it was an anti-system party within the Sartorian definition: its founding mission was to subvert the Gaullist Republic with its hated institutions, defining values and dominant political forces of right and left.[15] In keeping with that mission, the FN's electoral appeal has been based on popular disaffection with the mainstream parties, 'la bande des quatre (the gang of four)' in Jean-Marie Le Pen's favoured phrase, the 'UMPS' in Marine Le Pen's updated formulation. With their message of 'Tous pareils, tous pourris (They're all the same, all rotten)', they have sought to chip away at the political legitimacy enjoyed by the mainstream parties and to open a space for the FN large enough to change the dynamics of electoral competition.

We saw in Pascal Perrineau's opening chapter that the wider resonances of this anti-system message have been felt in many ways, but the FN has been the most potent force for disruption within the French party system. This disruptive capacity was dramatically shown in the 2002 presidential election. Although Jean-Marie Le Pen's shock election to the run-off at the expense of outgoing Socialist Prime Minister Jospin was part of a much wider picture of fragmentation in that election (with record vote dispersal across candidates, record abstention for a presidential election, record anti-system voting), it stands as the event which marks a rupture in the electoral norms of the Fifth Republic.

Yet the real significance of the FN since its emergence as an electoral challenger in the 1980s has not been as a fragmenting force but rather, perversely, as a force for consolidating the very bipolarism it sought to end. Already in the 1988 National Assembly elections, the concern of the RPR and UDF to close ranks not only against the left but also against an FN that had almost deprived them of their slender majority in 1986 was evident in their decision to present single joint candidates in the name of an Union du Rassemblement et du Centre (URC). The same tactical solidarity of the RPR–UDF, reconfigured as the Union pour la France (UPF), ensured the centre-right a sweeping victory in the National Assembly elections of 1993. This gave the FN its campaign focus for the subsequent elections of 1997, with its objective to inflict maximal damage on the outgoing centre-right coalition, provoke the 'implosion of the RPR–UDF bloc' and bring about a 'recomposition of the broad political landscape'.[16]

The election of Le Pen to the presidential run-off in 2002 seemed to take the FN a step closer to forcing such a recomposition, yet it merely gave new impetus to the bipolarisation of French politics. If the first round showed the FN's potential for disruption, the second round exposed the limits of its electoral capacity. The election of 2002 produced the wrong result for the FN. Le Pen had long built his hopes on eliminating the leading centre-right candidate then mobilising a broad coalition of the right against the Socialist front runner in the second round. Facing Chirac rather than Jospin removed all but the most marginal room for attracting support beyond his own core electorate. This restricted his advance between the two rounds to less than 1 per cent, some 720,000 votes, while a massive 'Republican front' rallied for the incumbent President. The 3 per cent (fewer than a million votes) that had separated Chirac from Le Pen in the first round swelled to a winning margin of over 64 per cent (some 20 million votes) in the second (82.2 per cent to 17.8 per cent).

In the wake of this aberrant presidential poll, the creation in 2002 of the UMP formalised the centre-right's strategy of increased internal cooperation and continued exclusion of the FN. The formation for the first time under the Fifth Republic of a single overarching centre-right party constituted arguably the most far-reaching outcome of the FN's impact on the French party system. No more would the first round of the presidential election be treated as a form of primary on the centre-right. The presidential elections of 2007 and 2012 would see the designated UMP candidate, Nicolas Sarkozy, neutralise competition within his own extended political family and seek to rally a unified coalition of centre-right support, with only the challenge of the non-aligned centre (in François Bayrou) recalling the previously open internecine rivalry within a nominally allied centre-right.

A restructuring impact was also exerted by the FN on the left. Chastened by the severe defeat of 1993, the parties of the left embarked on a renewed project of cooperation to compete against the greater intra-bloc cohesion of the centre-right. This would take concrete form in the government of the 'gauche plurielle' from 1997 to 2002. But unity through diversity is, as the left would discover, a risky strategy. Mortgaged to their observance of pluralism, the Socialists felt the fragmenting effects in 2002 of a surplus of left-wing presidential candidates, creating the conditions for Le Pen's elimination of Jospin. Following that débâcle, the need for tighter concertation was the driving force behind the electoral agreements between the Socialists, the Parti Radical de Gauche (PRG) and the Mouvement des Citoyens (MDC) in 2007, an approach that would be replicated and again deter the multiplication of leftist presidential candidacies in 2012.[17]

From the late 1980s, therefore, the FN acted as a spur to greater cooperation and partisan discipline on the centre-right, in National Assembly and other elections if not initially in the presidential contest. Though the response on the left was less urgent, it was accelerated by the heavy defeat of 1993. The 2002 presidential election marked a decisive moment. It confirmed the imperative, as urgently now on the left as on the right, to minimise fragmentation and promote intra-bloc cooperation over intra-bloc competition, favouring the consolidation of a two-pole system structured around the dominant parties of the UMP and the PS. The reduction from 16 presidential candidates in 2002 to 12 in 2007 and 10 in 2012 partly reflected this turn towards a more concerted bipolarity. The 57 per cent won by the UMP and PS candidates in the first round in 2007 (21 million votes) and their combined 56 per cent in 2012 (20 million votes), compared with only 36 per cent for Chirac and Jospin in 2002 (10.3 million votes), seemed to confirm this renewed assertion of bipolarism over fragmentation. The subsequent elections to the National Assembly amplified this picture, with the UMP and PS taking between them almost as large a share of the 577 seats in 2012 (474: 82 per cent) as they had in 2007 (499: 86 per cent) and seeming to bear out Grunberg and Haegel's argument for a two-bloc system centred on these hegemonic parties and their satellites.[18]

Real power and virtual power

So where does the FN sit within this bipolarised political space? The question invites two quite contrary answers. In terms of political influence, the FN has imposed itself as a third competitive bloc and intensified its challenge to the two-bloc dominance of centre-right and centre-left. Far from being a marginal far-right party exerting only nuisance power, the FN has acquired in Gilles Ivaldi's terms a 'central place' in French politics through its ability to set the policy agenda on certain issues and to compete for votes on both right and left of the political divide.[19]

Other analyses concur with this view of the FN as a central electoral competitor and argue for an increasing 'tripolarisation of French political life'.[20] 'We're moving towards a landscape that is effectively tripartite,' warned the Socialist deputy Jean-Christophe Cambadélis in summer 2013, calling on the various components of the left to unite and form 'the strongest pole'.[21] Reacting to the FN's elimination of the Socialist-backed PCF candidate in the cantonal by-election of Brignoles in October 2013 (an election the FN would go on to win in a run-off against the UMP), the PS first secretary Harlem Désir saw 'a very serious warning for the left'. Division, he urged, 'is not an option . . . In the prevailing conditions, the left must unite'.[22]

The same argument for unity in the face of the FN challenge ran through the vexed debates sparked by the leadership contest within the UMP in 2012 and the calls for the party to stay true to its 'founding pact' of bringing together diverse currents of the post-Gaullist and post-Giscardian centre-right. The FN had opened a 'fault line' in the UMP, warned former Prime Minister Jean-Pierre Raffarin, sounding a 'red alert' over the danger of the party fracturing. The UMP's internal divisions were also, for some, a factor in its electoral defeat by the FN in Brignoles.[23] Not the least of the fracture lines now running through the UMP is that between a national leadership firm in its refusal to countenance a deal with the FN and a majority of grassroots supporters who favour binding or occasional cooperation.[24]

All of this speaks to the *political power* of the FN as felt by the mainstream parties, and to its polarising effects on the party system. In terms of *executive power*, however, the FN has been effectively consigned to the margins. Here it is no more than a virtual force. It has failed with very few exceptions to convert its influence into representation and remains almost entirely bereft of institutional existence. For all its anti-establishment invective, it has barely made a dent in the UMP–PS duopoly and the stability of two-bloc politics as bolstered by the two-ballot majority voting system. Other factors too (the electoral calendar and reform of the voting rules for certain elections) have conspired to perpetuate the hegemony of the mainstream parties and the FN's exclusion from 'the system'. It exists as an increasingly potent electoral force, with its presence amplified through the media; but its lack of access to executive power at almost all levels is among the most serious obstacles to the systemic integration its leader now claims to seek.

Before considering in more detail the obstacles that impede the FN, let us first take some measure of its real, and growing, political significance. The FN emerged from the 2012 presidential and National Assembly elections stronger than ever in terms of support, having attracted a combined 10 million votes across both first ballots. Not only did Marine Le Pen, with 6.4 million votes, outdistance her father's first-round performance in 2002 (4.8 million); she exceeded the joint scores of both Jean-Marie Le Pen and Bruno Mégret in 2002 (5.5 million) and of Jean-Marie Le Pen and Philippe de Villiers in 1995 (6 million). More remarkably, she secured more first-round votes than Jacques Chirac in any of the four presidential elections he contested between 1981 and 2002 – two of which Chirac went on to win (1995 and 2002).

Of all the candidates in the 2012 presidential election, and of all the parties in the 2012 National Assembly elections, Marine Le Pen and the FN showed the strongest upward dynamic, gaining 7.5 per cent and 9.3 per cent respectively on the corresponding elections of 2007 (see Table 2.3). Over a longer time frame, the share of the vote on the right claimed by the FN in

TABLE 2.3 *Electoral ups and downs, 2007–12*

Candidate (presidential elections)	Percentage change of vote share between 2007 and 2012 (first round)
Ségolène Royal/François Hollande (PS)	+2.8
Nicolas Sarkozy (UMP)	–4
Jean-Marie Le Pen/Marine Le Pen (FN)	+7.5
François Bayrou (UDF/MoDem)	–9.4
Various far-left (Besancenot, Buffet, Laguiller, Bové/Mélenchon, Poutou, Arthaud)	+4.1
Party (National Assembly elections)	**Percentage change of vote share between 2007 and 2012 (first round)**
Parti Socialiste (PS)	+4.6
Union pour un Mouvement Populaire (UMP)	–12.4
Front National (FN)	+9.3
UDF/MoDem/Centre pour la France	–5.8
Various far-left (mainly PCF/Front de Gauche)	+0.2

presidential elections has risen from 1.5 per cent in 1974, through 28.3 per cent in 1988, to 38.2 per cent in 2012 (see Table 2.4). In National Assembly elections, the FN's share of the vote on the right has similarly risen from 0.4 per cent in 1981 through 17.6 per cent in 1986 to 28.4 per cent in 2012 (see Table 2.5). The elections of 2012 therefore represent (with the exception of 1997) a peak not just in votes cast for the FN but, more worryingly for the UMP, in the proportion of the combined right vote taken by Marine Le Pen and her party.

The map of FN support as drawn by Marine Le Pen in the first round of the 2012 presidential election had a broadly familiar look, with high points in the

TABLE 2.4 *Front National share of combined right vote in presidential elections (first round), 1974–2012*

Year	Combined right vote (%)	FN share of combined right vote (%)
1974	51.6	1.5
1988	50.9	28.3
1995	59.2	25.4
2002*	48.4	34.8
2007*	45	23.2
2012*	46.9	38.2

* Figures do not include François Bayrou with his posture of non-aligned centrism

TABLE 2.5 *Front National share of combined right vote in National Assembly elections (first or single round), 1981–2012*

Year	Combined right vote (%)	FN share of combined right vote (%)
1981	43.1	0.4
1986	54.7	17.6
1988	50.3	19.2
1993	56.9	21.8
1997	51.5	29
2002*	52.9	21
2007*	51.1	8.4
2012*	47.9	28.4

* Figures do not include François Bayrou's UDF/MoDem with its posture of non-aligned centrism

south-east, the north and the north-east of the country. She secured 20 per cent or more of the vote in 11 of France's 22 metropolitan regions and in 43 of the 96 departments. She won over 25 per cent in ten departments, including the south-eastern Vaucluse, where she recorded her highest score of 27 per cent, and the neighbouring Gard, where she led the poll with 25.5 per cent. Other strong scores were registered in the Provence–Alpes–Côte d'Azur and Languedoc-Roussillon regions: 24.8 per cent in the Var department, 24.2 per cent in Pyrénées-Orientales, 23.5 per cent in Alpes-Maritimes and 23.4 per cent in the Bouches-du-Rhône. An arc of departments across the north also saw scores well above Le Pen's national average: Pas-de-Calais (25.5 per cent), Somme (23.8 per cent), Oise (25.1 per cent), Aisne (26.3 per cent) and Ardennes (24.5 per cent). Le Pen voting was strong in north-eastern departments in or adjoining the border regions of Alsace and Lorraine, with 25.8 per cent in Meuse, 24.7 per cent in Moselle, 24.2 per cent in Vosges, 23.4 per cent in Haut-Rhin, 25.3 per cent in Haute-Marne and 25.1 per cent in Haute-Saône as in Aube. In only two departments of metropolitan France (Paris and Hauts-de-Seine) did Le Pen's score fall below 10 per cent.

Beyond these familiar geographical contours, a feature of the 2012 election was the growth of support in industrial and post-industrial areas of the north and north-east, with Le Pen competing more vigorously against the parties of the left than against the centre-right in working-class constituencies of some departments (Oise, Somme, Nord, Pas-de-Calais, Aisne, Moselle, Vosges, Haute-Saône, Bas-Rhin and Haut-Rhin).[25] Le Pen voting was particularly high in some former left-wing municipal strongholds: as examples, in the Nord department, Bruay-sur-l'Escaut (33 per cent), Anzin (29.4 per cent), Vieux-Condé (29.4 per cent) and Douchy-les-Mines (29 per cent); or in Pas-de-Calais, Harnes (31.8 per cent), Montigny-en-Gohelle (31.8 per cent),

Méricourt (30.7 per cent), Oignies (29.4 per cent), Sallaumines (29.3 per cent), Liévin (29 per cent) and Bully-les-Mines (29 per cent). In Le Pen's adopted political base of Hénin-Beaumont in the Pas-de-Calais coalfields, the FN leader came first with 35.5 per cent.[26]

In all of these locations, and in many more, the FN emerged as the main party of opposition to the PS and PCF. Other northern towns built on the production of coal, steel and iron voted strongly for the FN leader, such as Freyming-Merlebach (33.9 per cent) and Stiring-Wendel (33 per cent) in the Moselle department and Wittelsheim (32.5 per cent) in Haut-Rhin. Such results attest to the FN's penetration of areas where industrial recession, unemployment and economic hardship have taken a heavy toll and where, as Sylvain Crépon's fieldwork in the Pas-de-Calais shows, the FN has replaced the PCF as the 'voice of the people' against élites of right and left who have failed to respond adequately to the concerns driving voter choice.[27] What also marked this election for the FN was the support won by Marine Le Pen in some departments of the centre and west of France, with scores of 19 per cent to 23 per cent across Eure, Eure-et-Loir, Loiret, Loir-et-Cher, Orne, Cher and Sarthe. Gains were also made further west, with scores of 12 per cent to 16 per cent in coastal departments from Calvados through Manche, Côtes d'Armor, Finistère, Morbihan and Loire-Atlantique to Vendée and Charente-Maritime. Similarly, in a number of departments in and around the Massif Central (Dordogne, Corrèze, Cantal, Lozère, Allier) the Le Pen vote made significant ground.

This map of support gave evidence of some recomposition of the Le Pen vote between 2002 and 2012. In more than a fifth of metropolitan departments, support receded – by some margin at times in traditional areas of strength such as the Mediterranean littoral (–2.5 per cent in Alpes-Maritimes), Rhône-Alpes (–4.2 per cent in Haute-Savoie) and Ile-de-France (–4.2 per cent in Seine-Saint-Denis). This erosion of support in areas of established FN strength combined with growth in areas with no history of strong FN voting provided some measure of Marine Le Pen's success in 'nationalising' her appeal and reducing the once sharper divide between a France receptive to the FN and a France of weak FN support separated by a line running north-west to south-east.[28]

A further aspect of Marine Le Pen's success was the support she attracted in many rural areas. In the tiny village of Brachay in Haute-Marne, over 70 per cent of the votes cast went to Le Pen (31 of 43); in the nearby village of Flammerécourt, the figure was 55 per cent (24 of 44 votes). Though exceptionally high, these results were not unique. Some of the most arresting scores for Le Pen in this election were recorded in similarly small communes. The Haute-Marne department alone yielded further striking examples: Doulevant-le-Petit 46 per cent, Baudrecourt 44 per cent, Montreuil-sur-Blaise 44 per cent, Nomécourt 43 per cent, Fays 42 per cent – five villages with a combined electoral register of barely 400.[29] These resounding scores from *la France profonde* confirmed that FN voting could no longer be adequately defined by its urban character and issues, with immigration and crime eclipsing other concerns. As a post-election IFOP study led by Jérôme Fourquet showed, support for Le Pen was optimised in peri-urban zones located between 20 and 50 kilometres from large urban agglomerations, while her vote in some urban locations dropped below levels achieved by her father.[30] These peri-urban zones most receptive to Le Pen are those described by the geographer Christophe Guilluy as a 'fringe France', the new locus of a de-urbanised working and lower-middle class exposed to the economic effects of globalisation and averse to its social and cultural implications.[31] This is a France that combines economic hardship with limited social mobility, cultural conservatism and rising political disaffection, and where concerns over jobs, crime, immigration and Europe make fertile terrain for populism.

Alert to the potential for expanding and diversifying her electorate, Marine Le Pen made a determined effort to appeal not just to this 'fringe France' but to the wider rural France into which it has extended, a France 'despised by Parisian élites' and desolated by 'shameful European directives'. She pledged to restore local services hit by cuts, to reduce the price of fuel, and to scrap the Common Agricultural Policy (CAP) in favour of a 'French Agricultural Policy (FAP)'. In the purest populist tradition of defending *les petits* against *les gros*, she claimed to be the voice of the 'invisible' and the 'forgotten', those at 'the bottom of society', the many nameless victims of open borders, globalisation and the 'excesses of capitalism and the free market'.[32] Nor is 'populist' a label Marine Le Pen rejects: 'If populism means, as I think it does, defending the people against the élites, defending the forgotten ones against élites that are in the process of strangling them, then yes, in that case I am a populist'.[33] Although there are echoes here of a right-wing tradition running from Maurice Barrès to Pierre Poujade, Marine Le Pen combines this posture with a left-leaning repertoire of anti-capitalism, economic redistribution and social welfare provision.

In terms of voter profile, an Ipsos poll carried out for the first round of the presidential election showed support for Le Pen at 29 per cent among blue-collar workers (higher than for any other candidate), 25 per cent among shopkeepers, artisans and small business owners, 21 per cent among low-skilled non-manual employees, and 18 per cent among unemployed voters.[34] These findings were consonant with other polls which indicated strong support for Le Pen among the same categories, with higher levels recorded at times for blue-collar workers and unemployed voters (31 per cent and 28 per cent respectively for Cevipof, 35 per cent and 26 per cent for OpinionWay).[35] These polls also showed a closing of the gender gap in the Le Pen vote, highest levels of support in the 25–49 age group, and a strong appeal among the most poorly educated and those with the lowest earning power.

The 2012 elections confirmed the 'proletarisation' of the FN electorate that has been underway since the early 1990s;[36] they also confirmed FN voting as an expression of political choice defying neat left–right categorisation. An OpinionWay survey from April 2012 found that Le Pen drew support from across the full spectrum, with 13 per cent of Sarkozy's 2007 electorate, 9 per cent of Bayrou's centrist support, 4 per cent of former

Royal voters, 8 per cent of voters of the non-Socialist (mainly Trotskyist) left, and 19 per cent of those who had abstained or spoilt their ballot in 2007. The same poll found that Le Pen drew 32 per cent of those with confidence in 'neither left nor right' to govern the country.[37] This political 'polymorphism' has become a defining feature of the FN electorate,[38] chiming with the party's former slogan 'Ni droite, ni gauche – Français!' In the run-up to the 2012 presidential election, Marine Le Pen gained more new support from the left than from the right.[39] This partly explains the difficulty faced by Nicolas Sarkozy in seeking to attract Marine Le Pen's voters for the second round. Estimates of first-round Le Pen voters transferring to Hollande, abstaining or spoiling their ballot in the run-off vary from 42 per cent to 56 per cent, confirming the highly composite nature of her electorate and providing a seemingly incongruous key to the Socialist candidate's victory.[40] Some polls estimated the transfer of votes from Le Pen to Hollande at 21 per cent, 1.3 million; but even if one retains the lower estimate of 13–14 per cent (some 850,000), their transfer not to Sarkozy but to Hollande was decisive in securing the latter's victory margin of 1.1 million votes.[41]

There has long been a perverse element in vote transfers from far-right candidates in presidential elections. Part of Jean-Louis Tixier-Vignancour's ultra-nationalist support base preferred the Socialist Mitterrand to General de Gaulle in 1965, and some Le Pen supporters in subsequent elections transferred to the Socialist candidates Mitterrand, Jospin or Royal rather than to their post-Gaullist opponents, Chirac or Sarkozy. With Marine Le Pen, however, there is another explanation beyond political cynicism to account for the left-leaning tendency in part of her electorate.

In the wake of the 2008 financial crisis and in a context of economic austerity, rising unemployment, falling purchasing power and widespread pessimism, the FN under Marine Le Pen has effected a strategic shift towards an economically protectionist discourse embracing state interventionism, government spending on welfare, the expansion of public services and income redistribution. These classically 'left-wing' economic emphases now sit alongside the social illiberalism and ethno-cultural exclusionism of the FN's programme.[42] A leftward shift on economic policy began tentatively in the 2002 presidential campaign then developed in 2007, but it has been given stronger expression under Marine Le Pen's leadership since 2011. It has, as Gilles Ivaldi argues, 'taken the FN closer to fitting the "welfare chauvinist" profile' identified by Herbert Kitschelt as a strategy combining xenophobic authoritarianism with welfare-oriented social policies and protectionist economics.[43] The electorate that responds to this blend of economic and social protectionism is one of economic hardship, with a large component of what is now defined as the 'precariat class', typically those in insecure, interim or insufficient employment living in disadvantaged communities. An IFOP poll from April 2012 showed that Marine Le Pen won the largest share of the presidential vote among those who found it very difficult to get by on their earnings (32 per cent), with Hollande a distant second (24 per cent). It also found Le Pen voters to be almost unanimous (91 per cent) in calling for a more economically protectionist France.[44]

A much more extensive sociological survey by OpinionWay in 2012 showed Marine Le Pen's highest share of the vote (24 per cent) to be in the lowest-earning category (less than 999 euros per month) and also among social housing tenants (27 per cent). The same survey credited Le Pen with 35 per cent support among blue-collar workers, 25 per cent among low-skilled non-manual employees and 26 per cent among unemployed voters. It also found support for the FN leader at 24 per cent among voters on temporary employment contracts and at fully 38 per cent among those in interim jobs.[45] Small wonder that purchasing power should have risen to feature among the top three priorities of Le Pen voters in 2012, rivalling or displacing law and order as the second most urgent priority after immigration.[46]

Opportunities and obstacles

The foregoing discussion points to a number of important 'opportunity structures' which argue for their place in explanations of the FN's enduring resilience.[47] These would suggest that, in the current context of economic crisis and disaffection with mainstream politics, the party is well placed to consolidate and extend its electoral challenge. Yet, viewed through another lens, the FN has made little headway in moving from its marginal isolation to a genuinely central role in French politics. To judge by column inches and media airtime, and compared with a deeply unpopular Socialist administration and a divided UMP opposition, the FN was *the* successful party in France in 2013. It stole the headlines in two National Assembly by-elections, which its candidates came close to winning with 48.6 per cent (Beauvais) and 46.2 per cent (Villeneuve-sur-Lot) of the run-off vote.[48] Yet it emerged from the year having gained just one cantonal seat in the by-election of Brignoles in the southern Var department, taking its total representation on France's departmental councils to two seats out of 4,052.[49]

Similarly, in the National Assembly elections of June 2012, the FN was at the centre of media attention yet won only two seats out of 577. As in the above by-elections of Beauvais and Villeneuve-sur-Lot, a number of FN candidates achieved very strong scores in two-way run-offs (Florian Philippot's 46.3 per cent in Forbach, Valérie Laupies' 48.7 per cent in Arles, Stéphane Ravier's 49 per cent in Marseille, and Marine Le Pen's 49.9 per cent in Hénin-Beaumont); but they lost. Across the last full cycle of elections from 2008 to 2012, the FN won not a single senator out of 348, not a single mayor out of 36,718, and some 85 municipal councillors from 519,417; it secured 118 regional councillors from 1,880 and three Members of the European Parliament from a French contingent of 72 (raised since to 74).[50] Put another way, the FN won some 200 seats from over 525,000 – or 0.04 per cent – across all levels of democratic representation in France.

This institutional non-existence may be advantageous for an anti-system party but it is surely a critical deficiency for a party seeking to accede to government. By other measures, too, the FN has failed to create the kind of dynamic required to impose itself as an irresistible force. If Le Pen and her party had the strongest upward dynamic between 2007 and 2012, a longer view gives a quite different picture. Since 1986, when the FN first emerged as a serious contender in National Assembly elections, it has increased its vote share by just 4 per cent, from 9.6 per cent to 13.6 per cent. Since Jean-Marie Le Pen's first significant presidential bid in 1988, the party has raised its share of the presidential poll by 3.5 per cent, from 14.4 per cent to 17.9 per cent. When relativised in this way, the performances of Marine Le Pen and her party in 2012 signify less a powerful surge than a very modest, creeping, ineffectual advance over a quarter-century of electioneering.

Over the same period, the PCF has almost disappeared from view but the PS has held its vote share in National Assembly elections at close to 30 per cent; and the centre-right, despite substantial erosion of support since the 1980s, could still command through the UMP over 27 per cent – precisely twice the score of the FN – in an unfavourable election following ten years in power. Setting that against the 1997 National Assembly elections, when the FN came within less than 1 per cent of being the party with the highest vote on the right (RPR 15.7 per cent, FN 14.9 per cent, UDF 14.2 per cent), it seems so much further now from imposing itself as an essential alliance partner. Even at the peak of its threat to the centre-right's prospects for a parliamentary majority in 1997, its power remained more virtual than real, with the above profile of results producing 139 National Assembly seats for the RPR, 109 for the UDF and one for the FN.[51] The performance of the FN in the 2012 National Assembly elections (13.6 per cent) should also be set against the vote share secured by its leader a few weeks earlier (17.9 per cent), marking a loss of 4.3 per cent. This has been a recurrent pattern that the FN has been unable to eradicate (–4.7 per cent in 1988, –5.7 per cent in 2002, –6.1 per cent in 2007), evidence of continued failure in its drive to professionalise and present candidates in National Assembly elections of sufficient number and quality to match or exceed the performance of its leader in immediately preceding presidential polls.

In its impact as a contender in National Assembly elections, the FN might even be argued to have regressed rather than progressed. It qualified in 2012 for run-offs in 61 constituencies, contesting 59 of these, but that number was well short of the 133 constituencies for which it qualified in 1997.[52] This drop was mainly due to a change of electoral rules in 2003 that required candidates to win 12.5 per cent of the electoral register rather than of votes cast in order to contest the second round. Although the FN went on to win two seats in 2012 compared to one in 1997, its influence on the election outcome was much reduced. Analysis of its performance in all 59 run-offs showed the FN's limitations. Of the 28 three-way run-offs (in which the FN's chances of election were strongest), 14 were won by the left, 12 by the centre-right, and only two by the FN. In two-way run-offs against candidates of the left, the FN increased its score on average by some 16 per cent between the two rounds, but this left it far short of rallying the full combined right vote. In two-way run-offs against centre-right candidates too, the FN gained over 16 per cent on average between the rounds, confirming that its reserves of support extend beyond the right, but again it fell short in all cases.[53] Although the 'Republican front' that once united centre-right and left to block the FN no longer reliably functions, the FN continues almost without exception to encounter insurmountable difficulty in rallying a majority in head-to-head run-offs.

The punitive effects of the FN's isolation are clearer still from votes–seats ratios showing its gains in the 2012 elections relative to those made by smaller, or much smaller, parties. With 13.6 per cent of the first-round vote, the FN went on to win 0.3 per cent of seats in the National Assembly – the same proportion of seats as that gained by the Alliance Centriste and the Regionalists with 0.6 per cent of the first-round vote, while the Greens with 5.5 per cent took 17 seats (see Table 2.6).

A further marker of the FN's political isolation was the apparent difficulty encountered by Marine Le Pen, like her father before her, in securing her 500 elected sponsors' signatures. That sponsors' names are published by the Constitutional Council might explain the reluctance of many to take the step of publicly endorsing an FN candidate; but Marine Le Pen's much reported struggle to muster barely 1 per cent of 47,500 potential sponsors says much about the FN's continued ostracism by the political establishment. Of a piece with that ostracism is the fact that, despite its leader's ambition to 'de-demonise' the party and give it a Republican varnish, the FN continues to espouse policies that defy the essential pluralist and egalitarian values of the French Constitution. It has softened its image but has not undertaken any real ideological revision. Its core policy of *priorité nationale* – preferential allocation of jobs, housing and welfare support to French nationals over foreigners – was tested in the mid-1990s by Catherine Mégret as FN mayor of Vitrolles.[54] Her attempt to

TABLE 2.6 *Votes and seats for Front National and smaller parties in National Assembly elections of 2012*

Party	Votes (first round)	% (first round)	Seats (over 2 rounds)
Front National	3,528,663	13.6	2
Front de Gauche	1,793,192	6.9	10
Greens (EELV)	1,418,264	5.5	17
Nouveau Centre	569,897	2.2	12
Centre pour la France	458,098	1.8	2
Alliance Centriste	156,026	0.6	2
Regionalists	145,809	0.6	2

institute a special child allowance for parents of French or EU nationality was ruled illegal and incurred a suspended prison sentence, a fine and a temporary ban from public office, yet the same policy featured in Marine Le Pen's 2012 presidential manifesto.[55] An elected FN seeking to implement its programme in full would be on a collision course with the Constitution.

Attitudinal surveys of FN voters also argue against the FN's claim to be a 'normal' party now. A CSA poll from April 2012 found that, while only 7 per cent of Le Pen voters were motivated by attachment to her as a candidate and 10 per cent by attachment to the FN as a party, 44 per cent voted for her in order to express their 'opposition to other candidates'. The same poll found that only 36 per cent of Le Pen's electorate voted so that their candidate 'be elected president', compared with 85 per cent of Sarkozy's electorate and 76 per cent of Hollande's.[56] Other polls showed Marine Le Pen's electorate to have the highest proportion of those with no interest in the election and high proportions of those with neither interest nor faith in politics generally.[57] Such findings suggest a deep negativity and protest tendency among Le Pen and FN voters. More generally, support for the FN is tempered by scepticism about the party's credibility. While a TNS Sofres poll in January 2013 found 32 per cent of respondents in agreement with the ideas of the FN, 81 per cent disagreed with the solutions proposed. The same poll showed only 24 per cent agreeing and 73 per cent disagreeing with the FN's key policy of *priorité nationale*, while 35 per cent saw the FN as fit to join a government against 54 per cent judging it to be merely a protest party.[58]

Conclusion: What prospects for the Front National?

What place, then, does the FN occupy within the contemporary French political space, and what are its prospects? This chapter has argued that the FN vote is a vote beyond right and left – or, in Nonna Mayer's terms, 'between' right and left – with the FN challenging the centre-right but also being the major threat to the Socialist and Communist parties in some former strongholds of the left.[59] Blending authoritarian, exclusivist nationalism with economic and social protectionism, the FN has adapted its policy proposals to appeal across the traditional cleavage structure of French politics. If the foregoing pages acknowledge the strengths of the party under Marine Le Pen, however, they also show the enduring obstacles barring its path. The FN has the potential to play an increasingly influential role in the French party system, but it faces major difficulties in order to realise that potential and to develop from a party of political influence to a party of executive power.

Over three decades, the FN has mounted the most significant and sustained challenge to the established political order of the Fifth Republic. It has played a major role in reshaping the party system, replacing the PCF at least partly in what Georges Lavau famously called its 'tribune function' and driving both centre-right and centre-left into tighter bipolarity.[60] The party system within which it competes today has become more unfavourable, structured as it now is around two rather than four hegemonic parties. The space for a challenge by a party from outside this bipolarised majoritarian system is severely restricted, as shown by the FN's two National Assembly seats in 2012 compared with the UMP's 194 and the Socialist Party's 280. Moreover, as this chapter has argued, the FN set out to disrupt the two-bloc party system, only to become a catalyst for reinforcing the very duopoly it sought to end. Within that logic, the FN remains what it has been since its emergence in the mid-1980s: a party with almost no elected power base and with the negative capacity to spoil but not the positive capacity to impose itself as a viable alternative.

Can the FN emerge from this impasse? As Pascal Perrineau argues, there are three routes by which an anti-system party can come to power: force, alliance or a conversion to respectability.[61] Discounting the non-democratic dimension of the first, the institutional impediments built into the Fifth Republic are such that even a forceful electoral presence can be nullified if a party is sufficiently isolated; the second route has been barred, to date, by the UMP's resistance to formal cooperation with the FN; and the third has been only partly embarked upon through a change of style but the retention of the authoritarian, discriminatory and xenophobic-nationalist policies at the heart of the FN's programme.

The examples of Austria and Italy show how mainstream acceptability can be gained by radical right-wing parties with the complicity of the conservative right. For that complicity to be forged in France, the FN would have to abandon some of its key policies – *priorité nationale*, the restoration of capital punishment, the expulsion of certain categories of foreigner, the rejection of the EU and return to the franc, border controls and trade protection. It would also have to reverse its leftward shift on economic and welfare policy, which has moved it further from the UMP and makes cooperation at a national level yet more difficult to envisage.[62] Even if the UMP leadership were willing (like most of its base) to countenance an alliance with the FN, that might merely replace one set of problems with another.[63] For radical parties, the process of deradicalising can be perilous, with greater respectability and systemic integration being bought at the price of ideological compromise, policy reorientation and possibly party unity.[64]

With the presidential and National Assembly elections of 2012, the FN may have reached the limits of what an outsider party can achieve nationally under the existing institutional constraints of the Fifth Republic. As France entered a new cycle of elections in 2014 with municipal and European polls, the FN gained considerable ground, winning control of 11 municipalities of over 9,000 inhabitants and coming top in the European election with almost 25 per cent of the vote and 24 of France's 74 seats in the European Parliament. Though they marked a spectacular advance on the corresponding elections of 2008 and 2009, however, these subnational and supranational elections did nothing to alter the incapacity in which the FN finds itself in terms of access to national representation, let alone national power. With only two parliamentary seats out of 925 across both houses, the FN retained a 0.2 per cent stake in the national legislative arena and found itself blocked still by the same immoveable barrier to its progression as an aspiring party of government. Nor did these elections of 2014 alter – rather, they accentuated – the question confronting Marine Le Pen and her party: whether, and how far, to moderate their programme in order to pass from a vote-oriented to an office-oriented strategy. The question confronting the UMP, too, remained unaltered: whether to continue to exclude the FN or to collude in its systemic integration. The answers to these questions will depend on inter-party dynamics and strategic imperatives that are still being worked out, but they could determine the future shape and direction not only of the French right but of politics and policy-making in France.

Notes

1 Electoral statistics, including those in tables, are from the French Interior Ministry website, accessed 6 February 2014, http://www.interieur.gouv.fr/ Elections/Les-resultats, and from the France Politique website, accessed | 6 February 2014, http://www.france-politique.fr/. National results are for all of France, including overseas territories. Some more detailed electoral results are taken from *Le Monde*.

2 Among an abundant literature on fragmentation and bipolarity, see the chapter 'Transformations of the party system', in Andrew Knapp and Vincent Wright, *The Government and Politics of France*, 5th edn. (London: Routledge, 2006), 254–80.

3 Direction générale des collectivités locales, 'Les collectivités locales en chiffres', accessed 6 February 2014, http://www.collectivites-locales.gouv.fr/collectivites-locales-chiffres.

4 Gérard Grunberg and Florence Haegel, *La France vers le bipartisme* (Paris: Presses de la Fondation Nationale des Sciences Politiques, 2007).

5 Alistair Cole, *French Politics and Society* (Harlow: Pearson/Longman, 2005), 137–50; David Hanley, *Party, Society, Government: Republican democracy in France* (Oxford: Berghahn, 2002), 168–89.

6 Alistair Cole and Peter Campbell, *French Electoral Systems and Elections since 1789* (Aldershot: Gower, 1989), 86, 93–4.

7 Maurice Duverger, *Le Système politique français*, 18th edn. (Paris: Presses Universitaires de France, 1985).

8 François Borella, *Les Partis politiques dans la France d'aujourd'hui* (Paris: Seuil, 1973, 1981), 33, 205.

9 James Shields, *The Extreme Right in France: From Pétain to Le Pen* (London: Routledge, 2007), 252, 255.

10 James Shields, 'Support for Le Pen in France: Two elections in *trompe l'oeil*', *Politics* 30, 1 (2010): 65–6.

11 Shields, *The Extreme Right in France*, see Note 9, 267–8.

12 Nonna Mayer and Henri Rey, 'Avancée électorale, isolement politique du Front national', *Revue politique et parlementaire* 95, 964 (1993): 47.

13 James Shields, 'The far right vote in France: From consolidation to collapse?' *French Politics, Culture and Society* 28, 1 (2010): 39–40.

14 Shields, *The Extreme Right in France*, see Note 9, 176.

15 Giovanni Sartori, *Parties and Party Systems: A framework for analysis* (Colchester: ECPR Press, 2005), 117–18.

16 Christiane Chombeau, 'Jean-Marie Le Pen réclame à nouveau la démission de Jacques Chirac', *Le Monde*, 3 June 1997.

17 Jocelyn Evans and Gilles Ivaldi, *The 2012 French Presidential Elections: The inevitable alternation* (Basingstoke: Palgrave Macmillan, 2013), 40–1, 53–5.

18 Grunberg and Haegel, *La France vers le bipartisme*, see Note 4, 11–42, 119–22.

19 Gilles Ivaldi, 'Front national: une élection présidentielle de reconquête', *Revue politique et parlementaire* 114, 1063–4 (2012): 101–18.

20 IFOP poll of October 2013, accessed 6 February 2014, http://www.ifop.fr/?option=com_publication&type=poll&id=2355.

21 François-Xavier Bourmaud and Nicolas Barotte, 'Hollande rappelle sa majorité à l'union', *lefigaro.fr*, 1 July 2013.

22 'Cantonale à Brignoles: l'UMP et le FN s'en donnent à cœur joie après le 1er tour', *lemonde.fr*/AFP, 7 October 2013.

23 Jean-Baptiste de Montvalon and Alexandre Lemarié, 'L'UMP se déchire sur sa stratégie face au FN', *lemonde.fr*, 16 September 2013; interview with Guillaume Peltier, *lefigaro.fr*, 11 October 2013.

24 Ipsos poll of May 2012, accessed 6 February 2014, http://www.ipsos.fr/sites/default/files/attachments/rapport_2ndtourelectionpresidentielle-6mai2012.pdf; IFOP poll of May 2012, accessed 6 February 2014, http://www.ifop.com/media/poll/1859-1-study_file.pdf; TNS Sofres poll of January 2013, accessed 6 February 2014, http://www.tns-sofres.com/sites/default/files/2013.02.06-baro-FN.pdf.

25 Pascal Perrineau, 'L'électorat de Marine Le Pen: Ni tout à fait le même, ni tout à fait autre', in Pascal Perrineau, ed., *Le Vote normal. Les Elections présidentielle et législatives d'avril-mai-juin 2012* (Paris: Presses de la Fondation Nationale des Sciences Politiques, 2013), 229–32.

26 *Le Monde*, 24 April 2012, Supplement 'Présidentielle: Résultats premier tour'.

27 Pascal Perrineau, 'Marine Le Pen: Voter pour une nouvelle extrême droite?', in Pascal Perrineau and Luc Rouban, eds., *La Solitude de l'isoloir. Les Vrais enjeux de 2012* (Paris: Autrement, 2012), 26–7; Sylvain Crépon, *Enquête au cœur du nouveau Front National* (Paris: Nouveau Monde, 2012).

28 Perrineau, 'L'Electorat de Marine Le Pen', Note 25, 235–6.

29 'Résultats de l'élection présidentielle des communes de la Haute-Marne', *lemonde.fr*, accessed 6 February 2014, http://www.lemonde.fr/resultats-election-presidentielle/brachay,52110/.

30 Jérôme Fourquet, *Le Sens des cartes. Analyse sur la géographie des votes à la présidentielle* (Paris: Fondation Jean Jaurès, 2012), 43–79.

31 Christophe Guilluy, *Fractures françaises* (Paris: François Bourin Editeur, 2010).

32 Marine Le Pen, *Mon Projet pour la France et les Français*, presidential programme 2012; Ivaldi, 'Front national: une élection présidentielle de reconquête', see Note 19.

33 Gilles Ivaldi, 'Permanence et évolutions de l'idéologie frontiste', in Pascal Delwit, ed., *Le Front National. Mutations de l'extrême droite française* (Brussels: Éditions de l'Université de Bruxelles, 2012), 107.

34 Ipsos poll of April 2012, accessed 6 February 2014, http://www.ipsos.fr/sites/default/files/attachments/rapport_svv_2012_-_23_avril_2012_-_10h.pdf.

35 Perrineau, 'L'Electorat de Marine Le Pen', see Note 25, 237; OpinionWay poll of April 2012, accessed 6 February 2014, http://opinionlab.opinion-way.com/dokumenty/Sondage per cent20jour per cent20de per cent20vote-SOCIOLOGIE per cent20DU per cent20VOTE per cent20VF per cent20OLAB_5.pdf.

36 Nonna Mayer, 'From Jean-Marie to Marine Le Pen: Electoral change on the Far Right', *Parliamentary Affairs* 66, 1 (2013): 170–1.

37 OpinionWay poll of April 2012, see Note 35.

38 Gilles Ivaldi, 'Législatives: Un bilan en demi-teinte pour le Front national', *Revue politique et parlementaire* 114, 1063–4 (2012): 175–89.

39 Pascal Perrineau, 'La Renaissance électorale de l'électorat Le Pen', *CEVIPOF: Les Electorats politiques* 5 (2012), accessed 6 February 2014, http://www.cevipof.com/rtefiles/File/AtlasEl3/NotePERRINEAU.pdf.

40 TNS Sofres poll of May 2012, accessed 6 February 2014, http://www.tns-sofres.com/sites/default/files/2012.05.06-jourduvote.pdf; CSA poll of May 2012, accessed 6 February 2014, http://www.csa.eu/multimedia/data/sondages/data2012/opi20120506-sondage-jour-du-vote-raisons-du-choix-et-profil-des-electorats.pdf.

41 For the higher estimate, see the CSA and IFOP polls of May 2012, at Notes 24, 40; for the lower estimate, see the TNS Sofres and Ipsos polls of May 2012 at Notes 24, 40.

42 Marine Le Pen's 2012 presidential programme *Mon Projet pour la France et les Français*, see Note 32.

43 Gilles Ivaldi, 'The successful welfare–chauvinist party? The Front National in the 2012 elections in France', paper delivered at the European Sociological Association's Research Network on Political Sociology, University of Milan (Nov-Dec 2012), accessed 6 February 2014, http://hal.archives-ouvertes.fr/docs/00/76/54/28/PDF/Paper_Ivaldi_ESA_RN32_Milano_2012.pdf; Herbert Kitschelt (with Anthony J. McGann), *The Radical Right in Western Europe: A comparative analysis* (Ann Arbor, MI: University of Michigan Press, 1997).

44 IFOP poll of April 2012, accessed 6 February 2014, http://www.ifop.com/media/poll/1848–1-study_file.pdf.

45 OpinionWay poll of April 2012, see Note 35.

46 CSA poll of April 2012, accessed 6 February 2014, http://www.csa.eu/
multimedia/data/sondages/data2012/opi20120422-sondage-jour-du-vote-
premier-tour-election-presidentielle-2012-raisons-du-choix-et-profil-des-
electorats.pdf; and Ipsos poll of April 2012, see Note 34.

47 See, for example, Jens Rydgren, *The Populist Challenge: Political protest and
ethno-nationalist mobilization in France* (New York: Berghahn, 2004), 226–32.

48 Patrick Roger, 'Dans l'Oise, le sentiment d'abandon profite au FN', *lemonde.fr*,
25 March 2013; 'Villeneuve-sur-Lot: le candidat UMP l'emporte face au FN',
lemonde.fr, 23 June 2013.

49 'Brignoles: le candidat du Front national remporte la cantonale', *lemonde.fr*/
AFP, 13 October 2013.

50 Direction générale des collectivités locales, 'Les collectivités locales en chiffres',
see Note 3. It is difficult to determine with precision the number of municipal
council seats held by the FN. The claim by the party's general secretary, Steeve
Briois, that the figure was not 85 but 170 still confirms how vanishingly small
was the FN's share of over half a million seats at municipal level (Rémi
Duchemin, 'Pourquoi le FN a déjà gagné les municipales', *europe1.fr*,
15 November 2013). Although it did not win control of any council in 2008,
a few mayors of small communes (such as Jean-Yves Narquin in Villedieu-le-
Château and Gérard Marchand in Brachay) subsequently rallied to the FN
under Marine Le Pen.

51 Shields, *The Extreme Right in France*, see Note 9, 264–65.

52 'Législatives: le FN se maintiendra partout où il est qualifié, annonce Marine Le
Pen', *lemonde.fr*/AFP, 11 June 2012; Pierre Jaxel-Truer and Abel Mestre,
'Législatives: 34 triangulaires et quelques accrocs aux consignes', *lemonde.fr*,
13 June 2012.

53 Perrineau, 'L'Electorat de Marine Le Pen', see Note 25, 245.

54 Shields, *The Extreme Right in France*, see Note 9, 263.

55 Marine Le Pen, *Mon Projet pour la France et les Français*, see Note 32, 6.

56 CSA poll of April 2012, see Note 46.

57 Ipsos and OpinionWay polls of April 2012, see Notes 34, 35.

58 TNS Sofres poll of January 2013, see Note 24.

59 Mayer, 'From Jean-Marie to Marine Le Pen', see Note 36, 167; Perrineau,
'L'Electorat de Marine Le Pen', see Note 25, 229–36.

60 Georges Lavau, *A quoi sert le Parti Communiste Français?* (Paris: Fayard,
1981). The FN's self-assigned role as 'tribune' or 'voice' of the people harks
back to the role fulfilled by the 'tribune of the plebs' in an ancient Rome ruled
by patrician élites.

61 Perrineau, 'L'Electorat de Marine Le Pen', see Note 25, 247.

62 Ivaldi, 'The successful Welfare–Chauvinist Party?' see Note 43.

63 See IFOP and Ipsos polls of May 2012, and TNS Sofres poll of January 2013,
see Note 24.

64 James Shields, 'Radical or Not So Radical? Tactical variation in core policy
formation by the Front National', *French Politics, Culture and Society* 29, 3
(2011): 78–100.

3

Class, Class Conflict and the Left:

The Place of the People in French Politics

Nick Hewlett

The notions of class, class conflict and the people, once the ideological and analytical staples of the major parties of the left in France, have for some time been distinctly out of fashion. For many French politicians and analysts, to raise such questions and talk in such terms is seen as suspect, old-fashioned or 'unscientific', and certainly out of touch with the modernised reality of advanced capitalist societies. For several decades, a great deal of energy has been expended arguing that class should no longer be seen as one of the ordering principles of society. In this view, society has changed so much that traditional notions of division into classes no longer have any meaning and the basis of the left needs to be re-thought in terms of a far more consensual society where the great question of capital versus labour has been resolved, or at least attenuated so much that it can largely be ignored. Certainly, mainstream politicians and analysts of politics will often speak of the middle classes or the middle class (*la classe moyenne*), but this is seen as the only remaining class, the benign vehicle via which almost everyone can enjoy the fruits of prosperity. This vast middle class has grown as French society has become more homogeneous, more 'globalised' and more culturally united, while the notion of the working class has become almost meaningless. At the same time, class conflict has supposedly diminished greatly, or disappeared, because the mass working class is not there to drive the conflict and has indeed largely been absorbed into the middle classes. The argument is that, in these post-industrial times, capitalism has produced the goods, at least for the vast majority, and will continue to do so. However, the recent economic crisis (since 2008) has brought into sharper focus underlying socio-economic and political trends, exposing myths and illusions that previously appeared as reality. Increasing inequalities due to neo-liberalisation and economic crisis are showing how wrong a simplistic approach to class has been. An examination of various developments in French society and politics over the past thirty or so years will show not only that class is still very much alive, but that the mainstream left's neglect of this fact has meant that it finds it increasingly difficult to appeal to hundreds of thousands of people who should be its staunchest supporters. The costs of the left abandoning some of its core historic principles include high levels of abstention at elections among poorer sections of society and the rise of the extreme-right in the form of the Front National (FN).

In order to explore these ideas in relation to the left in France, I use the French notion of *le peuple* (henceforth, 'the people'). Over the centuries, the idea of the people has, of course, been particularly associated with France because of the country's predilection for revolt. My argument is that the notion is very much a political – and a politically-committed – one, rather than a sociological or economic one. The people are active, in movement, or at least potentially so and this is what helps define them. The people are political because they are associated with struggle, freedom from domination, emancipation, equality, and active participation in politics. It is a collective notion, which assumes that the interests of one are the interests of all, and vice versa; in this sense it is opposed to a liberal emphasis on individualism and individual freedom. The people is a term which implies a relationship of subordination and exploitation regarding the socio-economic and political élite. Just as importantly, it is a term which is not confined by national boundaries. It is not 'the French people' or 'the British people' but an international concept.[1] This is particularly significant now that advanced capitalist economies are so profoundly global, in terms of the production and sale of goods and services, and in terms of the flow of labour between different nation states. Clearly, the notion of the people, because of its political connotations of struggle for freedom and equality, is associated with those who are among the least wealthy in society. There is therefore, in my discussion here, a clear connection with the sociological make-up of society, as well as an assumption that the political views and actions of the least well-off and the most dominated sections of society are particularly significant. In common with Marx's proletariat, Hardt and Negri's multitude and Ranciere's *sans part*, the people are the 'common people', in the sense that they do not hold positions of political, social or economic power except when they come together and assert their collective might.[2] The people thus have a relationship with the ruling class that is largely one of exclusion from power, except at times of collective action and revolt. It should also be said that there is never a 'pure' manifestation of the people, nor a strict empirical definition of it, precisely because it is in essence a political idea, not an empirically-defined reality; nevertheless, references to it relate to some of the least well-off, the most under-privileged, as well as to notions of emancipation, struggle against injustice, and the need for equality. The idea of the people is unpopular nowadays with mainstream parties and many analysts, except perhaps in the context of routine voting at elections every few years. In contemporary French politics, a more developed idea of the people tends to be the preserve of either the far-left or, in a divisive and populist sense, the far-right; the centre-left is now far more concerned with the idea of the freedom of the individual and individual prosperity than it was even thirty years ago.

This is no surprise given that an important goal of every liberal democratic society – and arguably, at least, almost every society to date – has been to limit the participation of the people in politics in order to achieve a socio-economic and political settlement in favour of the interests of the social, political and economic élite. Certainly, for capitalism to flourish, there needs to be little direct political involvement on the part of ordinary people, or at least involvement of a very limited form; there is a necessary degree of depoliticisation, which is in fact the antithesis of real democracy conceived as the ongoing, profound involvement of the people in politics. There is a constant tension, then, including on the centre-left, between limiting participation of the people in politics for fear that they might go too far in their demands, and including them (in particular at elections) in order to pacify them as the citizen-consumers so central to the needs of modern capitalism. In many capitalist (and in particular imperial) countries, this process of limiting political participation and quelling revolt took place from 1800 onwards, partly via various material concessions – typically in the form of higher pay and better working conditions to the most organised sections of the working class – in return for more conformist behaviour on their part and an agreement, explicit or otherwise, not to rock the establishment boat. An inactive, apparently passive people is nevertheless a constant threat, even in the most superficially stable and tranquil countries, and must continue to be placated in order to prevent it, or parts of it, from rising up and threatening the status quo.

This process of effectively reducing class struggle was more difficult to achieve in France than in many other advanced capitalist societies. The French people remained active and a real threat to the established order for the whole of the nineteenth century and arguably well into the twentieth century as well. One way in which this threat of uprising was handled was to bind liberal democracy – universal (albeit for many years only male) suffrage, regular elections, freedom to organise political parties – together with a formal republican ideology where values associated with the active people were brought to the fore, such as equality, collective action in pursuit of justice for all and the legitimacy of revolutionary insurrection (at least historically). This was an arrangement that allowed the capitalist economy to function and élites to rule, but it did not prevent sporadic and serious uprisings. A glance at aspects of this history will clarify these points and in turn help understand more recent developments in relation to the left and the people.

After the direct intervention of the people in no uncertain terms in the 1789 revolution, their predilection for revolt became legendary. In the nineteenth century, the people again and again took to the streets, revolted and overthrew regimes, most famously in 1830, 1848 and 1871, causing great fear in the ruling élite. The highly authoritarian and autocratic Louis Napoleon Bonaparte himself depended on populist appeal as a way of attempting to neutralise the people, organising plebiscites and making frequent and direct appeals to the people for support. Countless political clubs and societies were formed with the promotion of the people's interests at heart, and their almost mythical status was represented in Delacroix's famous painting, *Liberty Guiding the People* (1830), while Victor Hugo, for example, cast the people as a major actor in various works of literature. Counter-revolutionary and 'counter-popular' movements were also significant, and it is important to mention the extraordinarily violent *semaine sanglante* in spring 1871, when over 25,000 Communards perished at the hands of the Versailles troops and many thousands more were deported. Indeed, the nature of this single week is of great importance for any understanding of the role of the people in more recent French history. First, the Communards were a major threat to the status quo, as witnessed by their occupation of Paris for many weeks and their experiments with forms of direct democracy and egalitarian social organisation. Second, the Versailles government attacked the Communards without mercy and with far more violence than was necessary simply to recapture Paris; as Edmond de Goncourt put it gleefully at the time, 'such a purge, by killing off the combative part of the population, defers the next revolution by a whole generation'.[3] This meant that the republicanism of the Third Republic had physically destroyed or deported some of the most politically active among the people. In the land where, as Friedrich Engels put it, 'class struggles are each time fought out to a decision', Paris was the international epicentre of modern revolution, but also of counter-revolution and counter-attack.[4] During the nineteenth century, the idea of the people became a central concern and a rallying cry for political groupings on the left and individual thinkers of the late eighteenth and nineteenth centuries, like Rousseau, Proudhon, Babeuf and Blanqui. This political tradition, of course, drew in particular on the philosophical legacy of Rousseau, whose concept of the 'general will' and scepticism towards parliamentary practice was so central to his ideas of political progress and democracy.[5] Moreover, it was French thought of the nineteenth century that informed Marx's and Engels' politics (as opposed to their philosophy and economics, which were strongly informed by German and British thinkers, respectively), including the idea of ordinary working people, and in particular the urban proletariat, being the ultimate driving force behind human emancipation.

The end of the nineteenth century and much of the twentieth century were marked both by the active role of the people in France and by attempts to limit their ability to influence politics directly. As mentioned above, the nature of the formal, governing republicanism of the Third Republic was one way in which the ruling class attempted to keep the people at bay. The people became explicit actors as far as republican ideology was concerned, and equality became part of the declared goals of the republic. Moreover, the legitimacy of revolt in defence of the collective rights of ordinary people became enshrined in, for example, the annual celebrations commemorating the storming of the Bastille on 14 July and the Marseillaise, which has been the national anthem of all Republics apart from the Second and which champions the role of armed insurrection in the cause of popular justice. At the same time, however, such was the ruling class's fear of actual revolt that workers' organisations – and strikes – were outlawed soon after the Revolution in 1791, and only legalised piecemeal in 1864 and 1884. When the Confédération générale du travail (CGT) trade union confederation was founded in 1895, it was led by a frustrated and radical vanguard whose inclination was far more towards strikes and industrial sabotage than negotiation and compromise with employers and government. Moreover, in 1920 when Lenin called for the formation of parties whose role was to support the 1917 Russian Revolution, a majority of the more moderate Socialist members went over to the newly-formed Communist Party (PCF). The Communists became more powerful and the Socialist left found it difficult to establish itself in its own right, particularly after the Second World War when, between 1944 and 1978, it was the largest political party and received roughly one fifth of the vote at national elections. The social-democratic left was certainly very weak compared with its counterparts in many other countries, but nevertheless used a language of class struggle that was influenced by Marxism. In other words, it lived in the shadow of the PCF, since the latter was the party of the most organised, largely blue-collar sections of the working class, along with the CGT. Strikes in 1936 after the formation of the Popular Front government, widespread strikes in 1947 and a three-week general strike combined with workplace occupations in May 1968 were among the most forceful expressions of the continuing predilection for uprising and revolt on the part of the working class.

Let us now interrupt this historical overview and present a juxtaposition of two moments in the history of the Socialist current, one in the 1970s and the other in 2012. On the eve of what later became known as the Mitterrand era, the explicit challenge for the Socialists was to attract enough working class voters to the PS in order to win elections. Mitterrand had declared publically in 1972 that the PS needed to take votes from the PCF, stating that 'our fundamental objective is to rebuild a great Socialist Party on the terrain occupied by the Communist Party, in order to show that, out of five million Communist voters, three million can vote Socialist'.[6] The working class was clearly seen as the key to the success of the PS and in the following decade the party did indeed do all it could to steal the clothes of the Communists. Let us compare this position of seeking out the working class vote with the position of a report published in 2012 by the think tank Terra Nova, which is very close to the PS and was in support of Dominique Strauss-Kahn before his comprehensive fall from grace after events in a New York hotel room in May 2011. The report, entitled *Gauche: quelle majorité électorale pour 2012?*, argued that society had changed so much that:

> [i]t is not possible today for the left to seek to restore its historic class coalition; the working class is no longer at the heart of the left vote and is no longer in step with [the left's] general values and can no longer be, as it once was, the motor driving the construction of a left electoral majority. Any wish for the left to implement a class strategy based on the working class, and more generally the people [*les classes populaires*] would require a renunciation of the left's cultural values, in other words a break with social democracy.[7]

In other words, the working class had moved greatly to the right and had abandoned not only socialism but also anything resembling progressive thinking; the report went on to argue that the only way to pursue social democratic and progressive policy was in turn to abandon the working class to its reactionary ways and to target various groups, which together would form a credible electorate for the PS, namely the university educated, young people, ethnic minorities in 'sensitive' suburbs, non-Catholics, and those living in large towns and cities. These groups, it argued, share progressive values of openness and tolerance that are broadly those of the centre-left, by stark contrast with those of the working class. This report certainly caused a major debate within the PS, but it represented the views of a substantial proportion of leaders and grass roots members alike.

Before examining further the questions of class, class conflict and the left in the early twenty-first century, we should examine some of the changes which took place under the presidency of François Mitterrand (1981–95). This period was a watershed as far as the influence of the people on party politics and government was concerned and is crucial for understanding the argument in this chapter. Mitterrand was elected President in 1981 and a parliamentary majority was formed on the basis of a manifesto whose general direction as well as detail flew in the face of much of what the rest of the advanced capitalist world was attempting to do. Mitterrand himself commented after victory in 1981 that the sociological majority had become the political majority and there was some truth in this, at least in the short term. Based loosely on an electoral pact signed by the PCF and PS in the early 1970s, it was ultimately, however, an attempt to achieve a Fordist compromise between capital, labour and government resulting in less overt class struggle, which had been pursued in various other countries, including Britain, Germany and various Nordic countries.[8] Substantial material concessions were made to the working class in the form of job creation, higher pay, higher social security benefits and improved labour legislation regarding working conditions, alongside a substantial wave of nationalisations. The PCF was included in the new government, a move which was designed to keep the PCF and the PCF's close allies in the major trade unions on board. Crucially, however, the government (including the Communists, who remained in the cabinet until 1984) performed a dramatic about-turn in 1982–3, when austerity measures were introduced and the working class was obliged to bear the brunt of the economic and social problems of the time, including rising – and as it turned out enduringly high – unemployment. Mitterrand's Parti socialiste (PS) appeared to have abandoned any real commitment to the people in favour of a highly pragmatic approach to governing, effectively pursuing very similar policies to the centre-right. Now very much the dominant force on the centre-left, it became deeply electoralist in its outlook and practice and seemed to embrace the views of mainstream and centre-right analysts of the international economy and society.

Since the mid- to late 1980s, the dominant view of the socio-economic structures of advanced capitalist countries has been one that accepts the migration of industrial production to developing countries where labour is cheaper, and promotes the rise of the service sector in advanced capitalist societies. According to this view, the working class that once worked in manufacturing is in virtually terminal decline and the fruits of these heavily import-dependent economies, while by no means evenly distributed across a national economy, are sufficiently distributed for the vast majority of the population to live in material and spiritual comfort. I would argue that in France it was largely the PS that translated this view of the national and international political economy into political strategy and practice over the course of the 1980s. In economic policy terms, the party became far more supportive of private enterprise than it had been pre-1982 and it moved very rapidly away from the neo-Keynesian, demand management measures described above. For our purposes, and as argued by Laurent Bouvet, the changes in 'cultural' orientation – as opposed to economic or political orientation – are just as important.[9] Instead of an appeal to a class-based electorate, by the end of the 1980s the PS had largely reoriented itself in order to attempt to appeal to a rather disparate target audience made up on the one hand of liberal-minded, largely university-educated people who were fairly comfortably off, and on the other hand younger people and groups who suffered discrimination of various forms, including ethnic minorities, immigrants, and gays and lesbians. Women were also a particular target of this new orientation. It was, then, supposedly 'post-materialist' values and social structures which determined the new orientation of the PS, reflecting the view that material differences within society were diminishing fast. There was a new emphasis on the individual as victim who deserved a more equal share of the capitalist cake and better treatment, rather than concentrating on the traditional Socialist concern, namely the working class as a whole.

Crucially, the PS was no longer competing to the same extent with the PCF for the traditional working class vote, because the Party experienced severe electoral decline through the late 1970s and the 1980s. Indeed, part of the new narrative of the centre-left was that the PCF's base in the blue-collar working class had all but disappeared and that, with the end of the Cold War, global Communism had been defeated forever. The challenge was to find a 'modernising' orientation which would guarantee that what happened to the PCF did not happen to the PS. During the 1980s, the PS was thus in pursuit of a more composite electorate that reflected the changing membership of the party itself and in particular the leadership and its most active members, who even before the Mitterrand victory of 1981 had increasingly been young, media-savvy, university-educated professionals.

A good indicator of this transformation was the highly significant policy document that emerged from the PS Congress of 1991, entitled *Un Nouvel horizon: Un Projet socialiste pour la France*. It was a rare public acknowledgement that the PS had changed profoundly since it first came to power in 1981 and was a statement of the way the party now saw society, the economy and politics more generally. It argued that:

> [t]he huge political fractures which criss-crossed French society (left–right, proletariat–bourgeoisie, state education–religious education) have attenuated; French society seems to have reached the era of mass individualism, characterised by dwindling of passions, withering of collective aspirations, relative homogenisation of ways of life and of behaviours. A large 'central bloc' or 'salaried society' now unites two out of three French people, perhaps even three out of four . . .[10]

Therefore, the PS, 'too long associated with the tenets of collectivism, reassert[ed] that the autonomy of the individual, the right to happiness for every woman and every man are the goals which it set itself'.[11] In the realm of the economy, the market was now praised and seen as essential, although there was work to do in order to explain differences with the centre-right in this domain:

> Now that the market economy, albeit tempered, is the rule, and with the existence of long-term unemployment, a large body of public opinion cannot see any difference between right-wing management and left-wing management . . . Having moved on from some former rather simplistic approaches, it is up to us to define . . . the terms of opposition between conservatism and progressive politics.[12]

Any idea of collective emancipation from capitalism had completely disappeared, as had any concept of class being at the heart of Socialist politics. These notions had been replaced by ideas about individual escape from the worst effects of material hardship and ideological oppression. As the influence of a traditional PCF was left further and further behind in the 1990s, the idea of the people was replaced by a vague, liberal multi-culturalism, where a commitment to the working class was replaced by an emphasis on individual rights, tolerance and combatting exclusion. This was combined with greatly encouraging capitalist enterprise, albeit with some degree of redistribution. Pragmatism was increasingly the order of the day and, as Mitterrand commented in a speech regarding privatisation of state-owned industries in 1992, 'we act according to the circumstances'.[13]

There was a broader intellectual context to this shift. From the mid-1980s onwards, high-profile intellectuals produced work that supported a view of France and of advanced capitalist societies more generally as less conflictual, increasingly middle class, and politically consensual. This was a view of society where the traditional idea of the people had no place. A classic version of this argument came from the revisionist historian François Furet, along with Jacques Julliard and Pierre Rosanvallon, who argued in *La République du centre* (1988) that France was finally falling in line with other, less revolutionary countries and had learned to love centre-oriented politics, where class conflict was weak and where there was simply a slight difference of emphasis between centre-left and centre-right. The two sides of the political spectrum now 'cohabited' with each other quite happily and *alternance* between left and right in government had become almost an expectation.[14] In many ways, this was a variant (although not explicitly so) of Daniel Bell's 1960s 'end of ideology' thesis. Bell argued that ideological divisions in the West were diminishing and that ideology would be less and less relevant as time went by.[15] The sociologist Henri Mendras had also argued in *La Seconde Révolution française* (1988) that social classes in France had changed greatly, along with the decline of the importance of political parties, the Catholic Church and even the Republic.[16] On the left, André Gorz had published *Adieu au prolétariat* in 1980, in which he argued that the working class was no longer the only revolutionary class, but his thesis was widely interpreted as meaning that the working class was, in fact, in terminal decline.[17]

Meanwhile, there was a steady stream of books and articles that sought to re-interpret the events of May 1968 in such a way that they had nothing at all to do with class, or at least not the working class. Perhaps most famously, Gilles Lipovetsky argued that the 1968 uprising, far from being a popular revolt against oppression of various kinds, was in fact about the pursuit of individualistic desires and was an 'explosion of explicitly individualistic demands and aspirations',[18] which was reminiscent of Régis Debray's argument in the late 1970s that the May 1968 revolt had, paradoxically, consolidated capitalism.[19] Bizarrely, 1968 was becoming a watershed moment when the people finally became obsolete and the individual became the main agent for change as well as the main beneficiary of change. This tendency was reinforced in the realm of political thought and philosophy by a group of scholars who set out to consolidate such liberal thought that existed in France and create a new culture of liberalism. This group included Marcel Gauchet, Luc Ferry and Alain Renaut, all of whom sought to challenge more dominant intellectual traditions in France, namely republicanism, structuralism and Marxism.[20] The fall of the Berlin Wall in 1989 and the international success of Francis Fukuyama's 'End of History' argument gave further credence to this liberal viewpoint: it seemed to many incontrovertible that an American liberal-capitalist ideology had won the battle between capitalism and communism in the twentieth century.[21] In short, there was an attempt on the part of many politicians and intellectuals alike to convince their audiences that the difference between social classes had eroded to the point that class was no longer relevant to politics and that the people, if they still existed at all, were becoming irrelevant. The PS did not go quite as far as Tony Blair's New Labour would go in undermining much of what the centre-left had stood for after its election victory in 1997, but the French Socialists certainly took the mainstream left (including, to some extent the PCF) to a very different place from where it had been in the 1970s.

None of this was entirely mistaken in terms of social analysis and the way in which political economy had evolved, but it misunderstood long-term socio-economic trends. Certainly, living standards had risen greatly and continued to do so for the majority. Likewise, the changes in methods of production, transport and communication, together with changes in global patterns of manufacturing and consumption, had drastically altered the social structure of society and the huge expansion of higher education had been part of the process as well. But there were several ways in which this very widely-accepted analysis was profoundly mistaken. First, there continued to be a large number of people who remained at the margins of society financially, socially and politically; most obviously there were the long-term unemployed and many impoverished immigrant workers from the post-war boom, and their families, and of course their children and grandchildren. There were also many people who might not have been among the least well off, but who were nevertheless very far from being middle class, in terms of both income and level of education, for example. Then there was the assumption that the Western economies would, apart from the occasional blip, continue to thrive, which has now been spectacularly called into question by the economic crisis and its drastic social consequences. Finally, there was the assumption that the capitalist class and the most obvious defenders of its interests in politics, would continue to be relatively benign in relation to those who produced the wealth at the point of production. Regarding May 1968, it was in fact much more the eventual failure of the radical impulse born in May than the logic of the revolt itself that led to the rise of individualism and superficial consensus.

This view is borne out by the analysis of the geographer Christophe Guilluy in his important book *Fractures françaises* (2011). He argues that, by stark contrast with the dominant view that French society has become one vast middle class, a majority of the French are in fact part of what he terms the 'popular classes' (*les couches populaires*). Traditionally, blue collar workers are seen as the archetypal working class and white collar workers are placed in a different, more aspirational and less impoverished and exploited category. Since the end of the 1970s, however, and in particular over the past two decades, white collar workers have become increasingly impoverished, to the extent that in 2010 a majority of French people were earning less than 2,000 Euros per month and almost eight million were considered poor by official criteria. Various factors, including housing costs increasing far faster than household income, have contributed to the fragmentation of the middle classes, whose dominance characterised only the baby-boom generation of the 1960s and 1970s.[22]

Nevertheless, Guilluy argues, the relative invisibility of the popular classes has allowed successive governments to present the image of a pacified society where conflict no longer exists:

> the invisibility of the popular classes evacuates the very idea of conflict and conflict no longer forms part of politics; this is one of the main causes of the disaffection of a large number of voters for political parties. This allows the myth of a majority middle class to persist.[23]

Politicians fully buy into this view of society as being predominantly middle class; the various different mainstream parties agree on the essential and conduct debates which are often meaningless. Guilluy goes on to explain that the erroneous dominant discourse suggests that in place of traditional class conflict there is now a large middle class on the one hand and the 'excluded' on the other, many of whom are ethnic minorities who live in 'troubled' suburbs of large towns and cities. Notorious suburbs of cities and large towns, then, equate to ethnic minority exclusion, while the white middle classes live in 'pavillons' in other neighbourhoods. However, the empirical reality is that a majority of blue-collar workers, white-collar workers and other poorer families live in industrial or rural 'periurban' locations. There are numerous success stories relating to young people living in supposedly impossibly-difficult suburbs, but they are overlooked in favour of a view in which class relations disappear and are replaced by those who are 'out' – in 'ethnic minority suburbs' – and the rest who are 'in' – elsewhere. This ghettoisation, Guilluy argues, suits the ruling class. For the mainstream left in particular, the figure of the immigrant has replaced that of the blue-collar worker since the early 1980s and the young ghetto-dweller has become the new figure of revolt.[24] Élites are happy to talk of ethnic diversity, which is relatively unchallenging, but not of greater equality. In short, 'the erroneous representations of French society mean that another, in fact more prevalent, France becomes invisible, namely the France of the popular classes'.[25] The large parties of the left and the right, Guilluy argues, still rely heavily on this idea of a vast, homogeneous middle class, but this perception bears no resemblance to reality. Certainly, the working class has moved out of towns and cities, but it has not diminished in size. Moreover, although the left has lost many working class votes, the working class has not moved to the right. Rather, over the past two decades a majority of French people has become disillusioned with the major parties, in particular because they have failed to offer the benefits of globalisation to the working class yet continue to benefit from it and support it themselves.

The effects of the increasingly global economy, the greater dominance of the financial sector, the pressure to consume an ever greater number of commodities, all followed by economic crisis and falling living standards for many people, have further marginalised both blue-collar workers and many white-collar workers. Thus the myth of inevitable 'embourgeoisement' for virtually all those lower down the social hierarchy is, for the moment at least, dead, and many people are either experiencing a drop in living standards or are fearful of doing so. Therefore, in order to talk more meaningfully in sociological terms about the working class, we now need to include blue-collar workers *and* many white-collar workers. Rémi Lefebvre argues that the size of the working class (*les catégories populaires*) has in fact diminished very little over the past thirty years, particularly given that there are approximately eight million white collar workers whose place in society is very similar to that of blue collar workers; the misleading impression of a disappearance of the working class stems from substantial structural changes *within* the class, including geographical dispersion and relocation within more 'professional' organisations, rather than a decline of the class itself.[26] With (in 2013) overall unemployment at over ten per cent, youth unemployment at 23 per cent, and with living standards almost static overall and falling for many, there can certainly be no pretence at general well-being. This has been compounded by the decline of the organised labour movement, which has had a long-lasting effect on the way in which sociological change is – or is not – reflected in mainstream party politics. Or, to put it another way, with the decline of the unions, the people are far less well represented. With the working class increasingly fragmented and on casual contracts, the rate of union membership is well under 10 per cent of the labour force and this, alongside the decline of the PCF and the radical move to the right on the part of the PS, means that politicians on the left who accept the view of French society as homogeneous and largely middle class are not properly called to account.

In the run-up to the 2007 presidential elections, the right-wing candidate Nicolas Sarkozy appeared, paradoxically, to have understood these sociological developments discussed above better than the left and he waged a more class conscious campaign than any major party had done for many years. Breaking quite clearly with the idea that there was little difference between right and left, he talked of an 'unapologetic right' (a *droite décomplexée*) and went out of his way to distance himself from Chirac, whom he regarded as weak, ineffectual and, by implication, conceding too much to those who allegedly shied away from work. He insisted that there would be a 'fiscal shield' protecting the rich against high taxes, and at the same time, in populist fashion, insisted that those who worked hard would be rewarded more than they ever had been before, regardless of where they were placed in society. This did not come in the form of championing of the people – or at least not in a traditional left-wing sense – but rather in a way that acknowledged the importance of some of the preoccupations of ordinary working people and interestingly put more emphasis on the notion of work and labour than any centre-oriented party since the PS in the late 1970s and early 1980s. The first lines of Sarkozy's manifesto claimed that 'France is experiencing a moral crisis: a crisis of work. The rehabilitation of work is at the heart of my presidential project.'[27] For Sarkozy, the events of May 1968 became a virtual obsession as he promised to rid France of the constricting effect of 'political correctness' that he blamed in turn on the influence of May 1968. My interpretation of this obsession is that Sarkozy recognised the strong class element there was in the events of 1968 (most importantly, the largest and longest general strike in French history), but that his agenda was one of asserting the increased dominance of the capitalist class rather than the working class; beneath his much-repeated slogan 'work more to earn more' and appeals to 'the France that gets up early' was a desire to consolidate the power of capitalism. He did this in a populist and quasi-Bonapartist fashion, while all the time making it clear that he himself had got where he was because he was aspirant and was proud to count as his friends some of the richest business people and most successful (and ruthless) media tycoons. In short, Sarkozy sought to reassert the importance of work, remuneration (increasing his own salary by 140 per cent), and the right to become rich through hard work. He asserted the importance of the notion of class, from the point of view of someone who clearly identified strongly with the interests of the ruling class, and the right to make money.[28]

In the meantime, the left political landscape in the early years of the twenty-first century in France is one where the PCF is a very faint shadow of its former self, with an aging and diminishing activist base and extremely poor results at national (and many local) elections. At the same time, the PS, both before and after Hollande's election victory in 2012, has had difficulty in defining its ideological orientation, is unsure of its target electorate, and seems to adhere to little more than mildly 'progressive' policies. Jean-Luc Mélenchon's further-left Front de Gauche coalition has certainly attempted to appeal to the sections of the population that had largely been bypassed by the fruits of prosperity and which had then been hardest hit by the international crisis. Although Mélenchon did less well than expected in the 2012 presidential elections (with 11 per cent of the overall vote), the Mélenchon campaign struck a chord precisely because it championed the people from a left perspective and challenged the FN's own populist appeal to ordinary working people. For which parties, then, does the working class vote at national elections? A certain proportion goes to the PS and a little to the PCF as well. But many analysts have pointed out that much of the blue-collar vote now goes to the extreme-right National Front. At the 2012 presidential elections, some 29 per cent of the blue-collar electorate (that is, 29 per cent of those blue-collar workers who went to the polls) voted Le Pen, which was one percentage point higher than for Hollande. Perhaps even more importantly, for the first time the FN managed to make significant gains in rural France and in the suburbs of large towns and cities, picking up many votes in increasingly deprived areas. As one FN leader commented, what worked was a campaign oriented towards rural areas and the greater suburbs – in other words, 'la France pauvre'.[29] Does this mean that the working class has become intrinsically right wing, as Terra Nova seems to suggest, or should this trend instead be interpreted as a sense of abandonment of the people by the left, a feeling that the mainstream left has now become largely a force that protects the interests of certain sections of the middle classes, not those of the people, and is above all concerned with gaining office? My argument above is that we must draw the latter conclusion. Moreover, after many years when the dominant view of society and politics was that the French population was becoming increasingly homogeneous, we appear to be witnessing a certain return of the people as an acknowledged force in French society, including in the political domain. With blue-collar voters voting FN in large numbers, and the persistence of the Mélenchon phenomenon, mainstream politicians and analysts have begun to realise that many poorer people feel passed over by government policies and unrepresented by mainstream parties.

More generally, one of the problems with much interpretation on the part of the left in relation to voters is that its analysis has had a resolutely national focus. The world taken as a whole has never been so industrialised; not only are the newly industrialising economies catching up fast with 'post-industrial' countries such as France, but advanced capitalist countries have never before imported and consumed so many commodities. But while the contemporary world economy is increasingly global, most forms of politics, including trade union organisation, operate at a national level. This, in effect, both offers a tremendous advantage to capital over labour and tends to weaken nationally-based organisations designed to defend and promote the interests of the people; some of the developments discussed above stem from this. While the centre-left in France and in many other countries has invested politically in a 'modern' notion of the French which says that the working class on which the conventional notion of the people was based has changed enormously and has indeed largely disappeared, capital remains resolutely class-conflictual and probably more so than at any time since 1945.

There are currently clear echoes of the 1930s, with high unemployment, increasing hardship, stronger class allegiances and polarised politics, with parties appealing to the people on the far-left but also the extreme-right, and the centre-right moving towards populism and alliances with the extreme-right. In this context, the PS struggles to understand the situation and only the presence of a strong FN and high abstentions allow it to win some national and local elections. However, an important difference between the present situation and the 1930s (not to mention the post-war period), is that the working class is more atomised and alienated; it does not work in large plants with a unified culture, it does not work and live in the centre of towns and cities, it feels little affinity with the centre-left parties led by middle-class professionals, and perhaps most importantly, it is not organised into trade unions, clubs and parties in the way it was in the early and mid-twentieth century. Although the working class is not significantly smaller than in the 1930s, it is far more dispersed, divided and more easily dominated. The recent economic crisis has exposed the injustice – and ultimately the folly – of the PS pursuing the politics of pragmatism and compromise laid down in the Mitterrand era, rather than defending properly the medium- and longer-term interests of the people. This is a problem which, if confronted, can be addressed in the interests of ordinary working people, but if it is not, there is a risk that politics in France will tip still further in favour of the extreme-right.

Notes

1 For an interesting discussion of this point, see Alain Badiou, 'Vingt-quatre notes sur les usages du mot "peuple"', in Alain Badiou et al, *Qu'est-ce qu'un peuple?* (Paris: La Fabrique, 2013).

2 Karl Marx and Friedrich Engels, *The Manifesto of the Communist Party*, in Karl Marx and Friedrich Engels, *Selected Works* (London: Lawrence and Wishart, 1968), 35–63; Michael Hardt and Antonio Negri, *Multitude* (London: Penguin, 2004); Jacques Rancière, *Disagreement: Politics and philosophy* (Minneapolis: University of Minnesota Press, 1998).

3 Edmond de Goncourt, *Paris under Siege, 1870–1871: From the Goncourt Journal*, ed. George J. Becker (Ithaca, NY: Cornell University Press, 1969), 312.

4 Friedrich Engels, 'Preface to the third German edition of "The eighteenth Brumaire of Louis Bonaparte", 1885', in Karl Marx and Friedrich Engels, *Selected Works in One Volume* (London: Lawrence and Wishart, 1968[1865]), 94.

5 Jean-Jacques Rousseau, *The Social Contract and Discourses* (London: Dent, 1973 [1762]).

6 Quoted in Jean Lacouture, *Mitterrand: Une Histoire de français, vol. 1* (Paris, Seuil, 1999), 372.

7 Bruno Jeanbard, Olivier Ferrand and Romain Prudent, *Gauche: Quelle majorité électorale pour 2012?* Accessed 12 August 2013. http://www.tnova.fr/essai/gauche-quelle-majorit-lectorale-pour-2012

8 Nick Hewlett, *Modern French Politics: Analysing conflict and consensus since 1945* (Cambridge: Polity Press, 1998), 60–91.

9 Laurent Bouvet, *Le Sens du peuple. La Gauche, la démocratie, le populisme* (Paris: Gallimard, 2013), 167–228.

10 Parti Socialiste, *Un Nouvel horizon. Le Projet socialiste pour la France* (Paris: Gallimard, 1992), 52.

11 Parti Socialiste, *Un Nouvel horizon*, see Note 10, 131.

12 Parti Socialiste, *Un Nouvel horizon*, see Note 10, 122.

13 Quoted in Alain Gélédan, *Bilan Économique des années Mitterrand, 1981–1994* (Paris: Le Monde Éditions, 1993), 249.

14 François Furet, Jacques Julliard and Pierre Rosanvallon, *La République de centre* (Paris: Calmann-Lévy, 1988).

15 Daniel Bell, *The End of Ideology* (New York: Free Press, 1960).

16 Henri Mendras, *La Seconde Révolution française* (Paris: Gallimard, 1988).

17 André Gorz, *Adieu au prolétariat* (Paris: Éditions Galilée, 1980).

18 Gilles Lipovetsky, '"Changer la vie" ou l'irruption de l'individualisme transpolitique', *Pouvoirs* 39 (1986): 93.

19 Régis Debray, *Modeste contribution aux discours et cérémonies officielles du dixième anniversaire* (Paris: Maspéro, 1978).

20 Marcel Gauchet *Le Désenchantement du monde* (Paris: Gallimard, 1985); Luc Ferry, *Philosophie politique, 3 vols.* (Paris: Presses universitaires de France, 1988); Alain Renaut, *L'Ere de l'individu: Contribution à une histoire de la subjectivité* (Paris: Gallimard, 1989).

21 Francis Fukuyama, *The End of History and the Last Man* (New York and London: Free Press and Hamish Hamilton, 1992).

22 Christophe Guilluy, *Fractures françaises* (Paris: François Bourin, 2010), 79–82.

23 Guilluy, *Fractures françaises*, see Note 22, 9.

24 Guilluy, *Fractures françaises*, see Note 22, 33–35.

25 Guilluy, *Fractures françaises*, see Note 22, 89.

26 Rémi Lefebvre, 'Les Contours flous du peuple de gauche', in Laurent Baumel and François Kalfon, *Plaidoyer pour une Gauche populaire. La Gauche face à ses électeurs* (Paris: Le Bord de l'eau, 2011), 94.

27 Nicolas Sarkozy, *Mon Projet. Ensemble, tout devient possible* (2007), 1.

28 Nick Hewlett, *The Sarkozy Phenomenon* (Exeter: Imprint Academic, 2011).

29 Arnaud Leparmentier and Vanessa Schneider, 'M. Sarkozy joue son va-tout en pariant sur l'électorat FN', *Le Monde*, 24 April 2012.

4

The Melancholy of Post-Communism:

François Furet and the Passions

Christophe Prochasson

Translated from the French by Emile Chabal

The 1970s were an age of transition in French intellectual and political life. They not only marked the highpoint of a polarised ideological struggle, but also the beginning of a slow atrophy of political reference points. The left was the first to be affected by these changes. This is hardly surprising since it was the left that had traditionally been most receptive to systems and theories, above all those of Marx and his disciples. As the latter fell out of favour, the French left found itself searching for an identity. To use the words of Gilles Lipovetsky, whose 1983 essay was one of the first to analyse France's new political configuration, politics was entering an 'age of emptiness'.[1] This sense of absence was reinforced that same year when the Socialist government 'forgot' to celebrate the centenary of Marx's death: even the single most important figure in the political architecture of the left was losing his symbolic power.

Many commentators have subsequently deplored this depoliticisation of French intellectual life.[2] Amid the generalised polemic and nostalgia, one figure is held to be particularly responsible for the ideological changes of the recent past: François Furet. The famous historian of the French Revolution had already earned the suspicion of the left by openly confronting his Marxist colleagues in the 1960s, but his name returned to prominence in the following decades. The historiographical debate surrounding the Revolution at the time of the bicentenary in 1989 reopened old ideological wounds. Was the Revolution about the Rights of Man or the Terror? Was it a revolution for the bourgeoisie or the people? What, if any, was the relationship between the French and Bolshevik Revolutions? Furet had already tackled some of these questions in his controversial essays in *Penser la Révolution française* (1978) but he reiterated his central claim – that the Revolution was 'over' – in the late 1980s.[3] He maintained that French politics had 'normalised'; there was no longer cause to believe in a mythical French 'exceptionality'.[4] The fall of the Berlin Wall and the collapse of Communism gave further strength to his argument. Indeed, Furet was one of the first historians to theorise the end of the Communist 'illusion' and the weakening of the revolutionary passion that had dominated the left since 1917. But, to his enemies, this willingness to write Communism's obituary merely confirmed their suspicions that Furet was actually rather comfortable with the advent of a new post-ideological age of uncertainty.

Of course, the changing intellectual landscape of the late 1980s and early 1990s also had a wider impact. The diminishing hold of Marxism and a revival of interest in liberalism forced French academics and intellectuals to rethink their work. The analytical frameworks of the previous three or four decades were abruptly refashioned. The rigorous scientism that had been the hallmark of the social sciences and the humanities was shattered. Historians who accepted the bankruptcy of Marxism began to reconsider the haphazard nature of *histoire évenementielle*, the role of individual actors, and the significance of political symbols rather than socio-economic structures. Furet's work, particularly in his later years, responded to these emerging trends; he, too, was affected by the anxiety that accompanied uncertainty.

Furet's theory of political passion reflected this new intellectual climate. It drew on alternative approaches to politics that had influenced him in his youth, and did not rely on Marx or Marxism. By the end of his career, 'passion' (*passion*) and 'feeling' (*sentiment*) had become constitutive elements of Furet's interpretation of modern politics.[5] At the broadest level, he maintained that 'fear' was the overwhelming passion of the right and 'resentment' the defining passion of the left.[6] In his last major book, *Le Passé d'une illusion* (1995), he referred to 'the feelings of patriotism that drove soldiers to the front in August 1914', as well as the 'passion for the universal', 'national feeling' and 'national passion', all of which were part of a wider 'democratic passion'.[7] Following Tocqueville and Rousseau, he also classed 'envy' and 'jealousy' among the 'democratic passions'. These were the result of a fundamental contradiction at the heart of democracy between the principle of equality and the realities of personal enrichment, a contradiction that Furet considered both irreconcilable and intolerable in modern society. 'Passion' and 'feeling' were thus intimately linked to the development of political thought, even if the latter implied a wider range of emotions such as the 'feeling of progress', 'religious feeling', 'national feeling', 'modern democratic feeling', 'class feeling' or 'modern feeling of class belonging'. Nevertheless, Furet generally preferred to use the term 'passion'. In 1980, during a lecture to the Colloque Tocqueville on the conceptual framework of Tocqueville's *Democracy in America* he presented equality as a 'passion', although he later clarified that it was simultaneously like a 'feeling' and an 'ideology'.

This deliberate semantic confusion had two important functions. First, it allowed Furet to differentiate a history of 'passions' from a history of 'mentalities' (*mentalités*). He had long been sceptical of 'mentalities' on the grounds that they implied a static emotional state whereas 'passions', by definition, fluctuated. Moreover, 'passion' incorporated an explicitly social dimension: for Furet, political 'passions' were almost always collective. Second, Furet's overlapping use of words was meant to expand and complicate our political vocabulary. 'Passions' are a mix of 'feeling' and 'ideology' in the same way that 'ideology' is a mix of 'ideas' and 'passions'. One of Furet's most famous concepts – that of political 'illusion' – was dependent on the volatility of the passions. He defined 'illusion' as an all-consuming psychological investment in a political cause. In this sense, 'illusion' and 'ideology' are similar: in *Le Passé d'une illusion*, he described the latter as an explanatory system 'through which the actions of men take on a providential character, shorn of divinity'.[8] This would appear to place ideology in the camp of reason rather than 'passion'. But Furet argued that there were also 'ideological passions' that could stir up the 'enthusiasm' of the popular classes and educated classes alike. National-socialism, which he saw as the 'intoxicating blend of the autodidact', was more potent than Marxism–Leninism, which retained a certain 'philosophical pedigree', but they both belonged as much to the emotional realm of 'passion' as the rationality of 'ideology'.[9]

There were occasions when Furet's liberal use of terms made it difficult to identify exactly what he meant. In 1996, the philosopher Paul Ricœur asked him: 'Where do you situate yourself? And, by extension, what kind of history do you do? A history of mentalities? A history of passions? A history of beliefs (*croyances*)?'[10] It was an awkward question, to which Furet gave no response. Still, it is clear that there were fewer passions than there were 'feelings' or 'emotions', and that the passions were governed by a clear hierarchy. The primary passion, from which all the other passions derived, was the 'egalitarian passion'. Below this, there were a number of subsidiary passions: 'revolutionary passion' and, specifically, 'a French passion for permanent revolution';[11] 'ideological passion', of which there was both a Communist and fascist variety; and 'national' or 'patriotic' passion. Alongside these political passions, there were those of a more societal orientation: the 'hatred' (*haine*) of the bourgeois; the 'anti-aristocratic' passion that anticipated the French Revolution; 'money', which is the great passion of the bourgeoisie; and the 'passion for well-being' (*bien-être*) that dominates modern society.[12]

These passions were not simply confined to the past. He mobilised three of them to explain the precipitous collapse of Communism in Eastern Europe:

> The passion for liberty did not, on the whole, play a determining role in the fall of Communism. The passion for well-being, yes, but this cannot be satisfied in the current configuration of productive forces. What remains is patriotic passion, which was in most cases sustained by the Stalinist regimes [of Eastern Europe].[13]

The idea of a 'patriotic' or 'national' passion was central to Furet's oeuvre. For instance, it is to this that he attributed the outbreak and longevity of the First World War. At the same time, he maintained that the intensity of patriotic passion in the early twentieth century was something of an 'enigma', incomprehensible to a young man or woman coming of age in the 1990s. This makes it all the more paradoxical that Furet should have elevated it to the status of a primary passion (along with the passion for well-being) in his discussion of the fall of Communism. Why was patriotic passion more important than the passion for liberty in late-twentieth-century Eastern Europe when the reverse was true in the West? In fact, Furet went so far as to recognise the passion for 'well-being' and the desire to emulate Western consumer society as the main motivations behind the toppling of the Communist regimes. Was it simply that Eastern Europeans were not yet fully aware of the passion for liberty? The answer is unclear.

Of all the democratic passions, however, it is the 'egalitarian' passion that is 'the mother of all passions in modern democracy'.[14] In this, Furet was largely reiterating a point made by Tocqueville more than a century earlier in *Democracy in America*; one might even say that he set out to test Tocqueville's prophesy about the dangers of egalitarianism using the history of the twentieth century. For Furet, democracy is both a social and political construct; by making equality its defining feature, democracy promotes a political form that can integrate the greatest number of people, but also establishes an absolute equivalence between all human beings: this was the emphatic message of the Declaration of the Rights of Man in 1789. The problem is that equality is a bottomless pit. It is an inextinguishable passion. Democracy produces inequality that cannot fully be eliminated without putting basic liberties at risk. This core tension between the egalitarian passion and the passion for liberty lies at the heart of the democratic polity and gives rise to the open contradiction between political equality and social inequality in contemporary society. Yet, despite this contradiction, the French Revolution ensured that the egalitarian passion would become the heart and soul of democracy – its primary, pre-eminent passion. The very fact that equality is unattainable gives democracy its inexhaustible strength: the difference between what Marxists call 'real' equality and political equality is irrelevant since the lesson of the revolutionary moment is that all humans are 'equal before the law' and that no one person can claim natural superiority over another. The Declaration of the Rights of Man refers only to 'distinctions' between men, but never inequality. Equality is thus the archetypal example of a passion since it is always beyond reach. As Furet put it himself: 'I believe very deeply that a modern democracy which promises liberty and equality, which promises the earth, is a form of utopia.'[15]

Furet returned time and again to this problem in his historical writing and his commentaries on contemporary society. He was scathing, for example, about what he considered to be the manipulation of the idea of equality among the American feminist and ethnic minority movements that he encountered in the 1970s and 1980s. How many times is it possible to reformulate equality? And for whom? Furet suggested that the incessant desire to apply equality would eventually result in such ludicrous concepts as 'equality for children' or the 'rights of nature'. But, for all its absurdity, he recognised that the incessant quest for equality was what gave democratic society its dynamism – and constituted its greatest weakness:

> If we consider the central predicament of modern democracy, we realise that there is a gap between the expectations it creates and the solutions it offers to those same expectations. There is, in theory, a point where total liberty and total equality meet and bring together the ideal conditions for individual autonomy; but this point is always out of reach. Democratic society is never democratic enough, and the expectations of its supporters are more numerous and more dangerous than those of its enemies. The promise of democracy is infinite [but] it is impossible to prioritise liberty and equality simultaneously, or even to reconcile them durably, in a society of individuals. This exposes all democratic regimes, not only to the excesses of demagogy but also to the constant reproach that they have betrayed their founding principles.[16]

Thus, in contrast to aristocratic societies – where political hierarchy corresponds to social inequality – democratic societies are perpetually torn between two poles. This contradiction feeds an insatiable appetite for further equality which explains the never-ending revolutions of nineteenth-century France and Europe. This frustration was reflected in bourgeois society, which was, in Furet's words, 'hard, sad and lonely'.[17]

An emphasis on the 'egalitarian passion' as the pre-eminent (and unattainable) democratic passion of the modern age encouraged a growing sense of melancholy in Furet's writing in the 1980s, which coincided with what appeared to be the terminal phase of France's revolutionary culture. The question is whether his pessimistic critique of political passion was designed to expel the passions from politics altogether, or whether he was willing to accommodate the passions in order to tame the 'illusions' they carried within them. The latter seems a more plausible interpretation, despite the fact that Furet's polemical style often made it look as if he wanted to break definitively with any political tradition or ideology that remained stubbornly attached to egalitarianism. At the time of the Bicentenary of the French Revolution in 1989, Furet was asked to explain his position to an audience at the Société française de philosophie:

> I will not be the advocate of the world in which we live and the way in which we, as citizens, experience politics. I only know that Marx thought he could solve an insoluble problem. I think there is something in modern democracy that is desperately abstract but with which we have to grapple every day. The fact that we inhabit a world that believes firmly in equality when we are all unequal is an idea we have to live with. I think [egalitarianism] is a noble and beautiful idea, but I don't think we can resolve the contradiction, intrinsic to modern democracy, between the aspiration to equality and the concrete reality of inequality. We can limit it, but we cannot eliminate it altogether, unless we eliminate liberty.[18]

Such a pessimistic analysis naturally led Furet to the conclusion that egalitarian passion was inextricably tied up with revolutionary passion. The two belonged together as vital elements of modern democracy.

Furet described the 'revolutionary passion' as the 'subject of his life'.[19] He argued that revolutionary passion expresses itself first and foremost in a belief in the omnipotence of political will, which pushes men and women to seize state power and use it to transform society in a short space of time. Simply by willing change, revolutionaries effect change. This does not, however, mean that revolutionary passion always develops in the same way, as Furet made clear in his discussion of the French and Bolshevik Revolutions. In the case of the French Revolution, the passion for revolution emerged from the movement of history: it was the revolutionary process itself that created revolutionary passion. Or, to put it another way, it was the Revolution that made revolutionaries. On the eve of 1789, none of the political figures who would come to prominence in later years thought that they were initiating a revolution, nor did they see themselves as revolutionaries. Their passion and fervour grew as events unfolded. In the Bolshevik Revolution, by contrast, Lenin and his comrades knew that they would start a revolution and believed that this was the only way to change Russian society. The passion and violence that the revolution unleashed were necessary in order to fulfil the revolutionary dream of the eighteenth century. The Bolsheviks were already inhabited by revolutionary passion before the event. Furet was nevertheless adamant that revolutionary passion was born during the French Revolution: this was the founding moment of a political culture that would be divided between those who would take up arms to destroy oppressive regimes and those who would denounce the inevitable destruction and tyranny that accompanied revolution.

In an essay from 1994, which would later become the first chapter of *Le Passé d'une illusion*, Furet offered a clear definition of 'revolutionary passion'. It was, he argued, a phenomenon similar in character to belief:

Revolutionary passion demands that every action be political: everything is part of history, starting with man, and everything can be improved in a good society, on condition that it is created [by the will of man]. But modern society is characterised by a political deficit with respect to the private existence of individuals. It cannot create an idea of the common good because men create their own common good within their subjective worlds. The only way for modern society to imagine the common good is through the idea of wellbeing, which divides people as much as it unites them, and therefore destroys the community it was intended to create. The revolutionary ideal is the result of this unfortunate situation. The most remarkable aspect of the French Revolution, apart from giving birth to democracy in Europe, was that it exposed the contradictory tensions and passions that emerged from this unprecedented social context. The event was so rich that European politics continued to live on its legacy for almost a century. But, in the minds of the people, it was far longer, for what the French Revolution invented was less a new society founded on political equality and representative government than a privileged model of political change, an idea of human will, and a messianic conception of politics. We need to understand the distance that separates the temptation of the revolutionary idea after 1914 and what the French were able to achieve, in terms of historical change, at the end of the eighteenth century.[20]

One of the most striking aspects of this passage is the conflation between revolutionary 'passion' and revolutionary 'idea'. The former is something akin to a black box from which the latter draws its inspiration. Likewise in the case of the Communist 'passion' and the Communist 'idea', both of which appear to have similar meanings in the opening pages of *Le Passé d'une illusion*. Furet himself does little to clarify his use of words by maintaining that 'I am less concerned with analysing concepts than I am with recreating a particular sensibility (*sensibilité*) and attitude (*opinion*)'.[21] The meaning of the two new words he uses here – 'sensibility' and 'attitude' – is hardly transparent. Moreover, contemporary social science has made us wary of these nebulous terms that now appear rather dated (as we know, Furet was not referring to the history of mentalities, about which he was sceptical; nor was he referring to the field of social psychology, about which he knew little). But the ambiguity was no accident: Furet was convinced that, regardless of social scientific explanations, there was always an enigma at the heart of every revolution.

The most substantial manifestation of revolutionary passion in the twentieth century was the Communist passion. What were the key components of this potent 'liqueur' that clouded even the most rational minds?[22] The 'enigma' of the Communist idea was that it was able to penetrate the sharp critical intelligence of the intellectual – and this despite the constant revelations about its tragic violence. According to Furet, the reason for this lay in the paradoxical combination of two forces: the triumph of political will and a submission to the inexorable laws of history. But the Communist passion, and revolutionary passion more generally, also depended upon a secondary passion: the hatred (*haine*) of the bourgeois. This was one of the most arresting claims in *Le Passé d'une illusion* and attracted a good deal of critical attention after the book's publication. Furet's argument was that an 'anti-bourgeois passion' developed in European political thought and culture from the late eighteenth-century onwards, particularly in the writings of Rousseau. This hatred of the bourgeois – that was 'as old as the bourgeois himself' – depended on the contradictions that gave rise to the 'egalitarian passion'.[23] Since bourgeois society was based on a spirit of competition, its values seemed to be directly opposed to the values of egalitarianism. As a result, the egalitarian passion was quickly transmuted into an anti-bourgeois passion. This was not simply an external problem; the bourgeois himself was divided between egalitarianism and the need to compete. Over time, the hatred of the bourgeois became 'self-hatred':

> at the heart of the anti-bourgeois passion lies the omnipresent remorse and guilty conscience of the bourgeois . . . The bourgeois is condemned to live in an open system that balances contradictory and powerful passions. He is caught between the calculated egotism that is required for personal enrichment, and compassion, which binds him to his fellow human beings, or at least, his fellow citizens. He is torn between the desire to be equal, and therefore the same as everyone else, and the obsession with difference that encourages him to pursue the tiniest form of distinction. He is torn between fraternity, the horizon of humanity, and envy, which constitutes his essential psychological motive.[24]

In this passage, Furet comes close to describing a form of social psychology that might explain the strength of the anti-bourgeois passion in the past two centuries. Of the multiple passions that act on the bourgeois, those which appear most forcefully are those of fear and terror, both of which existed in the political discourse of the extreme-right and the extreme-left. Furet maintains that these were specifically French traits: the American Revolution was also defined by an 'egalitarian passion' but it did not give rise to an obsessive hatred of the bourgeois, almost certainly because the American people quickly defined themselves as a 'bourgeois people'. In Europe – and especially in France – things were different. Here, the anti-bourgeois passion had a broad appeal among the 'rejects of modernity' and became a major theme in the greatest literary and philosophical texts of the nineteenth century.[25] For Balzac, the bourgeois was a 'parvenu'; for Stendhal, a 'rogue'; for Marx, a 'philistine'. In every context, the bourgeois appeared as a pitiful wretch:

> Far from being the embodiment of universal values, he has only one concern, his interests, and only one symbol, money. It is because of money that he is most hated; it is money that attracts the prejudices of the

aristocracy, the jealousy of the poor and the disdain of the intellectual. The bourgeois is petty, ugly, miserly, blinkered and parochial, while the artist is great, handsome, generous, brilliant and bohemian.[26]

These psychological attributes had a profound impact on modern European history for it was ultimately the bourgeoisie that produced individuals who 'detested the very air that they breathed'.[27] They turned against themselves by openly supporting regimes that promised the obliteration of their own class. During the nineteenth century, there were still powerful remnants of aristocratic rule, but the entire history of the twentieth century seemed to prove Furet's point about the centrality of bourgeois self-hatred.

It is no coincidence that Furet was making these observations at a time when Europe's revolutionary passion appeared to have run its course. The 'egalitarian passion' was still alive and well but, by the 1990s, Furet's famous claim that the French Revolution had 'come into port' was widely accepted, even among his erstwhile detractors on the left. Furet analysed this steady decline of revolutionary passion through a number of key moments in modern French history.[28] The 1880s were a decade of republican reconciliation in which the violent memories of the French Revolution appeared to have been consigned to history. But the First World War reactivated revolutionary passion and extended it to the right of the political spectrum. Where the counter-revolutionary right before the war had been fearful of revolution and discreet in its criticism of the bourgeois, the inter-war extreme-right was infused with revolutionary passion. The same was true of the left. Before 1914, the French Revolution had become little more than a soft symbol to be manipulated by half-hearted Socialists but the Bolshevik Revolution brought it into the limelight once again. 'The universal charm of October [1917]' represented the apogee of revolutionary passion – its climax and the beginning of its inexorable decline. Ultimately, the fall of the Berlin Wall was simply another nail in the coffin: by then, the revolutionary idea – and the passions that accompanied it – had died.

But was this truly the end of revolutionary passion? This question haunted Furet and contributed to his growing sense of melancholy. Was it possible to eliminate political passion altogether? Could democracy survive without the egalitarian passion from which it was born? Furet clearly believed that it could not. He thought politics was made up of three fundamental elements: interests, ideas and passions. Time and again he stated that the end of the Communist illusion did not mean the end of utopian ideas. Democratic ideals give rise to their own critique. Humans cannot but hope for a different (and better) society, even if the state of the world in the 1990s strongly suggested that the utopian eschatologies of nineteenth-century socialism, anarchism and communism had been definitively put to rest. As Furet himself put it:

We are all a bit depressed by the banality of our political life, but it would still be just too depressing to think that man can only get passionate for destructive and savage utopias.[29]

Even before *Le Passé d'une illusion* was published – a book which ends by discussing these ambiguities of contemporary politics – Furet's melancholy was increasingly apparent in his articles and lectures. It was as if he could not reconcile himself to the passing of a Communist ideal he had shared in his youth and subsequently fervently fought against in his career as a historian. The collapse of Soviet Communism marked the end of an era but it did not – could not – put an end to the new utopias that would emerge out of democracy. Of course, it was not possible to predict exactly what these would be, nor the form they would take. The old ideas that had given shape to the left since the French and Bolshevik Revolutions no longer had any credence but the dream of a post-capitalist society had not yet disappeared.

He addressed some of these themes in Sofia in 1996, in front of an audience that had only recently emerged from the shadow of Communism. His message was a mix of hope and uncertainty. Even though he was 'persuaded that the societies in which we live are inseparable from a vision, a recourse to an alternative society', he remained cautious about the future:

> for me, one of the positive aspects of the fall of Communism is that a long period has finally been dealt a sucker punch; this absurd idea [of Communism] that reigned supreme for so long, has received a killer blow. And, this being the case, it has made the world we live in more complicated and difficult since the future has become a sort of dark tunnel; we go forward, we do something, but the consequences of our actions are uncertain and unplanned. This is why we must all be humble and exercise humility when we manipulate ideas and think we understand something. This is my wisdom in a few words.[30]

He continued to develop this idea in one of his last public lectures in Lisbon in 1997, often using the same words and phrases. The passage is worth citing at length:

> Communism did not imagine any jury other than the jury of history, and it has been condemned by history to be stripped of its body and assets. Its failure is incontrovertible. But must we then conclude that all utopias should be driven from the public sphere of our societies? This would perhaps be too hasty for we would break one of the great sources of civic energy. If the social order cannot be any other way, then why make the effort? The end of the Communist idea has taken from before our eyes the most important alternative model of collective happiness that has ever existed for modern man. At the same time, it has aggravated the political deficit that is one of the foundational traits of modern liberalism . . . History has once again become a tunnel through which human beings move in darkness, without knowing where their actions will lead, uncertain about their destiny, dispossessed of the illusory security of what they do. For the most part without the help of God, the modern democratic

citizen at the end of the [twentieth] century must nevertheless contend with the decomposition of history: this anxiety is one that we will need to ward off. [We] find [ourselves] before a closed future, incapable of defining even notionally the horizon of a society other than the one in which we live, since this horizon has become impossible to imagine. It is enough to see the crisis of political language in today's democracies to understand this. The right and left still exist, but they are shorn of their reference points and, to a very large extent, their substance: the left no longer knows what socialism is, and the right, deprived of its master narrative of anti-Communism, is also searching for what distinguishes it [from the left]. The political scene in France and Italy give good examples of this situation. Will this situation last? For how long will the end of Communism deprive democratic politics of a revolutionary horizon? I leave you with this question.[31]

This is the fate of the European citizen of the late twentieth century, deprived of a future after weaving together the hope for a reconciled humanity for more than two centuries.

Furet was nevertheless adamant that the desire for a 'just society', inherent to democratic passion, 'will survive the collapse of Communism'.[32] This view was rather different to that of Francis Fukuyama, who used Hegel and Kojève to argue that the 'end of history' had arrived.[33] Indeed, Furet was openly sceptical about Fukuyama's thesis. When asked to comment on it, he argued that:

What is coming to an end is 'History' with a capital H, of the kind that was elaborated by nineteenth-century Marxism and twentieth-century Marxism–Leninism: in other words, the idea that capitalism is condemned by its own social organisation to disappear and give way to a new kind of society founded on the abolition of private propery. For a century and a half, the European left, even when it wasn't Communist, believed in the 'scientific' axiom that socialism would succeed Communism, and that the dictatorship of the proletariat would succeed democratic pluralism.[34]

According to Furet, this was the ideological configuration that had come to an 'end', rather than history *tout court*:

Today, I cannot find anywhere parties that are fighting in the name of a post-bourgeois horizon [but] I see no reason to call this the end of history since no one is obliged to be Hegelian or Kojèvian. There will still be a history after this one, even if ours – by which I mean the history which began two or three hundred years ago in Europe – appears to be 'closed'. But the history that is yet to come is unpredictable. We have already made progress by not trying to predict it, and devoting our time to explaining it.[35]

In an interview shortly after Furet's death, Paul Ricœur recalled a number of letters written by Furet in which he expressed concern about the future of revolutionary passion. What kind of outlet would it find now that democracy had become procedural and disenchanted? Along with Ricœur, Furet believed that the exercise of public liberty without passion would suffocate democracy. At the same time, we have seen how he vigorously criticised the new claims to equality that were emerging among women and sexual minorities in the United States of the 1970s and 1980s. He argued that this kind of radical demand for equality – driven by political correctness – was 'both significant and ridiculous', but he nonetheless realised that it represented 'the most important social movement of the last quarter century'.[36] Furet's principal objection was that American feminism had elevated rights to the status of an 'ideology' by inserting them indiscriminately into every aspect of social and private life. We might almost say that rights were on the way to becoming a blind passion at a time when other ideological passions were breaking down.

How to reenergise a lifeless democracy whose atrophy threatens its very existence? How to reintegrate a young generation that has lost faith in the value of political participation? These are some of the questions that preoccupied Furet after the collapse of the great political passions of the modern age. However, he was not willing to restore public debate at any cost. In his words:

> If it is to rekindle old revolutionary passions or historical orthodoxies, French intellectuals have already had their say – have said too much – and even where they have not examined their own conscience, they are on their guard. If it is to offer up to citizens repackaged versions of the national narrative, such as the Jacobin Republic or the founding fathers of the Third Republic, this will come across as little more than a mix that has been hastily cobbled together, without any relation to reality and, moreover, historically inaccurate. The real [solution] is that, deprived of our utopias, and too disconnected from our past to build any models from it, we simply learn to inhabit the world in which we live.[37]

In his interview with Ricœur, Furet maintained that 'the mystery I have perhaps better described than explained is that of the political passions of democratic man'.[38] He was surely right. And yet, for all that the passions appeared with ever greater frequency in his writing, they remained a Pandora's Box of possibilities; they retained an enigmatic and ineffable quality, which Furet did little to dispel. So, for instance, the difference between passions, feelings, ideas, ideologies and emotions was never entirely clear. But this is to miss the point: whatever their lack of conceptual clarity, the passions offered an alternative means to describe the social world using a language that had, for the most part, been cast aside by post-war French social science.

Notes

1 Gilles Lipovetsky, *L'Ere du vide. Essais sur l'individualisme contemporain* (Paris: Gallimard, 1983).

2 See for instance, Perry Anderson, *La Pensée tiède. Un Regard critique sur la culture française, suivi de La pensée réchauffée. Réponse de Pierre Nora* (Paris: Seuil, 2005); François Cusset, *La Décennie. Le Grand cauchemar des années 1980* (Paris: La Découverte, 2006); and Michael Scott Christofferson, *French Intellectuals against the Left: The antitotalitarian moment of the 1970s* (Oxford: Berghahn, 2004).

3 François Furet, Jacques Julliard and Pierre Rosanvallon, *La République du Centre. La Fin de l'exception française* (Paris: Calmann-Lévy, 1988).

4 François Furet, *Penser la Révolution française* (Paris: Gallimard, 1978).

5 Translator's note: It is difficult to render the French terms 'sentiment' and 'passion' consistently in English. I have opted here to translate them as 'feeling' and 'passion' respectively. I have retained this usage throughout, even where the English 'sentiment' might have been a more idiomatic rendering of the French 'sentiment'. In cases where there might be ambiguity about the exact meanings of other words, I have included the French in brackets.

6 Interview with Paul Ricœur, transcribed in spring 1996, Archives François Furet, Centre d'études sociologiques et politiques Raymond Aron (CESPRA), École des hautes études en sciences sociales (EHESS). A shorter version of the interview was published in François Furet, *Inventaires du communisme* (Paris: Éditions de l'EHESS, 2012).

7 François Furet, *Le Passé d'une illusion. Essai sur l'idée communiste au XXe siècle* (Paris: Robert Laffont/Calmann-Lévy, 1995), 72.

8 Furet, *Le Passé d'une illusion*, see Note 7, 18.

9 Furet, *Le Passé d'une illusion*, see Note 7, 18–19.

10 Interview with Paul Ricœur, spring 1996, see Note 6.

11 France 2, *Bouillon de culture*, presented by Bernard Pivot, first broadcast 27 January 1995.

12 *L'Humanité-Dimanche*, 7–14 January 1996.

13 François Furet, 'Dialogue sur la signification et la nature du communisme', *Commentaire* 71 (Spring 1995): 101.

14 Furet, *Le Passé d'une illusion*, see Note 7, 25.

15 Typed retranscription of 'Recherches sur l'époque communiste. A propos du livre de François Furet. *Le Passé d'une illusion*: Essai sur l'idée communiste au XXe siècle', a lecture given in Sofia, 12–13 April 1996. Archives François Furet. The proceedings of the conference were published in *Divinatio* 5 (Spring–Summer 1997).

16 Lecture given in Lisbon, probably 1992, Archives François Furet.

17 France Inter, *Les Guetteurs du siècle*, presented by Jacques Chancel, first broadcast 19 March 1995.

18 *Bulletin de la Société française de philosophie*, 83e année, 3e séance (1989): 321.

19 In a discussion of *Le Passé d'une illusion*, he explained to the TV presenter that the book was the 'livre de ma vie parce que la passion révolutionnaire, c'est le sujet de mon existence'. France 2, *Bouillon de culture*, 27 January 1995, see Note 11. See also, Hamit Bozarslan, Gilles Bataillon and Christophe Jaffrelot, *Passions révolutionnaires. Amérique latine, Moyen Orient, Inde* (Paris: Éditions de l'École des hautes études en sciences sociales, 2011).

20 'La passion révolutionnaire au XXe siècle. Essai sur le déclin du communisme' in François Furet, *La Révolution française* (Paris: Gallimard, 2007), 969–70. Originally published as François Furet, 'La passion révolutionnaire au XXe siècle. Essai sur le déclin du communisme', *Notes de la Fondation Saint-Simon*, 63 (May 1994).

21 Furet, *Le Passé d'une illusion*, see Note 7, 26.

22 France 2, *Bouillon de culture*, 27 January 1995, see Note 11.

23 Furet, *Le Passé d'une illusion*, see Note 7, 24.

24 Furet, *Le Passé d'une illusion*, see Note 7, 29–30.

25 Furet, *Le Passé d'une illusion*, see Note 7, 25.

26 Furet, *Le Passé d'une illusion*, see Note 7, 28.

27 Furet, *Le Passé d'une illusion*, see Note 7, 31.

28 In a television interview, he suggested that there were four key dates in the decline of revolutionary passion: 1799, 1814, 1880 and the 1980s. Antenne 2, *Apostrophes numéro 643*, presented by Bernard Pivot, first broadcast 28 October 1988.

29 France Inter, *Les Guetteurs du siècle*, 19 March 1995, see Note 17.

30 'Recherches sur l'époque communiste. A propos du livre de François Furet. *Le Passé d'une illusion*: essai sur l'idée communiste au XXe siècle', a lecture given in Sofia, 12–13 April 1996.

31 François Furet, 'Démocratie et utopie', a lecture given in Lisbon, 28 May 1997, Archives François Furet.

32 Furet, 'Dialogue sur la signification et la nature du communisme', see Note 13, 102.

33 Francis Fukuyama, *The End of History and the Last Man* (New York, NY: Free Press, 1992).

34 'The tyranny of revolutionary memory' in *Fictions of the Revolution*, corrected proofs of an interview, undated, Archives François Furet.

35 Unidentified and undated document (probably an interview for a foreign newspaper), Archives François Furet.

36 'L'Amérique de Clinton II' in François Furet, *Penser le XXe siècle* (Paris: Robert Laffont, 2007), 477–8. Originally published as François Furet, 'L'Amérique de Clinton II', *Le Débat* 94 (March–April 1997): 3–10.

37 Jean-Marie Colombani and Pierre Lepape, 'Un Entretien avec François Furet', *Le Monde*, 19 May 1992.

38 Interview with Paul Ricœur, Spring 1996.

PART TWO

The Politics of Post-Colonialism in Contemporary France

5

The Cost of Decolonisation:

Compensating the *Pieds-noirs*

Yann Scioldo-Zürcher

Translated from the French by Emile Chabal

Addressing the then finance minister, Jacques Chirac, on 29 June 1970, the Socialist *député* and mayor of Marseille, Gaston Defferre, had this to say about his fellow parliamentarians:

> Your youth – that some may envy – did not allow you to be part of the government or to sit in the National Assembly [at the time of Algerian independence in 1962]. It would therefore be interesting, if it were possible, to do a psychoanalysis of the mindset of some members of the present government who appear today to be deeply uncomfortable because they feel guilty that, many years ago, they promised the French in Algeria that they would never abandon the country; that they would always be wholly separate citizens (*citoyens à part entière*); and above all that, when the time came to leave, they would be fully compensated. According to a reflex well known in psychology – and psychoanalysis – this group [of *députés*] does not seek to repair the damage that was done, but instead resents all those who witnessed their broken promises. This is not how we will achieve national reconciliation . . .[1]

The context for these particularly pungent remarks was the heated discussion surrounding the final reading of a law designed to provide 'a national contribution to compensation for French citizens dispossessed of their assets situated in a territory formerly under the sovereignty, protection or administration of France'.[2] The tone of Defferre's intervention was not unusual for a confrontation between an opposition politician and the ruling party but it does capture the intensity of emotion surrounding the issue.[3] It is also a reminder that there was hardly any agreement in parliament about what exactly compensation was supposed to achieve. For some, it was part of a larger desire to 'atone' for the independence of Algeria. Others argued that it was a continuation of a project to 'pacify' the large number of French citizens displaced by the process of decolonisation, officially known as *rapatriés* (of whom the best known are the so-called *pieds-noirs* from Algeria).[4] Finally, there were those who saw repatriation and reintegration into metropolitan France as straightforward administrative issues.

But, whatever one's opinion, there was little doubt that the issue of compensation was profoundly political. During the presidential election of 1969, *rapatrié* pressure groups and organisations had vocally expressed their grievances to the main candidates. After canvassing vigorously among the *rapatrié* population, the newly-elected Gaullist president Georges Pompidou began to put together a compensation law. One year later, on 3 June 1970, the government presented draft legislation to a sympathetic parliament. But even though the legislation was formally declared 'of immediate importance' by a *déclaration d'urgence* on 12 June the parliamentary debates quickly turned into a fiasco. The text of the legislation was unanimously criticised in the National Assembly, it was rejected by the Senate on its second reading, and it was only because the majority party agreed to support the government that it became law on 30 June to howls of protest from the public gallery.[5] Even before it was officially published in the *Journal Officiel* on 15 July it was already being dismissed as obsolete by those who had voted for it.

It was not the principle of compensation itself that was at issue; nor was this a case of the resurgence of the poisonous politics of the Algerian War – the so-called 'Algerian ghost' – that had strangled earlier parliamentary debates about what to do with the *rapatriés*. Rather, it was the vague definition of 'compensation' that caused problems. The proposed legislation made it seemingly impossible to determine exactly what repatriation – as a policy of reintegration and social regulation – actually meant for the one million or so French citizens who had previously been resident in French territory overseas. The two previous laws relating to repatriation were those of 26 December 1961, which organised the integration of *rapatriés* into metropolitan France, and 6 November 1969, which suspended punitive judicial proceedings (but not the debt) of all those who had taken loans for assets subsequently lost. Both of these were designed to placate the *rapatrié* community and ensure that they were not plunged into immediate poverty.[6] But there were two main reasons why the question of compensation could not be dealt with in the same way. First, compensation was not coterminous with the protection of the most vulnerable since many *rapatriés* did not own property and would not therefore receive any compensation. Second, to compensate the *rapatriés* for the full value of their lost assets was not necessarily conducive to a broader project of national solidarity since any legislation would not apply to citizens who had always resided in metropolitan France. The 1970 law – and the debates surrounding it – captured all of these ambiguities. The justifications for the law oscillated between a desire to regulate and integrate the *rapatriés* through state subsidies, and the need to expiate French colonial guilt through compensation and reparation. The law sought to treat the *rapatriés* as a distinct (and victimised) community but, at the same time, as an integral part of the nation and an important electoral constituency.

These uncertainties, which exploded into full view in the late 1960s, have persisted on all sides of the political spectrum to the present-day. What role does compensation play in the wider management of the *rapatrié* population? To what extent should compensation be seen as part of a broader policy of repatriation and internal migration? The intense debates surrounding the first compensation law give us a privileged insight into the roots of this debate. And they illustrate perfectly the unease of the main political parties in the face of a new post-colonial age, in which France would have to redefine its relationship to its *rapatrié* population and the newly-independent nation-states that emerged out of the violence of French decolonisation.

'Solidarité correlative': The French state's definition of solidarity

The principle of compensation for lost assets had already been enshrined in article four of the repatriation law of 26 December 1961. It was included in this broader piece of legislation – which was passed in the run-up to the negotiations over the independence of Algeria – in an attempt to reassure those French citizens resident in Algeria who were concerned about their future and strongly mobilised in favour of 'Algérie française'. But the provisions for compensation were consistently ignored by the French state, which in any case devoted a substantial proportion of the national budget to supporting the resettlement and integration of the *rapatriés* in metropolitan France after the end of the Algerian War.[7] Nevertheless, some state structures were created to facilitate claims of compensation for lost assets from 1962 onwards. An asset service was set up in August 1962 and a government directive the following month led to the creation of a specific agency within the Ministry of Rapatriés – the Agence de défense des biens et intérêts des rapatriés – which was charged with 'safeguarding or re-establishing the link between an individual and his or her assets left overseas'. This task became much more complicated once the Algerian state began to reclaim French-owned assets from autumn 1962. Over the coming years, it nationalised agricultural land and industrial plant, and declared that all property held by *rapatriés* had become 'vacant'. In this context, the Agency's task was simply to process compensation requests and verify that these corresponded to actual lost assets in Algeria.[8] It did not distribute compensation, nor was it designed to look after the entirety of French assets in Algeria; on the contrary, its aim was to prevent the latter from being lost entirely. To this end, it received applications for compensation from *rapatriés* who had suffered material damage to their property before independence, and managed requests for reimbursement from farmers who had been forced to leave their farms before 1 January 1963. It also handled similar requests for reimbursement of costs for industries and businesses that had been nationalised.[9] Finally, it was the organisation to which *rapatriés* could apply if they wanted to authorise the French state to take all necessary measures to reclaim their assets in Algeria. A 1966 amendment to the original directive would have made the Agency responsible for determining the circumstances in which assets were lost and estimating their value with a view to providing adequate compensation, but this proposal was vetoed on procedural grounds. In short, it served no discernible function, except to show that the French state was concerned with the fate of the *rapatriés*.

Its limited mandate notwithstanding, the Agence de défense des biens did manage to put together some of the first official evaluations of lost assets. In March 1965, a report estimated that 20,000 farms, occupying 2,000,000 hectares and worth approximately 8 billion francs, had been abandoned in Algeria.[10] The value of buildings and livestock was estimated to be 650 million francs. Of the 260,000 dwellings that belonged to French citizens in 1962, 220,000 had been declared 'vacant', 30,000 had been sold at a very low price and 10,000 were still available to their owners. Moreover, there were a large number of commercial properties that had been abandoned or repossessed. Estimates of the value of this lost property again ran to about 8 billion francs. Of course, physical assets were only one part of the equation; there was also the question of the substantial debts incurred by the French in Algeria. *Rapatriés* were still expected to pay off their loans, even if they no longer had any control over the assets they had acquired using these loans. The 1969 law had suspended punitive measures against those who could no longer pay, but the debts of the *rapatriés* remained substantial. At the time, the Crédit foncier d'Algérie et de Tunisie estimated their value at 61,269,000 francs for building projects, 50,050 francs for commercial and industrial operations, and 1,023,000 francs for consumer goods.[11] As had been the case in metropolitan France, the favourable conditions attached to loans and mortgages after the Second World War had encouraged a *pied-noir* middle class to become homeowners in Algeria. This meant that the generation that entered working life in the 1950s had contracted significant debts.[12]

While the *rapatriés* themselves were under pressure from the banks, the French state was keen to put an end to the thorny issue of compensation as quickly as possible. Shortly after Pompidou's victory in 1969, an inter-ministerial commission for the *rapatriés* was set up under the authority of the Prime Minister. It brought together the government and the main *rapatrié* assocations and pressure groups (the largest of which was the Association Nationale des Français d'Afrique du Nord et leurs Amis (ANFANOMA)). But it was impossible to reconcile the demands of the latter with the budgetary constraints of the former. Associations sought complete compensation for lost assets, while the government opposed such a measure because of the prohibitive cost and because it would favour one particular group over another. It was in this divided context that legal definitions of compensation began to take shape in the late 1960s. Ultimately, the debates over the 1970 law did little more than render public the struggles that had previously taken place in the privacy of ministerial offices. And, as discussions stalled, disgruntled *rapatrié* pressure groups increasingly began mobilising their members against elected officials, a pattern that would continue into the 1990s and beyond.

The proposed definition of compensation reflected this lack of consensus. On 11 June 1970, the Prime Minister Jacques Chaban-Delmas put forward in parliament the idea of 'social compensation (*indemnisation à caractère social*)'. This was intended to avoid three possible dangers of compensation legislation: first, that the French state would unrealistically commit itself to reconstituting the complete fortunes of *rapatriés*; second, that compensation would recreate in metropolitan France the economic inequalities between property holders and non-property holders that had existed in Algeria and elsewhere; finally, that the enormous cost of a compensation law would threaten budget stability and affect French international competitiveness.[13] Significantly, the Prime Minister wanted to distinguish any compensation package for the *rapatriés* from the principle of war reparations that had, according to him, hampered France's economic development since 1945.[14] Likewise, he resisted the idea that compensation might be tied to the idea of 'expropriation' since it was not the French state but newly-independent post-colonial states that had repossessed French-owned assets overseas. Instead, any discussion about compensation needed to take into account the significant material assistance that the French state had already given to the *rapatriés* (16 billion francs since 1962), which had made it possible for them to integrate quickly into the French labour market and had protected the most socially vulnerable from the deleterious consequences of forced migration. In the eyes of the government, then, compensation was a form of national solidarity towards those French citizens displaced by decolonisation; its priority was to protect those who were in the most precarious economic circumstances. But any such solidarity had its limits: as the Finance Minister and future president Valéry Giscard d'Estaing repeated on numerous occasions, there would be no question of additional taxes to pay for compensation.[15]

The terms of the proposed law further limited potential access to compensation. Only individuals who had resided for five or more years in former French territories would be entitled to apply for compensation. This restriction was designed to exclude those who had made speculative acquisitions without ever residing in a former French territory; in any case, such individuals did not fit the definition of *rapatrié* since they themselves had not been displaced. Corporate bodies were also excluded from the law; instead, compensation would be distributed to individual members based on their shares or assets.[16] Compensation would be calculated using a decreasing coefficient: small property-owners would be fully compensated, whereas those who owned significant assets would not be able to receive more than 500,000 francs. The budget allocated to the law was 500 million francs per year, for a period of 'ten or so years'.[17] In order to manage claims, the law would also set up an Agence d'indemnisation under the auspices of the Finance Ministry. This would ensure that priority was given to repayments to the elderly and those who needed it the most. The Pompidou government's proposed law thus remained close to the idea of compensation as a form of reparation, rather than an attempt to reimburse the *rapatriés* for the full cost of their lost assets.

There was immediate criticism of this notion of compensation as 'correlative solidarity (*solidarité corrélative*)' by the two major left-wing groups in parliament. The smaller of these was the Communist Party (PCF), which could not play a major role in discussions since it had been reduced to only 34 *députés* after its catastrophic performance in the 1968 legislative elections. Its spokesperson was Paul Cermolacce, a *député* from the Bouches-du-Rhône (in the south of France). He reiterated the party line since the end of the Algerian War in 1962, namely that any compensation law should not be applied to 'those who had profited from colonisation'. These remarks were aimed at large landowners and supporters of the pro-Algérie française terrorist organisation, the Organisation de l'Armée Secrète (OAS). In addition, Cermolacce requested that a special 'national solidarity tax' be imposed for five years on those with large incomes or significant assets. Again, this was a proposal consistent with Communist policy.[18] By contrast, the Socialist bloc tore up the rule book and threw itself vigorously into discussions of the law.[19] In the first instance, they tried to force an immediate vote on whether the bill should be presented to the National Assembly at all (the so-called 'Question préalable'). This would have killed the bill at the first hurdle and made it possible for the Assembly to present its own law instead. When this initiative failed, the Socialist *députés* launched into a lengthy critique of the law on the grounds that the 'sacred' right of property was enshrined in the Declaration of the Rights of Man of 1789 and the French constitution of 1958 (which referred to the preamble of the 1946 constitution).

This principled stand led to a veritable flurry of more or less outlandish alternative propositions. On 29 June 1970, the Socialist bloc (led by Gaston Defferre) put forward the idea of a huge state-backed loan that would be made available to the Agence d'indemnisation for the benefit of those who had 'exported their capital [overseas]' and who intended to 'reinvest it for national benefit'.[20] Another proposal was for a specific *rapatrié* 'investment company' that would be in charge of large public works initiated by French state planners under the 'Sixth Plan'. It would be funded by state loans, investments by 'wealthy *rapatriés*' and the first set of compensation payments. As the debate progressed, the suggestions became more utopian and, in some cases, frankly bizarre. The Socialists suggested that the state build a '*rapatrié* motorway' that would link Marseille and Bordeaux, 'passing through areas with a high concentration of *rapatriés*'. They even argued for the creation of a chain of hotels that would be exclusively run by *rapatriés*![21] These ideas must have appeared decidedly odd to Giscard d'Estaing, whose policies were the embodiment of budgetary rigour, but the Socialists were determined to give compensation an 'economico-patriotic' quality that would make it comparable to other state subsidies, for instance the 3,500 million francs that the French state had provided to the Nord region for the reconversion of its coalfields. Lastly, the Socialists rejected the proposed legislation because it worked against a process of reconciliation between the metropolitan French and overseas French citizens who had supposedly been the victims of 'segregation' since their arrival in France.[22]

There were further criticisms of the law from the centre-right. Despite their proximity to the ruling party, the Républicains indépendants (RI) proposed yet another solution in the form of a national compensation fund, similar to the Caisse autonome d'amortissement that had been used since the French Revolution as a way of spreading the national debt. It would be funded, not by tax revenue, but by investment in rapidly-expanding sectors of the economy. In theory, this would cover the totality of compensation claims for lost assets. The logic behind such a proposal was clearly articulated by Pierre Baudis, RI *député* and mayor of the south-western city of Toulouse, who emphasised that a fund would not unduly raise expectations among the *rapatriés* and would thereby minimise resentment and anger towards the French state. As he put it:

> We understand that the disjunction between the words [of the government] and the corresponding raised hopes, and the actions [of the government], should have provoked a vigorous reaction among already traumatised *rapatriés* – [this reaction will be stronger] if their disillusionment grows.

Baudis, like many others, feared that anger among the *rapatriés* would lead to a repeat of the kind of violence France had experienced during the period of OAS terrorism. His was both a plea for greater compassion and a warning to the French state that it should take the resentment of the *rapatriés* seriously.

Ultimately, the government proved to be inflexible. It accepted only three of the many amendments to the proposed law. First, the Finance Ministry recognised that the compensation coefficient was likely to 'penalise middle-income households' and agreed to raise the percentage of compensation for which *rapatriés* would be eligible.[23] There would be no change in the maximum amount of possible compensation (500,000 francs) but assets valued at the time of loss at 40,000 francs would be compensated at 100 per cent, those valued at 60,000 francs at 86.6 per cent and those valued at 80,000 francs at 77.5 per cent. A wide range of assets were incorporated within the scope of the legislation, including those that had been nationalised, confiscated or destroyed, but there was an unwillingness to compensate for inflation, in large part because some assets had been lost as much as thirty years previously.[24] Second, the government agreed to amend the law so that compensation would be distributed to individuals rather than households. As a result, a couple married under the regime of the separation of property would count for two individuals, thereby doubling the potential compensation they could receive. Third, in a highly symbolic move, the law was amended in order to prevent the state from claiming back more than 50 per cent of the subsidies that had been provided to *rapatrié* households on arrival in metropolitan France. Originally, these had been designed to facilitate professional and economic reintegration.[25]

This tinkering around the edges was supposed to give the National Assembly the illusion that it had influenced the writing of the law. But few *députés* were convinced and there was growing frustration on the benches. Over the course of the debate, two fundamentally opposed positions emerged. On one side, there was the government position, which stressed the importance of strict budgetary controls and was defended particularly by the Finance Ministry and the main state auditing body, the Cour des Comptes. On the other, there was the view widely held by members of parliament that compensation should be less symbolic and more generous. This divide exposed the lack of clarity in the definition of compensation. The Finance Ministry was concerned to keep costs down and, on this occasion, the ministries in charge of social questions were in agreement since they too did not want to be put in charge of large and complex compensation claims. Even though most low- and middle-income households would be fully compensated, the French state would still be reclaiming some of the subsidies it had earlier provided for resettlement.

The question of compensation was not, therefore, constructed with reference to the economic situation of the *rapatriés*. Nor was it related to what Pierre Bourdieu has called the 'sharing of risk' by the state.[26] The French state saw no need to make the entire French population bear the burden of compensating the *rapatriés* as the latter were no longer adjudged to be a danger to a broader project of 'republican solidarity'. Rather, the justification for the 1970 law was of a more obviously philanthropic nature: the government was willing to contribute sometimes quite considerable sums, while remaining well aware that this could not resolve all of the *rapatrié*'s financial difficulties. By contrast, the opponents of the law, all of whom were *députés* in the National Assembly, positioned themselves in relation to their electoral agenda. It is no coincidence that the fiercest criticism of the law came from politicians who represented constituencies in the south of France, where many *rapatriés* lived. Politicians from these regions knew perfectly well that their outlandish suggestions had little chance of becoming law but they understood the importance of being seen to oppose the law. In any case, the Finance Ministry imposed such stringent budgetary limitations that the government always had the upper hand. This explains why the debate increasingly turned towards symbolic questions. Of these, one of the most significant was the issue of the 'debt' that was owed to France by the former colonies. By confiscating the assets of French citizens, the latter were now deemed to have 'dispossessed (*spolié*)' the French state as well.

This symbolic struggle over the post-colonial symbolism of 'debt' was reflected in the wording of the legislation. Article 62 of the 1970 law stated that compensation was 'an advance on the debts owed to French citizens dispossessed [of their assets] by foreign states'. The right, in particular, were adamantly and unanimously in favour of inserting this clause. They repeatedly asserted that the French state should not provide compensation for assets over which it did not have any control, especially if this was on behalf of a foreign state. Of course, all those who maintained this position were well aware that post-colonial nation-states formerly under French control had neither the funds nor the political will to entertain such a proposal. The mere fact of talking about this impossibility nonetheless had an invigorating effect on politicians, the majority of whom had been in office at the end of the Algerian War and remained troubled by its outcome. It is worth noting that no specific foreign state had featured prominently in discussions surrounding the law up to this point, but the debt question put Algeria squarely in the firing line.

Four RI *députés* – Olivier Giscard d'Estaing (the brother of Valéry, the Finance Minister), Pierre Baudis, Guy Begué and Jean Poudevigne – argued that a specific clause should be inserted into the law to guarantee that the French state would open negotiations with the Algerian state to reclaim the compensation.[27] Jean Royer, a non-aligned conservative *député*, went one step further by playing the national unity card. He exhorted the government to

> open direct negotiations with [the President of Algeria] Monsieur Bourmédienne [sic.] and the state over which he presides in order to obtain additional resources that can be used to make up for the current lacunae in compensation provision. In so doing, [the government] will be supported by the entire nation, whatever the parties that divide it, and whatever the direction of public opinion.[28]

As discussions become more heated, the rhetoric became more confrontational. Jean Bonhomme, a non-aligned centre-right *député* elected from the southern Tarn-et-Garonne constituency, firmly rejected a negotiated settlement. The only solution to this problem was a legal ruling:

It cannot be over-emphasised that the *rapatriés* have been dispossessed (*sont des spoliés*) and that they are victims of a lost war, the consequences of which must be borne by the [entire] nation. This is not about individual debts but debts owed to a whole nation; we cannot simply tell each *rapatrié* to get a good lawyer and seek redress from the Algerian state. I want it to be explicitly indicated [in this law] that the French state takes on individual debts and becomes the only creditor for those states that have dispossessed French citizens (*états spoliateurs*).[29]

The fact that such a thing would have been legally impossible was not the point; the logic was one of revenge rather than rationality. So pervasive was this feeling that Pierre-Charles Krieg, a right-wing *député* from the ruling party, shocked his fellow party members by demanding that the French state 'suspend all transfers of funds to Algeria'.[30] As for the left, it mostly avoided the issue, maintaining only that it was illusory, if not hypocritical, for the French state to cast compensation as an advance on debts due by post-colonial nation-states.[31]

Faced with the dissatisfaction of the ruling right-wing majority, Valéry Giscard d'Estaing sought to reassure parliamentarians that the government was in complete agreement on the principle of post-colonial debt. He did not, however, accept any of the amendments proposed by his colleagues. He argued that it was not worth exacerbating the 'tensions' between France and Algeria and endangering cooperation policies that had been put in place.[32] More importantly, the French state had neither the military nor the diplomatic means with which to impose forced debt repayments from its former colonies as it had done after the independence of Haiti 166 years earlier.[33] Quite apart from a lack of funds, the governments of all the former French colonies maintained that imperial violence, economic expropriation and legal discrimination were the source of French wealth. There was no question, then, of 'compensating' the *rapatriés* for their 'lost' assets. Finally, Giscard d'Estaing reassured his colleagues that, even after the passing of the law, the French state would continue to play its role as the defender of private interests in any subsequent negotiations. But this last point was a risky one to make: the Finance Minister was implicitly recognising that the proposed compensation package was inadequate and, crucially, that it was only a temporary solution. By positioning himself firmly within current budgetary constraints and acknowledging that the present legislation offered only partial compensation to the *rapatriés*, he was also ensuring that the issue of compensation would return to haunt future legislatures.

Compensation or integration?

The aim of the 1970 law was that it should be both unprecedented and exceptional. And yet, compared to other compensation and insurance laws for French citizens that had been passed since the Second World War, it appeared decidedly incomplete.[34] Moreover, for all its supposed novelty, the debates surrounding the law were, in the words of the historian Marie-Claude Smouts, 'strongly marked by the legacy of colonialism on the past and present relations between ex-colony and metropolitan France'.[35] On the one hand, the French state cast the *rapatriés* as victims and even, in some cases, as economically 'precarious' citizens. On the other, the policies towards them were reduced to a form of condescending 'solidarity' that was deemed a threat to budgetary stability, despite the fact that the principle of compensation had been set in stone by the very same government in 1961.

It is clear that, political rhetoric notwithstanding, the 'social condition' of the *rapatriés* was not really at the heart of the debate. The actual realities of poverty were never discussed, except through the emblematic figure of the 'elderly' *rapatrié*. At no point during the parliamentary debates did anyone refer to a report or study in order to support their arguments. The *députés* and the government were happy simply to rehash an 'empathetic' and victimising discourse that betrayed their unease towards an exiled population to whom they had promised everything. Two omissions are particularly striking in this regard. First, there was no mention of the *harkis* or any other former colonial soldiers who counted as some of the most economically marginalised *rapatrié* populations in France.[36] Second, there was no mention of the significant proportion of non-property owners, even though the law was supposed to respond to the needs of all *rapatriés*. The 'social question' was little more than a distraction from the main thrust of the law, which was to protect and guarantee property rights.

It is also noteworthy that discussion of compensation made no reference to historical precedent. No attempt was made to mobilise the history of property in the French empire or the history of wars of independence and their consequences. Indeed, parliamentarians did not even ask why Algeria had lost its French population. No additional historical, factual or analytical work was done in advance of the elaboration of the 1970 law that might shed light on the circumstances in which French citizens had lost or been stripped of their assets. Rather, compensation was viewed solely as the responsibility of newly-independent post-colonial states, over which France asserted an (imagined) right through claims for lost assets so modest that they scarcely reflected the value of those assets.

This silencing of history extended to government policy as well. At no point in the debate was there a discussion of the various *rapatrié* reintegration policies pursued by successive governments since 1962 and how these might relate to the proposed compensation package. This was proof that the diversity of *rapatrié* experiences had been reduced in the minds of parliamentarians to their potentially threatening electoral weight, which simultaneously reinforced the view that any compensation legislation was the result of clientelism. Worse still, by creating (and maintaining) official structures that incorporated *rapatrié* pressure groups and associations like the ANFANOMA, the French state legitimised a highly-partisan interpretation of state policy. In subsequent years, these pressure groups and associations would succeed in minimising the various forms of state intervention in favour of the *rapatriés* and fostering a climate of seething resentment among activists. Since the 1970 law did not set out a clear definition of compensation, the French state made itself vulnerable to the claim, repeated *ad nauseum* by *rapatrié* groups, that it had 'not done enough'. And, inevitably, the result was that these same groups would be consulted whenever there was talk of legislation.

Taking into account these various silences and elisions, it is easier to see how the question of compensation was, in fact, rather different to the social policies put in place to facilitate the reintegration of the *rapatriés* in the mid- to late-1960s. For the French state, the 'return' of Algerian *pieds-noirs* in 1962 required that the welfare state deploy its resources in order to safeguard this economically-fragile migrant population. This was especially evident with respect to the reintegration of state employees into the metropolitan civil service and access to social housing. These policies were characterised by a constant search for stability since protecting the *rapatriés* also meant protecting the French state from the OAS, which found its most enthusiastic support among angry *rapatriés*.[37] State assistance was thus a form of social and political regulation. This created a highly unusual context where economic and budgetary calculations played a key role but did not necessarily undermine other, more important, social and political priorities. The financial burden of integrating over one million *rapatriés* was justified in the name of a universal 'national solidarity' that was seen to be at the heart of the constitution of the Fifth Republic.[38]

The issue of compensation for lost assets, however, did not belong within the same conceptual framework. For a start, it dealt only with those who had owned property and those who had encountered difficulties in reintegrating themselves into metropolitan France. The government was therefore caught in a double bind: the principle of compensation was formally recognised in the law of 26 December 1961, which meant that it had to be implemented. Compensation had an obvious (albeit limited) social function and the French state also hoped that it would silence once and for all *rapatrié* pressure groups that had clamoured for redress. But an analysis of the parliamentary debates surrounding the 1970 law demonstrates unambiguously that the way in which compensation was defined was not a continuation of earlier social policies. It did not apply equally to all *rapatriés* and it could not be justified as a form of protection against the threat of a now virtually non-existent OAS. Instead, it was perceived to be a political, moral and symbolic obligation. The result was that the government adopted a condescending attitude towards the *rapatriés*: it had heard their pleas, and would put forward legislation, but they could only ever expect partial compensation. Meanwhile, the *députés* in the National Assembly indulged in polemical rhetoric that cast the state as an obstinate entity unwilling to 'repair' an obvious injustice (although this did not prevent them from voting for the legislation that they had spent so much time criticising).

As for the *rapatriés* themselves, they viewed compensation as an entitlement. They were unconcerned with budgetary constraints. The 1961 law that had officially designated them *rapatriés* had made provisions for compensation. It was not a question of whether they would be entitled to such compensation, but how fast it would be paid. Here, too, there was confusion. For the overwhelming majority of *rapatrié* – above all, the *pieds-noirs* from Algeria – compensation meant the complete reimbursement of their assets. This was supported by the widely-held view that the responsibility for the 'loss of Algérie française' lay solely with the metropolitan French, who had voted for the self-determination of Algeria in the referendum of 8 January 1961, and the Evian Accords that ended the war in the referendum of 8 April 1962 (those resident in Algeria could not vote in the latter). In addition, there was a strong sense among *pieds-noirs* that the loss of property was the fault of the Debré government and especially the President, Charles de Gaulle, who was seen as the 'grave-digger of Algeria'. It was only natural, therefore, that a Gaullist government under Pompidou and the entire French population should 'take responsibility' for their choice.

Over and above these strictly political concerns, the question of compensation was also intimately related to the autonomy of *rapatrié* families. It symbolised the restoration of family ties and the reinstatement of social positions inherited from previous generations, most of which had been washed away in the chaos of decolonisation and forced migration. Last but not least, there was real financial need. Ever since it was passed, the very partial repayments provided for by the 1970 law have been a source of bitter disappointment. Still today, elderly *pieds-noirs* remember the compensation package as a betrayal: 'it's a scandal'; 'they didn't give a damn about us; we lost everything and the government couldn't have cared less'; 'charity, that's what they offered us: charity!'[39] The payments offered appeared all the more derisory because the damaging psychological effects of flight, imposed exile and the exoticisation of an Algerian 'homeland' gave lost property a powerful emotional quality that was difficult to quantify. Resentment was only compounded by 'scandalous' inefficiency in handling applications for compensation: processing times were long and *rapatriés* who had waited for years became increasingly impatient. In the end, the 1970 law, which was supposed to resolve an awkward administrative problem, did exactly the opposite.

Conclusion: An uncertain compensation

On 11 June 1970, the Prime Minister Jacques Chaban-Delmas opened the debates on the compensation law by appealing for calm:

> The word 'compensation' and its emotional content seem to carry an almost magical quality to interested parties, which has sometimes led to unattainable expectations. The passing of time and the distancing in

space has led [some people] to idealise what they lost or forget what they have already received. But let me say this as clearly as possible: yes, it is true that we will never be able to do everything, abolish everything, erase everything. Who will ever pay the price of the regret, the pain, even the tears? I say this with the truthfulness and the honesty of human nature: we are doing what we can so that our fellow *rapatriés* can claim what is rightly their place in the national collective (*collectivité nationale*) and in our hearts . . .[40]

Nineteen days later, at the time of the final vote on the law, Jacques Limouzy, the secretary of state in charge of relations with parliament, urged parliamentarians to vote for the law by assuring them that 'you have not been asked whether, in voting for this text, you are turning a page and definitively resolving [the issue]'.[41] In the space of a few days, the spirit of the law had changed significantly. The almost unanimous hostility meant that it was now being defended as little more than a stopgap measure.

The ambiguities of the 1970 law ensured that debates over compensation would be a fixture in subsequent parliamentary sessions, especially given that the law empowered *rapatrié* associations who vigorously championed their cause. Not surprisingly, further compensation laws were passed in 1975 and 1987. This chain of events suggests that we would be wrong to see the 1970 law as simply another part of a project of national integration for 'returning' migrants. Rather, it should be seen as a purely domestic policy that expressed the desire of the French state to 'reimburse' its overseas citizens for lost assets, while simultaneously recognising the electoral power of the *rapatrié* community. Despite claims to the contrary, it had almost nothing to do with social policies that promoted integration. It was only thirty years later, in the 1990s, that compensation laws began to incorporate a social element, designed to assist the most vulnerable *rapatriés*. However, this could only take place once compensation was tied, not to property and assets, but to the social inequalities that were born out of displacement, migration and exile.

Notes

1 *Journal Officiel* (henceforth *JO*), Débats de l'Assemblée nationale, 1ère séance du 29 juin 1970, 3238.

2 The original title of the law in French was 'Loi relative à une contribution nationale à l'indemnisation des Français dépossédés de bien situés dans un territoire antérieurement placé sous la souveraineté, le protectorat ou la tutelle de la France'.

3 It is ironic that, eight years earlier, Defferre himself had told the thousands of *rapatriés d'Algérie* arriving in Marseille that they 'should find a place to settle [somewhere other than in Marseille]' in the pages of the local newspaper

L'Intransigeant. See Valérie Esclangon-Morin, *Les Rapatriés d'Afrique du Nord de 1956 à nos jours* (Paris: L'Harmattan, 2007), 160.

4 The term *rapatrié* is used to describe all French citizens formerly residing in a French colony who were displaced by decolonisation. The specific term *pied-noir* is widely used to describe those *rapatriés* of European origin who resided in Algeria up to (and shortly after) independence in 1962. Unlike the term *rapatriés*, however, *pied-noir* has no official legal definition.

5 The parliamentary session on 29 June was interrupted because of riotous behaviour in the public gallery; discussions continued the following day in a calmer environment.

6 On this, see Yann Scioldo-Zürcher, 'La Discrète mais réelle anticipation du rapatriement des Français d'Algérie: La Construction de la loi du 26 décembre 1961', in Abderrahmane Bouchène et al., eds., *Histoire de l'Algérie à la période coloniale 1830–1962* (Paris/Alger: La Découverte/Barzakh, 2012), 564–9.

7 More detailed discussion of this question can be found in Yann Scioldo-Zürcher, *Devenir métropolitain, politique d'accueil et d'intégration des rapatriés d'Algérie en métropole, 1954–2005* (Paris: Éditions de l'EHESS, 2010).

8 Archives du ministère des Affaires étrangères (henceforth AMAE), secrétariat d'État chargé des Affaires algériennes, box 40.

9 AMAE, secrétariat d'État chargé des Affaires algériennes, box 40.

10 AMAE, secrétariat d'État chargé des Affaires algériennes, box 41.

11 AMAE, secrétariat d'État chargé des Affaires algériennes, box 201.

12 Sylvie Effosse, *L'Invention du logement aidé en France, l'immobilier au temps des trente glorieuses* (Paris: Éditions du Comité pour l'histoire économique et financière de la France, 2003).

13 *JO*, Débats de l'Assemblée nationale, 1ère séance du 11 juin 1970, 2488.

14 It is worth noting, of course, that at the time the Algerian War was not officially considered to be a 'war' at all. No member of parliament appears to have made this point.

15 *JO*, Débats de l'Assemblée nationale, 1ère séance du 11 juin 1970, 2491.

16 As the Prime Minister made clear, the only individuals who could claim 'corporate' compensation were those who were in management roles in companies such as family businesses, which were considered to be similar to other non-financial corporate bodies such as associations. See *JO*, Débats de l'Assemblée nationale, 1ère séance du 11 juin 1970, 2488.

17 We should remember that the minimum wage (SMIC) in metropolitan France in 1970 was 600 francs per month.

18 *JO*, Débats de l'Assemblée nationale, 1ère séance du 11 juin 1970, 2492.

19 At this time, the socialist bloc called itself the Fédération de la gauche démocrate et socialiste. The present-day Parti Socialiste had just been founded in 1969.

20 *JO*, Débats de l'Assemblée nationale, 1ère séance du 29 juin 1970, 3237.

21 *JO*, Débats de l'Assemblée nationale, 1ère séance du 29 juin 1970, 3240. This idea was mostly of rhetorical value – it remained undeveloped.

22 *JO*, Débats de l'Assemblée nationale, 1ère séance du 29 juin 1970, 3238.

23 *JO*, Débats de l'Assemblée nationale, 1ère séance du 29 juin 1970, 2566.

24 See Article 12 of the 1970 law. On the debates, see *JO*, Débats de l'Assemblée nationale, 1ère séance du 12 juin 1970, 2566. Without ever explicitly naming them, the reference here is clearly to the few *rapatriés* from Lebanon and Syria.

25 Scioldo-Zürcher, *Devenir métropolitain*, see Note 7, 249–50.

26 See Pierre Bourdieu, *Sur l'État, cours au collège de France, 1989–1992* (Paris: Le Seuil, 2012).

27 All four *députés* were elected from southern constitutencies: Olivier Giscard d'Estaing from the Alpes-Maritimes, Baudis from the Haute-Garonne; Begué from the Lot-et-Garonne and Poudevigne from the Gard. *JO*, Débats de l'Assemblée nationale, 3ème séance du 12 juin 1970, 2576.

28 *JO*, Débats de l'Assemblée nationale, 1ère séance du 11 juin 1970, 2499.

29 *JO*, Débats de l'Assemblée nationale, 3ème séance du 12 juin 1970, 2577.

30 *JO*, Débats de l'Assemblée nationale, 3ème séance du 12 juin 1970, 2577.

31 *JO*, Débats de l'Assemblée nationale, 3ème séance du 12 juin 1970, 2576.

32 It is interesting that the Ministry of External Affairs remained silent on this point.

33 On these issues, see Jean-François Mouhot, *Les Réfugiés acadiens en France (1758–1785): L'Impossible ré-intégration?* (Rennes: Presses Universitaires de Rennes, 2012).

34 Jean-Marie Fecteau and Janice Harvey, *La Régulation sociale, entre l'acteur et l'institution, pour une problématique historique de l'interaction* (Sainte-Foy: Presses de l'Université du Québec, 2005).

35 Marie-Claude Smouts, 'Les études postcoloniales en France: Emergence et résistances', in Achille Mbembe et al., eds., *Ruptures postcoloniales. Les Nouveaux visages de la société française* (Paris: La Découverte, 2010), 310.

36 I use the term 'harki' in its generic sense to mean 'former Muslim French (*ancien français musulman*)', according to colonial terminology. For more on this, see the recent special issue of *Les Temps Modernes*, edited by Fatima Besnaci-Lancou ('Harkis. 1962–2012. Les Mythes et les faits', *Les Temps Modernes* 666 (November–December 2011)).

37 Frédéric Gros, *Le Principe de sécurité* (Paris: Gallimard, 2012).

38 Alain Supiot, *Grandeur et misère de l'État social* (Paris: Fayard, 2013).

39 These opinions were frequently expressed in the twenty interviews I conducted among *pieds-noirs* on the subject of compensation between 2011 and 2013.

40 *JO*, Débats de l'Assemblée nationale, 1ère séance du 11 juin 1970, 2489.

41 *JO*, Débats de l'Assemblée nationale, 1ère séance du 30 juin 1970, 3331.

6

From Militancy to History:

Sans Frontière and Immigrant Memory at the Dawn of the 1980s

Daniel A. Gordon

A major sign of France's 'age of uncertainty' was the transition it experienced from the anti-capitalism of *les années 68* (the 68 years) to the identity politics of the 1980s. In this chapter, we will be exploring an important, but until recently relatively overlooked, sign of this transition. The relationship between immigration and French politics has been a very familiar one in post-1980s France, albeit one too often considered both negatively (immigration as a problem) and passively (immigrants as an object of debate by a supposedly homogeneous host society). Yet for a fuller understanding, we need to appreciate how immigrants' own activism was already interacting with wider currents in both French and international politics even before the 1980s began. For the well-known aid agency Medécins sans frontières was not the only organisation in post-68 France to use the 'without borders' motif so evocative of *soixante-huitard* internationalism.[1] In 1979, a group of North African and former Maoist militants based in the well known immigrant neighbourhood of Barbès in northern Paris founded *Sans Frontière*, which they advertised as France's first widely-circulated newspaper by immigrants for immigrants.

Some examples give an indication of the magazine's importance, now that it can be seen in a more *longue durée* perspective. In 2007, the founders of *Sans Frontière* were partly responsible for the creation of the Cité Nationale de Histoire de l'Immigration, France's first national immigration museum. And in 2011, as a result of the 'Arab Spring', one of the magazine's founders, Driss El Yazami, was put in charge of Morocco's first official human rights watchdog, the Conseil National des Droits de l'Homme.[2] Yet these outcomes resulted from no smooth historical inevitability. Rather, they represented a historic turn-around that was the culmination of difficult decades of cultural and political activism. Between 1972 and 1976, the future founders of *Sans Frontière* were the leading lights in a militant leftist organisation known as the Mouvement des Travailleurs Arabes (MTA). This group was led by post-May 1968 immigrant radicals such as the Tunisian activists Faouzia and Saïd Bouziri, and had sought to organise 'first generation' North African migrant workers in France.[3] The organisation was frequently the target of intertwined state repression in France (such as the attempted deportation of the Bouziris in 1972), and in the countries of origin of its militants. In 1975, for example, as a result of Driss El Yazami's activist role in support of a hunger strike by Moroccan *sans-papiers* in Montpellier, where a Protestant church in which they had been sheltering was stormed by CRS riot police, Interior Minister Michel Poniatowski ordered that El Yazami be deported back to Morocco. Back in the Moroccan capital of Rabat, El Yazami was tied up, kept blindfolded and sentenced to life imprisonment.[4] With a previous wave of militancy apparently facing short-term defeat, the cadres of the MTA had decided to wind up their political organisation for good in 1976. Yet three years later, after El Yazami had escaped to France on a sailing boat, they decided to regroup to launch a new venture, the magazine *Sans Frontière*.

Sans Frontière perfectly illustrated the situation of transition between the left-wing politics of the post-68 period and the 1980s. It was one example – others included an annual street carnival in the La Goutte d'Or neighbourhood in Paris – of the way that former cadres of leftist groups like the MTA gravitated into less overtly 'revolutionary' forms of activism at the end of the 1970s. Although superficially *Sans Frontière* bore some resemblance to a counter-culture publication of the early 1970s like *Tout!*, the style and content had clearly moved on from the *gauchiste* agitational newsletters of that era. It had an obviously modern feel, it was unencumbered by tortuous political jargon, and included (in the manner of London's *Time Out*) gig listings and a lonely hearts column alongside a trendy logo and lots of photographs. In short, it was the immigrant equivalent of *Libération*, the daily newspaper that had emerged from the post-68 left in 1973. Indeed, after reading the first issue of *Sans Frontière*, one trade unionist in the Confédération générale du travail wrote in to complain that '*Sans Frontière* is too much like *Libé*'. During the 'bulldozer affair' of 1980 – when the Communist local authority of Vitry-sur-Seine, a suburb of Paris, was accused of playing the race card to pander to anti-immigrant prejudice – *Sans Frontière*'s unsurprisingly robust response was characterised by some critics as 'anti-communism in the style of *Libé*'.[5] *Sans Frontière* was correspondingly less critical of the Socialist Party than the Communist Party. In June 1981, just after François Mitterrand's election as President, and shortly before the Socialist landslide victory in the parliamentary elections that followed, the magazine welcomed on a visit to its office the future Socialist Prime Minister Lionel Jospin. He was standing for election against a particularly anti-immigrant right-wing incumbent in the 18th arrondissement of Paris, where *Sans Frontière* was based.[6] Fundamentally, though, the magazine's approach was non-sectarian, and it opened its columns to a variety of political viewpoints. This was not always a blessing. On various occasions, it was denounced by ultra-leftists, who accused the editorial team of working for an impressively contradictory group of political masters, including the KGB, the CIA, the Gulf Emirates, Israel and the PLO.[7]

Of course, *Sans Frontière* was strongly marked by its founders' political backgrounds in post-68 *gauchisme*. In 1979, for example, a debate took place about whether to allow advertising in the paper.[8] This was a classic sign of a magazine run by 'recovering' *soixante-huitards* in the process of becoming professional journalists.[9] In the same year, the offbeat activist Pierre Goldman, who had become something of an icon for the *soixante-huitard* generation after being wrongly convicted of armed robbery, was assassinated.[10] He received fulsome tributes in *Sans Frontière* as a man of integrity who was on the side of immigrants against people with power. The fact that Goldman repeatedly emphasised his feeling of not belonging to French society contributed to this sympathy (Goldman was the son of Holocaust survivors and had skin sufficiently dark for a policeman to have confused him in an identity parade with a man from Guadeloupe). As the editors put it: 'It is perhaps that he was one of us because [he was] *sans frontière*.'[11] But this was not an uncontroversial position to take: a reader from Nanterre called Aziz wrote in to complain that *Sans Frontière*'s silence on the 'anti-fascist consensus between Zionists and yesterday's anti-Zionists' around Goldman's death gave the impression of 'a continued ideological dependence of certain Arab militants on French intellectuals of the Maoist era'.[12] In other words, *Sans Frontière*'s association with Goldman – who could scarcely be described as any kind of Zionist, but was certainly interested in exploring his Jewish identity – was unacceptable to some militants on Arab nationalist grounds.

Sans Frontière's task was further complicated by the fact that it had to serve two audiences with conflicting demands. The first was an older audience drawn from the first generation of immigrants to France.[13] This was reflected in the fact that, from October 1981, the publication carried the subtitle *Hebdomadaire de l'immigration et du tiers monde*. True to its name, it featured a good deal of information about events in North Africa, West Africa and the Caribbean, and the magazine could boast among its writers reputed intellectuals like the Algerian sociologist Abdelmalek Sayad, who had collaborated with Pierre Bourdieu.[14] At various points, it also included interviews with prominent cultural and political figures from the global South, and served as a forum for debates on such sensitive issues as Islam and sexuality,[15] the relationship of Jews to Arab societies,[16] the end of the 'myth of return' for immigrant workers and the hostility of Algerian society to returned migrants,[17] the situation of women in North Africa,[18] the first signs of an Islamist movement in Algeria,[19] and the critical revisionist history of the Algerian Front de Libération National (FLN) by the historian and former FLN militant Mohamed Harbi.[20] *Sans Frontière* could thus hardly be said to have conformed to the caricatured portrait of *tiersmondisme* as a vehicle for white guilt and uncritical support for Third World Stalinist regimes.

At the same time, *Sans Frontière* also sought to address a French-born second-generation audience that differed in crucial respects from the first generation militants who founded the magazine. First, they were untied spatially to the locations where previous immigrant militancy had taken place. They did not live in the classic inner Paris immigrant areas like Barbès and Belleville, but in the high-rise *banlieues* – where groups like the MTA had always been weaker.[21] Second, because they had been born or grew up in France and educated in the French school system, they unproblematically saw their future as French. Third, they differed markedly in cultural outlook: whereas the MTA's founders had been influenced by a mixture of their cultures of origin and European high culture, the new generation's cultural landscape was shaped by an Anglo-American youth culture shared with their peers. *Sans Frontière* did, to some extent, succeed in forging inter-generational links, but it was a tall order. For the situation of the *travailleur immigré*, which had underpinned the classic leftist view of immigrants as (predominantly male) workers exploited by capitalism, was melting away before them. With mass unemployment, the *travailleur immigré* was often no longer a *travailleur*; with the second generation he was no longer an *immigré*; and with family reunification 'he' was often 'she'.

Nevertheless, *Sans Frontière* sought to bridge these divides by engaging with the struggles of the new generation. It reported extensively on the case of Samid and Mogniss Abdallah, two brothers from Nanterre who had got into trouble for creating a political organisation of mixed groups of young people made up of French and non-French, and unemployed and students. In 1979, the government attempted to deport the Abdallahs, before being forced to back down after a large mobilisation in their favour.[22] Moreover, the magazine often carried interviews with second-generation youths. They talked frankly about their lives in a way that went beyond the simplistic 'miserabilist' dialectic of oppressive France and oppressed immigrants, which had been the stock-in trade of earlier *gauchiste* papers.[23] Indeed the *Sans Frontière* experience had a lasting impact on the oldest second-generation activists, born in the 1950s, many of whom wrote for the magazine in the 1980s. Farid Aïchoune was one such figure. He had been present as a child during the fateful demonstrations of 17 October 1961, he had participated himself in May 1968, he had been threatened with expulsion for Maoist activism, and he was a founder member of the MTA. But his decision to join

Sans Frontière as a contributor launched his career as a journalist, and he subsequently moved on to *Le Nouvel Observateur*, where he still works.[24]

These inter-generational links are important because, while France generally remembers the 1983 'Marche des Beurs' as the beginning of the political expression of 'second generation' children of North African immigrants (*beurs*), this is somewhat misleading. The prehistory of the *beurs* in fact goes back some years before the term was coined. As early as 1977, sociologists were identifying the existence of a 'second generation' with its own problems quite distinct from those of immigrants proper.[25] The generation of *soixante-huitard* North African intellectuals represented on the editorial team of *Sans Frontière*, however, were often quite ambivalent about the new generation, whose propensity to commit acts of violence against schools and public transport facilities they found rather worrying. The magazine talked of 'a wild and confused revolt against their social imprisonment'.[26] The *Sans Frontière* team were often uneasy with the *banlieue* movements, seeing them as lacking a historical awareness of previous struggles.[27] Some critics, though, detected a tendency on the part of *Sans Frontière* to sweep under the carpet some of the more negative aspects of the behaviour of young people out of embarrassment. In 1981, a right-wing journalist accused the magazine's editors of being 'old lefties, professional anti-racists', only interested in a portrayal of poor oppressed Arabs,[28] while the writer Leïla Sebbar, herself a contributor to the magazine, felt that *Sans Frontière* had changed from its earlier mission to present marginal cultures as they are, both good and bad, and was now disguising the truth 'so as "not to disappoint Billancourt"'.[29] In this instance, Sebbar was repeating a phrase from the 1950s (widely, though wrongly, attributed to Jean-Paul Sartre), when it has often been argued that left-wing intellectuals showed more deference towards the Communist beliefs of the skilled French workers of the Renault car factory at Boulogne-Billancourt, in the suburbs of Paris, than to inconvenient truths about Stalinist repression in Eastern Europe out of fear that Communist workers would lose faith if Communist ideology were disturbed by revealing such truths to them.[30] Sebbar's implication was, therefore, that the *Sans Frontière* editors were censoring reality. Out of a similar kind of ideological deference, they were presenting a one-sided view of immigrant minorities in order to preserve the fiction that migrants are only ever victims of an oppressive system.

Criticism notwithstanding, one of *Sans Frontière*'s most important roles was as a transmitter of immigrant heritage and memory. It is significant that it did not limit itself to functioning as a bulletin board for questions of current urgency in a way that activist newspapers often do. It also served as a kind of *lieu de mémoire* for earlier struggles.[31] Its issue for 1 January 1980 was a retrospective on '1970–80: Les Années Immigrés', wistfully recalling the glory days of the early 1970s when big-name intellectuals like Jean-Paul Sartre and Michel Foucault had marched alongside immigrants.[32] The memory theme continued throughout 1980 and into 1981 in the rubric *Mémoire Immigré* (or sometimes *Mémoire du Peuple*) that documented the lives of ordinary workers. These narratives, little known today, are an invaluable resource for historians, particularly now that Génériques, the immigration history NGO founded by the former editors of *Sans Frontière*, has digitised the complete collection of *Sans Frontière* on its website Odysséo.[33]

To take but one example, the story of the Algerian immigrant worker Saïd Meredef shows that *Sans Frontière* took an interest in how the histories of anti-colonial struggles in the sending countries tied together with those of the social history of working people and the political history of post-1968 radicalism. During the Algerian war of independence, Meredef had been a *maquisard* in the FLN's armed wing, the Armée de Libération Nationale, yet after Algerian independence came to work in France for ten years (an irony typical of the intertwined histories of France and its former colonies). Meredef worked between 1964 and 1974 as a miner in the North of France, where he came across French and North African Maoist activists, who were trying to turn the working class of the region into revolutionaries. Meredef's account of his experiences provides an original primary source for writing a history from below of relations between immigrant workers and Maoism. In particular, three themes to which I did not devote sufficient attention in my own book emerge from his narrative.[34] First, gender: Meredef underlines just how much of the work in Maoist activism was done by women, whereas the credit was claimed by male leaders. He also makes reference to complications created by sexual relationships between French activists and immigrant workers. Secondly, Meredef deals with the difficulties involved in trying to unite Moroccans with Algerians: nationalist consciousness cut across the revolutionaries' aspiration of bringing the most exploited elements of the working class together in common struggle. Finally, Meredef suggests that the MTA neglected the North of France: accounts of the group, including my own, have tended to be centred on the Paris and Marseille regions precisely because the MTA's own activities were concentrated there, but the greater weaknesses experienced elsewhere also require attention from historians.[35]

In their discussions of past events, the *Sans Frontière* team inevitably placed a certain emphasis on the recent past in which they had participated themselves. Key formative events of post-1968 immigrant militancy received much coverage: the Mohammed Diab affair of 1972 about an Algerian lorry driver who died in custody at Versailles police station;[36] the first *sans-papiers* hunger strikes of 1972–3;[37] and the 'general strike' against racism of September 1973, when the MTA organised a series of widely followed one-day strikes by North African workers and shopkeepers against a major wave of racist violence.[38] But the editors emphasised that this was

> not in order to reminisce as out of date veterans. After all we are too young for that, aren't we? [They were in 1980 only in their early thirties.] For us it is about opening up, through various testimonies, a debate about everything that immigration has been able to produce in its history.[39]

As a result, other articles investigated the history of immigration from long before the MTA generation, such as one entitled 'Between Messali Hadj and Léon Blum', that started before the First World War, grabbing the reader's attention by inserting the life story of a more obscure individual into a better known context of two big-name leaders from Algerian and French inter-war politics respectively.[40]

The *Mémoire Immigré* section provides further evidence of *Sans Frontière*'s more ecumenical approach to memory. For instance, women were much better represented here than had been the case in most *gauchiste* publications of the early 1970s. Most of the interviews were done by Leïla Sebbar. The individual profiles included Aline N'Goala's journey from the slums of Martinique to Trotskyism and Antillais activism in the Latin Quarter;[41] Salem Younse's account of his mother's difficult existence in La Goutte d'Or, the emblematic North African district near *Sans Frontière*'s own offices;[42] Mami Romain's quest from Guadeloupe to Mali via Paris;[43] an interview with the grandmother, mother and daughter of the same Algerian family;[44] and one with 'Kadjia', a woman of Moroccan origin from Trappes, about her forced marriage at the age of 17.[45] Nor did *Sans Frontière* restrict itself only to those of Arab, Muslim or Black heritage. Within the group that worked on the magazine, the mainly North African ex-MTA crowd were joined by members of other immigrant groups. As Driss El Yazami notes, such diversity was unusual among the minority press of the time.[46] One of the people interviewed for the *Mémoire Immigré* section was 'Linda', a Portuguese immigrant.[47] The newspaper celebrated the Nobel Prizes awarded to the Polish writer Czeslaw Milosz and the Argentinian human rights activist Adolfo Perez Esquirol.[48] It also published articles on the Armenian community in Marseilles, and the difficulties experienced with the French police by Jean-Claude Sarfety, a Tunisian Jew who had previously held an Israeli passport, over a breach of an order expelling him from France.[49] This prefigured the way that the Génériques NGO has recently sought to bring together different histories, including those of communities which are not usually considered 'of immigrant origin' in contemporary France.

An especially striking example of this diversity was the *Mémoire Immigré* interview by Leïla Sebbar of a woman referred to as 'Aïcha', whose life story contained so many overlapping identities that it could have been tailor-made to fit the description *Sans Frontière*. While the name Aïcha may appear typically North African – as in the song by the rai singer Khaled – this Aïcha insisted that she was really Aisra, a Hebrew name. Despite the fact that her father was an Algerian (though she uses the term 'Kabyle') soldier in the French army, she claimed that her mother was a Polish Jew and had given her a Jewish name. Her grandmother had come to France as an agricultural labourer in the Ariège (not an occupation that would stereotypically be associated with Eastern European Jewish immigrants). Aïcha's Jewish mother, who had participated in the Resistance, was deported and killed in a Nazi camp – a sadly more familiar story – but so was her Muslim father, a more marginalised memory. Aïcha appears to have dealt with her mixed heritage by identifying only ambiguously with either identity. On the one hand, she stated 'I have always said that I was Jewish and Arab', although she was drawn more to her Arab side as a result of experiencing anti-Arab racism as a teenager in Normandy. On the other hand, she insisted that having been drawn to atheism by her grandmother, 'I am neither Muslim nor Jewish'. She visited Israel, but was repelled by the treatment of the Palestinians. One might expect someone in this position to sidestep the question of identity by simply identifying as French, but this was not the case: Aïcha had communicated with her grandmother, who spoke little French, in a mixture of Polish, Yiddish and Occitan, and although she was educated by the French state as a *pupille de la nation* orphan, went on to refuse French nationality and remain stateless. By this point she had much reason to be angry, having been the victim of sexual abuse while working as an agricultural labourer, for which she sought revenge by an arson attack on the farm involved.

With all the makings of a rebel, her political itinerary was also the ideal template for the New Left-influenced politics of *Sans Frontière*. Aïcha joined the Jeunesses communistes at 15 but left the party in 1956 because the Communists voted for 'special powers' to be granted to the French authorities in Algeria. In Caen, she became a *porteuse de valises* (suitcase carrier) with the Jeanson network, during which she even crossed gender identities by using her short hair and deep voice to pass as a man to evade the police.[50] Aïcha subsequently went to independent Algeria, but became disillusioned and decided against taking Algerian nationality on account of disagreements with the government – particularly on women's rights, with which she had become involved as a result of meeting another Aïcha, Aïcha Khrémis, a former *moudjahida* nationalist resistance fighter. Disabled in a car accident, she went on to write a book published by Maspero about the inadequacies of French social services, with particular reference to discrimination against the mentally ill and black women.[51]

Leaving aside its specificities, Aïcha's story was typical of the way *Sans Frontière* sought to portray the complexity of the immigrant experience. It wanted to be a forum for free and wide-ranging debate about the multifaceted nature of immigrants' lived reality. Thus, each time Aïcha's story threatened to slip into a predictable identity-based essentialism (Jewish, Polish, Arab, Muslim, Algerian, Kabyle, French, Occitan, feminine, masculine, victim, activist, Communist, anti-Communist, etc.), it managed to scramble out: she was at one time or another all of these things, and none of them. The lesson of the story was that people perceived as 'of immigrant origin' can resist being pigeonholed by only one aspect of their identity. This suggested a more complex and subtle debate about identity within this early immigrant-activist discourse than has been the case in many of the debates about national identity in post-1980s France, where ideas of what it is to be 'French' or 'immigrant' are too often fixed. We could not be further from the impoverished dichotomy of 'French' versus 'Muslim' in which immigration has often been discussed in later decades.

The *Mémoire Immigré* feature should also be situated in its context: it reflected both international trends and developments within French politics and society. Across Europe, many *soixante-huitards* turned to oral history in the late 1970s as a way of accessing 'people's history' or 'history from below', a movement that was strong in Britain with the History Workshop Movement.[52] It is thus no coincidence that in the same period we see something akin to a 'memory turn' in *Sans Frontière* and its British equivalent *Race Today*, a magazine of comparable immigrant-leftist context and content in the UK. By the early 1980s, both came to place a high emphasis on history, and both sought to correct the tendency of some younger activists to reinvent the wheel, by showing them that 'the movement has a history of its own'.[53] Here, the concern was very similar to those of the editors of *Sans Frontière*, who were faced with the emergence of a *beur* movement that often represented earlier generations as passive. *Sans Frontière* aimed to correct this amnesia by being, as Farid Aïchoune put it, a 'political training school' and a 'bridge laid down between past struggles and the new generation'.[54]

Sans Frontière's interest in memory can also be situated within wider trends in France. As Sarah Farmer has argued, the late 1970s witnessed a remarkable vogue for peasant memory among urban bourgeois audiences – precisely because this was the point of disappearance of traditional peasant society.[55] Arguably something similar was happening among immigrants: urban migrant activists were also searching for their now disappearing roots. Indeed, this was the very period when the 'myth of return' – the notion that migrants' stay in France would be a temporary affair – was being punctured by new social realities. Post-independence dreams of economic development failed to materialise in sending countries, and tighter French government restrictions on migration inadvertently led to many male migrants, given increasing difficulties to travel back and forth, being joined by their wives and children to stay in France for good.[56] This moment of fluidity in the migratory situation was well captured by *Sans Frontière*.

So, even outside the *Mémoire Immigré* rubric, *Sans Frontière* was impregnated by a real historical consciousness. It tackled debates on controversial aspects of the Algerian war of independence, including through book reviews,[57] debates about the role of the *harkis*,[58] polemics on the history of the FLN and Algerian Communist Party,[59] correspondence on the Paris massacre of 17 October 1961,[60] and an obituary of Abdelhafid Boussouf, one of the prominent leaders of the FLN (the obituary supported the theory that Boussouf had killed Abane Ramdane, a key FLN activist who died under mysterious circumstances in 1957).[61] Similarly, articles in *Sans Frontière* went back over internal conflicts within the Association des Marocains en France, a group linked to opposition activism in Morocco,[62] and within the history of trade unionism in Tunisia.[63] The theme of memory was often present: a series of articles about Tunisian women insisted on the need to 'Rediscover our

mothers' memory'.[64] Anniversaries, too, were frequently commemorated. The
newspaper published articles on the twenty-third anniversary of the bombing
by French forces of the Tunisian village of Sakiet Sidi Youssef in 1958;[65] the
tenth anniversary of the strike by mainly immigrant semi-skilled car workers at
Renault in 1971;[66] the third anniversary of the Tunisian riots of 26 January
1978;[67] the first anniversary of the 'bulldozer affair' of 1980;[68] the sixth
anniversary of the death of the Egyptian singer Oum Kalthoum;[69] and the
twentieth anniversary of the death of Franz Fanon.[70] The importance of the
historical debates that took place in the pages of *Sans Frontière* is that they
undermine the widely held notion that there was no real discussion in France
of the legacy of colonialism until the controversies around torture in Algeria
that took off in the early 2000s. Well before then there was a debate about
relevant issues of colonial memory, but it was happening in a minority
publication, out of sight of mainstream opinion-formers. As is so often the case,
those with the most access to power were not necessarily the best informed.

But while *Sans Frontière* occupied a relatively marginal and precarious
position within the French cultural scene at the time, it could claim some
credit for changing attitudes over the longer term.[71] A challenge for radicals
generally, from which *Sans Frontière* was not exempted, was how to sustain
activism in a post-68 era of political pessimism. In some ways, it was not
successful in this objective. Although *Sans Frontière* was better distributed
than many of the leftist publications of the 1970s, printing some 20,000
copies every two weeks at its height, it suffered from the financial insecurity
endemic to publications of this nature.[72] It was not without legal difficulties,
such as when Jean-Pierre Pierre-Bloch, a local right-wing deputy in the 18th
arrondissement, tried to sue the magazine.[73] By 1984, *Sans Frontière* had
become a glossy monthly primarily concerned with Third World issues, and
less on the pulse with respect to the 'second generation' in the *banlieue*. In
1986, little noticed by the outside world, the magazine folded; a successor
title, *Baraka*, had a short life, in turn closing amid acrimony between different
factions on the editorial committee.[74] The second half of the 1980s was thus
both a moment of crisis for the traditional assumptions of radical politics,
and of transition and reconversion into cultural and intellectual work. While
some continued activism, it was increasingly accompanied by reflection on
the past (a bit like Slow Food, this was Slow Activism). During the 1990s, the
older generation of activists became especially concerned with memory and
educational work, to ensure that their experiences were at least not forgotten.

In this respect, they were rather more successful. Today the struggle for the
recognition of immigration history sits uneasily between its militant
background and its belated official recognition. Certainly, minority heritage is
more visible in mainstream culture and media now than was the case at the
time of *Sans Frontière*. Some of the credit for this can be claimed by Génériques,
founded by El Yazami and Bouziri in 1987. Génériques pursued many of the
same goals as *Sans Frontière*, but in a more rigorous, professionalised and
scientific way. Its initial aim was to prepare the exhibition *France des Étrangers,*

France des Libertés that took place in 1989.[75] In retrospect, that year seems like a turning point with the collapse of the Berlin Wall, the bicentenary of the French Revolution and the first 'headscarf affair'. El Yazami and Bouziri later played important roles in the origins of the higher profile, and more controversial, Cité National de l'Histoire de l'Immigration. And the work of Génériques continues today, with a major oral history archive project launched in 2012 that is recording the stories of activists who participated in immigration struggles between the 1960s and 1980s. Nevertheless, the engagement of the founders of *Sans Frontière* has continued to find direct political outlets as well, most notably in the *sans-papiers* movements, campaigns for immigrant voting rights, and the Ligue des Droits de l'Homme, France's oldest human rights association, of which Saïd Bouziri was the treasurer until his death in Paris in 2009. Bouziri's own legacy is a multifarious one that, like his life, spans both sides of the Mediterranean, including his long involvement with opposition movements in the country of his birth.[76] This legacy has now received some recognition. After the Tunisian Revolution of 2011, a number of veteran militants gathered at Bouziri's grave in Tunis to thank him for his part in the origins of a revolution that he never lived to see. Subsequently, on 23 June 2012, the Mayor of Paris, Bertrand Delanoë, renamed a square in the 18th arrondissement after Bouziri, whose hunger strike in a local church annexe in 1972 had started France's first movement of *sans-papiers*. Yet one of the most important links in this journey remains *Sans Frontière*, which embodied in the field of culture the major historical transition between *les années 68* and the 1980s. Reflecting the changing fortunes of the left during this period, it demonstrated how debates from the previous period of militancy both continued and changed (in style as well as substance) during the less politicised period that followed. Above all, it kept alive memories from that earlier period of immigrant activism against a countervailing tendency to forget them. Yet, for all its achievements, the road from immigrant militancy to immigrant history has been a long one – and it shows little sign of coming to an end.

Notes

1 On MSF, which had no links with the magazine *Sans Frontière* beyond the name, see Eleanor Davey, 'Famine, aid and ideology: The political activism of Médecins Sans Frontières in the 1980s', *French Historical Studies*, 34, 3 (2011): 529–58.

2 *Le Courrier de l'Atlas*, April 2011.

3 See Daniel A. Gordon, *Immigrants and Intellectuals: May '68 and the rise of anti-racism in France* (Pontypool: Merlin Press, 2012).

4 'Mémoires d'immigration: Driss El Yazami', *Le Courrier de l'Atlas*, September 2008; Driss El Yazami, in a radio interview with Emmanuel Laurentin in France 2, *La fabrique de l'histoire: Histoire des étrangers*, episode 1, first broadcast 7 January 2008.

5 *Sans Frontière*, 24 January 1981.

6 *Sans Frontière*, 6 and 13 June 1981.

7 *Sans Frontière*, 7 February 1981.

8 *Sans Frontière*, 18 December 1979.

9 To borrow a phrase from the British *soixante-huitard* Christopher Hitchens, who described himself as a 'recovering Marxist'. Sean O'Hagen, 'Just a pretty face?', *The Observer*, 11 July 2004.

10 Pierre Goldman, *Souvenirs obscurs d'un juif polonais né en France* (Paris: Seuil, 1975).

11 *Sans Frontière*, 2 October 1979. On the incident with the policeman, see Hervé Hamon and Patrick Rotman, *Génération* (Paris: Seuil, vol. 2, 1988), 601–2.

12 *Sans Frontière*, 20 November 1979.

13 For example, on the rent strike in SONACOTRA immigrant workers' hostels: *Sans Frontière*, 1 May, 31 July and 2 October 1979, 20 November 1981.

14 Saïd Bouziri and Driss El Yazami, 'Prendre la peine', *Migrance*, 14 (1999): 2–4.

15 *Sans Frontière*, 24 June 1980.

16 *Sans Frontière*, 30 September 1980.

17 *Sans Frontière*, 27 March 1979, and 22 April 1980.

18 *Sans Frontière*, 7, 14, 18 and 21 February 1981.

19 *Sans Frontière*, 26 February 1980.

20 *Sans Frontière*, 20–26 December 1980.

21 Abdellali Hajjat, 'Le MTA et la "grève générale" contre le racisme de 1973', *Plein Droit*, 67 (2005): 36–40.

22 *Sans Frontière*, 1 May 1979.

23 *Sans Frontière*, 4 September 1979; Jacques Simon et al, *L'Immigration algérienne en France* (Paris: L'Harmattan, 2002), 188.

24 Ahmed Boubeker and Nicolas Beau, *Chroniques métissées* (Paris: Alain Moreau, 1986), 122–4.

25 Georges Abou-Sada, 'Générations issues de l'immigration: Problèmes de définition et aspects démographiques', in Georges Abou-Sada and Hélène Milet, eds., *Générations issues de l'immigration* (Paris: Arcantère, 1986), 25.

26 *Sans Frontière*, 26 February 1980.

27 Saïd Bouziri, interview with the author, Paris, 6 November 2004.

28 *Sans Frontière*, 30 May 1981.

29 *Sans Frontière*, 13 June 1981.

30 See Tony Judt, *Past Imperfect: French intellectuals 1944–1956* (Berkeley: University of California Press, 1992); Ian Birchall, *Sartre against Stalinism* (New York: Berghahn, 2004).

31 Pierre Nora, *Les Lieux de mémoire, vol. 1* (Paris: Gallimard, 1984).

32 *Sans Frontière*, 1 January 1980.

33 The archive can be found at: http://odysseo.org/ead.html?id=FRAS075GNQ_0 00000218&c=FRAS075GNQ_000000218_e0000019&qid=sdx_q9. The newspaper is also held in the Bibliothèque nationale de France.

34 Gordon, *Immigrants and intellectuals*, see Note 3.

35 *Sans Frontière*, 29 January and 12 February 1980.

36 *Sans Frontière*, 20 May 1980.

37 *Sans Frontière*, 29 January 1980.

38 *Sans Frontière*, 30 September 1980.

39 *Sans Frontière*, 30 September 1980.

40 *Sans Frontière*, 26 February 1980.

41 *Sans Frontière*, 25 March 1980.

42 *Sans Frontière*, 6 May 1980.

43 *Sans Frontière*, 3 June 1980.

44 *Sans Frontière*, 24 June 1980.

45 *Sans Frontière*, 18 and 25 April 1981.

46 Driss El Yazami, 'France's ethnic minority press' in Alec Hargreaves and Mark McKinney, eds., *Post-Colonial Cultures in France* (London: Routledge, 1997), 122, 124.

47 *Sans Frontière*, 13 and 20 December 1980.

48 *Sans Frontière*, 28 October 1980.

49 *Sans Frontière*, 11 and 25 May 1980, and 6 December 1980.

50 French FLN sympathisers who engaged in direct action, such as those in the network led by Francis Jeanson, were known as 'carriers of suitcases' because their main task was to smuggle suitcases of cash out of the country.

51 *Sans Frontière*, 31 January and 7 February 1981.

52 Raphael Samuel, ed., *People's History and Socialist Theory* (London: Routledge, 1981).

53 *Race Today*, August–September 1979. For a comparison, see Daniel A. Gordon, '*Sans Frontière* et *Race Today*, des vecteurs parallèles de l'héritage de l'immigration?' in Louisa Zanoun, ed., *La Patrimoine de l'immigration en France et en Europe*, special issue of *Migrance*, Hors série (2013); Daniel A. Gordon, 'French and British antiracists since the 1960s: A *rendez-vous manqué*?' in Maud Bracke and James Mark, eds., *Between Decolonisation and the Cold War: Transnational activism and its limits in Europe, 1950s–1990s*, special issue of *Journal of Contemporary History* (forthcoming 2015).

54 Boubeker and Beau, *Chroniques métissées*, see Note 24, 125.

55 Sarah Farmer, 'Memoirs of French peasant life: Progress and nostalgia in post-war France', *French History*, 25, 3 (2011): 362–79.

56 Jacques Barou, *Travailleurs africains en France* (Grenoble: Presses Universitaires de Grenoble, 1978), 148; Salem Kacet, *Le droit à la France* (Paris: Belfond), 1991, 36–43; Zakya Daoud, *De L'Immigration à la citoyenneté* (Casablanca: Mémoire de la Méditerranée, 2003), 38–40; John Berger and Jean Mohr, *A Seventh Man* (London: Verso, 2010), 217–23; *Mémoires d'immigrés* (1997),

documentary directed by Yamina Benguigui and available on DVD, episode 1, *Les Mères*.

57 *Sans Frontière*, 5 December 1981 and 1 January 1982.

58 *Sans Frontière*, 24 January 1981. The term *harki* refers to Algerian Muslims who fought as soldiers in the French army against Algerian nationalists between 1954 and 1962.

59 *Sans Frontière*, 14 February 1981.

60 *Sans Frontière*, 28 October 1980 and 30 October 1981.

61 *Sans Frontière*, 14 February 1981.

62 *Sans Frontière*, 15 January 1982. On the AMF specifically, see Daoud, *De L'Immigration à la citoyenneté*, see Note 56.

63 *Sans Frontière*, 10 January 1981.

64 *Sans Frontière*, 14 February 1981.

65 *Sans Frontiere*, 14 February 1981.

66 *Sans Frontière*, 6 November 1981.

67 *Sans Frontière*, 24 January 1981.

68 *Sans Frontière*, 25 December 1981.

69 *Sans Frontière*, 14 February 1981.

70 *Sans Frontière*, 25 December 1981.

71 Gordon, *Immigrants and Intellectuals*, see Note 3, 158–176, 219–233.

72 *Sans Frontière*, 24 June 1980.

73 *Sans Frontière*, 26 February 1980.

74 El Yazami, 'France's ethnic minority press', see Note 46, 123.

75 Louisa Zanoun, '*Sans Frontière* and Génériques', paper presented at the Algeria Revisited Conference, University of Leicester, April 2012. See also Génériques, ed., *France des etrangers, France des libertés* (Paris: Éditions Ouvrières/ Génériques, 1990).

76 See the brochure, Génériques, ed., *Saïd Bouziri: L'Humain au coeur de la vie* (Paris: Génériques, 2012).

7

Algeria in Paris:

Fifty Years On

Isabel Hollis

In the aftermath of conflict, defining a neutral and inclusive cultural heritage can be a political minefield. Key players – such as political activists, representatives from minority groups, or heritage and museum workers – vie for space in a crowded political landscape. This has certainly been true of the Algerian War, where a broad collective malaise regarding French colonialism in North Africa has been reinforced by the competing claims of various memory groups. One might contrast, for example, the memories of the *pieds-noirs*, who felt disinherited of their homeland, and those of the French *porteurs de valise* (suitcase carriers), whose anti-colonial politics and complex involvement with the fight for Algerian independence compromised their relationship with public opinion at home.[1] By the same token, many private memories were buried away, too traumatic to bring to the public eye, including those of victims and perpetrators of torture, or those of persecuted *harki* soldiers.[2] After the independence of Algeria in 1962, multiple discourses of memory were constructed, and countless individuals developed their own narrative of the past. Yet the nature of memory is that it is incomplete or ravaged by the distorting passage of time. To return to an event like the Algerian War implies an unravelling of the intimate and collective processes that function to manipulate memory, in order to establish an inclusive historical narrative.

This makes it particularly useful to study anniversaries as key moments of fracture, division and reconciliation. The fiftieth anniversary of the end of the Algerian War in 2012 brought the conflict – and its legacy – into the public eye. By the time the commemorations were over, it was clear that a good deal of progress had been made on the difficult path towards constructing a public memory of colonialism in metropolitan France. Several key events occurred in Paris over the course of this period. Some were specifically linked to the demonstration of 17 October 1961, which brought the violence of the Algerian War to the streets of Paris; other events remembered the Algerian War; and still others commemorated the whole colonial project in Algeria, from its beginnings in 1830 to the acquisition of independence in 1962. This commemorative flurry was in sharp contrast to the reluctance, not only in political circles but also among those who lived through the war, to discuss Algeria in the decades following the conflict, a point of debate for a number of scholars of French history.[3] Since the late 1990s, however, there has been a shift in this trend. Several factors have contributed to this process – notably, the gradual emergence of a debate on the use of torture during the war in 1999–2000, as well as the curiosity of second- and third-generation Algerians in France who have actively sought a deeper understanding of their parents' background and origins. The fiftieth anniversary was, therefore, an opportunity to create a public and open engagement with the events of that took place in Algeria in the 1950s and 1960s.

The historian Herman Lebovics has discussed how, in contemporary France, a 'new official definition of the national heritage will henceforth incorporate something of its ex-colonial empire', but he acknowledged (in 2004) that this ' "something" remain[ed] to be determined'.[4] Between 2004 and 2011, an extensive re-imagining of France's cultural heritage saw some space opened up for the ex-colonial empire and its 'others'. In 2007, the opening of the Cité Nationale de l'Histoire de l'Immigration at Porte Dorée, just on the cusp between central Paris and the *périphérique*, signified at first glance a sea-change in the cultural landscape of the city. But the visitor must look past the colonial frescoes that decorate this rehabilitated exhibition space, constructed initially for the Colonial Exhibition of 1931, in order to accept it as symbolic of a desire to include immigrant populations within France's national heritage. Similarly, the inauguration in 2006 of the Musée du Quai Branly – a museum entirely devoted to 'indigenous' arts – has presented the visiting public with a difficult mixture of cultural inclusion and cultural othering. The museum's mission is to display what the French call 'les arts premiers', which implies an interest in (and openness to) other cultures but simultaneously hints at their primitive character. These controversial heritage practices in France have left interested parties eager to see when and how a more inclusive discussion of the Francophonie, the Empire and French colonial rule might take place.

As the site that typically accommodates memories, the museum has been described by Andreas Huyssen 'both as a burial chamber of the past – with all that entails in terms of decay, erosion, forgetting – and as a site of possible resurrections'.[5] Despite the protracted process of memory emergence surrounding colonial Algeria and the Algerian War, the fiftieth anniversary saw the mobilisation of a number of public sites in France to exhibit this uncomfortable story. This use of public space to remember Algeria was in itself a turning point. As Joshua Cole has demonstrated, the polemic in 2001 surrounding the installation of a plaque on the Pont Saint Michel in Paris commemorating 17 October 1961 was clear evidence of the continued tension between official memories and the claims of minority representatives seeking to tell 'their' story of the Algerian War.[6] It is noteworthy, then, that in 2011 and 2012 prestigious spaces opened their doors and their archives to tell the Algerian story, most notably, the colossal Musée de l'Armée at the Invalides (of which more below), but also such sites as the Réfectoire des Cordeliers at the Odéon, where an exhibition was held, and the Petit Palais museum, where a series of debates again brought the Algerian War to public attention.

The fiftieth anniversary commemorations also happened to coincide with the build-up to the 2012 presidential election. This added controversy to the discussions surrounding Algeria, which occurred alongside a political debate that seemed to stigmatise French Muslims in quite specific terms. Was the production of *halal* meat an acceptable practice? Were separate swimming times for men and women, to facilitate access for Muslims, a 'threat' to national identity? These questions pushed post-colonial politics further into people's daily lives, requiring them to consider how immigrant 'others' might be encroaching on the way they ate and exercised. Even before the election campaign, the Sarkozy presidency had been marked by a polarisation of opinions surrounding immigration, integration and colonialism. This took the form both of state-sponsored public debates, like the 'grand débat sur l'identité nationale' launched in October 2009, and of staged moments of national unity. A good example of the latter was the broad and non-specific commemoration of the end of the French Empire organised by Sarkozy on 14 July 2010. This could have been an opportunity to show solidarity with the nation's post-colonial others, but, as Patricia Lorcin demonstrates in Chapter 8, the display was criticised as more nostalgic than commemorative. More generally, Sarkozy's poor record in honouring immigrant populations has made it relatively easy for his successor, François Hollande, to adopt a more inclusive voice.

Nevertheless, for colonialism to find its rightful place in France's cultural heritage, more was required than simply a change of president. To get a clearer view, we need to look directly at how French colonialism has been memorialised. This chapter will examine two commemorative events that took place around the fiftieth anniversary in order to consider how each one contributed to the emergence and negotiation of memories surrounding the Algerian conflict. The first of these, and perhaps the most prominent of all the Algeria-related events in Paris, was an exhibition held from May to July 2012 at the Musée de l'Armée, which looked at colonial Algeria from its beginnings in 1830 to its conclusion in 1962. The second was less visible and less prestigious; indeed few will have encountered it. On the fiftieth anniversary of 17 October 1961, the artistic group Raspouteam launched a 'hidden' exhibition – accessible only by scanning unmarked QR codes pasted onto buildings around Paris, which directed interested parties to a website documenting the event's history and evoking its trauma. Both exhibits brought the uncomfortable memory of Algeria into the public gaze, but in contrasting ways.

Official memories: The exhibition at the Musée de l'Armée

I visited the exhibition on Algeria at the Musée de l'Armée in June 2012, but even before entering the exhibition space, I was struck by the surroundings. The Hôtel des Invalides, in which the museum is located, was built during the 1670s and commissioned by Louis XIV to house injured soldiers and military veterans, as well as for the manufacture of military equipment. The main edifice stands around a central courtyard where a selection of cannons sits proudly. Perhaps the most significant alteration made to the site since its construction was the addition of Napoleon's tomb in 1840, an edifice that draws in thousands of tourists every year, and which seems to add further gravitas to the site's military past. To the south side of the Invalides site, a military hospital still functions, while the main building, with its grandiose baroque architecture, is now home to a permanent exhibition detailing the military history of France, as well as temporary exhibits that elaborate this history.

But, despite its association with the army, the area around the Invalides – and the Invalides itself – is as much about French political grandeur as it is about the country's military successes. For instance, Napoleon's tomb is quite clearly a glorification of his role as the most extraordinary military leader that France has produced, but the main focus of the tomb's artwork is nonetheless on his Civil Code as opposed to his military exploits. This is in keeping with the broader urban character of the seventh *arrondissement* of Paris. Home to the National Assembly and to a number of ministries and foreign embassies, the area is at the heart of French political life. Demonstrators regularly gather here in the hope that their cause will be recognised, yet they are heavily policed. When a new president is elected, two cannons are rolled down from the Musée de l'Armée to fire celebratory shots down the road towards the river Seine. The sense of political power and prestige that pervades the area spreads to its commercial enterprises too. When I tried to order some books on French slavery in the Caribbean at a local bookshop, the owner gave me a wry smile: 'Are you really planning to order those here,' he commented, 'with Napoleon watching over us?' This was a reminder that the seventh *arrondissement* is not a space that welcomes those who call the status, legitimacy or actions of the French Republic into question. The symbolism of marking fifty years of Algerian independence from France in the heart of its most political *arrondissement* should not therefore be lost on us.

Yet the exhibition – entitled *Algérie: 1830–1962, avec Jacques Ferrandez* – was evidently not intended to be merely a reproduction of official memories of the Algerian War. With the help of striking images by Ferrandez – a cartoonist renowned for his work on Algeria and a *pied-noir* who lived through the period of decolonisation – the exhibition documented colonial Algeria in its entirety, distinguishing itself by not focusing on the war alone, and thereby contextualising that particularly violent episode within a complex history.[7] Its thorough treatment of the period acted as proof of the increasing dialogue and understanding around Algeria, a process that was gradually set in motion when the French state officially recognised the Algerian conflict of 1954–62 as a 'war' in 1999 and opened some of its archives to historians. Certainly, the exhibition's focus on the entire period, twinned with the centrality of its location, seemed to position the exhibition as the seminal commemorative narrative to document Algeria, although this did raise the question of whether such a domineering act of public remembrance would also be an inclusive one. Either way, it was a clear commercial success for the museum. In the three and a half months of its duration, 44,000 visitors attended the exhibition. By measure of comparison, the 2012 exhibition on Napoleon III and Italy only drew in 21,000, while the previous exhibition on the French art of armour production had more success, though still fell behind Algeria with 42,000 visitors.

Reactions to the exhibition were mostly positive. Nevertheless, while the French press praised the exhibition's bold subject matter and neutrality, informal discussion with academic colleagues who had attended the exhibition threw up some criticisms, the most prominent of which was of the exhibition's short duration, and the concern that this was intended to minimise impact and public awareness.[8] This does not hold up to scrutiny, however, as the museum only holds two exhibitions a year, and they are always three and a half months long. As a case in point, a recent exhibition on Napoleon and Europe was subject to the same time limit, despite the popularity and prestige of the topic, and the relationship between its subject matter and the building in which it was housed. A further criticism was of the emphasis, at certain points in the exhibition, on the voices of French anti-colonial thinkers. Quotations from French Algeria's critics were pasted in large letters on the exhibition walls. Again, though, I felt this detail added an important nuance to the exhibition. While post-colonial discourse has taken pains to unveil the crimes committed by colonial powers, it has at times neglected the anti-colonial voices that existed among inhabitants of colonial nations. Of course, it is also important not to overstate the influence of anti-colonial thought, especially in a conflict as complex as the Algerian War.

The entrance to the exhibition reflected the difficulty of commemorating a distressing and, for many, shameful period in French history, in a building that celebrates French military glory. Within the vast space of the Invalides, the entrance seemed understated for what was such a significant act of historical recognition. The underwhelming, utilitarian staircase that led to the exhibition was a disappointment after the splendid cobbled walkways and cannons that welcome the visitor to the building itself, as was the cramped lift inadequate for the number of visitors that were attending at the time of my visit. The building's elaborate seventeenth-century architecture contrasted strongly with the minimalist entrance to the exhibition. In many ways, this contrast reflected the dual character of the exhibition, with Ferrandez's cartoons and orientalist images adding a pleasing aesthetic to some parts of the exhibition, while others were deliberately stark, corresponding with their sinister subject matter. Visitors began by entering the section of the exhibition documenting colonisation and colonial rule. Here, the quotations from anti-colonial thinkers came into their own – their prominence ensured that the visitor continuously questioned the ethical dimensions of the colonial enterprise. The second, separate section of the exhibition was dedicated to war, both the involvement of Algerians in the First and Second World Wars, and the Algerian War itself. The horrors of the latter were laid bare using a more contemporary aesthetic: photographs, film footage and recorded voices through headphones created an unsettling contact with the realities of the war.

In the French left-wing newspaper, *Libération*, the exhibition was reviewed as forcing those involved to examine their consciences.[9] This did not seem to me to be the overarching aim. Instead, the intention was to stick to facts, without pointing fingers. Indeed, in an interview in May 2012, the director of the Musée de l'Armée recalled welcoming organisations representing *anciens combattants* to talk through the exhibition. He described the exhibition's aim to them as: 'neither to conceal nor to insist too heavily on anything or cause unnecessary offence.'[10] This was an ambitious statement, given the subject matter. The exhibition committee also travelled to Algeria, where some ex-FLN members were interviewed, and Algerian historians were involved in the creation of the exhibition. Clearly, the committee took the necessary steps to achieve 'neutrality' in their coverage, although the exhibition was not irreproachable in this respect.

On the polemical subject of torture, for example, there was a tendency to acknowledge certain abuses while simultaneously excusing them by emphasising the difficulty of avoiding abuse given the context. In the exhibition, the violence employed by both French and Algerians was discussed with few concessions and the prevalence of the French military's use of torture was made explicit with photographic evidence. Yet close reading of the book that accompanied the exhibition suggests an underlying narrative that stresses the lack of military autonomy. Faced with a political majority who initially could not conceive of losing French Algeria, the military were, the text suggests, obliged to act accordingly. This interpretation goes some way to exonerating the French perpetrators of violence, as the responsibility appears to lie instead with key political figures, who are condemned for their failure to discourage or forbid the practice of torture. Where the French army are concerned, we read of their fear of denouncing colleagues or of destroying the army's image of unity, lessening the apparent gravity of individual acts of violence committed by French soldiers. The exhibition also highlighted the distinction, and even conflict, between political and military will from the start. One of the first displays quoted General Bugeaud's intervention in the National Assembly in 1840:

> The possession of Africa is a mistake. Since you are set upon doing it anyway, then you will need to go all out.

Bugeaud believed that there was a general political disregard for military opinion in the decision-making process and the decision on the part of the curators to bring this to the fore early in the exhibition strongly suggested that the military were not agents of the state, but victims of its whims.

While it was impossible for the organisers not to consider the context of the exhibition's situation in a building that has traditionally housed and supported retired French soldiers, the relatively 'indulgent' view of practices of army violence did not extend to atrocities committed by the Front de Libération Nationale (FLN). The FLN was denounced for its indiscriminate acts of terror committed on both French and Algerian victims, men, women and children. In the book accompanying the exhibition, the political cause of the FLN is undermined by emphasising the fact that the majority of their victims were Algerian Muslims. The language is emotive, referring to a 'veritable carnage' and a 'cortege of atrocities'. No such terms were applied to the French. In the exhibition, specific FLN massacres were highlighted, with place names and numbers of people killed, while the description of French violence remained generalised, reducing audience identification with the victims. Acts of violence clearly became relative in the exhibition. When perpetrated by the FLN, they were atrocities; when perpetrated by the French, they were regretful but obligatory. Quite apart from the historical bias that this suggests, such a narrative flirts dangerously with the ethical problem of quantifying violence – some of the violent deaths were, it seems, worse than others.

This is not to say, however, that the French military were entirely excused or whitewashed by the exhibition, merely that the emphasis on their lack of political agency might lead the visitor to conclude that they were essentially 'pawns' in a political battle that raged overhead. It is certainly the case that the question of individual responsibility was far from clear-cut. A number of French soldiers were conscripts, but does this liberate them from individual responsibility? Equally, the FLN put considerable pressure on Algerians living both at home and in France to support their cause, seeking Algerian unity in the struggle or independence. How did pressurising Algerians compromise the broader political vision of the FLN, or lead individuals to commit acts of violence they abhorred? In France, the defensive argument of just 'doing one's job' has become a trope – famously, it was Maurice Papon's defence when he was tried for his involvement with the deportation of Jews during the Second World War and the suppression of the 17 October 1961, demonstration.[11] It is perhaps not entirely surprising, then, that this same narrative was discernable between the lines of the exhibition.

Still, *Algérie: 1830–1962* was a striking departure for its open, public overview of the colonial period and its complexities. It was significant because of its location – the centrality and status of the Hôtel des Invalides gave it additional legitimacy – and because of its proximity to France's major political institutions. With the National Assembly on its doorstep, it hinted at a changing relationship between an uncomfortable past and the state institutions that played an active role in concealing that same past. Few events coinciding with the fifty-year celebrations of Algerian independence were as visible as this, and it was the heightened visibility that made it remarkable.

Hidden memories: Raspouteam's commemoration of 17 October 1961

If the Musée de l'Armée attempts to commemorate the Algerian War were designed to attract large crowds, other memorial projects were distinctive for their invisible and underground character, echoing in the very style of installation the trend of obfuscation that has hindered the emergence of colonial memory, and thus subverting it. Commemorations of the anti-colonial protests of 17 October 1961, in Paris have often typified this alternative style. Although the brutal repression of Algerian demonstrators on that day was only one among many violent episodes during the era of decolonisation, it has received particular attention as a number of Algerians were killed in central Paris (estimates range from 30 to 300).[12] Notably through the work of documentary films that now exist about the event, the police and the French state have come under considerable criticism for the rehearsed cover-up of the atrocities that they committed on that day.[13] Commemorative gestures relating to the event have brazenly called the state into question, the best known of which was a graffiti message emblazoned across the Pont Saint Michel by left-wing activists several weeks later, reading 'Algerians were drowned here'. This graffiti has set the tone for an altogether different approach to remembering the Algerian War – one which fits in well with Raspouteam's 'underground' philosophy.

The Raspouteam group was founded in 2005 and is comprised of two web designers and a history student, who describe themselves as 'urban artists'.[14] Their mission is to 'manipulate new technology for a political and cultural end, by combining it with posters, stencils and graffiti'.[15] They have now masterminded three commemorative projects using this approach. The first of these was entitled 'Public Disorder', and remembered specific instances of police brutality committed on the streets of Paris; the second focused on the Paris Commune 140 years after the event; and the third commemorated the fiftieth anniversary of the protests of 17 October 1961.

All three projects were exhibited on the streets of Paris, in the very sites where the events they document occurred. Here, 'exhibited' refers to their usage of vast wall posters depicting historical events, pasted onto the urban space. Some exhibits were more discreet, with QR codes stuck to walls, inciting passers-by to scan and discover through their website the historical event that was being commemorated. The website made extensive use of maps, with links hovering over the locations in question. In this manner, unexpected, unpublicised urban frescoes were designed to lead the viewer into an online archive of state acts of brutality.

A major part of their project on 17 October 1961, was a webdocumentary produced in collaboration with Agat films. It was made up of a series of witness testimonies from Algerian labourers, FLN activists, and members of the French police. This formed part of an online site that remains accessible after the end of the commemorative period and incorporates primary historical sources, such as photographs and newspaper articles, as well as interviews with contemporary historians like Mohamed Harbi, Neil Macmaster and Emmanuel Blanchard. The defining characteristic of Raspouteam's commemorative work is their use of urban space to guide the public to their online archive. Today, the witness testimonies that make up the project '17 October 1961' can be accessed through an interactive online map that links through to their webdocumentaries recalling the event. However, when first released on 17 October 2011, the documentaries were accessible by scanning QR codes situated at seven different sites around Paris: Pont de Neuilly, Pont de Clichy, Palais des Sports, Étoile, Grands Boulevards, Saint Michel and Montreuil. Printed onto ceramic tiles, the codes were glued onto walls in each space. Word of mouth aside, members of the public discovered them only by chance as they walked through the streets of Paris. To encourage public interaction, film footage of the event was projected in a selection of the sites at night, but, for the most part, Raspouteam's urban art was characterised by a subversive and hidden engagement with the city.

This characteristic of their work should be understood within a broader polemical context of non recognition of grievances committed against minority groups and the alleged 'cover-up' that took place after the protests of 17 October 1961; and which came to a head on the same date in 2012. At the 51st anniversary of the event, recently elected President François Hollande made a speech that recognised on behalf of the French state the degree of violence committed:

> On 17 October 1961, Algerians who demonstrated for their right to independence were killed during a bloody repression. The Republic recognises lucidly this fact. Fifty-one years later, I pay homage to the memory of the victims.[16]

Prior to Hollande's declaration, there had been no formal state recognition of this specific moment in the Algerian War. But his political opponents did not share the same sentiments. In the words of Christian Jacob, the parliamentary leader of the centre-right UMP:

> Though there is no question we should deny the events of October 1961 or forget its victims, it is intolerable that the Republican Police, and subsequently the entire Republic, should be called into question.[17]

The far-right Front National, unsurprisingly, went even further. The party's leader, Marine Le Pen, had this to say:

> Don't you feel that all this repenting has an influence on the way in which new generations of French youth of Algerian origin now feel hostility and even hatred towards France, and that France owes them something, which some have come to claim back, by coercive or violent means?[18]

It is telling that both Jacob and Le Pen responded in time for their comments to be recorded in the papers the following day, indicating the persistence of political stakes surrounding colonial memory in general, and the Algerian War in particular.

This spat between leaders hints at a wider political disagreement over whether post-colonial European societies should be held accountable for the imperial atrocities committed by their predecessors. French writer Pascal Bruckner has, controversially, explored this phenomenon. He describes the relentless 'self-flagellation' of the West in stark terms: 'We hate ourselves much more than we love others. The malaise, ceasing to be supported by a political project, gnaws away at Western consciousness from within.'[19] Critics have claimed that his intolerance of Western masochism is a reactionary reflex that plays into the hands of the Front National. Yet Bruckner raises an important question about the nature of collective 'repentance': does the 'comfort of redemption' obtained by those who 'repent' provide a solution to the public discord created by contested memories?[20] In fact, neither Bruckner's scepticism nor Hollande's fervour is capable of resolving such discord. Raspouteam's subversive approach constitutes a creative response. It provides a more nuanced solution to the problem of contemporary society's collective responsibility. The furtive nature of their work raises questions in the public imagination, leaving each individual to construct his or her own response.

This is achieved largely through a spontaneous encounter with the past. Raspouteam's work is never fixed spatially, as they use the whole of Paris to create temporary commemorations in the same site that the event took place, and on the anniversary of its occurrence. Likewise, their work is not fixed temporally, as the duration of the exhibit depends on how long it takes for it to be noticed and removed. Raspouteam's projects give the (smartphone-wielding) public a choice of how to engage with, and therefore constitute, the urban space. The public become agents in the appropriation of city spaces, as their subjective experience of those spaces is altered. The subtle emergence of hidden narratives is dependent on their interaction. Those who choose to interact are able to experience a new temporal cartography of the city, activating the city as extending back through time, not just as extending through space. Members of the public construct a commemorative narrative and their own memorials. The action of scanning the QR code and reading the information excavates a buried narrative of obfuscated state crimes.

In this respect, the events commemorated by Raspouteam acquire a renewed presence on the urban landscape, due to this unexpected discovery of the event at the same site on which it occurred. This, as well as the 'Quick Response' medium through which commemorative narratives are accessed, gives a spontaneity to their work that contrasts with the forward planning, advertising, advanced ticket buying and generally structured approach that is characteristic of museum visits today. Moreover, their use of new technology creates new commemorative opportunities. While a museum exhibit that incorporates digital technologies to enhance the visitor experience may be hailed for its contemporary aesthetic and its encouragement of audience participation, this engagement is nonetheless limited to the confines of the museum – it does not so much revolutionise the museum experience as add gloss to it. The use of technology in museums facilitates and adds immediacy to our encounter with the exhibit, but usually does not transform the nature of that encounter. Raspouteam, on the other hand, use digital technologies to interrogate the nature of our relationship with a troubled past. By placing the onus on each individual to act upon their curiosity, or to ignore the artwork that appeals for their response, they have developed a new kind of commemorative practice that tries to bring in a different kind of public.

Yet these transformative technologies raise questions regarding public engagement. In contrast to the Musée de l'Armée, Raspouteam's purpose is to hold the French *forces de l'ordre* (police, army, security services, etc.) accountable for specific acts of injustice, which have in most cases been covered up. The strategy of placing QR codes around the city means that the commemorative project is hidden in plain sight, just like the acts of violence they commemorated. Access to information requires an action of decoding. The aim is to bring individual and otherwise unrecognised experiences of victimhood to public attention in a manner that is therefore befitting to the unveiling of hidden pasts. However, this spontaneous public engagement is limited by the very medium that it celebrates; it is only effective if the passing public is technologically 'switched on'. Raspouteam make demands of their public that are perhaps idealistic bearing in mind the purposeful mobility that characterises the average city dweller. As members of the public undertake their daily commute, trip to the shops, visits to friends or otherwise, they are required not only to have a smartphone and to know how to use it, but also to be sufficiently curious and have time to scan a QR code and listen to the webdocumentaries that they discover.

Indeed, though the eye is drawn to the codes by the posters installed on the same site, this does not guarantee their appeal to the passer-by. If city dwellers can be broadly categorised into visitors (who may not scan because of the cost of using internet on a smartphone when abroad) and locals (who probably will not scan because they are busy pursuing their daily lives), then the project's most innovative dimension – its element of surprise – might also be its downfall. Seen in this light, we could be tempted to view Raspouteam's inventive combination of urban and technological environments as little more than an elaborate exercise in public mystification. The clandestine nature of their work leads us to question its reach, appeal and subsequent legitimacy. Raspouteam's studied anonymity protects them from the reassuring processes of public scrutiny and criticism that are essential in questioning and then elaborating other portrayals of the past. One might argue that the webdocumentaries, available in the universally accessible space of the internet, go some way to resolving this problem. However, it is not the case that by placing something online, it is guaranteed to have a broad impact – in fact, a project as specific as that of Raspouteam is somewhat lost within the limitless space and scope of the World Wide Web. The Musée de l'Armée exhibition has a web page too – and undoubtedly a more popular one, due to the advertising and press coverage that the exhibition received. In the end, then, these apparently very diverse approaches to remembering Algeria are rendered banal by their online afterlife, the experience of the web-visitor being much the same in both cases. This undermines the innovative technological approach that Raspouteam take as their point of departure.

The webdocumentaries of Raspouteam and their use of urban art nonetheless have the effect of diminishing the museum's status as a favoured site of encounter with the past. Complex or unsightly pasts should not, Raspouteam seem to suggest, be dependent on the politics of the cultural spaces where they are exhibited. Despite the limitations surrounding access to Raspouteam's work, the originality of using technical media to create an unexpected encounter with the past is a refreshing and dynamic step away from the traditional museum exhibit. Moreover, by positioning the present-day public as a witness to a past injustice, that public is newly inscribed in the process of taking responsibility for that past, giving each act of violence a renewed contemporary valence. In this respect, Raspouteam engages our civic responsibility by hinting at our duty to remember. Meanwhile, the use of the museum as a space of encounter tends instead to place the exhibited subject firmly in the past by virtue of the institution that houses it. How the audience encounters that past depends on the museum's own history. As a site of memory, the museum space is invested with a certain status, wielding a degree of power over the past, over which narratives are unveiled or kept hidden, over the representation of those narratives, and over which voice is given priority. In this sense, the museum takes possession of the past. The historical and geographical status of the Musée de l'Armée, and its institutional authority as a space that documents military history might encourage the visitor to view an exhibition that is held there as canonical truth, as opposed to one of many possible representations. By contrast,

Raspouteam suggest that the age of uncertainty in France pertains not just to the unsettling nature of post-colonial memories, but also to the destabilising fashion in which they may be brought to our attention. We talk about the past 'haunting' us, but the chance encounter that Raspouteam sets out to create mirrors this process of haunting and brings the past that lingers in the shadows into a new light.

The commemorative years that surrounded the fiftieth anniversary of the end of the Algerian War saw the Parisian urban space altered by the incorporation of new geographies of memory. Despite their clear differences, the exhibitions at the Musée de l'Armée and the 'installations' by Raspouteam did have one thing in common: their success in shifting or questioning the surface grandeur of the Parisian landscape. While the seventh *arrondissement* became home to a historical narrative that its past inhabitants – politicians and presidents – had set out to deny, other sites of centrality and substance – such as the Pont Saint Michel and the Place de l'Etoile – were shown to conceal their own uncomfortable historical truths. Raspouteam brought the debate on memory, repentance and public responsibility for the past into the quotidian spaces of Paris, engaging unsuspecting passers-by as witnesses to a concealed history. So, while it is still too early to give a definitive answer to Lebovics's question about the incorporation of a colonial heritage into French national memory, we can already see that one characteristic of this process has been the appropriation of crucial French sites of memory as monuments to alternative narratives of the past. Over time, this new layer will be carved onto the urban palimpsest, and a more open and critical narrative of French imperialism and decolonisation will find its place in French history.

Notes

1 The *porteurs de valise*, led by Francis Jeanson, were left-wing French who helped the Algerian liberation movement by transporting money and papers for Algerians.

2 The term *harki* refers to Algerian Muslims who fought as soldiers in the French army against Algerian nationalists between 1954 and 1962.

3 Benjamin Stora is a key historian of Algeria, and his work *La Gangrène et l'oubli: La Mémoire de la guerre d'Algérie* (Paris: Éditions La Découverte, 2005) explores the complex process of both remembering and forgetting in relation to Algeria. Jim House and Neil Macmaster's book *Paris 1961: Algerians, state terror and memory* (Oxford: Oxford University Press, 2006) gives a detailed analysis of the process of remembering for Algerians in France. Anne Donadey has drawn inspiration from Henry Rousso's 'Vichy syndrome' to describe an 'Algeria syndrome', mapping patterns of repression and return in memories of Algeria: '"Une certaine idée de la France": The Algeria Syndrome and struggles over "French' Identity"', in Steven Ungar and Tom Conley, eds., *Identity Papers: Contested nationhood in twentieth century France* (Minneapolis: University of Minnesota Press, 1996), 215.

4 Herman Lebovics, *Bringing the Empire Back Home: France in the global age* (Durham: Duke University Press, 2004), 10.

5 Andreas Huysmans, *Twilight Memories: Marking time in a culture of amnesia* (New York and London: Routledge, 1995), 15.

6 Joshua Cole, 'Entering history: The memory of police violence in Paris, October 1961', in Patricia Lorcin, ed., *Algeria and France: 1800–2000, identity, memory, nostalgia* (New York: Syracuse University Press, 2006), 117–34.

7 Patricia Lorcin discusses Ferrandez's series *Carnets d'Orient* in Chapter 8 in this book.

8 See for example, Cyril Hofstein, 'Mémoires d'Algérie', *Le Figaro*, 10 May 2012, accessed 17 February 2014.

9 Thomas Hofnung, 'France-Algérie: L'Armée fait son exposition de conscience', *Libération*, 25 June 2012, accessed 17 February 2014.

10 Jean Guisnel, 'Le Directeur du Musée de l'Armée: L'Exposition Algerie 1830–1962 est un "travail historique"', *Le Point*, 29 May 2012, accessed 1 January 2014, http://www.lepoint.fr/editos-du-point/jean-guisnel/le-directeur-du-musee-de-l-armee-l-exposition-algerie-1830-1962-est-un-travail-historiq ue-29-05-2012-1466292_53.php.

11 See for example, Raphaëlle Branche and Sylvie Thénault, ed., *La France en guerre 1954–1962: Expériences métropolitaines de la la guerre d'indépendance algérienne* (Paris: Éditions Autrement, 2008).

12 For some sense of the controversy over the number of people killed at the demonstration, see Jean-Paul Brunet, 'Police violence in Paris, October 1961: Historical sources, methods and conclusions', *The Historical Journal* 51, 1 (2008): 195–204.

13 For instance, Yasmina Adi's film, *Ici on noie les Algeriens: 17 octobre 1961* (Paris: Agat Films, 2011).

14 I am yet to ascertain whether the name draws inspiration from Rasputin, the advisor to the Romanovs, though some held that he was a prophet and a visionary.

15 '17.10.1961: un webdoc de Raspouteam', accessed 15 January 2014, http://www.raspouteam.org/1961/credits/17_10_61_dp.pdf.

16 Thomas Wieder, 'François Hollande reconnaît la répression du 17 octobre 1961, critiques à droite', *Le Monde*, 17 October 2012.

17 Wieder, 'François Hollande reconnaît la répression', see Note 16.

18 Wieder, 'François Hollande reconnaît la répression', see Note 16.

19 Pascal Bruckner, *The Tyranny of Guilt: An essay on modern masochism*, trans. Steven Rendall (Princeton: Princeton University Press, 2010), 13.

20 Bruckner, *The Tyranny of Guilt*, see Note 19, 3.

8

France's Nostalgias for Empire[1]

Patricia M. E. Lorcin

The concept of nostalgia in relation to empire is usually analysed by scholars and lay persons alike as a longing for a period of former imperial and colonial glory thus eliding the full spectrum of hegemonic practices that are associated with empire. In the chapter that follows, which focuses on the narratives and practices of France's relationship to the territories of its former empire, I shall argue that there is a distinction to be made between imperial nostalgia and colonial nostalgia.[2] The former is associated with the loss of empire, that is to say the decline of national grandeur and the international power politics connected to economic and political hegemony; whereas the latter is associated with the loss of socio-cultural standing or, to be more precise, the colonial lifestyle. The frequent elision of the two concepts of nostalgia, imperial and colonial, no doubt arises from the fact that a colonial lifestyle, as experienced by settlers in the various corners of the nineteenth and twentieth century European empires, could not have existed without imperialism. Arguably, there is also a gendered dimension to the two concepts. To be sure, present-day indulgence in the emotion or expression of imperial or colonial nostalgia is neither the prerogative of men nor that of women, but, as I argue in my recent monograph, the formative periods of these concepts was contingent on gender.[3] The power brokers of nineteenth- and twentieth-century European empires were almost exclusively male, whereas women, as many scholars of colonialism have demonstrated, were essential to the creation of a sustained colonial lifestyle.[4] Indeed, the dedication of a recent book evoking colonial nostalgia, albeit about Kenya, acknowledged 'the outstanding contribution of the women of Kenya to the making of *their* Country'.[5] This is not to occlude men from the creation of a colonial setting that would give rise to the nostalgia of the post-independence period; rather it is to suggest that nostalgia for the 'great happy family of colonial relations' was closely related to women's vital role in establishing a viable social setting in which Europeans could lay down roots and thrive.

Theorising nostalgia

The concept of nostalgia has a long history. From its seventeenth century beginning as a medical condition described by Johannes Hofer, through its association with melancholy during the Romantic period, to its multiple present day iterations, the etymological origin of nostalgia in the Greek *nostos* (home) and *algos* (pain) suggested (and suggests) sufficient dislocation or discomfort with the present to necessitate an embellished recollection of the past. It is, as Andreea Decíu Rítívoí has characterised it, an imagined evocation of *Yesterday's Self*.[6] But the evocation is not merely personally subjective; it is a collective cultural experience, as Janelle Wilson has pointed out.[7] Fred Davis also distinguishes between the private and the collective, describing the former as shaped by the illusions and recollections of one's personal biography, while the latter is associated with the symbols and devices of a public, familiar and widely shared character, thus making it a deeply social emotion.[8] Finally, nostalgia has been characterised as the resistance of tradition to modernity, as in the culture of capitalism, which splinters the concept into diverse incarnations of class, power and economic displacements. Such are, according to Kathleen Stewart, the 'nostalgias of hegemony or resistance'.[9]

The literary scholar, Svetlana Boym, has complicated the analysis of nostalgia by arguing that the concept is made up of two constitutive parts: *restorative* and *reflective*. She links the former with *nostos*, or the home and the desire to reconstruct aspects of it even if such a goal remains elusive, and the latter to *algia*, or the pain of loss and rueful memory that ensues.[10] Her two-fold typology seeks to illuminate the manipulations and seductions of nostalgia, which, she argues, is both prospective and retrospective. For Boym, nostalgia is not just about displacement and loss of a cherished past, it is also about 'a romance with one's own fantasy', where fantasies of the past are defined by the exigencies of the present.[11] The duality suggested by Boym is particularly useful in elucidating the differences between imperial and colonial nostalgia. Although these two concepts contain aspects of both of Boym's definitions, the balance is different. Imperial nostalgia is more heavily weighted towards the *reflective* dimension, with the *algia* or loss being associated with a hegemonic past. Colonial nostalgia, on the other hand, is more readily associated with the *restorative* dimension, where the *nostos* or yearning for the home is for a past lifestyle.

How do these two nostalgias, imperial and colonial, diverge from neo-imperialism and neo-colonialism? To begin with, whereas the nostalgias of empire suggest an attenuated post-independence relationship that has anodyne overtones, the designation of 'neo' is not only deprecatory but also suggests economic or political ties that are unevenly matched. The difference between neo-imperialism and imperial nostalgia; between neo-colonialism and colonial nostalgia is contingent on time. The prefix 'neo' implies new forms of imperialism or colonialism, whereby the hegemonic practices of the past are redeployed in the sole interests of the former imperial or colonial power to the detriment, real or imagined, of the subordinate nation or area. Both neo-imperialism and neo-colonialism have been used extensively since decolonisation, sometimes with justification but often as a derogatory categorisation of an undesired relationship by critics of the regimes involved.

Post-independence leaders such as Houphouët-Boigny and Leopold Senghor were among a select group of élites from France's African colonies who had taken their seats as deputies in the French National Assembly after the Second World War and prior to independence. As leaders of their newly independent countries, they maintained close relations with France even as they shed the colonial mantle. The case of the Ivory Coast is a good example since the French government's long-time adviser on African affairs, Jacques Foccart – the 'Secret Mastermind in Africa', as the *New York Times* put it in 1997 – created a particularly strong tie with Houphouët-Boigny in the 1960s and 1970s.[12] Hence neo-imperialism, whether it was accurate or not, had a strong resonance in the early post-independence period. This was the golden age of France's privileged relationship with its former African colonies, or what became known as 'Françafrique'.[13] But, as the first generation of leaders died off or were replaced by coups d'états or elections, ties were loosened or broken. From the 1970s onwards, successive French Ministers of Foreign Affairs have announced the relinquishing of their hold on Africa or even suggested the demise of Françafrique, but a relationship, attenuated though it may be, remains: an imperial 'remembrance of things past'.[14] The robustness of the 'neo', with its overt collusion of African heads of state, has been overtaken by the amorphousness of nostalgia where ties still exist but are no longer predicated by the exclusive interests of France.

If the term neo-imperialism has its roots in vigorous post-independence collaborative interests, neo-colonialism is more ambiguous and, I would argue, implausible. It is a misnomer used interchangeably with neo-imperialism, albeit one that is often associated with the movement of people to and from former colonies. For instance, independence ushered in waves of migration between the former colonies and France, whether these were settlers, as in the case of the *pied-noir* exodus from Algeria, or the recently independent peoples who emigrated from the former French colonies for political or economic reasons. After the collapse of the Berlin Wall and the passing of the Schengen Agreement in 1995, emigration from former colonies increased further, creating a backlash in France as reverse colonisation was perceived to be taking place. While this became a leitmotif of the French extreme-right, it had nothing to do with neo-colonialism. At the same time, there was a migration of expatriates and political refugees, particularly to West Africa. Again, the Ivory Coast serves as a pertinent example. The economic boom of the late 1960s and the 1970s – the Ivorian miracle – was characterised by an influx of

French expatriates whose technical expertise, commercial connections and financial investment was encouraged by Houphouët-Boigny. The French presence increased to over 60,000, double the 30,000 of the colonial period. The French were not alone, however. The Palestinian exodus into Lebanon in 1971 following the conflict between the PLO (Palestinian Liberation Organization) and the Jordanian Armed Forces started a diaspora as Lebanese, many of them Maronites, left the country. During the 1975–90 Lebanese civil war, over one million Lebanese left as sectarianism took hold and their country appeared to be disintegrating. They scattered across the globe gravitating to territories such as West Africa where a Lebanese (and Syrian) presence had existed since the end of the nineteenth century. They became involved in commerce and trade helping to fuel the Ivorian economic 'miracle'. Moreover, a flourishing economy drew other investors from all over the world. These were expatriates, not colonials and they were there at the instigation of the Ivorian government, whatever the means they had used to get through the door. As long as the economy was healthy and the country politically stable, the cosmopolitan community of international and multi-national corporations and institutions did not dissipate. But the collapse of the price of cocoa, for which the Ivory Coast was the world's leading exporter, and the oil crises of the late 1970s put paid to the 'Ivorian miracle'. As the country became racked with political instability, the French presence diminished, as did that of the international expatriate community. The era of the 'neos', if it had ever truly existed, was over; had that of nostalgia begun?

Imperial nostalgia

On 7 February 1994, two months after his death, Houphouët-Boigny was laid to rest following a grandiose and very lengthy funeral in the Basilica of Our Lady of Peace in Yamassoukro, the world's largest church, which the defunct leader had had built to the honour of Africa and had subsequently bequeathed to the Vatican. The attendance was as lavish as the setting. Representatives of eighty countries, including twenty-seven heads of state, were among the 7,000 guests who filled the basilica. The seventy-person French delegation had arrived earlier in three passenger planes. A number of Russian transport planes carried the fifty black limousines for the guests from France and the motorcycles of the Republican Guard that would flank the motorcade as it snaked its way to the basilica. Headed by the then president, François Mitterrand, and his Prime Minister, Edouard Balladur, the delegation included every living former Prime Minister; the former President, Valéry Giscard D'Estaing; the President of the European Commission, Jacques Delors; Jacques Foccart, now in his eighties; his successor, Jean-Christophe Mitterrand, President Mitterrand's son; Jacques Chirac, then mayor of Paris and future president of France; and a host of other ministers and public officials. Eighty French journalists accompanied the dignitaries to report on the occasion and the French presence.[15] Also in attendance were Raphaëlle Leygues and Michel Dupuch, the two longest-serving ambassadors to the Ivory Coast, whose ambassadorial residence in Abidjan was adjacent to the Ivorian Presidential residence and who had met regularly with Houphouët-Boigny to discuss 'matters of mutual importance'. Following the funeral, Mitterrand and Balladur held a mini-conference with all the heads of state of the Francophone African countries for discussions about the regional currency, the CFA franc.[16] The funeral appeared to be the swan song of Françafrique. It was also a monumental show of imperial nostalgia, echoing, as it did, the grandiose arrival of French governors and their retinue when, in bygone days, they took up their posts in the colonies. The plumed hats, horse-drawn carriages and military bands, those colourful and awe-inspiring symbols of the power of France's colonial-era presence, had disappeared. But the large French contingent, dressed in suitable shades of mourning, spilling out of multiple aircraft, and arriving in a seemingly endless line of official black limousines was, if not as colourful, certainly no less awe-inspiring. The French still knew how to make their presence felt overseas.

France's imperial nostalgia, however, has not been confined to spectral demonstrations of past imperial force at the state occasions of former colonies, even if they are its most apparent representation. The country's numerous military interventions in Africa over the years are an indicator of France's desire to maintain the prestige associated with its past imperial power. Whether to prop up dictatorial regimes such as that of Omar Bongo (1935–2009) of Gabon, to intervene in Rwanda in 1994 or the implementation of Opération Épervier in 1986, which established a defence agreement between France and Chad to help the former colonial territory contain the encroachment of Libya into Chadian territory, these activities served to send a message to the French public, if not to the world, that France was still a power to be reckoned with in Africa.[17] John Darnton summed it up when writing in the *New York Times* about the French intervention in Rwanda:

among the colonial powers that once ruled Africa, France stands out for its readiness and ability to dispatch troops to a besieged country on the continent . . . France is able to pull off such a manoeuver with swagger and élan. No apologies, no obeisance to sensitivities over sovereignty. The helicopters swoop low over the banana trees and disgorge the patrols of closely cropped camouflaged young men in broad daylight, almost as a matter of right.[18]

The apparent success of the post-independence *pax gallica* in former French colonies in limiting internecine conflict and civilian casualties may well account for the 'swagger and élan' of such unrepentant activity.[19] Nevertheless, Françafrique and France's repeated interventions in Africa, many of which occurred outside the aegis of the United Nations, provided a recurring reminder of her imperial past and intimated a continuation of world-power status.

Two international events changed the shape of France's relationship to its former colonies: the collapse of the Berlin Wall and the attacks on the World Trade Centre on 11 September 2001. Both of these sharpened the concept of French imperial nostalgia. The collapse of the Wall heralded the end of the Cold War and transformed the United States into the sole superpower, perhaps only temporarily but nonetheless ominously for those countries that had relied on the Soviet Union to countermand the ideological and economic encroachment of global capitalism. As a result, France's role as Western gatekeeper to its former territories, primarily in Africa, lost some of its political and diplomatic relevance, even if it continued to maintain a military presence in some of them.[20] Significantly, institutions such as the OAU (Organization of African Unity) or the United Nations now became involved in the relationship between France and its African colonies. In the case of Opération Épervier, for example, the OAU brokered a peace treaty between Chad and Libya in 1988 thus removing the main justification for the operation. The demise of the Cold War changed the paradigms by which the West appraised non-Western territories and its relationship to them. Whereas keeping communism at bay had shaped prevailing Western political and diplomatic paradigms, now maintaining human rights and introducing Western concepts of democracy reconfigured them. Buttressing despotic or brutal heads of state was no longer as necessary or, equally importantly, as desirable. Thus, it was not of interest to prop up leaders such as the President of Chad, Hissene Habré, whose record of human rights left much to be desired. Although Opération Épervier remained in force, France took a backseat position and remained supposedly 'neutral' in subsequent skirmishes between Chad and Libya.

Following the catastrophe of 9/11, France's activities in, and its relations with, its former colonies took a back seat to American endeavours to retaliate for the physical and psychological wounds it had sustained as a result of the attack. What started out as punitive measures to redress the wrong inflicted on its people and wipe out the nerve centre of the attackers in Afghanistan ended up as an exercise in US imperialism, as American forces moved into Iraq in 2003 on the supposed pretext of weapons of mass destruction. Unlike Britain, which allied itself with the United States, France, to its temporary economic detriment in the United States, did not.[21] Ultimately, Iraq's nuclear weapons were shown not to exist and the mismanagement of the 'occupation' produced disastrous results as the social fabric of the country disintegrated, thousands were killed and the country descended into sectarianism and acute instability. Iraq was not, and had never been, the purview of France. Involvement, nostalgic or otherwise, was not *de rigueur*. Since 2010, when it became clear that Barack Obama's overseas activities would not depart radically from those of his predecessor, France has once more started to reconfigure its relationship with areas of former imperial influence. Like other former imperial powers, it operates in the shade of US imperialism. As France has reduced its troops in the various posts in Africa, the United States has increased its presence. France's neo-imperialism, if it exists at all, is much attenuated. By contrast, French imperial nostalgia lingers on.

On 14 July 2010, to mark what President Sarkozy declared was the fiftieth anniversary of the end of the French Empire, the Bastille Day military parade included troops from thirteen of France's former African colonies. The decorum of the event was marred by extensive criticism of what was deemed to be an unpardonable display of nostalgia, an unseemly demonstration of continued French interference in Africa, and a betrayal of Sarkozy's pre-election promise that France would cease to 'meddle' in African affairs.[22] One of the few African leaders whose troops boycotted the event was the then Ivorian President, Laurent Gbagbo. One year later, following Gbagbo's ousting and the accession – with a little help from France – of Alassane Outtara to the Ivorian presidency, a French mission headed by Prime Minister, François Fillon, arrived in Abidjan to redress the low point in Franco-Ivorian relations suffered under Gbagbo.[23] 'We are determined to remain your closest partner and the many companies that came with me will tell you so,' Fillon declared during his visit.[24] The new relationship was to be complex-free (*une relation décomplexée*), although he reminded his interlocutors that it was a relationship based on a 'very long-standing friendship' (*une amitié très ancienne*) and an equally long-standing historical connection.[25] When the Ivorian paper, *Notre Voie*, described the visit as France calling on one of its sub-prefectures, Fillon responded that France's involvement in the Ivory Coast was by no means 'the return of the colonialists' and to call it such was using 'out-dated software'.[26] Africa, he concluded, was evolving towards modernity and it was France's ambition to assist the Ivory Coast in becoming even more modern.[27] The evocation of out-dated software was no doubt calculated to situate a 'modern' Fillon in the technological mainstream, but the suggestion of bringing modernity to less-than-truly-modern places brought to mind a leitmotif of the *mission civilisatrice*. Nostalgia, it seemed, would cling resolutely to evocations of relationships past.

In May 2012, François Hollande was elected president and France's relationship to her former colonial territories shifted again. The advent of a Socialist president crystallised the hopes of a number of African leaders. Immediately following the election, the Senegalese Francophone web portal, *Rewmi*, posted the following headline: 'François Hollande, President. A new hope for Africa'. The daily newspaper *Les Dépêches de Brazzaville* hopefully anticipated that the new president might provide 'a different face to the historic relations' that existed between the two countries and create a more balanced relationship by putting an end to the 'relations of opaque influences (*relations d'influence opaques*) between France and its ex-Francophone colonies'. The *Gabon Libre*, on the other hand, was more clear-sighted, declaring that it was 'illusory to imagine' that the past would be put to rest by 'the apparition of a *deus ex machina*, by the name of Hollande, as a number of Africans from the continent and the diaspora naively believe'.[28]

Nevertheless, Hollande appeared to be fulfilling African hopes for a change during his October 2012 official visit to Senegal, his first to Africa. In his address to the National Assembly in Dakar on 12 October he elaborated on the West's particular preoccupations since 9/11: democracy and the respect for equal rights. He reminded his audience that Africa was the cradle of humanity. He commended Senegalese democracy and stated that 'the time of Françafrique [is] over, [for] there [is] Africa [and] there [is] the partnership between France and Africa based on respect, openness (*clarté*) and solidarity'. Unlike Sarkozy, whose arrogance and lack of sensitivity had led him to declare that 'African man had not yet entered history', Hollande emphasised the fact that Africa was 'the birthplace of humanity' and stressed that he had no intention of preaching morality to Africans, who 'were partners and friends'. He raised the question of the crisis in Mali and, pointing to the horrors perpetrated there, stressed the fact it had to be resolved by Africans. The support of international organisations such as the OAU, the EU and the UN would help to achieve a resolution, but France would restrict itself to 'logistical support'.[29] This would not be long in coming.

In the meantime, in December 2012, Hollande attempted to lay France's imperial past to rest by choosing to pay his first North African official visit to Algeria, rather than Morocco, formerly the venue of choice for visits by French heads of state. Addressing the Algerian parliament on 20 December he denounced the injustices and brutality of France's colonial past in Algeria but did not go as far as apologising for them. This mollified some of France's detractors but dashed the hopes of those who had wanted an outright apology.[30] If interring one of the worst chapters of French colonial history was the apparent aim of Hollande's visit, French economic interests were, if less discernible, nonetheless salient. For the first time since independence China had surpassed France in aid to Algeria, a fact that was certainly at the back of Hollande's mind.[31] Additionally there was the need to maintain good relations to safeguard the continued flow to Europe of Algerian gas through the TransMed pipeline running from the complex that lay along the border with Mali, a factor that was significant in France's upcoming intervention in the country.

Within weeks of the Algerian visit, France was once more flexing its military muscles in Africa. Following the Malian President, Dioncounda Traoré's, request for assistance in early 2013 to combat 'Islamist jihadists', who were in control of the north of his country, Hollande responded that 'a fatal blow had been dealt to the very existence of Mali'. He added that it was unacceptable for France and the international community to sit by and let the country be overrun. Although the UN passed the resolution Hollande had sought to sanction international intervention, action was not envisaged until an international force could be mustered.[32] As the situation escalated, Hollande took the decision to instigate Operation Serval to beat back the 'terrorists' who were threatening the country. By 11 January, French troops were in Mali. In early February, Hollande, accompanied by his foreign and defence ministers, paid a triumphal visit to Timbuktu and Bamako. The delegation was greeted by cheering crowds waving French flags. A member of the welcoming committee, Moustapha Ben Essayati, seemed to sum up the general enthusiasm when he declared: 'If I had only one wish it would be that the French army stays in the Sahara, that they create a base here.'[33] Imperial nostalgia in the form of a perceived past *pax gallica* was not only the prerogative of France and the French.

In an interview in June 2013, Isabelle Lasserre and Thierry Oberlé, two journalists from *Le Figaro*, were interviewed about their book, *Notre guerre secrète au Mali*.[34] Lasserre stated that French intervention in the area had been on the cards since 2008–9, and that various scenarios had been envisaged if an opportune moment occurred that merited intervention. The 2013 'jihadist' activity in the north was that opportunity. Terrorists had to be kept at bay, of course, but there were also valuable uranium deposits that needed to be safeguarded, to say nothing of the Algerian gas complex. France's concerns about safeguarding the Aïn Amenas gas field had materialised when the rebels had captured the complex in retaliation for France's intervention in Mali. The 'jihadist' attack prompted the deployment of a further 3,500 troops. Nevertheless, in spite of reservations from scholars like Immanuel Wallerstein and criticisms from the public, Hollande did not envisage France's military remaining indefinitely and anticipated a quick handover to African-led troops.[35]

By May 2013, Hollande considered Operation Serval to have achieved its goal. In a television interview broadcast on 31 May he stated that the intervention had been 'a military and practical success', adding that with forthcoming elections in the Sahel these achievements would be followed by 'political success'. He reminded his viewers that the object had been to liberate Mali from the hold of 'terrorists' and that the UN would soon be taking over the peacekeeping.[36] On 5 June, Hollande was awarded the 2013 Felix Houphouët-Boigny UNESCO peace prize for his initiative in Mali and, in particular, for saving the World Heritage site of Timbuktu, ancient seat of Islamic learning. The ceremony was attended by a number of presidents from former French African colonies.[37] In presenting the prize to Hollande, the director general of UNESCO, Irina Bokova declared:

> Your decision to stand by Mali – at the request of President Traoré and with the support of the United Nations – and to protect the peoples and culture of the country inspires us all. This is a reminder that what brings us together is greater than that which sets us apart, be it our identity, language or religion . . . UNESCO saved the temples of Egypt and rebuilt the Mostar Bridge. UNESCO will rebuild the mausoleums of Mali.[38]

What, if anything, does saving a World Heritage site tell us about imperial nostalgia? Saving historic sites for posterity has not been the sole prerogative of UNESCO. In the mid-nineteenth century, the French explorer, Henri

Mouhot, stumbled on Angkor Wat. By the end of the nineteenth century when the area had been absorbed into French Indochina, the 'rediscovery' of Angkor was being vaunted as an example of imperial prowess. The French had 'saved' a vital part of Cambodia's heritage, implying that Cambodia needed France to protect its national interests and, by becoming part of Indochina, it would be safeguarded in more than one way by the French.[39] Saving the magnificence of civilisations past, whether it comprises edifices, documents or any other significant markers, is a commendable pursuit and should be actively encouraged. Unlike the colonial period where a measure of pillaging was part of the 'conservation' and there was limited access to 'saved' sites, World Heritage sites can be enjoyed by anyone with the wherewithal to visit them. What is unsettling in this case is the hype, imperial or otherwise, that suggests that the West is paramount in the accomplishment of such activities. There were discomforting echoes of such a sentiment in Bokova's citation for Hollande.

Still, we might legitimately ask whether France's operation in Mali, sanctioned as it was by the UN and including the involvement of an African military force, can be considered an exercise in imperial nostalgia. A number of aspects of the operation make it so. The first is the renewal (and strengthening) of its gatekeeper ties with a former colony. The second is the international kudos that accrued to France as a result of the operation, demonstrating its political and diplomatic impact beyond the borders of Europe. Finally, in much the same way as the Falkland war gave Margaret Thatcher a popularity boost in the early 1980s, so too the French invasion of Mali gave Hollande a temporary boost in his popularity ratings, which had plummeted during his first six months in office. France could, it seemed, still command international respect reminiscent of times past.

Colonial nostalgia

How is colonial nostalgia different from imperial nostalgia and in what ways do the two intersect? Unlike imperial nostalgia, which concerns the practices, activities and utterances of politicians and statesmen with an eye on the world stage, colonial nostalgia is connected to reminiscences and evocations of a past lifestyle and an idealised vision of the inter-cultural relations within the colony that existed at that time. It is important, at this juncture, to distinguish between colonial myths, and the themes and activities inherent to nostalgia. The basic difference, as I interpret it, is that colonial nostalgia is the embellished memory of lived experience, whereas colonial myth is either the misinterpretation or incomprehension of the colonised territory and its people or the fabrication of a non-existent dimension of the colonial experience.[40] To be sure, colonial nostalgia can incorporate colonial myths, but it is a collective sentiment that remains grounded in personal or familial experience in a way that myth does not. Unlike imperial nostalgia, which is all-encompassing insofar as it harks back to, or echoes, periods of global hegemony when manifestations and discursive patterns were fairly consistent, colonial nostalgia is more regionally specific being predicated on differences in the colonial 'heritage', on the variations of colonial paradigms and on generational distinctions. Whereas the central premise of colonial nostalgia is relatively constant whatever the metropolitan or regional focus, namely the occluded memory of the exactions inflicted on the colonised people, the belief in benevolent modernity and relative bonhomie of the colonial lifestyle, the differences lie in the way in which such nostalgia is lived and articulated. The forms and genres by which colonial nostalgia is expressed are narrative, visual and, in some instances, even institutional.

Colonial nostalgia associated with any area was at its most intense immediately following decolonisation. Where decolonisation had been prolonged and violent, as in the case of Algeria, the nostalgia could also be extremely bitter as the early titles of settler memoirs such as *Déracinés* or *Et à l'heure de notre mort* suggest.[41] Indeed, the most extreme example of colonial nostalgia is associated with the *pied-noir* communities in France. Shaped originally by the Algerian war of independence, when over one million settlers flooded back to France in the space of a few months, it developed a veritable credo, which was eventually dubbed *nostalgérie*. Over the ensuing fifty years, resentment over exile and loss has been tempered with a concomitant proliferation of fiction, non-fiction, coffee-table books, films, monuments, and websites. There is even a religious dimension to *nostalgérie*: every year, pilgrimages take place to sites reminiscent of, or related to, the colonial past in Algeria.[42] More complex than the colonial nostalgia of most other areas, its myriad ramifications and, on occasion, acute bitterness are due to the splintering of every faction of colonial society during the eight ferocious years of conflict and the ensuing settler exodus.[43] In comparison with other forms of colonial nostalgia, the most striking aspect of *nostalgérie* is that it has not dissipated over time. From expressing the sentiments of a marginalised component of French society, the nostalgia of the *pied-noir* community has morphed into a discourse that has permeated the cultural, social and political mainstream. It is not possible, in a short chapter, to cover the extensive manifestations of *nostalgérie*, but one indication of the way in which it is being absorbed into the cultural fabric of France is evidenced by the ten-volume graphic novel series by Jacques Ferrandez, *Carnets d'Orient*, covering the history of colonial Algeria from conquest to decolonisation.[44]

The significance of the graphic novel to historical representation has engaged scholars from a wide range of disciplines. Since the publication of Art Spiegelman's two *Maus* volumes and Joe Sacco's *Palestine*, scholars have deconstructed the aesthetic and narrative dimensions of such works to elucidate historical moments and events.[45] As Edward Said stated, in the preface to *Palestine*, what set Sacco [and Spiegelman's] work[s] apart from the usual graphic novel and set a new trend was the focus on 'history's victims'. Most comics, he added 'routinely conclude with someone's victory, the triumph of good over evil, or the routing of the unjust by the just, or even the marriage of two young lovers'.[46] If Spiegelman and Sacco eschewed triumphalist or heroic narratives, it was their engagement, head on, with contemporary historical and political issues that made their work so relevant; issues that were not only the preoccupation of scholars but also of a wider public. The visual nature of graphic novels responds to a generation for whom visual representation has achieved unprecedented power to shape ideas and opinions. Thus their popularity rests on the fact they are 'empathetic reflections of today's communicative mode . . . distributed across media'.[47] As Seamus O'Malley states in an article on the graphic novel, *From Hell*, about Jack the Ripper, historical representation in the graphic novel 'deftly registers the presentness of the past because of the language of comics'.[48] Such a statement is particularly relevant to Ferrandez's series, in which history and memory are interwoven in nostalgic depictions, which respond to the *pied-noir* predicament of being part of, yet apart from, French society. French by nationality but 'Algerian' by historical memory, *pied-noir* memory has been consciously kept alive as nostalgia.

Jacques Ferrandez was born in Algiers in 1955 but grew up in the south of France, where he was trained at the École nationale d'art decorative in Nice. In addition to his graphic novels on Algeria, Ferrandez, who considers himself to be a 'Mediterranean', has converted literary classics into graphic novels, in much the same way as *Classics Illustrated* converted English classics into comics between 1941 and 1971.[49] With the exception of *Djemilah*, the first book of the *Carnets d'Orient* series, each volume is prefaced by a well-known personality, most of whom are in some way connected to Algeria. Their prefaces serve to endorse the authenticity of the narrative.[50] Algerians are certainly not absent from the series, but the narrative is that of the French history of Algeria.[51] Nor does Ferrandez avoid showing the cruelty and racism of his compatriots in their relations with the local population, whether Arab, Berber or Jew, although such negativity is nearly always mitigated by the presence of a close relationship between an Algerian and a French person, whether it is in the form of male companionship or in a sexually-charged heterosexual relationship. The series opens in 1830 with Joseph Constant, a French artist, falling in love with an Algerian woman, Djemilah, and ends in the last four volumes with a love affair between Octave, a former French paratrooper and Samia, an Algerian medical student, who eventually has his child. Whereas in the first instance the love affair between Joseph and Djemilah leads to frustration as Jacques cannot marry or even live with Djemilah, it ends well for Samia and Octave who end up together in Paris, thus mirroring the alleged evolution of the relationship between the 'coloniser' and the 'colonised'. The aesthetic tone of the early novels is reminiscent of nineteenth-century Orientalist imagery, mimicking the Orientalism of the time. Jacques, who keeps a diary, which eventually resurfaces in the final volumes of the series, ends the first book with the following entry:

Following my experience in Algeria, I have unceasingly sought to paint the mysteries and the beauties of the Orient . . . The Orient is a woman, who sometimes offers herself and sometimes refuses to do so. The Orient is a woman one wants to take and possess, going as far as rape. The Orient is a woman who will always elude us.[52]

The last sentence of the 'entry', which foretells the end of both the historical and narrative sagas, encapsulates the nostalgia that is threaded through the series; a nostalgia of the missed opportunity of successful and permanent co-habitation. The series follows the historical trajectory of the colony fairly faithfully but it is a French story. Furthermore, six of the ten volumes concern the period 1954–62, although only four focus specifically on the events of the war mirroring one of the major historiographical predilections of scholars of colonial Algeria. Many of the narrative images in these latter four volumes appear to be reproductions of scenes from Pontecorvo's film, *The Battle of Algiers* and Camus' unfinished novel (and the film) *Le Premier homme*, even if post-1960 events that have recently been the subject of debate or scholarship, such as the October 1961 massacre of Algerians in Paris, are also included. The narrative of Samia and Octave, which is threaded through the final volumes, is a constant reminder that a union of the two culturally different peoples might have been possible. That Ferrandez focuses so much of his 'history' on the period 1954–62 is hardly surprising. It was, after all, the crucible of *nostalgérie*.

Unlike the works of nostalgia written by the first generation of the settler 'diaspora', Ferrandez's work has the distance and detachment of the second or third generation *pied-noir*, who grew up in France but was nonetheless nourished by the nostalgic reminiscences and historical memories of the community.[53] He does not apportion blame, as did many of the works – pro- or anti-colonial, nostalgic or otherwise – that emerged in the post-independence period. Rather, he tries to present a picture of human foibles and passions, both negative and positive. In doing so, he attenuates the strain of nostalgia that runs through the series. It is a powerful work that will serve to inform generations of BD fanatics, young and old, of France's Algerian 'adventure', emphasising what could have been but wasn't. Is it intentional – or merely unfortunate – that the periods of conquest and colonial apogee are reduced to four of the ten volumes? The glossing over of the excesses of colonisation – the smoking in caves of the Ouled Riah tribe, the rapacious land expropriations in particular after the Kabyle revolt of 1870–1, the waves of violent anti-Semitism and ferocious repressions such as that after Sétif – help to create the nostalgic vision of opportunities lost by both sides instead of a more clear-sighted one of freedom lost by one and power gained by another.

If Algeria was subject to the longest period of French colonial rule in the nineteenth and twentieth centuries, it was not the only site of violent decolonisation. French Indochina presents an additional paradigm of colonial nostalgia. The transformation of French Indochina into present-day Vietnam was as complicated as it was protracted, involving not only the French, but also the presence of the Japanese during World War Two and, after 1954, the Americans. Nostalgia in the immediate aftermath of the departure of the French, following Dien Bien Phu, was clouded by the events of the 1940–5 period and the ensuing struggles of the Cold War. By 1975, when the Vietnamese had won their war against the Americans and united their country, French colonial nostalgia had the advantage of being filtered through an opaque lens caused by the atrocities and devastation of the American war. A good example of this is Marguerite Duras' fictionalised autobiography, *L'Amant*, first published in 1984, which does not entirely fit into the canon of pure colonial nostalgia, as it presents some of the seamier sides of colonial existence. The novel recounts the affair of a young, nubile French girl from the lower echelons of colonial society with an unattractive but wealthy Chinese man. The novel depicts colonial racism as an inferiority complex, whereby the girl's family, psychologically diminished by its class and relative poverty in comparison to the lover's wealth, is not only disparaging but also truculent or hostile in their behaviour towards him. The film of the novel, for which Duras wrote the screenplay, creates a more compelling picture of the relationship. It transforms the homely lover of the novel into a handsome and desirable suitor (as portrayed by Tony Leung Ka-fa) thus diminishing the evident class cupidity of the girl's family and highlighting the erotic appeal of the affair. In so doing, the film creates a nostalgic metaphor of France's desire for the riches and beauties of Indochina. The transposition of the novel to the film brings to the fore a colonial nostalgia that is less apparent in the novel.

Films are a privileged genre for the depiction of colonial nostalgia. This is true even when they problematise the colonial moment by including conflictual situations, whether these are revolts and their aftermath or the tensions and racism of everyday life. In Régis Wargnier's *Indochine* (1992), for example, the focal event of the film is the 1930 Yen Bay uprising and its aftermath. The central relationship, which is written like a palimpsest over the film's politics, is between the wealthy plantation owner, the beautiful Éliane Devries, and her equally beautiful adopted daughter, Camille, a scion of the Nguyen dynasty whose parents were killed in an accident. It is a parable of the colonial relationship and its dénouement. The two women symbolise their respective nations and it is this connection that constitutes the underlying current of colonial nostalgia. Éliane brings up Camille as her own daughter inculcating her with French values and providing her with a French education. But she is 'betrayed' in the end for Camille joins the resistance and ends up in the upper echelons of the political élite of what eventually becomes the Democratic Republic of Vietnam. During the metamorphosis from pampered protégé to hard-headed revolutionary, Camille has a son whom she abandons and who is brought up by Éliane. At the end of the film, when Camille's son has the opportunity of meeting – and perhaps reuniting with – his birth mother it does not work out and he returns to Éliane, acknowledging her as his 'true' mother. Wargnier's critique of French colonialism in Indochina, as depicted by the events of Yen Bay and the ensuing repression, is attenuated by the overlying representational narrative of a beneficently maternal France faced with the faithlessness and deception of its wayward colonial 'child'.[54]

Alongside film, colonial nostalgia has been renewed by tourism. As Michael Hall and Hazel Tucker have aptly remarked, tourism 'both reinforces and is embedded in post-colonial relationships'.[55] Intrinsic to the tourist industry is the promotion of an area's heritage. Colonial nostalgia in this context extends further than that expressed by former settlers or colonial officials as it attracts travellers, most of whom have never experienced life in the colonies. In the immediate aftermath of independence, newly-created countries sought to eradicate the traces of colonialism by letting colonial buildings fall into ruin or changing street names and other vestiges of colonisation. Towards the end of the twentieth century, however, governments realised that there was profit to be made by attracting tourists in search of their colonial 'heritage'. The result was the rapid commodification of colonial nostalgia.[56] Two examples from the possible choices of former French colonies will suffice for our purposes: the Ivory Coast and Vietnam.

FIGURE 1 *Former Governor's House, now a museum in Grand Bassam, Ivory Coast.*

Photograph by the author.

FIGURE 2 *Former colonial residence in Grand Bassam, Ivory Coast.*
Photograph by the author.

FIGURE 3A *Monument commemorating the 1893 yellow fever epidemic in Grand Bassam, Ivory Coast. The monument was renovated in the summer of 2012, and this picture was taken after the renovation.*

Photograph by Affoh Guenneguez; reproduced with permission.

FIGURE 3B *A close-up of the yellow fever memorial. The caption reads 'France remembers its children, fallen in Côte d'Ivoire'.*

Photograph by Affoh Guenneguez; reproduced with permission.

FIGURE 4 *Ruins of colonial residences along Grand Bassam Beach.*
Photograph by the author.

FIGURE 5 *An Ivorian wood sculpture.*
Photograph by the author.

FIGURE 6 *Town Hall, Ho Chi Minh City, Vietnam.*
Photograph by the author.

FIGURE 7 *Colonial Institute, Ho Chi Minh City, Vietnam.*
Photograph by the author.

FIGURE 8 *Opera House, Hanoi, Vietnam.*
Photograph by the author.

FIGURE 9 *Government Guest House, Hanoi, Vietnam.*
Photograph by the author.

In sub-Saharan Africa one of the most evocative tourist destinations, both for its colonial vestiges and for the symbolic dimension of its crumbling ruins, is Grand Bassam, the first French capital of the Ivory Coast. Visiting the Governor's House, now a museum (Figure 1); ambling through the dilapidation of the old French quarter along rue Treich-Laplane (Figure 2) (named after the explorer and first colonial governor); stopping at a monument commemorating the 1893 yellow fever epidemic (Figures 3a and 3b); or wandering through the crumbling colonial ruins along the beach (Figure 4). These all evoke strong feelings of a past once distinguished but now faded. A few former colonial houses have been restored, usually by wealthy Ivorians for their personal use, others have been, or are about to be, restored with the aid of overseas funds. In 2012, for example, the French, under the aegis of UNESCO, undertook to renovate the Bassam sub-prefecture and the yellow fever monument. Grand Bassam had, that year, been designated a World Heritage Site, elevating this former colonial capital to one of the world's most desirable tourist destinations.[57] The commodification of colonial nostalgia continues in the local arts and craft. These cater to the tourist souvenir trade and create artefacts redolent of the colonial period that tourists take home as souvenirs of their holiday and times past (Figure 5).

In Vietnam the atmospheric evocation is different. There is little sense of a dilapidated past. Former colonial buildings, most of which were built in the French architectural style of the early 1900s, have been carefully restored and maintained for present-day use. In Ho Chi Minh City, for example, there is a noticeable similarity between the town hall (Figure 6) and its equivalent in Paris. The republican friezes and symbols, which adorned official buildings, have not been removed but refurbished (Figures 6 and 7). Similarly, in Hanoi, the opera house (Figure 8) or the present Government Guest House (Figure 9) are examples of buildings restored for governmental or public use. Tourists who visit the well-kept former colonial residential quarters get a flavour of the way in which the French lived and asserted their socio-economic identity on this beautiful city. In spite of its distance from France, the draw of nostalgia is apparent in the increasing number of French visitors (99,000 in 2001 and 219,721 in 2012).[58] Apart from Southeast Asian and Pacific tourists, whose preponderance is due to their residential proximity to Vietnam, the two most representative nations are the United States and France, both with strong imperial links to the country. For some tourists, the attraction of former colonial sites is shaped by a quest for exoticism. This is often a consequence of wealth: it is now possible to mimic the power of former times through travel. For others, tourism is an attempt to recapture history, to relive nostalgically a moment in the past. The commodification of 'colonial heritage' by the governments of former colonies exploits this type of nostalgia by allowing tourists to indulge their fantasies of what colonisation was (or should have been).

One of the consequences of these overlapping forms of French colonial nostalgia has been a growing interest in 'protecting' the memory of colonialism. The desire to institutionalise colonial memory started fairly soon after decolonisation. The impulse went beyond the lodging of official documents in the national archives, in particular for the *pieds-noirs* from Algeria. The Centre du Documentation historique sur l'Algérie (CDHA) grew out of a 1974 organisation established to collect documents and memorabilia connected to the colonial period. Today, it is housed in the Maison du Maréchal Juin in Aix-en-Provence and has extended its collections to include the whole of the Maghreb and its peoples during the colonial period.[59] Additionally in France, the Sainte Claire convent in Perpignan, which now houses the 'Wall of the Disappeared [of the Algerian War]', is the projected site for a *pied-noir* museum. Although the main objective of these institutions is historical insofar as they serve as a repository of documentation for historians, all contain a significant number of personal documents, memoirs and reminiscences of 'times past' that blur the boundaries between historical memory and colonial nostalgia, between fact and fiction.

The institutionalisation of nostalgia took another turn in 2005 when the nostalgic trope of colonial benevolence came close to being written into French law. Article 4 of the law of 23 February stated:

That University research programs should grant the French overseas presence, notably in North Africa, the place it deserves in history.

That the school curriculum in particular should acknowledge the positive aspects of the French overseas presence, particularly in North Africa, and acknowledge the history and sacrifices of the combatants from those areas who fought in the French armed forces.

That cooperation to access oral and written sources between France and its former overseas territories be encouraged.[60]

Its abrogation, following a widespread campaign, prevented its ratification but it was nonetheless an indication that the need to institutionalise colonial memory and colonial nostalgia had acquired a significant political dimension.

Beyond nostalgia?

A sentiment of loss of power or status underpins the nostalgias of both empire and colony. Whereas the former is manifested at the national level by statements and practices associated with lost transnational dominance and international supremacy, evidence of the latter is more personal and is associated with socio-economic deprivations or changes. Both are, of course, manifestations of a historical memory whose 'memory excisions' serve to occlude or diminish the histories of dominated lands and peoples and the manner in which that domination took place. As such, they differ from the 'forgetting' involved in the narrower historical memory of the nation whose erasures are territorially specific and are concerned with the consolidation of the historical template of the nation rather than its global outreach.[61] Furthermore, the occlusion or highlighting of episodes, events and personalities involved in national historical memory are contingent either on their relevance and importance to present-day events, which usually involve the need to bind national groups or the actual nation together (such as national, political party or religious commemorations and celebrations), or are concerned with the healing of national wounds (such as the memory of the two World Wars). Imperial nostalgia and colonial nostalgia, on the other hand, are concerned only with loss and the concomitant need to recover prestige or a sense of self-worth in the face of quasi-universal condemnation of Europe's imperial and colonial episodes.

The *nostalgérie* of the *pied-noir* community in France has made it a point of honour to keep the memory of Algeria alive.[62] Colonial nostalgia associated with other territories, however, will inevitably weaken as colonial actors and their progeny disappear. First-generation colonial nostalgia will be swept into the archives even while its commodification in an attenuated and anodyne form continues to cater to France's colonialist epigones. Imperial nostalgia, on the other hand, has potentially longer staying power, waxing and waning in response to national exigencies, whether they are geared to underline national prestige, as in the case of the French presence at Houphouet-Boigny's funeral, or French interventions in Africa that take place in the face of international hegemonic decline. As the European imperial epoch recedes, the manifestation of imperial or colonial nostalgia is merely a stage in the historicising trajectory of a past whose true definition has yet to be properly incorporated into the history of the nation.

Notes

1 Parts of this article appeared in *Historical Reflections/Réflexions historiques* 39, 3 (2013) under the title 'Imperial nostalgia; Colonial nostalgia: Differences of theory, similarities of practice'. Whereas that article focused on Britain and France, this article is a much-expanded version of the French focus. The previously published sections appear here with the permission of *Historical Reflections*.

2 Imperial nostalgia in the context of this article is the nostalgia associated with nineteenth- and twentieth-century European overseas imperialism, not with the imperial nostalgia that is associated with empires internal to Europe such as the Austro-Hungarian or Russian Empires. I do not discuss European legacies in former imperial territories, the works on which are legion. For a very recent example, see Kwasi Kwarteng, *Ghosts of Empire. Britain's legacies in the modern world* (London: Bloomsbury, 2011).

3 Patricia M. E. Lorcin, *Historicizing Colonial Nostalgia: European women's narratives of colonial Algeria and Kenya 1900-Present* (New York: Palgrave, 2012).

4 For women's role in the foundation of colonial nostalgia, see Lorcin, *Historicizing Colonial Nostalgia*, Note 3. For women's roles in the French colonial enterprise, see Julia Ann Clancy-Smith and Frances Gouda, eds., *Domesticating the Empire: Race, gender, and family life in French and Dutch colonialism* (Charlottesville, VA: University Press of Virginia, 1998); Yvonne Knibiehler and Régine Goutalier, *Les Femmes au temps des colonies* (Paris: Stock, 1985); Nupur Chaudhuri and Margaret Strobel, *Western Women and Imperialism: Complicity and resistance* (Bloomington, IN: Indiana University Press, 1992); Jeanne Faure-Sardet, *Mosaïques: Impressions, contes, nouvelles et souvenirs*, (Algiers: Fontana, n.d.); Rebecca Rogers, 'Telling stories about the colonies: British and French women in Algeria in the nineteenth century', *Gender & History* 21, 1 (2009); Rebecca Rogers, *A Frenchwoman's Imperial Story. Madame Luce in nineteenth-century Algeria* (Stanford, CA: Stanford University Press, 2013).

5 Nigel Pavitt, *Kenya, a Country in the Making 1880-1940* (London: W.W. Norton & Co., 2008), emphasis added.

6 Andreea Decíu Rítívoí, *Yesterday's Self: Nostalgia and the immigrant identity* (Lanham, MD: Rowman & Littlefield, 2002).

7 Janelle L. Wilson, *Nostalgia: Sanctuary of meaning* (Lewisburg, PA: Bucknell University Press, 2005), 31.

8 Fred Davis, *Yearning for Yesterday. A sociology of nostalgia* (London: The Free Press, 1979), 122.

9 Kathleen Stewart, 'Nostalgia – a polemic', *Cultural Anthropology* 3, 3 (1988): 227–41.

10 Svetlana Boym, *The Future of Nostalgia* (New York: Basic Books, 2001), xviii.

11 Boym, *The Future of Nostalgia*, see Note 10, xiii–xvi.

12 Charles Whitney, 'Jacques Foccart dies at 83; Secret mastermind in Africa', *New York Times*, 20 March 1997.

13 Houphouët-Boigny was the first leader to use the term Françafrique in a positive sense.

14 For the progression of the changing attitudes, see James-William Gbaguidi, 'Françafrique. La rupture commencera-t-elle par le Tchad?', *Courrier International*, 13 July 2011; and Julia Küntzie, 'Afrique. Avec Hollande, la fin de la françafrique?', *Courrier International*, 11 May 2012.

15 My thanks to Claude Philippe Lorcin, then Press Attaché at the French Embassy in Abidjan and organiser of the activities of the press contingent of the delegation, for information regarding the transport details. See also Jean-Karim Fall, 'Le dernier homage à Houphouët-Boigny', *Le Monde*, 3 February 1994; Frederic Fritscher, 'Le dernier et long voyage de Félix Houphouët-Boigny', *Le Monde*, 8 February 1994; Kenneth Noble, 'For Ivory Coast's founder. Lavish funeral', *The New York Times*, 9 February 1994; and on the tenth anniversary of his death, Muhammed Junior Ouattara, 'La Mort d'Houphouët Boigny', *Jeune Afrique*, 6 December 2004.

16 Fall, 'Le Dernier homage à Houphouët-Boigny', see Note 15. The Acronym CFA now means Communauté financière africaine. It originally stood for Colonies françaises d'Afrique.

17 Operation Épervier took place on the nights of 13–14 February 1986 at the
    behest of the Chadian President Hissène Habré and the French Defence
    Minister at the time, Paul Quilès, to contain the encroachment of Libya into
    Chadian territory. The bone of contention was the uranium-rich Aozou strip.
    The Chadian Operation Épervier should not be confused with a similarly
    named 2004 anti-corruption operation in the Cameroons, which did not
    involve French intervention.

18 John Darnton, 'Intervening with elan and no regrets', *The New York Times*,
    26 June 1994.

19 In the period 1960 to 1990 the number of victims of repressions or massacres
    per 10,000 in former French colonies was 35; in former Anglophone colonies it
    was 790; in former Belgian colonies it was 3,000; and in former Portuguese
    colonies it was 4,000. Stephen Smith, 'Nodding and winking: Françafrique',
    London Review of Books 32, 3 (2010): 10–12.

20 In Chad, Senegal, the Ivory Coast, Central African Republic and Djibouti.

21 This was the time of 'freedom fries' and wholesale disposal of French wines
    down the drain.

22 Lizzy Davies, 'Nicolas Sarkozy accused of colonial nostalgia over Bastille Day
    parade', *The Guardian*, 13 July 2010. In my view if nostalgia were to be
    imputed to the event, it constitutes imperial not colonial nostalgia. Sarkozy's
    ambiguous attitude to Africa and to France's colonial past was evident in the
    speech he gave at the University of Dakar on 26 July 2007 when he
    acknowledged the violence and injustice of the colonial period while
    patronisingly declaring that 'African man had not yet entered history' but still
    remained 'nostalgically wedded to the lost paradise of childhood'. 'Allocution
    de Nicolas Sarkozy, prononcée à l'Université de Dakar', 29 July 2007, accessed
    22 May 2012, http://www.afrik.com/article12199.html (author's translation
    from the French).

23 For an account of Fillon's visit see: Philippe Bernard, 'A Abidjan, François Fillon
    celebre le retour de la France, "Partenaire de reference" de la Côte d'Ivoire', *Le
    Monde*, 16 July 2011 and Thomas Hofnung, 'Offensive Française à Abidjan',
    Libération, 16 July 2011.

24 AFP Correspondent, 'French PM in Ivory Coast to pledge support', *Agence
    France Presse*, 14 July 2011.

25 Diarrassouba Sory, 'François Fillon (Premier Ministre Français): "Aujourd'Hui,
    Nos Deux Pays, Engagent Une Relation Décomplexée"', *Le Nouveau Réveil*,
    16 July 2011.

26 D.D., 'François Fillon à Abidjan aujourd'hui: La France vient visiter sa "Sous-
    Préfecture"', *Notre Voie*, 14 July 2011. Republished on *Abidjan.net*, accessed
    12 March 2011, http://news.abidjan.net/h/404466.html.

27 Abdoulaye Touré, 'Coopération France–Côte D'ivoire / François Fillon: "Ceux
    qui parlent de françafrique doivent changer de vocabulaire et de logiciel"',
    L'Intelligent d'Abidjan, 16 July 2011. Republished on *Abidjan.net*, accessed
    12 March 2012, http://news.abidjan.net/h/404662.html?utm_
    source=lesbuzz&utm_medium=site.

28 Küntzie, 'Afrique. Avec Hollande, la fin de la françafrique?', see Note 14.

29 The full text of Hollande's speech can be found in 'François Hollande à
    Dakar: "Le Temps de la Françafrique est Révolu"', *Le Monde*, 12 October
    2012.

30 Melissa Bell (video) and Assiya Hamza (text), 'Hollande faces France's bitter
    colonial past in Algeria', France 24: *International News*, accessed 11 June 2013,
    http://www.france24.com/en/20121218-hollande-visit-algeria-france-colonial-
    bouteflika. See 'François Hollande à Dakar: "Le temps de la françafrique est
    revolu", *Le Monde*, 19 December 2012; 'Minute par minute – Hollande en
    Algérie: "Un Nouvel Âge" et des accords', *Le Monde*, 19 December 2012. See
    also 'Hollande en Algérie, la page est loin d'etre tournée? (Analyse)', *L'Humanité*,
    23 December 2012. An illustration of the diverse responses to Hollande's
    declaration can be seen in the blog entries following the article 'Minute par
    minute – Hollande en Algérie'.

31 Bell and Hamza, 'Hollande faces France's bitter colonial past in Algeria',
    see Note 30.

32 Afua Hirsch, 'French troops arrive in Mali to stem rebel advance',
    The Guardian, 11 January 2013.

33 'French President greeted by jubilant crowds in Mali', *Dawn (Pakistan)*,
    3 February 2013. See also Faith Karimi and Pierre Meilhan, 'French leader
    makes jubilant trip to Mali to thank his troops battling militants', *CNN
    Online*, accessed 7 June 2013, http://www.cnn.com/2013/02/02/world/africa/
    mali-conflict/index.html.

34 Interview by Virginie Herz with Isabelle Lasserre and Thierry Oberlé, authors
    of 'Notre guerre secrète au Mali: Les Nouvelles menaces contre la France',
    France 24, first broadcast 6 June 2013.

35 Immanuel Wallerstein, 'The very risky bet of Hollande in Mali: The probable
    long-term disaster', 1 February 2013, accessed 3 June 2013, http://www.
    iwallerstein.com/risky-bet-hollande-mali-probable-longterm-disaster/. For a
    view on the end of the operation see, Christian Thiam, 'La Fin de l'opération
    epervier semble se préciser', *Yolele.com*, accessed 3 June 2013, http://www.
    yolele.com/spip.php?article54.

36 'François Hollande juge l'operation "Serval" au Mali, "Réussie Militairement"',
    Le Monde, 31 May 2013.

37 Thomas Boni Yayi of Benin; Blaise Compaoré of Burkina Faso; Alassane
    Ouattara of Côte d'Ivoire; Dioncounda Traoré of Mali; Mohamed Ould Abdel
    Aziz of Mauritania; Idriss Déby Itno of Chad; and Macky Sall of Senegal. Niger
    was represented by its Prime Minister, Brigi Rafini.

38 'French President François Hollande awarded UNESCO Peace Prize for action
    in Africa. United Nations Educational, Scientific and Cultural Organization',
    UNESCO Media Services, accessed 10 June 2013, http://www.unesco.org/new/
    en/media-services/single-view/news/french_president_francois_hollande_
    awarded_unesco_peace_prize_for_action_in_africa/.

39 For discussions of the significance of Angkor to French colonial ideology and
    activities, see Tim Winter, *Post-Conflict Heritage, Postcolonial Tourism: Culture,
    politics and development at Angkor* (London: Routledge, 2007), Ch. 2. See also
    the introduction to Panivong Norindr, *Phantasmatic Indochina: French colonial*

ideology in architecture, film, and literature (Durham: Duke University Press, 1996).

40 I am not using myth in the Barthian sense of 'depoliticised speech'. Roland Barthes, *Mythologies*, trans. Annette Lavers (New York: Hill & Wang, 1972), 145.

41 Francine Dessaigne, *Déracinés!* (Meaux: Éditions du Fuseau, 1964); Marie Elbe, *Et à l'heure de notre mort* (Paris: Presses de la Cité, 1963).

42 Since independence the *pieds-noirs* have initiated a number of pilgrimages to religious edifices in France that bear the same name as former colonial religious sites. Among the best known are those to Notre Dame de Santa Cruz in Nîmes and to the statue of Notre Dame d'Afrique at Théoule-sur-Mer. The former is undertaken at Ascension each year by the *pieds-noirs* of Oran. It is the oldest of these pilgrimages, having recently celebrated its 51st year. The Théoule pilgrimage occurs on 1 May and is not specific to one colonial region but connects the pilgrims from the former colony to Algiers where there used to be a similar statue at the cathedral of that name. Professor Abderrahmane Moussaoui of the University of Aix-en-Provence is at present working on these pilgrimages.

43 For an analysis of the shifting themes and practices, see Lorcin, *Historicizing Colonial Nostalgia*, Chs. 6 and 7, see Note 3.

44 Jacques Ferrandez, *Carnets D'Orient. 1, Djemilah* (Paris: Casterman, 1994); Jacques Ferrandez (preface by Jean-Claude Carrière), *L'Année de feu* (Paris: Casterman, 1994); Jacques Ferrandez (preface by Jules Roy), *Les fils du sud* (Paris: Casterman, 1994); Jacques Ferrandez (preface by Benjamin Stora), *Le Centenaire* (Paris: Casterman, 1994); Jacques Ferrandez (preface by Louis Gardel), *Le Cimetière des Princesses* (Bruxelles: Casterman, 1995); Jacques Ferrandez (preface by Gilles Kepel), *La Guerre fantome* (Tournai: Casterman, 2002); Jacques Ferrandez (preface by Bruno Étienne), *Rue de la Bombe* (Bruxelles: Casterman, 2004); Jacques Ferrandez (preface by Michel Pierre), *La Fille du djebel amour* (Bruxelles: Casterman, 2005); Jacques Ferrandez (preface by Mohamed Fellag), *Dernière demeure* (Bruxelles: Casterman, 2007); and Jacques Ferrandez (preface by Maïssa Bey), *Terre fatale* (Brussels: Casterman, 2009).

45 Joe Sacco, *Palestine* (Seattle, WA: Fantagraphics Books, 2001); Art Spiegelman, *Maus: A survivor's tale* (New York: Pantheon Books, 1978); *Maus II: A survivor's tale: and Here my troubles began* (New York: Pantheon Books, 1991). For analysis of graphic novels, see Michael A. Chaney, ed., *Graphic Subjects: Critical essays on autobiography and graphic novels* (Madison, WI: The University of Wisconsin Press, 2011); Matthew J. Costello, *Secret Identity Crisis: Comic books and the unmasking of Cold War America* (New York: Continuum, 2009); Hugo Frey, 'History and memory in Franco-Belgian *Bandes Dessinées*', *Rethinking History* 6, 3 (2002): 293–304; Joseph Witek, *Comic Books as History: The narrative art of Jack Jackson, Art Spiegelman, and Harvey Pekar* (Jackson, MS: University Press of Mississippi, 1989); and Richard Iadonisi, ed., *Graphic History: Essays on graphic novels and/as history* (Newcastle upon Tyne: Cambridge Scholars Publishing, 2012).

46 Edward Said, 'Preface' to Sacco, *Palestine*, see Note 45, v.

47 Maheed Ahmed, 'Historicizing graphic novels: The welcome subjective g(l)aze', in Iadonisi, ed., *Graphic History*, see Note 45, 148–201, 198.

48 Seamus O'Malley, 'Speculative history, speculative fiction: Allen Moore and Eddie Campbell's From Hell', in Iadonisi, ed., *Graphic History*, see Note 45, 162–83, 64.

49 For example, Jacques Ferrandez and Albert Camus, *L'Hôte* (Paris: Gallimard, 2009); Jacques Ferrandez and Marcel Pagnol, *Jean de Florette. Manon des sources* (Paris: Casterman classiques, 1997); Jacques Ferrandez and Robert Louis Stevenson, *Le Cas étrange du Dr Jekyll et de Mr Hyde* (Paris: Éditions du chêne, 1994).

50 For example, Benjamin Stora, Louis Gardel, Jules Roy, Mohamed Said Fellag.

51 Chapter 5 in *Djemila*, see Note 44, for example, is devoted to Abd-el-Kader and his efforts to rid the area of the French.

52 Ferrandez, *Carnets d'Orient. 1, Djemilah*, see Note 44, 70 (author's translation from the French).

53 For an extensive analysis of first generation *pied-noir* narratives, see Lorcin, *Historicizing Colonial Nostalgia*, Chs. 6 and 7, see Note 3.

54 For some works on films dealing with the colonies, see Carolyn A. Durham, 'Strategies of subversion in colonial nostalgia film: Militarism and marriage in Brigitte Roüan's Outremer', *Studies in French Cinema* 1, 2 (2001): 89–97; Rachael Langford, 'Colonial false memory syndrome? The cinémémoire archive of French colonial films and mémoire d'Outremer (Claude Bossion, 1997)', *Studies in French Cinema*, 5, 2 (2005): 99–110; Alison Murray, 'Women, nostalgia, memory: Chocolat, Outremer, and Indochine', *Research in African Literatures* 33, 2 (2002): 235–44; David Henry Slavin, *Colonial Cinema and Imperial France, 1919-1939: White blind spots, male fantasies, settler myths* (Baltimore, MD: Johns Hopkins University Press, 2001); Peter J. Bloom, *French Colonial Documentary: Mythologies of humanitarianism* (Minneapolis, MN: University of Minnesota Press, 2008); and Norindr, *Phantasmatic Indochina*.

55 Colin Michael Hall and Hazel Tucker, eds., *Tourism and Postcolonialism: Contested discourses, identities, and representations* (London: Routledge, 2004), 2.

56 For other discussions of tourism and postcolonialism, see Jessica Jacobs, *Sex, Tourism and the Postcolonial Encounter: Landscapes of longing in Egypt* (Farnham: Ashgate, 2010); and Robert Aldrich, *Vestiges of the Colonial Empire in France: Monuments, museums, and colonial memories* (New York: Palgrave Macmillan, 2005).

57 UNESCO World Heritage Centre, 'Historic town of Grand-Bassam – Unesco World Heritage Centre', accessed 20 June 2013, http://whc.unesco.org/en/list/1322; Ministère de la Défense, 'Côte D'ivoire: Rénovation de la Sous-Préfecture de Grand-Bassam', accessed 20 June 2013, http://www.defense.gouv.fr/operations/cote-d-ivoire/actualites/cote-d-ivoire-renovation-de-la-sous-prefecture-de-grand-bassam.

58 Kaye Sung Chon and Arthur Asa Berger, *Vietnam Tourism* (London: Routledge, 2005).

59 The collection of settler memoirs and documentation was not limited to the French. The Oxford Colonial Records Project is at present in Rhodes House, while the Netherlands-Indies Tea and Family Archives is a foundation set up by the descendants of settlers in the Dutch East Indies for a similar purpose.

60 'Loi n° 2005–158 du 23 février 2005 portant reconnaissance de la Nation et contribution nationale en faveur des Français rapatriés (1)', *Journal officiel*, accessed 27 March 2012, http://www.legifrance.gouv.fr/affichTexte.do?cidTexte=JORFTEXT000000444898.

61 The historical memory of a nation can of course include the 'forgetting' of imperial or colonial activities that took place on the national territory through a rewriting of historical narratives, as in the case of the US discourse of Manifest Destiny, which justified the conquest of the West and the eradication of most of the native American population.

62 In 2009, the deputy mayor of Perpignan, Jean-Marc Pujol, declared that France was 'a country that took 50 years to say we bear responsibility for what happened to the Jews during World War II, [o]ne day I think we will have to take responsibility for what happened to the *pieds-noirs*.' Michael Kimmelman, 'Footprints of *pieds-noirs* reach deep into France', *The New York Times*, 5 March 2009.

PART THREE

Republicanism, Liberalism and the Changing Contours of French Intellectual Life

9

Justifying Capitalism in an Age of Uncertainty:

L'Association pour la Liberté Économique et le Progrès Social, 1969–73

Michael C. Behrent

The view that the 1970s represent a major turning point in global history, and particularly economic history, is increasingly common among historians and other scholars. Nixon's suspension of the dollar's convertibility into gold in 1971, the 1973 oil shock, stagflation, Petrodollars, and deregulation not only left the economy created during the post-war decades in tatters, but ushered in an era of economic, social, and political uncertainty. The historian Charles S. Maier has observed that 'the turmoil of the 1970s provoked a fundamental rethinking of the economic and political axioms that had been taken for granted since the Second World War. It closed the 'post-war' era and its policy premises. What might replace them would be in dispute.'[1] For David Harvey, the decade's closing years brought the most decisive change. Considering the impact of Deng Xiaoping's economic reforms in China, the new monetary policy pursued by Paul Volcker as chairman of the US Federal Reserve, and the elections of Margaret Thatcher and Ronald Reagan, Harvey concludes: 'Future historians may well look upon the years 1978–80 as a revolutionary turning-point in the world's social and economic history.'[2] For France, too, the 1970s was the decade in which 'la crise' began. The country reeled from the onslaught of rampant inflation, declining production, devastating unemployment, intense social conflict, at the same time that it watched with increasing desperation as the French government experimented with economic medicine old and new in its effort to find a cure for the nation's predicament, lurching from Jacques Chirac's cautious 'relance' to the 'rigueur' and the avowed economic liberalism of the successive plans proposed by Raymond Barre.

For France, as for much of the Western world, the 1970s slump was more than a particularly painful cyclical crisis: it represented a transformation in the very nature of capitalism. While a comprehensive overview of this paradigm shift is beyond the scope of this essay, several of its most important features deserve mention. First, the structure of corporations underwent dramatic change. As Luc Boltanski and Ève Chiapello have argued, the 1970s marked the transition from an economic landscape dominated by large, bureaucratised, and hierarchical companies in which investors increasingly shared decision-making with university-trained and technically-proficient 'managers', to a 'third phase' of capitalism, which witnessed the ascendency of tighter, leaner, and less top-down corporations, in which executives working in decentralised, rhizomatic 'networks', and using high-speed telecommunications, pursued an array of business 'projects' across a globalised world economy. Second, as Boltanski and Chiapello demonstrate, the transformation of the global economy over the past three decades, and the resulting restructuring of the corporate world, has given birth to a set of arguments for justifying this changing economic order. They call this the 'new spirit of capitalism'.[3] This spirit successfully absorbed much of the 1960s discontent with capitalist society, which was articulated with particular vigour (if not always coherence) in the student and workers' riots of May 68. The belief that hierarchical and bureaucratic organisations were inefficient, that they created 'one-dimensional' thinking, and that all human beings have a need for meaningful and imaginative work had already made inroads among France's mid-level managers by the mid-1960s, well before they inspired the slogans that *soixante-huitards* brandished on their banners and spray-painted onto the Latin Quarter's walls. While neo-managerialism did not coalesce into a coherent ideology until the early 1990s, some of the arguments upon which it would subsequently build – particularly its critique of the 'organisation' capitalism of the 1960s – had entered public discourse by the late-1960s and had become increasingly widespread over the course of the 1970s. Yet as Boltanski and Chiapello note, while the 'new spirit of capitalism' incorporated much of 1968's anti-authoritarian and libertarian tendencies, it primarily integrated what they call the aesthetic critique of capitalism (that capitalism produces disenchantment and selfishness) rather than the social denunciation of it (that capitalism is oppressive and reduces much of society to misery). In this way a new set of arguments emerged to justify capitalism as it was reconstituted in the wake of the crisis of the 1970s. These arguments co-opted the critiques of capitalism that were least threatening to its existence, thus ensuring that capitalism's resurgence in the 1980s would elicit relatively little opposition.

This chapter will consider the emergence of a new capitalist spirit by examining an organisation of French businessmen, academics, and politicians that sought to promote the interests of French business and reinvigorate liberalism. In the late 1960s and early 1970s, the Association pour la liberté économique et le progrès social (ALEPS) aimed to reintroduce liberal economic thought into public discourse and critique the statist and collectivist doctrines that, it believed, dominated French economic thought. In doing so, ALEPS and its members also attempted to determine how those who had identified with the spirit of 1960s radicalism – and particularly the young people who participated in May 68 – might be drawn over to the liberal cause. Ultimately, however, the enthusiasm of ALEPS for economic freedom was too deeply rooted in a fundamentally conservative outlook for such a rapprochement to occur. The study of ALEPS during its early period (1966–73) thus sheds light on some of the ideological constraints that prevented the emergence in France of a significant political movement organised around the principles of economic liberalism. If indeed there was a 'new spirit of capitalism' in this period, it was very incomplete in the French case and failed to coalesce in the mid-1970s as it did in the United States or the United Kingdom.

The beginnings of ALEPS

Compared to the history of French republicanism or socialism, the story of French liberalism presents itself as one of starts and fits. French liberals periodically fret that their movement is in abeyance, leading them to declare that the time for renewal has arrived. French neoliberalism is one such periodic renascence. While a French liberal tradition was established in the nineteenth century with political thinkers like Benjamin Constant, Alexis de Tocqueville, and François Guizot and economic theorists such as Jean-Baptiste Say and Frédéric Bastiat, French neoliberalism is now largely considered to have been born in Paris in 1938, on the occasion of a gathering to celebrate the publication of the French translation of the American journalist Walter Lippman's essay, *The Good Society*. The 'Colloque Lippmann', as it was eventually called, was the brainchild of the philosopher Louis Rougier, who taught at the University of Besançon. The guests were an international 'who's who' of prominent liberals, including the leading figures of the Austrian school of economics, Friedrich Hayek and Ludwig von Mises; Wilhelm Röpke and Alexander Rüstow, German economists associated with the so-called *Ordo* school; and an American trustee of the Rockefeller Foundation, Tracy B. Kittredge. Many of the participants were French: besides Rougier himself, they included the writer André Maurois, the economists Bernard Lavergne and Jacques Rueff, the liberal intellectual

Raymond Aron, the political scientist André Siegfried, and several business executives (Auguste Detoeuf, Louis Marlio, and Ernest Mercier) and *haut fonctionnaires* (Robert Marjolin). As François Denord has argued, while the attendees were all alarmed by the rise of collectivism and state interventionism, they were split between defenders of 'old' liberalism and proponents of 'neoliberalism', who were critical of the doctrine of laissez-faire in its purest form.[4] The following year, many of the colloquium's participants joined the Centre international d'études pour le renouveau du libéralisme (CIRL), which brought together academic economists, corporate managers, and several leaders of the CGT trade union. The CIRL would subsequently play a major part in shaping the policies of the Daladier government (1938–40).

The fall of France in 1940 not only dispersed the advocates of economic liberalism, but pushed their ideas to the sidelines. Even so, after the Liberation, the French liberal network was gradually reconstituted, encouraged by the Cold War and the Fourth Republic's turn to more liberal policies in the late 1940s. For instance, in 1947, the Centre national du patronat français (CNPF) established the Association de la libre entreprise (ALE) to 'highlight the misdeeds of state intervention . . . and to denounce it as the cancer of France'.[5] Economic liberals could also turn to the Centre national des indépendants (CNI), founded a year later in 1948. Finally, the Centre des jeunes patrons (CJP) was the home of economic liberals who were sympathetic to the teachings of social Catholicism. Thanks to these organisations, French economic liberals managed to cross the desert of the post-war years, mirroring in this way the international movement of which they were the local chapter (the Mont Pèlerin Society was founded in 1947). By the mid-1960s, there was once again an acute sense among French liberals that their ideas were in abeyance (despite the fact that one liberal-inspired Rueff-Armand committee played a critical role in launching the 'new franc' in 1960). Evidence of this apparent eclipse of liberal thought could be found in the pages of *Les Temps modernes*: in a 1959 article, Serge Mallet dubbed Raymond Aron 'the last liberal'.[6]

The sense that liberal values needed once again to be rekindled spurred the creation of ALEPS. Acknowledging liberalism's eclipse during this era, a French economist observed in 1965:

> In France, most economists (professionals, amateurs, or unconscious ones) accept very deep state intervention as a self-evident hypothesis and speak only of planning, systematic development, and methods of action; there is a tendency to erect a science of (the state's) economic policy on the ruins of a science of spontaneous mechanisms. France continues down the path of socialism, *dirigisme*, and planning. Contrary to what one might have expected after the Liberation, France underwent no economic conversion; controls were maintained and at times were even reinforced, and inspiration was more readily found in the East than the West.[7]

Hoping to reverse these trends, ALEPS was founded in 1966 at the initiative of André Arnoux (1895–1971), an industrialist who ran a family company, Chauvin-Arnoux, specialising in measurement technology.[8] Arnoux also fancied himself as a philosopher and a humanist: he wrote books bearing such inspirational titles as *The Call from Within* or *The Path to Happiness*.[9] Arnoux's goal, as he explained in a 1968 account of the organisation's history, was 'to encourage, by all the means at its disposal and in all forms that it can imagine, the enrichment and diffusion of liberal ideas, considered from their theoretical and practical aspects, insisting in particular on the possibilities they offer for social progress'.[10]

At the same time, the founders of ALEPS saw themselves as involved in an intellectual struggle to save France from the prevailing illiberal climate:

> Confronted with the quasi-universal propagation of Marxism – usually in a bastardised form – which moulds minds, often without their knowledge, and to which one refers out of intellectual conformity, so that one can think like everyone else, the Association pour la liberté économique et le progrès social has assigned itself the task of introducing, teaching, and imposing liberal thought, enriched by its great past and rejuvenated, renovated, and adapted to the realities of today's world.[11]

Even as it sought to appeal to the younger generation, the new association rounded up many of France's older and more established economic liberals. While Arnoux was the founding president of ALEPS, the first acting president was the economist Daniel Villey (1910–68). First at the University of Poitiers, then at the University of Paris, Villey was a tireless defender of the liberal tradition, intent on imparting its teachings to his students. Above all, Villey maintained that true liberty was impossible without economic liberty. For its honorary president, ALEPS chose a figure whose background was strikingly different to that of Villey: Hyacinthe Dubreuil (1883–1971). He was a self-educated *ouvrier mécanicien* and union activist who, in 1929, became a bestselling author when he published *Standards, le travail américain vu par un ouvrier français*,[12] an account of fifteen months living and working in factories across the United States that presented new American industrial models as promising solutions to Europe's economic difficulties and strained industrial relations. According to Martin Fine, Dubreuil remained committed throughout his career to the neo-Saint-Simonian dream of a 'new France, capable of sustained economic growth and greater industrial efficiency while preserving its social cohesion'.[13] Yet without abandoning this ideal, Dubreuil's relationship with the Socialist left quickly soured. In 1938, he bemoaned the 'fatal influence of Marx' and, after the war, Dubreuil helped to promote the latest American industrial fad – the human relations movement – and joined the CJP.[14] By 1966, Dubreuil was prepared to join forces with industrialists like Arnoux and liberal economists such as Villey to defend 'economic freedom and social progress'.

ALEPS declared that it was 'honoured to have at its helm two "producers", a boss and a worker'.[15]

The first public event organised by ALEPS was a prize competition, named after its founder, for books dedicated to economic liberalism. In 1967, the first 'Grand prix André Arnoux' was awarded to France's pre-eminent liberal economist, Jacques Rueff (1896–1978) for the entirety of his oeuvre. In return, Rueff agreed to chair the prize committee in the following and subsequent years. The committee assembled by Rueff added further members to ALEPS' widening circle: Jean Fourastié (1907–90), an economist for the Comissariat general du plan who later coined the phrase 'les trente glorieuses'; the economist Gaston Leduc (1904–79), a specialist in the theories of the great marginalist Léon Walras and a future head of the Mont Pèlerin Society; and Luc Bourcier de Carbon (1913–79), an economist who taught at the Paris law faculty and succeeded Daniel Villey as ALEPS' president.

In 1968, the committee awarded the André Auroux prize to the economist Maurice Allais (1911–2010). An engineer trained at the École polytechnique, Allais entered the field of economics as a self-described amateur when, during the Occupation, he read everything he could find by Léon Walras, Irving Fischer and Vilfredo Pareto.[16] He eventually became one of France's most innovative and prestigious economists, winning the Nobel Prize in 1988 in recognition for his contributions to such questions as market efficiency, monetary dynamics, and the economics of uncertainty. An extraordinary polymath, Allais also found time to do research into economic history as well as theoretical and experimental physics. Yet even as he insisted on the scientific character of his research, Allais readily admitted that his thinking had 'unquestionably been greatly influenced by a philosophy of liberal (in the European sense of the word) inspiration, along the lines of Alexis de Tocqueville, Léon Walras, Vilfredo Pareto and John Maynard Keynes, to name but a few'.[17]

The group of individuals that founded ALEPS was thus in many ways quite diverse. It included industrialists, former union activists, and economists, some of whom were creatures of the university (such as Allais), while others had advised governments (like Fourastié and Rueff). For some, liberty was a philosophy or ethical end in itself, while for others it was a hypothesis that had to be proven through rigorous economic analysis and assessed from the standpoint of market efficiency. Some equated economic freedom with markets and entrepreneurship, while others associated it with decentralised economic decision-making and workplace creativity. What united this cast of characters was age (the organisation's founders were born between 1883 and 1913, meaning that by 1968 the youngest among them was 55) and a sense that whatever liberal dispositions may have taken root in France were now being threatened by *dirigisme* and economic planning at the political level, and the hegemony of Marxism at the intellectual and cultural level.

ALEPS decided to push back against these trends by organising a conference cycle entitled the 'Week of Liberal Thought' (*Semaine de la pensée libérale*), the first of which was held in Paris in November 1968. This event was intended as a liberal answer to the *semaines de la pensée marxiste* which, since 1962, had been organised by the philosopher Roger Garaudy under the auspices of the French Communist Party. By the time the first 'liberal week' opened, however, a new set of issues was shaping public discourse, arising from the student and worker movement that had exploded the previous May. Cautiously, ALEPS saw May 68 as an opportunity: were not the young people who had rallied behind slogans such as 'il est interdit d'interdire' and 'l'imagination prend le pouvoir' expressing, however confusedly, an incipiently liberal worldview? The trick would be to show that the Marxist solutions embraced by many students were more likely to vitiate rather than fulfil this aspiration for freedom. As the organisation's president, Luc Bourcier de Carbon, explained:

The first week of liberal thought proposed to alert public opinion, which had fallen asleep, so that it might better feel the dangers that threaten our free and progressive society, to draw attention to the fragility of our wellbeing and its causes, to denounce the fallacious promises of those who offer to trade our economic liberty for vain hopes of wellbeing [a remark that distantly echoes the May 68 graffiti: 'We don't want a world where the guarantee of not dying of starvation brings the risk of dying of boredom'], to call on young people to reflect upon the experience of enchained countries, [and] to define a modern liberal order offering man every opportunity for fulfilment.[18]

Put differently: could the conception of freedom espoused by economic liberals offer a social and political programme for post-May 68 France?

ALEPS and the liberal case for May 68

The Première Semaine de la Pensée Libérale assembled on 14 November 1968 at the Maison de la Chimie in Paris. The organisers sought to present its agenda in a topical light. Specifically, they set out to make the case that liberalism was both the inner tendency and ultimate cause of the *mouvement de mai* that had rocked the country six months earlier. The first panel was entitled 'The Thirst for Liberty in the Modern World'. In his account of proceedings, Claude Harmel left little doubt that this 'thirst for liberty' was a reference to the events of May:

this theme of the first day had in a sense been imposed by the event which rocked the French university system five or six months previously: were not the clearest demands of the students in revolt demands for liberty? If one saw flying above these crowds, forgotten and unexpected, the black flag of anarchy, was it not because they wanted to take as far as possible their protest against the constraints, which they saw as excessive and pointless, of a society they considered oppressive?[19]

Even as they acknowledged the students' Marxist and anarchist proclivities, the conference participants expressed broad sympathy for the protestors' longing for liberty and denunciations of the repressive character of French institutions. The first speaker was Claude Bruaire (1932–86), a Catholic theologian who taught philosophy at the University of Tours. Bruaire, who had recently completed a dissertation under Paul Ricœur at the Sorbonne, would become one of France's most prominent contemporary Catholic thinkers, developing close ties with fellow theologians Xavier Tilliette and Jean-Luc Marion as well as with the *nouvelle théologie* of Henri de Lubac and Hans Urs von Balthasar and their journal, *Communio*, to which Bruaire became a frequent contributor.[20] Bruaire described the student movement as a spiritual struggle: 'To many students, to many intellectuals, the world seemed like a logical straitjacket. There was nothing left to say and, particularly, nothing left to do.' Their 'unlimited desire' expressed itself in a spirit of revolt, in an aspiration for an intangible 'complete otherness (*tout autre*)', which occurred in a state of complete 'ideological and doctrinal indetermination'.[21]

The next speaker approached the student uprising from what would appear to be a rather different perspective. He was Michel Crozier (1922–2013), the acerbic critic of the 'bureaucratic phenomenon'.[22] While teaching sociology at Nanterre, Crozier had witnessed the initial skirmishes of the May 68 movement first-hand. Unsurprisingly, he described the events as a revolt against the country's inflexible institutions, of which none was more sclerotic than the university itself. 'In the gallery of bureaucratic monsters in which this old country of customs officials and accountants takes pride,' he remarked, 'the most caricatural specimen is and remains its university.' Yet even as he sympathised with these efforts to free society from bureaucracy's grip, Crozier feared that the student revolt was part of the problem rather than the solution. 'This tolerant movement that aspires to expression and complete release' depends on 'absolutist demands that impose on all true psychological terror'.[23]

The first session's final speaker was Michel Drancourt, the editor of one of the era's leading business magazines, *Entreprises*. Drancourt studied economics under François Perroux, who was himself a student of the Austrian school (notably Ludwig von Mises) before gravitating towards *pétainisme* during the Occupation.[24] In the 1950s, Drancourt helped to launch *Entreprises*, a business magazine that was deliberately modelled on American publications such as *Fortune* and *Business Week*.[25] As someone who believed he was promoting the creative dynamism of the business world against French society's more conservative inclinations, Drancourt, too, could muster some sympathy for the student radicals. He observed: 'The student revolt and its consequences are, in part, a reaction against the sclerosis of the University and an old-fashioned style of authority, in all its forms.' The movement had, moreover, 'revealed a refusal of some forms of group discipline'. Still, he ultimately saw the political and cultural attitudes of the protestors as self-contradictory. They denounced the 'civilisation of machines' for being soulless, even as they used machines as tools of liberation. They critiqued consumer society, while considering material progress as a *fait accompli* that created opportunities for more just and meaningful social relations. Finally, he noted that while the students were quick to denounce 'Americanisation', many of their aspirations were 'very curiously turned towards American reality', including demands relating to the independence of universities, the right of managers to participate in corporate decision-making, and the demand for a more humane system of industrial relations. He wondered, ultimately, if a disturbing complicity did not exist between 'the most dynamic intellectuals [and] the most adventurous young people', on the one hand, and 'the most traditional power', on the other. The former's claim to originality was a mask under which 'very French traditions' were preserved, including: 'distrust of companies; scorn for technology; egalitarianism; admiration for authority when it is political or intellectual, and disdain for authority when it is economic.'[26]

This ambivalence toward the student movement resurfaced in later sessions. On a panel entitled 'From Centralisation to a Plurality of Decision Centres', Maurice Allais observed with apprehension: 'Everywhere states have become more and more centralised, centralising, and bureaucratic' to which he immediately added: 'the majority of the youth has detached itself from liberal thought, to the point that one wonders if it even has any knowledge of it.'[27] In the concluding session, Maurice Roy returned to the theme of higher education. While some look to the university to train economic leaders, 'this same university', he lamented, 'has remained for the most part consistent with its original vocation: that of being a machine for producing intellectuals [*clercs*]'.[28] The Sorbonne epistemologist René Poirier (1900–95) warned against seeing the student radicals as champions of an inchoate liberalism:

> The university agitation uses liberal or libertarian slogans. It is fashionable to use words such as 'autonomy', 'independence', 'liberty', but defenders of liberal thought would be making a serious mistake if they believed that their philosophy could benefit from this fashion. For the liberties that the agitators boast of are 'equivocal, poorly defined, and imperialistic' and 'devour one another'.[29]

In his introduction to the printed version of the proceedings, Claude Harmel, responded to Poirier's critique of the student movement. Poirier would surely agree, he wrote, that

> by assigning it tasks that are not its own and that force it to intervene incessantly in each and everyone's life, economic *dirigisme*, authoritarian planning, and economic and social statism have shorn the state of the moral authority that, in great liberal periods, allowed them to ensure its fundamental function of preserving order and defending liberties without hardly ever having recourse to force.

When the state violates the 'natural order' in this way, Harmel continued, it

> is not a coincidence that, in response to totalitarian despotism, and at the
> very moment when its most brutal incarnation has started to decompose,
> we see a reappearance of the belief, which is just as murderous, that
> individual spontaneity suffices to preserve a fraternal social bond.[30]

The discussion of May 68 and the student movement at ALEPS' first week
of liberal thought was thus characterised by a number of tensions. On the
one hand, many of the liberals gathered at the Maison de la Chimie saw the
students, if not as fellow travellers, at least as critics of many of the trends
in French society that they too found troubling. While some, like Harmel,
seemed willing to see the student movement as endorsing a certain
'misunderstood liberalism', most saw the movement as quite alien to their
beliefs. Crozier suggested that, despite their anti-authoritarianism, students
may have inculcated far more of the institutional culture (with its
bureaucratic and illiberal proclivities) than they realised. Drancourt saw
them as hypocrites, eager to profit from the material benefits and personal
freedom that the post-war economy had made possible while still
accumulating the cultural capital earned from engaging in an aesthetic
critique of consumer society. Others were frankly conservative in their
assessment, seeing the May events as the very opposite of the liberal
conception of freedom exercised responsibly. ALEPS saw, in short, May 68
as presenting a valuable opportunity to make the case for the relevance of a
liberal programme to contemporary France. But even in the way they
articulated their own views, this group of liberals were unquestionably wary
towards the *mouvement de mai*.

A new capitalist spirit? Justifications for an emerging order

Yet however much personal distaste they might have felt for May 68, many
of the participants at ALEPS forums recognised that the student and worker
upheaval was not an historical accident or an isolated occurrence, but rather
a symptom of the profound forces that were transforming the industrialised
world. If this were the case, then the issue became not only whether youth
culture could be brought over to the liberal cause, but also whether capitalist
economies were themselves being altered by the very factors that had made
the social tensions of the 1960s possible. Was a new form of capitalism
being born? And if so, did it require a new set of arguments and 'a new spirit
of capitalism'?

For the economist Robert Marjolin (1911–86), the answer was mostly
'yes'. Marjolin had played an integral role in France's post-war reconstruction,

notably through his involvement with the implementation of the Marshall Plan and in the negotiations that created the European Economic Community (he had also, it is worth recalling, attended the *Colloque Lippmann* in 1938). It is perhaps not surprising, then, that Marjolin told an ALEPS audience in October 1969 that liberalism's true message was not simply liberty, but also relentless change and opposition to conservatism. Asking 'what is truly, in our days, a liberal?', he noted that 'in French . . . the word "liberal" evokes the idea of a certain passivity towards economic affairs'.[31] Searching for a better definition, he consulted an American dictionary and was surprised to find the answer: 'A liberal is an opponent of a conservative.' He noted that for Americans, one could 'almost say that [a liberal] was a man of the left', despite the fact that, in economic affairs, liberals favoured 'the refusal of restrictions on exchange when they were not strictly indispensable'.[32] However confused Marjolin's conception of American liberalism may have been, what mattered is the lesson he drew from it. He explained: 'I have always felt myself close to this American liberalism, which has always been progressive, reformist, and animated by a spirit of justice and change.'[33] Liberalism therefore meant a political vision that embraced and harnessed the change that was transforming society.

Recognising this kind of change meant acknowledging the considerable uncertainty pervading contemporary society: 'We started from something we thought we knew,' Marjolin mused, 'we will arrive at something about which we have absolutely no idea, and we do not know the path by which we will get there.'[34] If liberalism had a future in France, he argued, it was insofar as it ceased to be identified with economic complacency, and became, rather, the advocate of change: 'Let us be clear: if we want liberalism to find something of an audience among the popular masses, it must appear as a factor of change' – but he added 'change acting in favour of great equality'.[35] In short, Marjolin appeared to acknowledge that the nature of French society was changing, both because of the social transformations of the 1960s and the first steps towards globalisation. He attempted, moreover, to make the case that liberalism's legitimacy now depended on its ability to present itself as promoting change and resisting 'conservatism'. But the problem with his defence of liberalism (in addition to the inherent vagueness in the term 'change') rested on a confusion between American progressivism (with its suspicions of unfettered markets) and a purer conception of free-market liberalism. Marjolin recognised perhaps that a new spirit of capitalism was being born, yet he made sense of it in terms borrowed from the post-war model in which his own career was so invested.

A different and perhaps more prescient analysis of capitalism's newly emergent spirit was made two years later by Michel Poniatowski (1922–2002), the general secretary of the Républicains indépendants, the right-wing liberal party most closely associated with the future president Valéry Giscard d'Estaing. Speaking at the fourth ALEPS conference, held in December 1971, Poniatowksi very clearly spoke of the present moment as one in which society found itself on the brink of a major transformation. 'Today,' he reflected, 'the consequences of the changes before which we find ourselves are not predictable.'[36] Part of the reason for this uncertainty lay in the fact that the very nature of French society – and, in particular, its capitalistic economy – was being revolutionised. Without using the term, Poniatowski, in so many words, announced the imminent demise of the so-called 'trente glorieuses'.[37] France found itself 'on the cusp between two civilisations: one that is quantitative, which is ending, and one that is qualitative, which is being prepared'. The society coming to a close was marked by 'man's effort to free himself from material constraints'.[38] While this civilisation made possible a 'dazzling liberation', its 'search for efficiency moulded a hard society, governed by relationships based on force and interest'. In this society, he added, 'man finds himself thrown into the future (*lancé dans une fuite en avant*), in which, to have more, he feels himself being less'.[39] Dissatisfaction with the quality of life offered by post-war society's quantitative achievements explains the contemporary crisis in authority: 'In all societies, to the East as to the West, youth's attitude of refusal attests to the present incapacity of offering reasons of living to those who seek the realisation of an ideal.'[40] For this reason, the alternative before which France finds itself is a 'society of constraint' – that is, socialism – or a 'society of choice' – that is, liberalism.

In Poniatowski's vision, the forces transforming modern society announced the advent of an economy which, however 'traumatic' it might be in its novelty, nonetheless offered the individual far more autonomy and opportunity for self-realisation. Developments in the organisational sciences would make it possible 'gradually to substitute prediction and incentives for constraint'. Rapid advances in computer technology would facilitate 'the decentralisation of decision-making'. The development of social relationships based on increasingly complex and diverse bonds between individuals operating in multiple, overlapping 'systems' would, in turn, enhance 'the individual's autonomy of judgement and choice'. Meanwhile, the demand for high-skilled jobs – specifically, for '*techniciens*' and '*cadres*' (technicians and managers) would grow exponentially.[41] Finally, the civilisation that arose from these changes would 'conceive of itself as a society open to the world and would refuse national societies that are closed and withdrawn into themselves'.[42] In Poniatowski's view, liberalism was the political philosophy ideally suited to this context of greater uncertainty, more fluid hierarchy, increased decentralisation, heightened social complexity, the rise of an information and knowledge-based economy, and globalisation – traits that are fully consonant with Boltanski and Chiapello's characterisation of the 'new spirit' of capitalism's self-image. Poniatowski concluded: 'What are we lacking to change direction?' His answer was clear: 'political will' and a 'political project', namely, liberalism. Liberalism was the philosophy that best understood the new global society.

Although Poniatowski intuited that this new phase of capitalism would be based on less hierarchy and greater individual autonomy, it was far from evident that these developments had yet to transform capitalism's core unit: the company. Indeed, one sign of a new capitalist spirit might well be found in the disgruntlement of French *cadres*. They were becoming increasingly central to French business culture even though they often felt that the unique experience and expertise they embodied was ignored by their paternalistic bosses. Boltanski and Chiapello observe that concern about the dissatisfaction of the *cadres* pervaded French corporate discourse during this period.[43] These concerns surfaced on several occasions during ALEPS encounters. At the 1970 conference, a representative of the Confédération générale des cadres, the main *cadres* trade union:

> In the modern world, salaried employees (*les salaries*), and in particular *cadres*, feel more and more the need to be associated with the company's operations; in other words, to be informed, to be consulted, to participate in decisions. And our new company leaders do not involve most *cadres* any more than older capitalists once did.[44]

Philippe David, the vice-president of the Centre national des jeunes cadres, made this point even more strongly, specifically connecting the *cadres'* discontent with May 68: 'From whence comes this kind of malaise that affirmed itself in a spectacular way in May 68, which had existed in a latent state for a long time, and which is a genuine reality among *cadres*?'[45] For David, the answer lay in different conceptions of the modern company's purpose (*la finalité de l'entreprise*). 'In a fine élan of liberalism,' David remarked, 'some have affirmed that profit is the company's purpose. For me, this is not true.' Profits, he maintained, are a means, not an end. In fact, a company is a community that serves the needs of its various constituencies: 'The goal is to serve clients, to offer them quality products at a better price, and to prove a living to men who are stakeholders, through capital or through work.'[46] While certainly no revolutionary, David nonetheless sought to translate some of the critiques of the *soixante-huitards* into a corporate idiom: business, he believed, needed to offer work that was personally meaningful – not only for businessmen, but for all concerned. And just as the student movement's discontent expressed itself in generational terms, so did the young *cadres* of the early 1970s complain about their older superiors.[47] A new spirit of capitalism was discernible not only in the discourse of politicians and business leaders, but also, and perhaps even more so, in the critical outlook of French *cadres*, who in some instances frequently sympathised with the student movement's critique of French society's hierarchy, rigidity, and formality.

The debates at ALEPS meetings reveal an awareness that French society and specifically French capitalism found itself at the dawn of a new era. A number of aspects of the previous system that had been targeted by the cultural criticism of the 1960s – hierarchical workplace relations, the emphasis on efficiency at the expense of all other factors, 'one-dimensional' thinking – were seen as increasingly unviable. It was beginning to occur to some, at least, that a new spirit of capitalism would emphasise decentralisation rather than concentration; personal meaning and fulfilment as much as monetary success; and, in particular, autonomy and creativity instead of obedience and discipline. In this way, ALEPS conferences in this period confirm Boltanski and Chiapello's insight that capitalism, in the early 1970s, was seeking new ways to justify itself, notably by co-opting the aesthetic (but not the social) critique of capitalism levelled by the 1960s counterculture. Even so, this perspective remains partial. For alongside this more progressive and liberal vision of capitalism, far more conservative instincts continued to prevail.

Liberalism's conservative lining

Between 1969 and 1973, ALEPS' 'weeks of liberal thought' explored a number of themes that its members believed could form the basis of a liberal project – themes that demonstrated that not only freedom, but specifically economic freedom, could be the touchstone for reforming French society. At the October 1969 meeting, panels were organised on: 'the market economy and the condition of the working class'; Catholics and liberal economics; industrial policy in a 'liberal Europe'; 'liberty and rigour in professional life'; and current conditions for economic growth.[48] The conference held the following year, in November 1970, adopted as its theme: 'Liberalism: Emergency Exit from Socialism.' Its panels included a reprise of the previous year's examination of 'the market economy and the working class' (this time with the participation of Raymond Aron); a panel specifically dedicated to the year's theme of liberalism as socialism's primary alternative; and panels devoted to *cadres* and economic power, responsibility and freedom, and 'individual success and the general interest'.[49] The idea of liberalism's 'social efficacy', around which the gathering of December 1971 was organised, provided an occasion for discussing nationalisations; 'standards of living: socialist failures, liberal successes'; liberal responses to the challenge of industrial growth; and liberalism in power.[50] In December 1972 ('current problems, liberal answers'), ALEPS discussed the relationship between human liberty and economic liberty, 'free enterprise for a free Europe', and social guarantees under a liberal system.[51] In November 1973, the association felt confident enough to dedicate its week-long meeting to considering liberalism as a 'societal project (*un projet de société*)'. To this end, they discussed the contemporary relevance and realism of the liberal project; the idea that a free society requires a strong state; the role of companies in society (including a presentation by Serge Dassault); and the economy's ultimate purpose ('l'économie pour quoi faire?').[52]

    As we have seen, the ideas explored at these meetings frequently sought to articulate the principles of a new capitalist spirit. Yet it would be a mistake to exaggerate its presence. While some speakers foresaw the advent of a more dynamic, knowledge-based, decentralised, and globalised version of capitalism, others were far more concerned with articulating a vision of liberalism that not only harmonised with the achievements and social model of the post-war economy, but could be justified in terms of the prudent and often staunchly conservative solutions it offered to the uncertain age that France seemed about to enter. At times, this meant that speakers expressed some sympathy for socialist or social-democratic ideas, precisely because they saw a fully free-market society as too disruptive or unstable; at others, it led ALEPS sympathisers to adopt the conservative position that true freedom required a stiff dose of discipline to flourish. These reservations were particularly apparent in debates surrounding three issues: work and the 'condition of the working class'; the role of Christianity in contemporary society; and the relationship between freedom and order.

The simple fact that they again organised panels on 'the market economy and the working class', as they did in 1969 and 1970, makes it clear that ALEPS' organisers still saw the refutation of Marxism and other forms of socialism as central to the task of building a liberal project. Yet in the very process of demonstrating the shortcomings of Marxist economics, many speakers found themselves claiming that capitalism actually fulfils socialism's goals better than the programmes of Socialists were ever likely to do. The 1969 panel opened with a lengthy analysis of Marx's arguments about the inevitable pauperisation (or at least relative pauperisation) of the working class. The presenter was Louis Devaux (1907–95), the former CEO of Shell-France and sometime confidante of the Jesuit philosopher Pierre Teilhard de Chardin.[53] The problem with Marx's claim that capital accumulation necessarily results in the impoverishment of workers, Devaux argued, was that it reflected only one, relatively brief stage in the history of capitalism. Technical progress and the monetisation of the economy had brought this zero-sum game to an end: thanks to Henry Ford and John Maynard Keynes, it was now clear that high wages benefit both business and the economy as a whole, linking, through the market mechanism, the interests of employers and employees. There is, however, one possible wrinkle in this otherwise virtuous circle: inflation, spurred by wage increases, but which can ultimately wipe out the relative income of the working class. Consequently, while Devaux sought to refute Marx's ideas by showing how modern capitalism largely benefits workers, he also acknowledged that it was potentially unstable and destructive.[54]

The next paper was by Claude Harmel (d. 2011), whose views on May 68 were examined above. Harmel was a critical figure in the history of ALEPS, who was responsible for editing the published proceedings of the annual 'liberal weeks'. In the 1930s, Harmel (whose real name was Guy Lemonnier) had been an activist with the SFIO before joining Marcel Déat's fascist and ultimately collaborationist Rassemblement national populaire (RNP). After the war, he was sentenced to four years in prison and *dégradation nationale*, before being amnestied. He joined several former RNP members who sought to enlist their knowledge of the labour movement into the service of anti-communism through the *Bulletin d'études et d'informations politiques internationales* (which allegedly worked with the CIA).[55] The paper he delivered at the 1969 ALEPS conference drew on the same wealth of knowledge: it was entitled 'Liberal Thought and Union Action'. Harmel's intention was to dispel the myth that liberal, free-market policies had had a disastrous effect on labour relations and that liberals were unconcerned with social questions. According to Harmel, liberals, as a result of their attachment to free enterprise and market relations, had managed to create a series of policies and institutions that improved the life of the working class: *caisses d'épargne, bourses de travail*, work accidents insurance, and even the legalisation of labour unions. He presents liberalism less as an individualist alternative to socialism than as a doctrine with its own distinctive approach to social policy. He goes so far as to refer to a '*collectivisme libéral*'.[56] Liberalism's appeal seems to lie, for Harmel, in what he calls an '*état d'esprit nouveau*, this ethos of production, of productive labour', which he contrasts to a 'clerical spirit' that in France regards everything that is not ' "disinterested" intellectual work' as 'ignoble'.[57] Interestingly, though, Harmel's proposed solution does not lie in the creativity of the market or the rationality of competition, but a peculiar kind of corporatist order. Unions, he maintains, can play a valuable role in a liberal society, offering workers forms of social insurance, provided they do not try to throw their weight around inside companies themselves. In the past century, he argues, the major institutions of French society – 'the *patrie*, the state, the church, the commune, the school, the family, itself' – have undergone a process of 'universal decomposition'. The only institution that has 'held fast' is the company (*l'entreprise*), which is why, he explains, 'one turns to it as towards an anchor of salvation, a haven of grace, a shipwreck survivor's lifesaver'.[58] The company, he hopes, could serve as a model to which France's weakened institutions might turn as they seek to revive themselves.

What stands out in Devaux's and Harmel's reflections on the condition of the working class and liberalism is, first, how deeply they are committed to a vision of liberalism's *social* implications and, second, how different these visions are from what we have come to associate with neoliberalism. Devaux presents the Fordist economy and Keynesian policies of the *trente glorieuses* as triumphs of *liberalism* (something that, presumably, would trouble many a member of the Mont Pèlerin Society), while Harmel attempts nothing less than to square a kind of Vichy corporatism with the circle of capitalist entrepreneurialism. None of the virtues that either speaker attributes to these arrangements inheres solely in the market mechanism itself, but only in its secondary traits or effects. Far from extending personal autonomy, capitalism's virtues lie in its capacity to establish security and order.

Further evidence for the conservative character of ALEPS' liberalism can be found in debates surrounding the role of Christianity in modern society.

At the October 1969 meeting, Pierre de Calan (1911–93), a CEO active in the CNPF, chaired a panel on 'Catholics and Economic Liberalism'. Calan declared that the relevance of economic liberalism had to be assessed from the standpoint of two 'indisputable' trends: the collapse of socialism and the resurgence of Christian thought:

> Between these two major facts – the triumph of economic liberalism on the one hand, and Christian thought, the influence of which has never been more intense, on the other – is there opposition, articulation, or subordination? . . . Has the Church condemned liberalism?

Calan offered a tentative answer to his own question:

> Many of us think and feel that if the answer was a categorical and un-nuanced 'yes', we would find ourselves in a situation that is both tragic and absurd. For it seems impossible to us Christians that the order established by the creator-God be opposed to the ends offered us by the God who is our supreme purpose and the people's legislator.[59]

A methodical examination of this problem was undertaken by Albert Garand (1912–86), an economist at the CNPF who clearly laid out the points of agreement between economic liberals and the Catholic Church. Garand made it clear that the economic liberalism he intended to address was not that of the nineteenth century, but 'today's liberalism, or neoliberalism such as it has manifested itself in the German Ordoliberal school of Walter Eucken and his friends'.[60] From this perspective, economic liberalism would seem to have much in common with the Catholic Church's teachings. He quoted Pope John XXIII's encyclical on Christianity and social progress, *Magister et Magistra* (1961), which asserts:

> It should be stated at the outset that in the economic order first place must be given to the personal initiative of private citizens working either as individuals or in association with each other in various ways for the furtherance of common interests.[61]

For this reason, the Church has always affirmed the principle of private property of the means of production (as evidenced in Leo XIII's condemnation of socialism's denial of this right in *Rerum Novarum*), and, by extension, the legitimacy of salaried labour. The problem, in Garand's view, was that the Church was inclined to see the pursuit of self-interest as egotistical and, more generally, that it could never accept the very concept of the market, which placed an 'enormous mass of conflicts of interest' at the heart of the social order. Garand in particular bemoaned the Church's blindness to the fact that 'the only peaceful way to settle these conflicts in keeping with the national and international general interest was the system of the market economy'.[62] Instead, the Church is attached to an 'organic economy', based on the 'image of Christ's mystical body', consisting of a 'number of social bodies which, like the organs of the human body, would each have their role and would have to agree to coordinate their functions'.[63] Consequently, the Church remains committed to the misguided idea (in Garand's eye) that a 'third way' between liberalism and socialism could still be found. For Garand, in short, the Catholic Church, by refusing to endorse the principle of the market, had opened itself to Socialist principles that in fact violated its core beliefs. His hope was that it would still be possible to persuade the Church that its theology should commit it to economic liberalism.

So central were the concerns that Garand addressed in his paper that ALEPS actually organised an entirely separate colloquium on the subject in late 1970 entitled 'The Church Faced with the Problems of our Time'. Participants included Bourcier de Carbon (the ALEPS president), Henri Guitton (an economist and the brother of Catholic philosopher Jean Guitton), Michel Villey (the natural law historian and brother of Daniel Villey, the association's first president), Achille Dauphin-Meunier (an economist close to Bertrand de Jouvenel and to the collaborationist press during the Occupation), Garand, and Calan.[64] Perhaps what is most remarkable about the discussion of Christianity in the early years of the association's history is how seriously they took the matter, at a time when religious belief was in decline and France was well on its way to becoming a secular society. If anything, ALEPS' speakers often sounded more sanguine about the prospect of enlisting the Catholic Church in the liberal cause than they were about reaching out to the free-thinking radicals of May 68. If its members saw Catholicism as liberal, it was in part because they still seem to have seen liberalism as Catholic (or at least Christian).

A final clue to the ultimately conservative outlook of ALEPS is the way it conceived of the relationship between economic liberalism and social order. This concern was integral to the way in which many of their members viewed May 68: try as they might to muster up some sympathy for the students' free-spiritedness and critique of the country's sclerotic institutions, the economists and businessmen who attended the gatherings could not refrain from describing the protestors as threats to the social order. The 'creative destruction' that Joseph Schumpeter believed was inherent to capitalism was not, in other words, a principle they were eager to expand into a social principle. In his introduction to the proceedings of the 1969 'liberal week', Claude Harmel wrote: 'Contrary to anarchism, [liberal thought] knows that man cannot be free outside an organised society [and] that there is no organised society without a state.'[65] At the 1970 conference, the philosopher René Poirier expressed anxiety that the modern need for freedom would result in a 'sort of generalised freedom', which would soon result in the 'freedom to be violent, the freedom of brutal action and of revolutionary flair', giving birth to 'a kind of small-time Nietzscheanism'.[66] To the same panel, Raymond Aron offered his customary measured insight.

More than anything, he conceded that the 'cultural revolution' that was transforming the Western world presented a challenge to liberal thought:

> There can be no free polity as long as men lack a spontaneous, affective respect for the law [and] respect for one another; however, we are today faced with a new kind of cultural revolution, which is not liberal but *libertaire*, and, confronted with this revolution, the liberal is very troubled! What should liberals think about drug use? What should liberals think about Woodstock? Should liberals think of students who scorn, in the sexual realm, the prohibitions and obligations that their parents respected?[67]

To these questions, Aron offered the judicious reply that liberals must adopt a 'mixed attitude'. The liberal should not oppose a 'brutal, blind, categorical refusal' to intellectual and moral quests that may help humanity to 'free itself in a way from some of its secular prejudices'. At the same time, liberals cannot deny 'the danger confronting a society which, having lost all religious sanctions in its system of prohibitions and obligations, is in the process of losing all capacity to command and forbid'.[68] Aron's concern with identifying the point at which freedom conflicts with the need for social order undoubtedly belongs to a longstanding tradition of liberal thought. Yet his remarks, like those of other participants, suggest the extent to which the liberalism discussed at ALEPS was often forthrightly conservative in tenor: its debates about freedom were more focused on the constraints that are constitutive of true freedom than they were on the nature of freedom itself.

Conclusion: Neo-liberalism à la française?

Between 1966 and 1973, ALEPS made a robust case for reinvigorating French society through the principles of economic liberalism. Its members advocated unleashing the creativity of the market from state regulation and intervention, bolstering the legal and economic status of companies, promoting competition and entrepreneurialism, and decentralising bureaucratic decision-making processes. This was accompanied by a relentless critique of Marxism, collectivism, and economic planning. In these ways, they helped to inject into French public discourse a vocabulary that would ultimately serve to rationalise, in the 1980s and 1990s, the adoption of neo-liberal policies and the globalisation of the French economy. Moreover, in response to the economic transformations that France was then undergoing, they began to articulate a new set of justifications for capitalism, corresponding to what Boltanski and Chiapello have described as the 'new spirit of capitalism': a newly emergent form of capitalism that, compared to the system that had prevailed in the 1950s and 1960s, was less hierarchical and paternalistic, more decentralised, and more focused on ensuring the 'self-fulfilment' of top managers. Yet what

remains striking about ALEPS in its early years is how different its conception
of economic liberalism was from neoliberalism as we now understand it.
Despite the fact that some of the association's members sought to tap into the
emancipatory aspirations of the student movement, many of them instinctively
tethered their commitment to economic freedom to a conservative conception
of the social order and devoted considerable energy to the quixotic task of
resting economic liberalism on a Christian foundation. One consequence of
the reluctance to go down the road of full-blown free-market economic
liberalism à la Hayek was that many of its members were hardly relentless or
dogmatic in their criticism of state intervention and social welfare policies.
Quite a few of the economists involved with ALEPS identified more with the
Ordoliberalism of Röpke and Eucken than with the 'pure' liberalism of Hayek.
The economist Gaston Leduc, for instance, confessed to the 1973 gathering:
'for my part, I recognise that in a modern economy . . . state intervention is
absolutely necessary and in many cases indispensable.'[69]

If ALEPS members were at times softer on policies that Friedrich Hayek and
his disciples might have regarded as 'collectivist', it was in part because some
had once subscribed to explicitly collectivist ideologies. Indeed, one of the most
puzzling and disturbing characteristics of ALEPS is that a number of its most
prominent figures had flirted with fascism or the Vichy regime in the 1930s and
1940s. Claude Harmel had been the *secrétaire général adjoint* of Marcel Déat's
collaborationist RNP. And Hyacinthe Dubreuil, who at the 1968 conference
called for a 'new liberalism' in which 'the organisation of work' would be
founded on 'liberty',[70] had in 1941 hailed Philippe Pétain as 'a venerable chief
who, like a knight of times of old, protects today a suffering France'.[71] Nor
were these dalliances merely youthful indiscretions. They continued (at least in
some instances) to shape the pool from which economic liberals sought fresh
recruits: Harmel, according to his *Le Monde* obituary, 'took under his wing'
Alain Madelin (b. 1946) and Hervé Novelli (b. 1949), both of whom had been
active in the 1960s in the far-right student organisation Occident, shepherding
them towards the promised land of economic liberalism.[72] Madelin subsequently
became France's most prominent neo-liberal spokesmen with his involvement
in the economic policies of the Chirac government in 1986–8 and his
(admittedly disastrous) presidential bid in 2002.

ALEPS began to free itself of its heavier conservative baggage in the mid-
to late 1970s, with the arrival of a new generation of Chicago School-
inspired economists. In his 1978 book *Demain le capitalisme*, one such
economist, Henri Lepage, submitted that 'the liberal message will be effective
only if it proves that there is a gulf separating it from conservatism', adding:

> the liberal's goal is not to enforce an *end*, but to preoccupy himself with
> the *means* that make it possible to achieve the best possible arbitration
> between different individual and collective preferences and ends that, at
> a given moment, constitute the matrix of the social body's conflicting
> interests and wills.[73]

With these words, Lepage echoed Hayek's famous 1960 essay 'Why I Am not a Conservative', in which he observed: 'to the liberal neither moral nor religious ideals are proper objects of coercion, while both conservatives and socialists recognise no such limits.'[74] In many respects, the early history of ALEPS captures a moment when convergences seemed possible between French capitalism and the emancipatory politics of the 1960s. At the same time, the participants of the 'liberal weeks' often seemed more intent on defending economic liberalism's moral and religious virtues than on arguing that the market offered a superordinating (and thus 'liberating') framework for integrating individuals into a social order that nonetheless gives them extensive latitude in making their own moral and lifestyle choices. Consequently, many liberals involved with ALEPS seemed uneasy about the prospect of what, in more recent years, the French left has come to denounce as '*ultralibéralisme*'. The true significance of ALEPS in these years is the way in which it attests to the uncertainty on the part of champions of French capitalism as to how to justify their conviction at a time when the post-war economy was dying and neo-liberalism was struggling to be born.

Notes

1 Charles S. Maier, '"Malaise": The crisis of capitalism in the 1970s', in Niall Ferguson, Charles S. Maier, Erez Manela and Daniel J. Sargent, eds., *The Shock of the Global: The 1970s in perspective* (Cambridge, MA: The Belknap Press of Harvard University, 2010), 26.

2 David Harvey, *A Brief History of Neoliberalism* (Oxford: Oxford University Press, 2005), 1. On the late 1970s – and particularly 1979 – as a major historical turning point, see Christian Caryl, *Strange Rebels: 1979 and the birth of the 21st century* (New York: Basic Books, 2013).

3 Luc Boltanski and Ève Chiapello, *The New Spirit of Capitalism*, trans. Gregory Elliott (London: Verso, 2005 [1999]).

4 François Denord, 'French neoliberalism and its divisions: From the Colloque Walter Lippmann to the Fifth Republic', in Philip Mirkowski and Dieter Plehwe, eds., *The Road from Mont Pèlerin: The making of the neoliberal thought collective* (Cambridge, MA: Harvard University Press, 2009), 19. See also Denord, *Néolibéralisme version française: Histoire d'une idéologie politique* (Paris: Demopolis, 2007); Denord, 'Aux origines du néo-libéralisme en France: Louis Rougier et le Colloque Walter Lippmann de 1938', *Le Mouvement social* 195 (2001): 9–34; and Serge Audier, *Aux Origines du néo-libéralisme: Le Colloque Walter Lippmann* (Paris: Éditions du Bord de l'eau, 2008).

5 Quoted in Denord, 'French neoliberalism and its divisions', see Note 4, 53.

6 Serge Mallet, 'Raymond Aron ou le dernier des "libéraux"', *Les Temps modernes* 165 (November 1959): 931–40.

7 Robert Mossé, review of François Bilger, 'La pensée économique libérale dans l'Allemagne contemporaine', *Weltwirtschaftliches Archiv* 95 (1965): 89.

8 An overview of Chauvin-Arnoux's history is available at the company's website: http://www.chauvin-arnoux.com/Groupe/historique.asp (accessed 1 September 2012).

9 André Arnoux, *L'Appel intérieur: pour ceux qui ne croient pas, pour ceux qui doutent, pour ceux qui voudraient croire* (Paris: Spes, 1945) and *La voie du bonheur* (Paris: Nouvelles Éditions Latines, 1956).

10 'A. L. E. P. S.', in *Première semaine de la pensée libérale. Paris. Maison de la Chimie. 14, 15, 18, 19, 20 novembre 1968* (St. Brieuc: Presses universitaires de Bretagne, 1969), 4.

11 See Note 10.

12 Hyacinthe Dubreuil, *Standards, le travail américain vu par un ouvrier français* (Paris: Grasset, 1929). The book was translated into English as *Robots or Men? A French workman's experience in American industry*, trans. Frances and Mason Merrill (New York and London: Harper & Brothers, 1930).

13 Martin Fine, 'Hyacinthe Dubreuil: Le Témoignage d'un ouvrier sur le syndicalisme, les relations industrielles et l'évolution technologique de 1921 à 1940', *Le Mouvement social* 106 (January–March, 1979): 46.

14 Denord, 'French neoliberalism and its divisions', see Note 4, 54.

15 'A. L. E. P. S.', see Note 10, 4.

16 Maurice Allais, 'An outline of my main contributions to economic science', *The American Economic Review* 87, 6 (December 1997): 3.

17 Maurice Allais, 'My life philosophy', *The American Economist* 33, 2 (1989): 10.

18 Luc Bourcier de Carbon, quoted in 'Conclusion', *Première semaine de la pensée libéral*, see Note 10, 39.

19 Claude Harmel, 'La soif de liberté dans le monde moderne', in *Première semaine de la pensée libérale*, see Note 10, 7.

20 Antonio López, F.S.C.B, *Spirit's Gift: The metaphysical insight of Claude Bruaire* (Washington DC: The Catholic University Press of America, 2006), 7–9.

21 Claude Bruaire, quoted in 'La soif de liberté dans le monde moderne', see Note 19, 7.

22 Michel Crozier, *Le Phénomène bureaucratique* (Paris: Seuil, 1964).

23 Crozier, quoted in 'La soif de liberté dans le monde moderne', see Note 19, 8.

24 Guy Thuillier, 'Comment François Perroux voyait la politique en octobre 1943', *La Revue administrative* 56 (September 2003): 477–86.

25 Michel Drancourt, 'L'Entreprise au cœur: Entretien avec Michel Drancourt' (interview with Bernard Colasse and Francis Pave), *Annales des mines* (December 1998): 6.

26 Drancourt, quoted in 'La soif de liberté dans le monde moderne', see Note 19, 8–9.

27 Maurice Allais, paraphrased by Claude Harmel in 'De la centralisation à la pluralité des centres de décision', in *Première semaine de la pensée libérale*, see Note 10, 19.

28 Maurice Roy, quoted in 'Pour un ordre libéral' in *Première semaine de la pensée libérale*, see Note 10, 34.

29 René Poirier, quoted in *Première semaine de la pensée libérale*, see Note 10, 36.

30 Claude Harmel, in *Première semaine de la pensée libérale*, see Note 10, 37.

31 Robert Marjolin, 'Intervention et liberté dans la politique économique européenne', in *Le Renouveau de la pensée libérale. 2e Semaine de la pensée libérale Octobre 1969. Texte intégral des débats* (Paris: Nouvelles éditions Latines, 1970), 172.

32 Marjolin, 'Intervention et liberté', see Note 31, 173.

33 Marjolin, 'Intervention et liberté', see Note 31, 173.

34 Marjolin, 'Intervention et liberté', see Note 31, 174.

35 Marjolin, 'Intervention et liberté', see Note 31, 176.

36 Michel Poniatowski, 'Qu'en sera-t-il du libéralisme en France', in *L'Efficacité sociale du libéralisme. 4e Semaine de la pensée libérale Décembre 71. Texte intégral des débats* (Paris: Éditions Albatros/Étapes, 1972), 313.

37 This term only entered the mainstream after it was coined by the economist Jean Fourastié, in Jean Fourastié, *Les Trente glorieuses, ou la révolution invisible de 1946 à 1975* (Paris: Fayard, 1979).

38 Poniatowski, 'Qu'en sera-t-il du libéralisme en France', see Note 36, 314.

39 Poniatowski, 'Qu'en sera-t-il du libéralisme en France', see Note 36, 314–15.

40 Poniatowski, 'Qu'en sera-t-il du libéralisme en France', see Note 36, 315.

41 Poniatowski, 'Qu'en sera-t-il du libéralisme en France', see Note 36, 316–17.

42 Poniatowski, 'Qu'en sera-t-il du libéralisme en France', see Note 36, 318.

43 Boltanski and Chiapello, *The New Spirit of Capitalism*, see Note 3, 62–3.

44 M. de Hesdin, 'Qu'est-ce qu'un cadre', in *Le Libéralisme, sortie de secours du socialisme. 3e semaine de la pensée libérale Novembre 1970. Texte intégral des débats* (Paris: Éditions Étapes, 1971), 121.

45 Philippe David, in *Le Libéralisme*, see Note 44, 124.

46 David, in *Le Libéralisme*, see Note 44, 124.

47 David, in *Le Libéralisme*, see Note 44, 126–7.

48 *Le Renouveau de la pensée libérale*, see Note 31.

49 David, in *Le Libéralisme*, see Note 44.

50 *L'Efficacité sociale du libéralisme*, see Note 36.

51 *Liberté économique et progrès social. Problèmes actuels, réponses libérales. 5e semaine de la pensée libérale Décembre 72. Texte intégral des débats* (Paris: Éditions Albatros, 1973).

52 *Liberté économique et progrès social. Le Libéralisme, un projet de société. 6e semaine de la pensée libérale 26–29 Novembre 1973. Texte intégral des débats* (Paris: Éditions Albatros, 1973).

53 Jacques Baron, 'Louis Devaux: Les Leçons d'une carrière à l'américaine', *L'Entreprise* 641 (23 December 1967): 45–53. Devaux would later serve as the head of the CNPF.

54 Louis Devaux, 'Un Impératif social: La Croissance économique' in *Le Renouveau de la pensée libérale*, see Note 31, 47.

55 Abel Mestre, 'Claude Harmel, figure de l'anticommunisme, fondateur de l'Institut supérieur du travail' (obituary), *Le Monde*, 29 November 2011.

56 Harmel, 'La Pensée libérale et l'action syndicale', in *Le Renouveau de la pensée libérale*, see Note 31, 59.

57 Harmel, 'La Pensée libérale et l'action syndicale', in *Le Renouveau de la pensée libérale*, see Note 56, 54.

58 Harmel, 'La Pensée libérale et l'action syndicale', in *Le Renouveau de la pensée libérale*, see Note 56, 69.

59 Pierre de Calan, 'Allocution d'ouverture', in *Le Renouveau de la pensée libérale*, see Note 31, 107.

60 Albert Garand, 'L'Église a-t-elle condamné le libéralisme économique?', in *Le Renouveau de la pensée libérale*, see Note 31, 109.

61 Garand, 'L'Église a-t-elle condamné le libéralisme économique?', see Note 60, 110. An English version of *Magister et Magistra* is available on the Vatican's website at http://www.vatican.va/holy_father/john_xxiii/encyclicals/documents/hf_j-xxiii_enc_15051961_mater_en.html.

62 Garand, 'L'Église a-t-elle condamné le libéralisme économique?', see Note 60, 118.

63 Garand, 'L'Église a-t-elle condamné le libéralisme économique?', see Note 60, 118.

64 Liberté économique et progrès social, *L'Église face aux problèmes du temps* (Paris: Nouvelles éditions Latines, 1971).

65 Harmel, 'Introduction', in *Le Renouveau de la pensée libérale*, see Note 31, 3.

66 Poirier, 'Les Aspects divers de la liberté', in in *Le Renouveau de la pensée libérale*, see Note 31, 21, 22.

67 Raymond Aron, 'Civilisation moderne et liberté', in *Le Renouveau de la pensée libérale*, see Note 31, 34.

68 Aron, 'Civilisation moderne et liberté', see Note 67, 35.

69 Gaston Leduc, 'Les interventions économiques de l'État', in *Le Libéralisme, un projet de société*, 76. On p. 78, Leduc also affirmed the principle, dear to Ordoliberals, that 'the state must define the rules of the [economic] game'.

70 Dubreuil, 'A chacun sa chance', in *Première semaine de la pensée libérale*, see Note 31, 37.

71 Quoted in Fine, 'Hyacinthe Dubreuil: le témoignage d'un ouvrier', see Note 13, 61.

72 Mestre, 'Claude Harmel', see Note 55.

73 Henri Lepage, *Demain le capitalisme* (Paris: Livre de poche, 1978), 418.

74 Friedrich Hayek, 'Why I am not a Conservative', in *The Constitution of Liberty* (Chicago: The University of Chicago Press, 1960), 402.

10

France's Anti-68 Liberal Revival

Iain Stewart

In the tenth anniversary issue of the intellectual journal *Commentaire*, the economist Christian Stoffaës remarked that, since the journal's birth in 1978, France had undergone a 'liberal revolution' in which Marxism had been displaced from its position of ideological dominance by the rediscovery of the country's liberal heritage.[1] As the intellectual historian Mark Lilla has noted, other continental European countries experienced a similar collapse in the intellectual respectability of Marxism during this period, but only in France was this accompanied by a major revival of the domestic liberal tradition.[2] Both Stoffaës and Lilla viewed this development with considerable satisfaction, but of course the ideological reorientation of the French intelligentsia in these years was not always so warmly received. In 1983, Perry Anderson famously remarked that in the space of a few years Paris had made the transition from a beacon of revolutionary politics to 'the capital of European intellectual reaction', an argument that continues to echo on the contemporary French left in the work of Daniel Lindenberg and François Cusset.[3]

Yet radical evaluative disagreement over France's 'liberal revolution' exists alongside a basic empirical agreement over the extent of the ideological transformation that occurred in France between the late 1970s and 1980s: whatever they think of its content, all the commentators mentioned above would agree that something akin to an ideological revolution occurred in France in these years. The need to develop our understanding of the content and complexities of this phenomenon is a major priority for contemporary intellectual historians of France since the 1970s.[4] Much of the work published on this topic in the 1990s tended to reduce the complexities of France's intellectual revolution to an 'anti-totalitarian turn' in the mid- to late 1970s. In this narrative, the French publication of Alexander Solzhenitsyn's *The Gulag*

Archipelago in 1974 triggered a collective epiphany among France's intellectuals, leading them to abandon Marxism and to embrace a half-forgotten liberal tradition.[5] Although there is an element of truth in this argument, such narratives obscure more than they reveal. There were, for instance, different kinds of anti-totalitarianism. While some anti-totalitarian intellectuals championed the cause of human rights, others regarded this as a utopian illusion.[6] Indeed, not all anti-totalitarian intellectuals claimed to be liberals, and those that were active in the recovery of France's liberal tradition in these years entered into this project with significantly different objectives. Like the Revolution of 1789, the historiography of which was being fundamentally contested in this period, France's liberal revolution was not a bloc.

   This chapter builds on, and is a contribution towards, the new historiography of France's intellectual transformation in the 1970s and 1980s. In particular, it follows recent work by Michael Scott Christofferson and Julian Bourg in de-emphasising the importance of a mythical 'anti-totalitarian moment' and stressing the importance of longer-term factors in the transformation of the French intellectual landscape, particularly the impact of the *événements* of May–June 1968.[7] Unlike Bourg or Christofferson, however, the focus here will be specifically on the revival of the French liberal tradition in these years. Through a historical analysis of the contribution made by the journals *Contrepoint* and *Commentaire* to this revival, I identify a specific form of liberal revivalism that emerged as a hostile response to the upheavals of 1968.[8] In line with their explicit commitment to intellectual pluralism, contributors to *Commentaire* and *Contrepoint* sometimes cooperated with other liberal revivalists and anti-totalitarians; however, the two journals' anti-68 origins clearly shaped their interpretation of the French liberal tradition that they were programmatically committed to reviving. What distinguished the liberal revivalism of these journals was that it was tied to a specific project aimed at reforming French political culture. Anti-totalitarianism played an important rhetorical role in this project. But it was the interrelated critiques of radical egalitarianism, relativist 'anti-humanism', and intellectual 'irresponsibility' that fundamentally shaped the liberal revivalism promoted by *Contrepoint* and *Commentaire* and marked it out from alternative readings of France's liberal tradition in the 1970s and 1980s.

Raymond Aron and the roots of the French liberal revival

During an interview in 1981, the political sociologist and commentator Raymond Aron remarked with amusement that for the first time his work was on the verge of becoming fashionable.[9] At this point, towards the end of his life, he was undergoing a reputational transformation. Ever since his conversion to militant anti-communism at the onset of the Cold War had caused him to break with his friend Jean-Paul Sartre, Aron had been shunned by a French intellectual left where it was supposedly considered 'better to be wrong with Sartre than right with Aron'. The relative popularity of these two men has often since been used as a kind of shorthand for the ideological orientation of the French intelligentsia. The historian Tony Judt summed up the dramatic political changes that swept the French intellectual landscape in the late 1970s and 1980s as the building of 'a monument to Aronian reason' upon 'the funeral pyre of Sartrean radicalism', an analysis echoed in 2005 by the then French Prime Minister Jean-Pierre Raffarin, who noted with satisfaction that 'the majority of intellectuals [now] prefer to be right with Aron than wrong with Sartre'.[10] However, the origins of Aron's reputational transformation lie not in any radical change in his own work, but rather in France's 'anti-totalitarian moment' of the mid- to late 1970s.[11] The revival of the French liberal tradition, which accelerated amid this anti-totalitarian turn, also contributed to Aron's intellectual ascendency in these years. Not only was Aron one of France's earliest theorists of totalitarianism, but he had pioneered the rediscovery of the French liberal tradition long before this became fashionable in the late 1970s and 1980s. French liberal revivalists such as François Furet, Marcel Gauchet and Pierre Manent read authors like Tocqueville and Constant through the prism of their contemporary anti-totalitarianism, and in doing so some of these figures were influenced by Raymond Aron.[12] Nevertheless, just as it would be a mistake to regard the liberal revival and anti-totalitarianism as two sides of the same coin, Aron's own liberal revivalism cannot be simply reduced to his anti-totalitarianism.

Aron's earliest work on the subject of totalitarianism was published on the eve of the Second World War, but it was not until the late 1950s that his reflection on this issue began to draw explicitly on the French liberal tradition for inspiration.[13] A central and influential contention of his theory was that democracy and totalitarianism were not opposites but rather that the latter was the pathological product of a malfunctioning democratic political culture. Although he originally developed this argument under the influence of radically anti-liberal thinkers such as Carl Schmitt, in the late 1950s Aron turned to Montesquieu's *The Spirit of the Laws* to rework his theory for the book *Democracy and Totalitarianism* (1965).[14] Here Aron maintained his earlier emphasis on the problem of political culture, but articulated this by using Montesquieu's vocabulary of the 'principle' of a regime and the problem of its corruption. He followed Montesquieu by defining the principle of a political regime as a set of social attitudes without which such a regime cannot function. For liberal democracies, this principle was a combination of respect for legality and a spirit of compromise, and the underlying importance of these attributes remained implicit in his subsequent work that engaged more substantially with France's liberal tradition.[15] As we shall see, some of these later instances of Aron's French liberal revivalism also involved a corresponding shift away from some of his formative German intellectual influences.

Democracy and Totalitarianism was the last in a trilogy of books based
upon lectures given at the Sorbonne between 1955 and 1958, which was
the period in which Aron first began seriously to study Montesquieu and
Tocqueville.[16] Ironically, given the title of this book, these were years in which
the language of international anti-communism was moving away from the
aggressive and emotive anti-totalitarian discourse of the early Cold War and
towards an ostensibly more objective comparative analysis of Capitalist and
Communist forms of 'industrial society'.[17] One of the features of this rhetorical
shift was the emergence of what came to be known as 'end of ideology' theory.
In the mid- to late 1950s, Raymond Aron was France's leading proponent of
this theory.[18] The degree of optimism with which it was articulated varied, but
proponents of the end of ideology shared the fundamental assumption that
sustained economic growth, managed by a moderately interventionist state
in cooperation with labour and enterprise, could simultaneously deliver
increasing levels of wages, benefits, profits and investment.[19] By thus aligning
the interests of workers and employers, a new 'politics of productivity' would
replace the old politics of class conflict, rendering traditional ideological
distinctions between left and right redundant in the process.[20] Because it
embraced the mixed economy and a moderate degree of state economic
planning, end of ideology theory received a hostile reception from neoliberals
committed to a revival of classical economic liberalism.[21] But for liberals like
Aron, this post-ideological vision was the basis on which a healthy democratic
political culture of legality and compromise could be built in France.

   Françoise Mélonio has linked France's post-Second World War Tocqueville
revival to the emergence of this end of ideology theory.[22] Given Tocqueville's
famous concerns over the extension of the powers of the centralised state,
this is not an obvious connection to make even if Tocqueville could be
mobilised in support of end of ideology theory in other ways.[23] In Aron's
case, instead of referring to the author of *Democracy in America* to support
the detail of his analysis, he set up a comparison between Tocqueville and
Marx's predictive accuracy in relation to the issue of equality. The point here
was to suggest that, under the influence of sustained economic growth, the
development of post-Second World War western democracies confirmed
Tocqueville's predictions of rising social equality in democratic capitalist
societies and contradicted Marx's opposite vision of the pauperisation of the
working class.[24] Another way in which Tocqueville resonated with Aron's end
of ideology argument was in his critique of intellectuals' alleged propensity
for a moralising and unrealistic form of 'literary politics'.[25] One of the
principal obstacles to a political culture of legality and compromise that Aron
consistently identified and critiqued throughout his career was the alleged
irresponsibility of France's public intellectuals, and it is significant that he
first articulated his end of ideology theory in the conclusion to his famous
polemical work *L'Opium des Intellectuels* (1955).[26] However, it is important
to recognise that Aron's theorisation of intellectual irresponsibility predated
his encounter with Tocqueville in the 1950s; instead, it originated in his

reading of Max Weber's work on the political ethics of responsibility and conviction during the early 1930s.[27] As with his adaptation of Montesquieu to reformulate his comparative analysis of democratic and totalitarian states, Tocqueville was not a formative influence but rather an adaptive one.

If Aron used aspects of Montesquieu and Tocqueville's work to inform elements of his own theories of totalitarianism and the end of ideology between 1955 and 1958, it was not until 1959–60 that he positioned his work more explicitly and comprehensively within this liberal lineage. The key text here, sometimes referred to as a foundational moment in the wider French liberal revival, is his *Les Étapes de la pensée sociologique*, published in 1967 but based upon lectures on the history of sociological thought given at the Sorbonne eight years earlier.[28] Here Aron cast himself for the first time as a 'belated descendent' of Montesquieu and Tocqueville, whom he identified as the founders of a 'French school of political sociology' that was in opposition to the influential positivist and Marxist traditions.[29] By claiming this lineage, Aron was attempting both to legitimise his own brand of anti-positivist, anti-Marxist political sociology and reinforce its epistemological basis.[30] In referring to himself as a 'belated descendent' of the liberal tradition, Aron tacitly acknowledged the fact that he had developed his sociological perspective in the 1930s entirely independently of these retrospectively selected French liberal predecessors. Before the Second World War, his main influences were a series of German thinkers including Wilhelm Dilthey, Edmund Husserl, Martin Heidegger and, above all, Max Weber.

In his second book, *Introduction à la philosophie de l'histoire* (1938), Aron combined these German influences to inform a relativistic critique of the epistemological position of Marxism on the basis of which he argued for a sociologically informed, gradualist and broadly liberal 'politics of understanding'.[31] This was Aron's version of Weber's ethic of responsibility. In his memoirs, Aron identified the *Introduction* as having established the fundamental basis of all his subsequent political thought, but the problem with this book was that its radically relativistic attack on Marxism and positivism seemed to remove the possibility of attaining the kind of objective knowledge upon which responsible, sociologically informed decision-making was to be based.[32] Furthermore, from a moral perspective, Aron's epistemological relativism provided an insubstantial normative basis for his defence of moderate liberal democracy.[33] It was partly to address these issues that Aron turned to a more comprehensive analysis of Montesquieu and Tocqueville in 1959.

Influenced in part by Leo Strauss's critique of Max Weber's moral relativism,[34] one of Aron's priorities in the late 1950s and early 1960s was to explore the possibilities for a modern political science that combined empirical rigour with a renewed sensitivity to the normative concerns of classical political philosophy. This is one of the things that attracted him to the work of Montesquieu and Tocqueville in these years. Like Weber, they were pluralistic, probabilistic thinkers who refused mono-causal determinism, but their interpretative pluralism did not overextend into a radical relativism that undermined empirical objectivity or denied the possibility of rationally grounded value judgements. For Aron, Montesquieu and Tocqueville were to be admired as political sociologists 'who never cease to judge at the same time as [they] describe'.[35] This concern with establishing a political sociology that combined modern empirical methods with a classical philosophical sensibility was partly a response to growing criticism of the end of ideology theory in the late 1950s. Because it apparently reduced a political problem to the technical issue of managing economic productivity, end of ideology theory came to be linked to growing concerns about a crisis of normative political philosophy in the late 1950s and early 1960s.[36] This critique of end of ideology theory on classical philosophical grounds was soon compounded by a more radical attack from the emergent New Left that led Aron to draw further upon Tocqueville in formulating his response.[37]

The ideological development of the New Left in France and elsewhere during the 1960s was partly a critical response to trends that end of ideology theorists had celebrated, notably the rise of the consumer society and the decline of the working class as a revolutionary force. This response involved highlighting the persistence of shocking inequalities within consumer societies, exploring the phenomena of alienation and anomie that accompanied growing prosperity, and critiquing post-war technocratic elitism in the name of a direct democracy that would extend beyond the traditional political arena to all spheres of social life through the promotion of self-management (*autogestion*). Aron responded to the new ideological challenge posed by the New Left through a theory of the 'dialectic of equality' that drew heavily upon Tocqueville for inspiration.[38] His main disagreement was with the influential neo-Marxism of Herbert Marcuse. Aron argued that the alienation and anomie that had accompanied the post-war economic miracle were not so much products of capitalism as they were inherent within the insatiable egalitarian appetite of modern democracy. This impulse was at once stimulated and frustrated by an industrial civilisation that provided rising material prosperity but whose inevitably hierarchical character obstructed the same egalitarian desires that growing productivity had helped to create. Although rising post-war prosperity served in part to lessen the appeal of revolutionary political ideologies, it could not provide reasons for living. Thus while in one sense it engendered social conservatism, at the same time it fed a spiritual revolt whose privileged expression during the 1960s was a rise in demands for enhanced participation and self-management and a critique of hierarchical bureaucracies that was keenly felt in the Gaullist Fifth Republic.

The explosion of such demands amid the libertarian contestation that marked the events of May and June 1968 in France prompted Aron to reformulate this Tocquevillian critique along more aggressively polemical lines.[39] He refused to take the actions of students and intellectuals during the crisis seriously and, convinced that they were indulging in pseudo-revolutionary agitation against a consumer society of whose material benefits they were among the principal beneficiaries, he labelled the events a 'psychodrama'.[40]

Although in this regard Aron's analysis was dismissive, in another sense he took the events of May 1968 extremely seriously. The explosion of discontent in 1968 signified a profound moral crisis, which he diagnosed by adapting Tocqueville's theory of the importance of religion in restraining the egalitarian impulse of democratic societies. By 1968, he suggested, the moral bases of a necessary minimum respect for legally constituted authority in France had been undermined not only by a long-term decline in the influence of religion over social mores, but also by the more recent erosion of atheistic humanism as an alternative source of moral principles with which to tame the insatiable egalitarian appetite of student radicals and the irresponsible intellectuals that indulged them.[41]

Aron's liberal revivalism, then, developed in a number of directions between 1955 and 1968, all of which were driven by his overriding preoccupation with the problem of developing and maintaining a democratic political culture based on the principles of legality and compromise. Aron first articulated this in the terminology of Montesquieu's *De l'Esprit des lois* when revising his theory of totalitarianism, but in most respects his recovery of the liberal tradition in these years cannot be reduced to his anti-totalitarianism. It was related to a project of epistemological revision undertaken in the context of a crisis of political philosophy, and it informed and legitimised both a critique of radical egalitarianism and of the postmodern anti-humanism with which Aron associated the emergence of radical egalitarian ideologies in France. Tocqueville was the primary point of reference for the latter critiques, and increasingly came to displace Max Weber as the inspiration for Aron's critique of intellectual irresponsibility and its pernicious influence upon French political culture.[42] Nevertheless, it is important not to overstate the role of Tocqueville: it is significant, for instance, that Aron largely ignored a number of key tenets of Tocqueville's thought, including his economic liberalism and his emphasis on the importance of associational life in maintaining a healthy democratic political culture. The latter point is particularly noteworthy because defenders of the legacy of May 1968 typically point to its positive impact on associational life in France during the 1970s.[43] Aron, however, was France's leading intellectual critic of the *événements*, and, as we shall see below, this was the single most important factor in bringing together a group of like-minded younger intellectuals that would form the core editorial teams of two 'Aronian' journals dedicated to reviving France's liberal tradition.

The origins and orientations of *Contrepoint* and *Commentaire*

Prior to the publication of his famous anti-68 essay, *La Révolution introuvable* (1968), Aron gave a running commentary on the events in his columns for the conservative daily *Le Figaro*. On 11 June 1968, he used this

column to publish an appeal for the formation of a 'Committee for the
Defence and Renovation of the French University'.[44] Although the committee
itself was short-lived, the group of intellectuals that rallied to Aron's appeal
continued to interact through his weekly seminar at the École pratique des
hautes études. It was through the network established there that the journal
Contrepoint was founded in May 1970.[45] *Contrepoint* was the first French
journal explicitly committed to reviving France's liberal tradition of political
thought, and its liberal revivalism was closely related to its origins in Aron's
intellectual reaction against May 68.[46] Timing the launch to coincide with
the second anniversary of the *événements* was a deliberate move, and the
journal, which carried a different quotation from Tocqueville on each of its
mastheads, regularly published articles devoted to studying aspects of the
moral crisis that Aron had diagnosed in *La Révolution introuvable*. Thus,
for instance, the editorial in the first issue of *Contrepoint* claimed that it was
committed to combating 'the nihilist anarchism of the dominant group of
intellectuals' and the radically egalitarian, anti-authoritarian ideologies
espoused by the various leftist groups that had sprung up in the wake of
1968.[47] Its early editions were special issues treating such themes as 'liberty
and authority', 'the state of the youth', 'the origins of the malaise' and 'the
situation of the intellectuals'. *Contrepoint* was particularly critical of those
intellectuals – most prominently Michel Foucault, Jacques Lacan, Gilles
Deleuze and Félix Guattari – whose relativist anti-humanism was regarded
as the philosophical basis for the nihilistic libertarianism of the *soixante-
huitard* radicals.[48]

   Contrepoint was an anti-totalitarian journal, but its anti-totalitarianism
was expansively defined in response to the post-68 landscape of left-wing
politics in France. A significant feature of this landscape was the crystallisation
of radical left-wing forms of anti-communism. Groups such as Gauche
Prolétarienne existed to the left of (and in opposition to) the French
Communist Party (PCF), often espousing a 'third worldist' ideology inspired
by the examples of Communist China, Vietnam or Cuba rather than the
Soviet Union. *Contrepoint*'s anti-totalitarianism therefore extended beyond
the PCF and USSR to embrace Communist regimes in the developing world
and the revolutionary leftism in France, which, notwithstanding its own
opposition to the PCF, was accused of opening the door to Communist
subversion by destabilising the liberal order.[49] These concerns intensified
from 1972 with the signing of the Common Programme between the PCF
and the Socialist Party, which established the prospect of Communists
entering government in France for the first time since the start of the Cold
War. The wider anti-totalitarian turn in France developed following the
scandal surrounding Solzhenitsyn's *The Gulag Archipelago* and media
coverage of atrocities and humanitarian crises in Cambodia and Vietnam,
but was itself in large part a response to the re-emergence of the PCF as a
potential party of government.[50] *Contrepoint*, however, was unable fully to
take advantage of the more propitious intellectual environment that began

to develop in 1974 because personal differences between the journal's directors, Georges Liébert and Patrick Devedjian, led to the former's resignation, the withdrawal of Raymond Aron's support for the project and, shortly thereafter, the journal's termination at the end of 1976.[51]

While *Contrepoint* never achieved a circulation that would enable it to compete with more established publications such as *Esprit* or *Les Temps modernes*, it nevertheless carried a degree of influence in the entourage of the centre-right politician Valéry Giscard d'Estaing, who admired the journal and wanted it to operate as a kind of think tank for the development of his brand of 'advanced liberalism'.[52] Although this invitation was declined, both *Contrepoint* and its successor *Commentaire* retained close links to Giscard d'Estaing and the governments that served under his presidency between 1974 and 1981. Jean-Claude Casanova, a key figure in the running of both journals, served as an advisor to Raymond Barre during the latter's time in office as Prime Minister between 1976 and 1981.[53] Raymond Aron served as an informal advisor during the election campaigns of 1978 and 1981 and had previously taught Giscard d'Estaing, Raymond Barre and Alain Peyrefitte (who was Minister of Justice between 1977 and 1981) at the École nationale d'administration and Sciences Po.[54] The close ties that existed between *Contrepoint*, *Commentaire* and Sciences Po were significant from an ideological as well as a sociological point of view. The latter institution originated from the École libre des sciences politiques founded in 1872 to train France's new political and administrative élite following the Franco-Prussian War. Its name had changed following its part nationalisation after the Second World War, when Raymond Aron joined its teaching staff, but across its different incarnations Sciences Po was closely associated with the preservation of France's liberal tradition of political thought.[55] The variety of liberalism with which this institution tended to be associated was one that was more or less elitist and for which the value of democracy was secondary to that of liberty.[56]

The journal *Commentaire* was founded in March 1978 and its editorial team was largely composed from the group that had coalesced under Aron's tutelage ten years earlier. Liébert and Devedjian, the younger alumni of Sciences Po that had driven the establishment of *Contrepoint*, were replaced by the more experienced and well-connected Jean-Claude Casanova, alongside the young political philosopher Pierre Manent and the historian Marc Fumaroli. Unlike at *Contrepoint*, where he played a fairly inconspicuous role, Raymond Aron was presented as the public face of *Commentaire*. The journal was advertised to prospective subscribers as an initiative taken by Aron with the aim of contributing to the intellectual and political reform of France. The means by which this reform would be pursued were the promotion of liberal pluralism and the rejection of dogmatic intellectual conformism.[57] The latter had been a prominent and recurrent theme in *Contrepoint*, which was more overtly combative than its successor and placed less of an emphasis on its intellectual pluralism.[58] This tonal shift was a reflection of the newly emerging intellectual landscape in France at the time. Still, there were limits to *Commentaire*'s embrace of alternative ideological outlooks. Although it positioned itself as an anti-totalitarian journal, its inaugural editorial was scornful of the 'telegenic' and 'lightweight' New Philosophers, former radicals such as Bernard-Henri Lévy and André Glucksmann who had become famous following their anti-totalitarian conversions.[59]

It is significant in this regard that *Commentaire* did not position itself merely as an anti-totalitarian journal; it was opposed to what it identified as the *two* major threats to liberal democracy: 'the inarticulate cry of pure revolt on one side; the absolute knowledge of total ideology on the other'.[60] In railing against the first of these enemies of liberty, it picked up from where *Contrepoint*'s condemnation of nihilistic libertarianism had left off in 1970. Thus, while its opposition to 'total ideology' situated *Commentaire* within a wider field of intellectual anti-totalitarianism, its conservative anti-libertarianism distinguished it from other anti-totalitarian journals like *Esprit* or *Le Débat*. The most significant direction in which *Commentaire* explicitly opened itself to outside collaboration was the anti-Communist, *autogestionnaire* current within the Socialist Party and the non-Communist trade union, the Confédération française démocratique du travail (CFDT). This section of the French left was praised in its inaugural editorial for having 'rediscovered civil society' and being ready to 'break the fatal equation of socialism and state control'. This olive branch proffered to a section of the left was, however, conditional upon it 'demonstrat[ing] that it can be something other than the impotent libertarian counterpoint to the statist left'.[61]

Anti-68 liberal revivalism in comparative perspective

As we have seen, the French liberal revivalism prosecuted by the intellectuals of *Contrepoint* and *Commentaire* originated primarily in their hostility to the events and legacy of May 1968 rather than in the critique of totalitarianism. However, this did not prevent them from applying the vocabulary of anti-totalitarianism to their readings of the French liberal tradition. Articles in *Commentaire*'s 'Classics of Liberty' section, which was devoted to the rediscovery of predominantly French liberal authors of the eighteenth and nineteenth centuries, are littered with references to 'Jacobin totalitarianism', the 'pre-totalitarian experience' of the First Empire, or the sensitivity to the totalitarian menace of authors such as Hippolyte Taine or Benjamin Constant (who 'somehow foresaw Hitler through Napoleon').[62] This anachronistic tendency was a feature of the wider liberal revival that accompanied the anti-totalitarian turn; it was not specific to authors associated with *Commentaire*.[63] An explicitly anti-totalitarian interpretation of Constant by the pro-68 philosopher Marcel Gauchet was praised in the pages of 'Classics of Liberty' by Pierre Manent in 1980, for instance.[64] Gauchet's mentor, Claude Lefort, was another pro-68, anti-totalitarian liberal revivalist whose work was praised by Manent in *Commentaire*.[65] Closer comparison of Manent and Lefort, however, indicates that, despite converging upon the language of anti-totalitarianism, they otherwise offered divergent interpretations of the French liberal tradition's contemporary significance.

Along with Cornelius Castoriadis, Lefort had been a founder of the anti-Stalinist journal *Socialisme ou Barbarie*, which had been influential in developing the direct democratic, left-wing anti-communism that was a major ideological inspiration for many activists in 1968.[66] That year he had been a prominent supporter of the student and workers' movements, a position for which he was criticised by Raymond Aron, who was Lefort's doctoral supervisor and with whom he otherwise had good relations.[67] Meanwhile, Pierre Manent was Aron's assistant at the Collège de France and a director of *Commentaire*. In 1968 he had begun to frequent Aron's seminar, which he has described as 'a refuge far from the nave of madmen' at the École normale supérieure where he studied philosophy in an environment dominated by Althusserian Marxism.[68] Reflecting back on the *événements* in 2010, Manent attributed them partly to a crisis in the teaching of political philosophy in France at the time.[69] He retrospectively defined his own intellectual project as an attempt at rehabilitating an 'authentic political science', reconnected to its classical philosophical roots and liberated from postmodernist relativism.[70]

The first major source of inspiration in this enterprise was the work of Raymond Aron, and it was Aron who introduced Manent to his second main intellectual influence, Leo Strauss.[71] Claude Lefort was also an admirer of Strauss and Aron, as well as being an important theorist of totalitarianism in the 1970s.[72] Lefort and Manent shared Aron's basic point of view that totalitarianism existed as a permanent possibility within democracy itself rather than something opposite and external to democracy.[73] And they both viewed France's liberal tradition, with the primacy that it afforded to the political domain, as a rich source of inspiration from which to approach this issue. The work of Tocqueville in particular was a common point of reference, but Lefort and Manent's readings of Tocqueville emphasised contrasting sides of his work, with Manent following Aron's lead in focusing on the problem of the insatiable egalitarian impulse at work in democratic societies and Lefort being more interested in Tocqueville's views on associational life as the guarantor of a strong civil society.[74]

This essential difference between Lefort and Manent became apparent in an article by Manent dedicated to Lefort's writing on democracy and totalitarianism, published in the winter of 1981. In this otherwise positive assessment of Lefort's work, Manent took exception to his sympathetic evaluation of the contribution made by new social movements committed to women's and gay liberation, ecology, and the causes of the Lip factory workers and the farmers of the Larzac. Whereas Lefort saw such movements in a positive light as having helped to reinforce the rights of individuals in the face of the state, Manent regarded them as ultimately reinforcing the power of the state, as the final guarantor of these rights, and eroding those traditional relations of authority – 'employer over employee, man over woman and children . . .' – belonging to civil society.[75] A year earlier, Manent had expressed his views on this issue in more polemical terms:

> All that is needed to make the water diviners of the rue du Mail feel civil society bubbling up beneath their feet is for three ecologists, two feminists, a community organiser and a pirate radio presenter to meet up somewhere. There is something more urgent than liberating civil society from the grip of the State: liberating minds from the sterilising grip of the comfort blanket concept of civil society.[76]

The concept of civil society makes for a useful point of comparison from which to develop a more specific sense of the ways in which *Contrepoint* and *Commentaire* instrumentalised anti-totalitarianism and the French liberal tradition to intervene in contemporary social and political debate. That anti-totalitarianism was unavoidably a pro-civil society position was made obvious by the foundation in 1980 of the independent Solidarity trade union in Poland. Yet while this development received significant positive coverage in *Commentaire*,[77] the journal's regular contributors were at best ambivalent towards recent developments in French civil society. Whether such developments were regarded with friendly scepticism or open hostility depended on an implicit distinction at work in 'Aronian' liberal commentary between 'radical' and 'moderate' ideal types of French civil society movements.

The landslide Gaullist victory in the elections of June 1968 marked the immediate political failure of 68 radicalism. In the wake of this failure, however, the generalised libertarian contestation of 68 was channelled into a wide variety of different single-issue protest organisations, which for the purposes of our analysis can be collectively defined as the emergence of a new radical civil society in France.[78] Two movements emblematic of this radical civil society were anti-psychiatry and the campaign for greater transparency in the running of France's prison system.[79] Michel Foucault and Gilles Deleuze were among the most prominent intellectuals to become involved in these movements, theorising a new form of 'specific' intellectual engagement in the process. By enabling marginalised groups to speak for themselves, the engagement of intellectuals like Foucault and Deleuze in these movements was intended to be highly practical, but at the same time the anti-psychiatry and prisons movements were informed by Foucault and Deleuze's complex poststructuralist theories of power and desire.[80] The anti-68 liberal critique of radical civil society often collapsed the critique of new social movements into an attack on structuralist and poststructuralist anti-humanism and its alleged propensity for irresponsible, libertarian nihilism.[81]

Tocqueville was again an important point of reference here, as he had been in 1968 and before, with Raymond Aron revisiting the nineteenth century liberal to critique the anti-psychiatry and prisons movements along with the theories of their intellectual advocates. 'By what aberration or ignorance of history,' Aron asked 'do so many intellectuals denounce as "repressive" the societies that legalise abortion, that tolerate homosexual relationships, that give consideration to unions in the armed forces?'[82] From the perspective of Deleuze's definition of men as 'desiring machines', he argued, all known forms of society must appear oppressive, but for Aron 'what threatens liberal Europe is not excessive repression, but license'.[83] In order to explain what he described as '[t]he conjunction of *paraded license* ... and of *denounced repression*' he drew upon Tocqueville's account of the origins of the French Revolution. In *The Old Regime and the French Revolution*, Tocqueville had underlined the paradoxical nature of the Revolution given the extent of the social liberalisation that had occurred under the absolute monarchy compared to in France's continental European neighbours. His counterintuitive explanation for this was that 'the very destruction of some of the institutions of the Middle Ages made those that survived seem all the more detestable'.[84] Aron turned this specific argument into a general principle, explaining that the anti-psychiatry and prisons movements were illustrative of what he called 'Tocqueville's Law'. Writing the year before legislative elections that the united Socialist and Communist parties were widely expected to win, the application of 'Tocqueville's Law' to France's radical civil society reprised Aron's previous theoretical critiques of insatiable egalitarianism while linking it to the practical possibility of a partially Communist government in France.

Aron was not the only liberal revivalist associated with *Commentaire* to draw upon the French liberal tradition to critique egalitarian ideology, its intellectual defenders and its influence on radical civil society. In his best-selling book *Le Mal français*, published in 1976, the Gaullist politician Alain Peyrefitte proposed an 'intellectual and moral reform' inspired by Ernest Renan, stressing the importance of intellectual and political 'responsibility' while lamenting French intellectuals' tendencies towards its opposite.[85] Peyrefitte, like Aron who had advised him during the preparation of the book, called upon Tocqueville to explain and critique the intensification of radical egalitarianism in the 1970s.[86] Rather than celebrate the growth of associational life in this decade, Peyrefitte bemoaned its negativity and the preponderance of 'anti-associations'.[87] In other texts published in *Commentaire*, Peyrefitte also used Tocqueville's writings on the penal systems in France and the United States to argue against the 'philanthropic illusions' of both moderate and radical promoters of liberalising prison reforms.[88] François Bourricaud, who had been Peyrefitte's advisor during the latter's ill-fated tenure as Minister of Education in 1968,[89] was another prominent liberal revivalist at *Commentaire*. A sociologist claiming the lineage set out by Aron in *Main Currents of Sociological Thought*, Bourricaud was a defender of meritocratic elitism. He was worried by a 'crisis of professional authority' whose origins he traced to May 68 and the influence of thinkers like Jacques Lacan and Michel Foucault, 'sophists' who paled in comparison with the great Tocqueville.[90]

If the anti-68 liberal revivalists who wrote in the pages of *Commentaire* were hostile towards the sort of radical civil society represented by the anti-psychiatry and prisons movements, they were somewhat more open towards the 'moderate' developments occurring within the non-Communist trade union the CFDT and the *autogestionnaire* tendency led by Michel Rocard within the Socialist Party. This 'second left' differentiated itself from the Socialist mainstream by its decentralising, anti-statist leanings and critique of the radical nationalising agenda set out in the Common Programme. Its chief theorist was Pierre Rosanvallon, who had been the head of the CFDT's youth wing in 1968.[91] Rosanvallon went on to play an important part in the French liberal revival, with his egalitarian, radically democratic liberal vision reflecting his activist background. As he put it in the mid-1970s:

> The original liberal project was to develop an authentic civil society against the project of a totalitarian State . . . Liberalism is thus above all a theory of the separation of powers and of the limitation of the power of the State, but in the framework of an egalitarian society.[92]

The anachronistic reference to totalitarianism in this passage from Rosanvallon's book *L'Âge de l'autogestion* (1976) situates it within the general context of France's anti-totalitarian turn, but its egalitarian emphasis sets it apart from the anti-68 liberal revivalists of *Commentaire* and aligns Rosanvallon with the radical democratic critique of Claude Lefort. After meeting Lefort and studying his work in the early 1970s, Rosanvallon was persuaded that the best way to theorise *autogestion* would be to do so in the light of reflection on the nature of totalitarianism and the latter's democratic origins. For Rosanvallon, as for Lefort, this entailed a reading of France's liberal tradition of political thought, which emphasised themes of decentralisation and civil association as bulwarks against the totalitarian menace. Whereas anti-68 liberal revivalists like Aron and Manent were preoccupied with tempering an insatiable egalitarian impulse inherent to modern democratic societies, Rosanvallon's theory of *autogestion* represented an attempt to harness this impulse in the service of a new, radically democratic form of political liberalism.

As we have seen, *Commentaire*'s attitude towards the second left was ambivalent: insofar as it was anti-Communist and sceptical of the statist socialism of the Common Programme, this was a section of the left to be welcomed into the journal's pluralist embrace.[93] But its egalitarian and direct democratic leanings also made it an object of suspicion; hence the suggestion in the journal's inaugural editorial that the second left must abandon irresponsible libertarianism and stop 'hoping eternally for vague things'.[94] The latter point was a reference to the theory of *autogestion*, which was subjected to a detailed philosophical critique by Jean Baechler in the same issue.[95]

Although respectful of Rosanvallon, whom he identified as one of the few 'serious' theorists of *autogestion*, Baechler ultimately concluded that his attempt to define *autogestion* as a new form of political liberalism failed. Whereas the absolute evil for liberals was tyranny, for the theorist of *autogestion*, Baechler claimed, this was capitalism. The source of this difference originated not in their respective political or economic theories, but in their attitudes to modernity, which the authentic liberal stoically accepted with all its opportunities and constraints, while *autogestionnaire* socialism rationalised its ultimate rejection of modernity in the name of anti-capitalism.[96]

The heterogeneity of the French liberal revival

As Baechler and Manent's critiques of Rosanvallon and Lefort show, there was significant disagreement between liberal revivalists in France during the late 1970s. Yet there was convergence on some key issues. A mutual preoccupation with the critique of totalitarianism conceived as the product of a failing democratic political culture was one such point of convergence; a shared sense that France's liberal tradition of political thought offered a superior means of engaging with this issue was another. Common to the authors discussed in this chapter was a sense that a key advantage of this liberal tradition was its recognition of the primacy of the political domain; studying its authors therefore offered a means of exploring the phenomena of democracy and totalitarianism without reducing them to products of structural economic forces. This rejection of economic reductionism not only distanced these French liberal revivalists from positivistic forms of Marxism, it also informed their common, if uneven, scepticism towards classical economic liberalism: notwithstanding its opponents' claims to the contrary, French neo-liberalism was far from being a facsimile of its Anglo-American counterpart.[97]

Among the authors covered in this chapter there existed sufficient common ground on which to develop institutional forms of collaboration that would have a lasting impact on the French intellectual landscape. In 1977, the historian François Furet, a major figure in France's late twentieth-century liberal revival, established a seminar at the École des hautes études en sciences sociales dedicated to political philosophy, largely as incarnated in the French liberal tradition.[98] This seminar was a forerunner of the Institut Raymond Aron, founded in 1985, which played an important role in consolidating France's liberal revival and the related reinterpretation of the French Revolution promoted by Furet and his colleagues; more broadly, it also helped to revive the previously moribund discipline of the history of political ideas in France.[99] Through this institute the name of Raymond Aron has come to be associated with an expansive, pluralist French liberal revival encompassing the work, not only of his close collaborators at

Commentaire, but also of individuals whose intellectual trajectories included taking positions on the events of 1968 that were opposed, sometimes radically so, to his own. As we have seen, Claude Lefort acknowledged Aron as an important influence on his intellectual development despite their differences over May 68; similarly, François Furet cited Aron as an important influence but did not share his views on the *événements*.[100] Does it, then, make sense to speak of a specific anti-68 liberal revival inspired by Aron's example?

The answer, I think, is yes. The most obvious factor to take into account here is the origin of the two journals, *Contrepoint* and *Commentaire*, in the milieu that developed around Aron following his appeal for the formation of a Committee for the Defence and Renovation of the French University in the summer of 1968. Within the pages of these journals in the 1970s and 1980s a specific reading of France's eighteenth- and nineteenth-century liberal authors predominated.[101] This interpretation of France's liberal heritage was linked to a project aimed at reforming the political and intellectual culture of late-twentieth century France through the interrelated critiques of radical egalitarianism, relativist 'anti-humanism', and intellectual 'irresponsibility'. These critiques were substantially inspired by Raymond Aron's Tocquevillian analyses of the 'dialectic of equality' and May 68. The anti-totalitarianism of these journals shared common characteristics with the wider anti-totalitarian turn that developed in France from the mid-1970s, including an anachronistic tendency to apply the language of totalitarianism to the analysis of authors writing in the nineteenth century and earlier. They also tended to regard totalitarianism as the product of a malfunctioning democratic political culture. But, while other liberal revivalists promoted the benefits of an effervescent associational life to counteract this, the regular contributors to *Commentaire* and *Contrepoint* emphasised the need to inculcate the right kinds of social and political *mœurs*, which typically entailed shunning radical egalitarianism as socially and politically pernicious. The positive side of this equation was the need for intellectuals to embrace an attitude of 'responsibility'. For anti-68 liberals this meant rejecting not only Marxism but also the radical relativism of 'French theory' in favour of a form of centrist 'realism' aimed at France's cultured political and administrative élite.[102]

The French anti-68 liberal revival has had specific intellectual and political legacies in France and through its reception in the United States. Thanks in large part to Pierre Manent, *Commentaire* became an important transmission belt for the introduction of American neo-conservative thought into France during the 1980s, particularly that of Leo Strauss and Allan Bloom.[103] The anti-egalitarian, anti-postmodernist leanings of the anti-68 liberal revival chimed with Straussians and other anti-postmodernist intellectuals in the United States, who tried, with limited success, to import it in the 1990s.[104] In the autumn of 1989 the publication in *Commentaire* of the first French translation of Francis Fukuyama's famous article 'The end of history?' signalled a post-Cold War revival of a more conservative, pro-market variant of end of ideology theory.[105] Debating an apparently post-ideological age actually pre-dated the end of the Cold War in French domestic politics, and was linked to the electoral decline of the PCF, the influence of Furetian revisionism in French revolutionary historiography, and the experience of political 'cohabitation' between 1986 and 1988.[106] Following the collapse of communism abroad and the revival of mass social protest at home, however, France's heterogeneous liberal intellectual alliance became increasingly fragmented during the 1990s. This process reached a low point in 2002 when a scandal broke out over the publication in a series edited by Pierre Rosanvallon of a book by Daniel Lindenberg attacking Pierre Manent as an intellectual reactionary.[107] The involvement of Nicolas Baverez, Raymond Aron's biographer and a regular contributor to *Commentaire*, in Nicolas Sarkozy's infamous campaign speech on the need to 'liquidate the legacy of 1968' again highlighted the specificity of the journal's liberal vision.[108] By this point, though, the intensity of *Commentaire*'s liberal revivalism, as measured by the frequency with which the 'Classics of Liberty' section ran in the journal, had slowed significantly since its peak in the 1970s and 1980s.[109] However, given that at the time of writing the latest two issues of *Commentaire* have focused on 'The Crisis of Liberalism', perhaps the late twentieth-century French liberal renaissance will itself be subjected to an early twenty-first-century revival.[110]

Notes

1 Christian Stoffaës, 'Apprivoiser le liberalisme', *Commentaire* 41 (1988): 46. All translations are my own, unless otherwise stated. I am grateful to Emile Chabal for his careful reading of, and comments on, an earlier draft of this chapter.

2 Mark Lilla, 'The other Velvet Revolution: Continental liberalism and its discontents', *Daedalus* 123 (1994): 129–57.

3 Perry Anderson, *In the Tracks of Historical Materialism* (London: Verso, 1983), 32; Daniel Lindenberg, *Le Rappel a l'ordre: Enquête sur les nouveaux reactionnaires* (Paris: Éditions du Seuil, 2002); François Cusset, *French Theory: How Foucault, Derrida, Deleuze, & Co. transformed the intellectual life of the United States* (Minneapolis: University of Minnesota Press, 2008), 309–27.

4 See for example, the innovative work of Michael Scott Christofferson, Julian Bourg, Michael Behrent and Samuel Moyn.

5 Mark Lilla, 'The legitimacy of the liberal age', in Mark Lilla, ed., *New French Thought: Political philosophy* (Princeton: Princeton University Press, 1994), 3–34; Tony Judt, *The Burden of Responsibility: Blum, Camus, Aron, and the French twentieth century* (London: University of Chicago Press, 1998), 137–82.

6 For different anti-totalitarian perspectives on human rights, see Raymond Aron, 'Sociology and the philosophy of human rights', in H. E. Keifer et al., eds., *Ethics and Social Justice* (New York: State University of New York, 1968), 282–99; Claude Lefort, 'Droits de l'homme et politique', *Libre* 7 (1980): 3–42;

Marcel Gauchet, 'Les droits de l'homme ne sont pas une politique', *Le Débat* 3 (1980): 3–21.

7 Julian Bourg, ed., *From Revolution to Ethics: May 1968 and contemporary french thought* (London: McGill Queen's University Press, 2007); Michael Scott Christofferson, *French Intellectuals against the Left: The anti-totalitarian moment of the 1970s* (Oxford: Berghahn Books, 2004).

8 On an alternative form of liberal revivalism developed by authors with roots in *soixante-huitard* activism, see Andrew Jainchill and Samuel Moyn, 'French democracy between totalitarianism and solidarity: Pierre Rosanvallon and revisionist historiography', *The Journal of Modern History* 76 (2004): 107–54; Samuel Moyn, 'The politics of individual rights: Marcel Gauchet and Claude Lefort', in Raf Geenens and Helena Rosenblatt, eds., *French Liberalism from Montesquieu to the Present Day* (Cambridge: Cambridge University Press, 2012), 291–310.

9 Raymond Aron, *The Committed Observer* (Washington D.C.: Regnery Gateway, 1983), 271.

10 Judt, *Burden of Responsibility*, see Note 5, 137; Jean-Pierre Raffarin, 'Allocution de M. Jean-Pierre Raffarin, Premier Ministre', in Élisabeth Dutartre, ed., *Raymond Aron et la democratie au XXIe siecle* (Paris: Éditions de Fallois, 2007), 237. See also Sunil Khilnani, *Arguing Revolution: The intellectual left in post-war France* (London: Yale University Press, 1993), 130–3.

11 I borrow this term from Christofferson, *French Intellectuals against the Left*, see Note 7.

12 On this point see for example, Helena Rosenblatt, 'Why Constant? A critical overview of the Constant revival', *Modern Intellectual History* 1 (2004): 439–53. Furet and Manent in particular acknowledged their intellectual debts to Aron. See Pierre Manent, *Le Regard politique: Entretiens avec Bénédicte Delorme-Montini* (Paris: Flammarion, 2010), 49–81; François Furet, 'La Rencontre d'une idee et d'une vie', *Commentaire*, 8 (1985): 52–4.

13 See Raymond Aron, 'États Démocratiques et États Totalitaires', in Raymond Aron, *Penser la liberté, penser la democratie* (Paris: Gallimard, 2005), 57–106.

14 Iain Stewart, 'Raymond Aron and the roots of the French liberal renaissance' (PhD diss., University of Manchester, 2011), 77–112.

15 Raymond Aron, *Démocratie et totalitarisme* (Paris: Gallimard, 1965), 170–8.

16 The first two books were Raymond Aron, *Dix-huit leçons sur la societe industrielle* (Paris: Gallimard, 1962) and Raymond Aron, *La Lutte de classes: Nouvelles leçons sur la societe industrielle* (Paris: Gallimard, 1964). Aron began to study Tocqueville in 1955 on the recommendation of the American sociologists Daniel Bell and Robert Dahl. See here Françoise Mélonio, *Tocqueville et les Français* (Paris: Aubier, 1993), 279.

17 On this point, see Ghita Ionescu, 'Raymond Aron: A modern classicist', in Kenneth Minogue et al., eds., *Contemporary Political Philosophers* (London: Methuen, 1976), 198.

18 Aron's key contributions to this theory are to be found in Raymond Aron, *L'Opium des intellectuels* (Paris: Hachette Littératures, 2002), 315–34; Aron,

Dix-huit leçons, see Note 16; Aron, *La Lutte*, see Note 16; Aron, *Démocratie et totalitarisme*, see Note 15. For the wider debate over end of ideology theory see Chaim Isaac Waxman, ed., *The End of Ideology Debate* (New York: Funk & Wagnalls, 1968). For a detailed account of Aron's contribution to end of ideology theory and his role in the Congress for Cultural Freedom see Stewart, 'Raymond Aron', see Note 14, 113–51.

19 At the most optimistic end of the spectrum Seymour Martin Lipset claimed in 1960 that in Western liberal democracies 'the fundamental political problems of the industrial revolution have been solved' and that such regimes represented 'the good society itself in operation'. Seymour Martin Lipset, *The Political Man: The social bases of politics* (London: Mercury Books, 1960), 403, 406.

20 The term 'politics of productivity' is taken from Charles S. Maier, *In Search of Stability: Explorations in historical political economy* (Cambridge: Cambridge University Press, 1987), 121–52.

21 Lipset, *Political Man*, see Note 19, 404–5.

22 Mélonio, *Tocqueville*, see Note 16, 274–85.

23 See Alexis de Tocqueville, *Democracy in America and Two Essays on America* (London: Penguin, 2003), 777–809.

24 Aron, *Dix-huit leçons*, see Note 16, 33–73. See also Raymond Aron, *Essai sur les libertés* (Paris: Calmann-Lévy, 1965), 17–72; Raymond Aron, *Trois essais sur l'âge industriel* (Paris: Plon, 1966), 108.

25 Alexis de Tocqueville, *The Old Regime and the French Revolution* (New York: Anchor Books, 1983), 138–48.

26 Aron invokes the 'end of the age of ideologies' in the conclusion to Raymond Aron, *L'Opium des intellectuels* (Paris: Hachette Littératures, 2002), 315–34.

27 See, e.g., Raymond Aron, 'Réflexions sur les problemes économiques Français', *Revue de metaphysique et de morale*, XLIV (1937): 793. The relevant text from Weber is Max Weber, 'Politics as a vocation', in Hans Heinrich Gerth et al., eds., *From Max Weber: Essays in Sociology* (London: Routledge, 1991), 77–128. On the importance of Weber's influence, see Raymond Aron, *Mémoires: 50 Ans de réflexion politique* (Paris: Julliard, 1983), 68 72.

28 Jean-Louis Benoît, 'Reading Tocqueville: Diachrony, synchrony and new perspectives', in Raf Geenens et al., eds., *Reading Tocqueville from Oracle to Actor* (Basingstoke: Palgrave Macmillan, 2007), 54.

29 The English translation of this these lectures was published in 1965, two years before the French version. References here are to the latter: Raymond Aron, *Les Étapes de la pensee sociologique* (Paris: Gallimard, 1967), 295.

30 A more detailed version of the following analysis is available in Stewart, 'Raymond Aron', see Note 14, 152–203.

31 Raymond Aron, *Introduction à la Philosophie de l'Histoire: Essai sur les limites de l'objectivite historique* (Paris: Gallimard, 1986), 413–14.

32 Aron, *Mémoires*, see Note 27, 125.

33 On these points, see Daniel J. Mahoney, 'Raymond Aron and the morality of prudence', *Modern Age* 43 (2001): 243–52.

34 For a discussion of Strauss's critique of Weber see Raymond Aron, 'Introduction', in Max Weber, *Le Savant et le politique* (Paris: Plon, 1959), 31–52. On Aron's admiration for Strauss, see Aron, *Mémoires*, see Note 27, 457.

35 Aron, *Les Étapes*, see Note 29, 239–40.

36 Andrew Vincent, *The Nature of Political Theory* (Oxford: Oxford University Press, 2004), 56.

37 See for example, C. Wright Mills, 'Letter to the New Left', *New Left Review* 1 (1960): 18–23; Herbert Marcuse, *One Dimensional Man: Studies in the ideology of advanced industrial society* (London: Routledge, 2002), 11.

38 Raymond Aron, *Les Désillusions du progres: Essai sur la dialectique de la modernite* (Paris: Calmann-Lévy, 1969), 19–90. This book was first published in English as an entry into the *Encyclopaedia Britannica* in 1964.

39 The notion of 'contestation' was central to the rhetoric of protest in 1968. It connotes a radically anti-authoritarian critique directed at wide range of social institutions, not just the State or the University but also the family, trade unions, schools, offices, factories, etc.

40 Raymond Aron, *La Révolution introuvable: Réflexions sur les évenements de Mai* (Paris: Librairie Arthème Fayard, 1968), 117–21.

41 Aron, *La Révolution introuvable*, see Note 40, 134–7. See also pages 122–3, 147.

42 Daniel J. Mahoney, *The Liberal Political Science of Raymond Aron: A critical introduction* (Lanham: Rowman & Littlefield, 1992), 15, 161.

43 See, e.g., Richard Wolin, *The Wind from the East: French intellectuals, the cultural revolution, and the legacy of the 1960s* (Princeton: Princeton University Press, 2010), 362.

44 Raymond Aron, 'La crise de l'Université: Une mise en garde et un appel de Raymond Aron', in Aron, *Révolution introuvable*, see Note 40, 169–70.

45 *Contrepoint* has been described by one of its regular contributors as a direct response to Aron's appeal for a committee in defence of the University in *Le Figaro* two years earlier. See Gwendal Châton, 'Désaccord parfait: Le *Contrepoint* liberal dans les configurations intellectuels des annees soixante-dix', in Jean Baudouin et al., eds., *Les Revues et la dynamique des ruptures* (Rennes: Presses Universitaires de Rennes, 2007), 145. On the links between Aron's seminar and *Contrepoint*, see Châton, 'Désaccord parfait', 138–59 and Rémy Rieffel, *La Tribu des clercs: Les Intellectuels sous la Ve République* (Paris: Calmann-Lévy, 1993), 245–6.

46 '*Contrepoint* was really founded in reaction to May 1968' – Jean Baechler quoted in Gwendal Châton, 'La Liberté retrouvée. Une histoire du liberalisme politique en France à travers les revues Aroniennes *Contrepoint* et *Commentaire*' (PhD diss., University of Rennes 1, 2006), 160.

47 Anon, 'Éditorial', *Contrepoint* 1 (1970): 4.

48 Châton, 'Liberté retrouvée', see Note 46, 228–9, 243–8.

49 Châton, 'Liberté retrouvée', see Note 46, 227.

50 This is a main argument of Christofferson, *French Intellectuals*, see Note 7. See also Khilnani, *Arguing Revolution*, Note 10, 149–50.

51 In 1977, Liébert went on to develop the collection *Pluriel* at the French publishing house Hachette, producing new paperback editions of classic texts from the liberal tradition as well as numerous works by contemporary liberals that had been affiliated with *Contrepoint*. He also maintained a place on the editorial board of *Commentaire*. See Rieffel, *La Tribu des clercs*, see Note 45, 260.

52 See Châton, 'Désaccord parfait', see Note 45, 161–2.

53 Rémy Rieffel implies that *Commentaire* was 'un club barriste'. See his *La Tribu des clercs*, see Note 45, 252–7.

54 Aron, *Mémoires*, see Note 27, 566–74; Nicolas Baverez, *Raymond Aron: Un Moraliste aux temps des ideologies* (Paris: Flammarion, 1993), 436–40, 474.

55 H. S. Jones, 'French liberalism and the legacy of the Revolution', in Tim Blanning et al., eds., *Historicising the French Revolution* (Newcastle: Cambridge Scholars Publishing, 2008), 192.

56 In both of its incarnations, this institution was founded amid the theorisation by some of its most respected teaching staff of élite renewal in response to national humiliation. See in the first instance, Ernest Renan, *La Réforme intellectuelle et morale* (Paris: Michel-Lévy Frères, 1871) and, in the second, Raymond Aron, *Chroniques de guerre: 'La France libre', 1940–1945* (Paris: Gallimard, 1990). On criticism of Sciences Po as elitist and undemocratic, see Philip Nord, *France's New Deal: From the thirties to the post-war era* (Princeton: Princeton University Press, 2010), 67–86, 130–44, 189–213.

57 See the advanced promotional flyer kept in *Fonds Raymond Aron*, Bibliothèque Nationale de France, NAF28060(130).

58 Anon, 'Éditorial', *Contrepoint*, 1 (May 1970): 3–5. On the theme of intellectual non-conformism, see Châton, 'Liberté retrouvée', see Note 46, 164–8.

59 Anon, 'Commentaire', *Commentaire* 1 (1978): 5. See also Raymond Aron, 'Pour le progres: Après la chute des idoles', *Commentaire* 1 (1978): 233–43.

60 Anon, 'Commentaire', see Note 59, 3.

61 Anon, 'Commentaire', see Note 59, 5.

62 Jean-Thomas Nordmann, 'Taine liberal', *Commentaire* 3 (1978): 364; Alfred Fabre-Luce, 'Benjamin Constant et ses partenaires', *Commentaire* 2 (1978): 193. See also Patrice Rolland, 'Équivoques du liberalisme: À propos de Benjamin Constant', *Commentaire* 16 (1981): 417; René Pomeau, 'Montesquieu: Le Vécu d'une politique', *Commentaire* 17 (1982): 127–8; Pierre Rétat, 'La Notion du principe chez Montesquieu', *Commentaire* 17 (1982): 131; Jean-François Revel, 'Pour lire Jouffroy', *Commentaire* 27 (1984): 546–7, etc.

63 On this wider tendency, see Rosenblatt, 'Why constant?', see Note 10.

64 Pierre Manent, 'Aux origines du liberalisme: Benjamin Constant', *Commentaire*, 11 (1980). Manent was commenting upon Marcel Gauchet, 'Introduction' in Benjamin Constant, *De la Liberté chez les Modernes* (Paris: Librairie Générale Française, 1980), 11–91.

65 Pierre Manent, 'Démocratie et totalitarisme: À propos de Claude Lefort', *Commentaire* 16 (1981): 574–83.

66 See for example, Daniel Cohn-Bendit and Gabriel Cohn Bendit, *Obsolete Communism: The left-wing alternative* (Edinburgh: AK Press, 2000), 23.

67 For Lefort's analysis of May 1968, see his contribution to Claude Lefort, Edgar Morin and Jean-Marc Coudray, *Mai 1968: La Brèche. Premières reflexions sur les évenements* (Paris: Fayard, 1968). On his relations with Aron, see Claude Lefort, 'Raymond Aron et le phenomene totalitaire', in Christian Bachelier et al., eds., *Raymond Aron et la liberte politique* (Paris: Éditions de Fallois, 2002), 87.

68 Manent, *Regard politique*, see Note 12, 35.

69 Manent, *Regard politique*, see Note 12, 39.

70 Manent, *Regard politique*, see Note 12, 11–15.

71 Manent, *Regard politique*, see Note 12, 49–81.

72 On Lefort and Strauss, see Claudia Hilb, 'Claude Lefort as reader of Leo Strauss', in Martin Plot, *Claude Lefort: Thinker of the political* (Basingstoke: Palgrave Macmillan, 2013), 71–88. On Aron and totalitarianism, see Lefort, 'Raymond Aron', see Note 67.

73 See Manent, 'Démocratie et totalitarisme,' see Note 65, 575.

74 Serge Audier, *Tocqueville retrouve: Genèse et enjeux du renouveau Tocquevillien français* (Paris: Vrin, 2004). On the 'Aronian' reading of Tocqueville, see pages 19–162; on the 'Lefortian' interpretation, see pages 163–232. See also Pierre Manent, *Tocqueville et la nature de la democratie* (Paris: Gallimard, 1982).

75 Manent, 'Démocratie et totalitarisme', see Note 65, 582.

76 Manent, 'Aux origines du liberalisme,' see Note 64, 484. Rue du Mail was home to the offices of the left-wing weekly news magazine, *Le Nouvel observateur*.

77 See for instance, Marcin Krol, 'Pologne: Une Révolution differente', *Commentaire* 12 (1980): 537–45.

78 The binary distinction between radical and moderate forms of civil society movements oversimplifies a more complex reality; it is used here simply as a means of clarifying the anti-68 liberals' different responses to different kinds of civil society movement, and corresponds with a similar distinction made by authors contributing to *Contrepoint* and *Commentaire*. For an example of this distinction, see Jean Baechler, 'Libéralisme et autogestion', *Commentaire* 1 (1978): 27–38.

79 On these movements, see Bourg, *Revolution to Ethics*, see Note 7, 79–176.

80 See here 'Intellectuals and power: A conversation between Michel Foucault and Gilles Deleuze' [1972]. Available at libcom.org, accessed 31 August 2013: http://libcom.org/library/intellectuals-power-a-conversation-between-michel-foucault-and-gilles-deleuze

81 See Michel Crozier, 'Les angoisses existentielles des intellectuels français', *Commentaire* 6 (1979): 169–80; François Bourricaud, 'La Crise de l'autorite professionnelle: Avocats, Magistrats, Médecins et Professeurs', *Commentaire* 7 (1979): 382–89; François Bourricaud, 'De la Psychanalyse a la revolution', *Commentaire* 36 (1986): 804–7. See also the positive reception afforded to Alain Renaut and Luc Ferry's controversial *La Pensée 68: Essai sur l'anti-*

humanisme contemporaine (Paris: Gallimard, 1985) in Raymond Boudon, 'Éloge du conformisme intellectuel', *Commentaire* 35 (1986): 535–7; Marc Beigbeder, 'La Bouteille a la mer: L'Heure des comptes?', *Commentaire* 33 (1986): 151–4.

82   Raymond Aron, *In Defense of Decadent Europe* (South Bend: Regnery Gateway, 1979). Originally published in 1977, all quotations here come from pages 236–7. On 'Tocqueville's Law' in general, see pages 236–43.

83   On 'desiring machines', see Gilles Deleuze and Félix Guattari, *Anti-Oedipus: Capitalism and schizophrenia* (London: Continuum, 2004).

84   Tocqueville, *Origins*, 31–32.

85   Alain Peyrefitte, *Le Mal français* (Paris: Plon, 1976), 463, 482–86.

86   Peyrefitte, *Le Mal français*, see Note 85, iv.

87   Peyrefitte, *Le Mal français*, see Note 85, 397, 407.

88   Alain Peyrefitte, 'Les Paradoxes de Tocqueville', *Commentaire* 10 (1980): 280–1; Alain Peyrefitte, 'Tocqueville et les illusions penitentiaires', *Commentaire* 30 (1985): 606–14.

89   Alain Peyrefitte, 'Un Intellectuel responsable', *Commentaire* 58 (1992): 433–4.

90   Bourricaud, 'La Crise', see Note 81; Raymond Bourricaud, 'L'Avenir de l'institution universitaire en France', *Commentaire* 11 (1980): 492–9; Raymond Boudon and François Bourricaud, 'La Sociologie aujourd'hui', *Commentaire* 19 (1982): 464–5, 470; François Bourricaud, 'De la Psychanalyse à la Révolution', *Commentaire* 36 (1986): 804–7.

91   The following discussion of Rosanvallon draws on Jainchill and Moyn, 'French democracy', see Note 8.

92   Pierre Rosanvallon, *L'Âge de l'autogestion* (Paris: Seuil, 1976), 44–5.

93   See for instance, Pierre Rosanvallon, 'Marx et la societe civile', *Commentaire* 4 (1978): 477–88; Michel Rocard, 'La Social-Démocratie et la liberte', *Commentaire* 19 (1982): 367–9.

94   Anon, *Commentaire*, see Note 59, 5.

95   Jean Baechler, 'Libéralisme et autogestion', *Commentaire* 1 (1978): 27–38. For a more sympathetic analysis of this subject, see Guillaume Guindey, 'L'Autogestion de l'économie', *Commentaire* 4 (1978): 512–14. Baechler was one of Raymond Aron's earliest 'disciples' – see Châton, 'Liberté retrouvee', see Note 46, 87–89; Jean Baechler, 'Maître et disciple', *Commentaire*, 8 (1985): 62–6.

96   Baechler, 'Libéralisme et autogestion', see Note 95, 38.

97   For a positive French perspective on economic liberalism, see Alain Madelin, *Aux Sources du modèle liberale français* (Paris: Perrin, 1997). For a critical perpective that mistakenly conflates French and Anglo-American neo-liberalism, see Philippe Lacoue-Labarthe, 'Neither an accident nor a mistake', *Critical Enquiry* 15 (1989): 482. In October 1984, Gilles Anquetil, writing in the left-wing weekly *Nouvel Observateur*, referred disparagingly to an 'arono-hayekian consensus' in French economics. See Luc Ferry and Alain Renaut, 'Droits-libertés et Droits-créances: Raymond Aron critique de Friedrich von Hayek', *Droits* 2 (1985): 75. On French neo-liberalism more broadly, see

François Denord, *Néo-libéralisme version française: Histoire d'une ideologie politique* (Paris: Demopolis, 2007).

98 Pierre Manent remembers this seminar as having been dedicated to the recovery of France's liberal tradition, whereas Rosanvallon has described it as a seminar in political philosophy. This confusion is significant in itself in indicating the politically oriented approach to the liberal tradition prevalent at the time. Among the regular attenders of this seminar were Pierre Rosanvallon, Pierre Manent, Claude Lefort, Marcel Gauchet, Cornelius Castoriadis, Bernard Manin, Philippe Raynaud and Krzysztof Pomian. See also, Manent, *Regard politique*, see Note 12, 112–13; Jainchill and Moyn, 'French Democracy', see Note 8, 116.

99 Jeremy Jennings, 'Le Retour des émigrés? The study of the history of political ideas in contemporary France', in Dan Castiglione et al., eds., *The History of Political Thought in National Context* (Cambridge: Cambridge University Press, 2001), 213–15.

100 Furet, 'La Rencontre', see Note 12. For a recent biography, see Christophe Prochasson, *François Furet: Les Chemins de la melancolie* (Paris: Éditions Stock, 2013).

101 This is not to suggest that alternative readings did not find their way into *Commentaire* in particular. See here Jean-Pierre Cot, 'Actualité et ambiguïtes du liberalisme', *Commentaire* 35 (1986): 403–11. That *Commentaire* did have a specific vision of the French liberal tradition is confirmed by the fact that this piece was preceded by an editorial note highlighting that Cot's vision of French liberalism differed from that of the journal in which it was published.

102 Note here the title of Judt, *Burden of Responsibility*, see Note 5.

103 On this, see Serge Audier, *La Pensée anti-68: Essai sur les origines d'une restauration intellectuelle* (Paris: La Découverte, 2009), 141–68. Audier offers an interpretation of Raymond Aron as a thinker less hostile to the legacy of 68 than is given in this chapter. On Aron, see also Serge Audier, *Raymond Aron: La Démocratie conflictuelle* (Paris: Éditions Michalon, 2004).

104 Cusset, *French Theory*, see Note 3, 275; Martin Jay, 'Lafayette's children: The American reception of French liberalism', *SubStance* 31 (2002): 9–26. Raymond Aron has been promoted sympathetically in the United States as the originator of neo-conservatism. See Brian C. Anderson, 'The Aronian renewal', *First Things* 6 (1995): 61–4. Authors from the wider liberal revival were also included in the 'New French Thought' series, edited by Mark Lilla, through which the French liberal revival was imported into the United States.

105 Francis Fukuyama, 'La Fin de l'histoire?', *Commentaire* 47 (1989): 457–69. I am grateful to Emile Chabal for raising this point.

106 See here François Furet, Jacques Julliard and Pierre Rosanvallon, *La République du Centre: La Fin de l'exception française* (Paris: Calmann-Lévy, 1988).

107 Lindenberg, *Rappel à l'ordre*, see Note 3. On this scandal, see Jeremy Jennings, *Revolution and the Republic: A history of political thought in France since the eighteenth century* (Oxford: Oxford University Press, 2011), 512–13.

108 Audier, *Pensée anti-68*, see Note 103, 54–5.

109 In the 1970s and 1980s, 68 per cent (32/47) of *Commentaire*'s issues contained a 'Classics of Liberty' section; in the 1990s this was 52 per cent (21/40), in the 2000s, 32 per cent (17/40); in the 2010s, as of September 2013, 7 per cent (1/14).

110 Pierre Manent, 'La Crise du libéralisme', *Commentaire* 141 (2013): 91–103; Pierre-Henri Tavoillot et al, 'Le Libéralisme politique: Victoire ou défaite?', *Commentaire* 142 (2013): 245–64.

11

Republicanism and the Critique of Human Rights

Camille Robcis

In the summer of 1980, Marcel Gauchet, the editor of the journal *Le Débat*, developed one of the most forceful post-war French critiques of human rights in an article entitled 'Human rights are not a politic'.[1] Gauchet contended that his piece was inspired by the sudden revival of human rights in French political and intellectual life during the late 1970s. As Gauchet argued, this revival was surprising since Marxists had, throughout the 1960s, denounced rights as formal fictions and alienating abstractions designed to mask class domination. Furthermore, during these same years, influential thinkers such as Lacan, Foucault, Derrida and Althusser had repeatedly called for the decentring of the human in philosophy and in politics. Yet, human rights were back, and not only in 'the East' where they were being deployed to fight totalitarianism, but in 'the West', where they were increasingly mobilised against governments that had not been particularly notorious for violating basic individual rights. But more than 'the West' in general, Gauchet's target was France and, specifically, two important currents within the French left. The first was minority groups such as homosexuals, feminists, immigrants, and environmentalists. Inspired by May 68 and the *droit à la différence* movement, these groups had begun to use the discourse of rights to make various political claims. The second was anti-totalitarian thinkers. Bound together by their disillusionment with Marxism and the 'Gulag effect', they too had begun to champion human rights during the 1970s as the best antidote to state bureaucracy. In both cases, Gauchet contended, the discourse on human rights served as a subterfuge to avoid tackling the real question haunting the French political and intellectual left at the end of the 1970s – namely, the problem of

imagining a new political and social model that could replace Marxism and
fill the void left by its demise. In this context, human rights were merely 'a
way of avoiding, by giving a prepackaged answer, the questions that emerge
with the collapse of the social project (*projet de société*) forged throughout
a century and a half of the workers' movement'.[2] 'Can and should human
rights constitute a politic (*une politique*), our politic?',[3] Gauchet asked,
adding the 'our' to emphasise that he was referring to France. The answer in
this article and in his subsequent work was an unambiguous no.

Gauchet's essay appeared in the third issue of *Le Débat*, the journal that he
had founded with the historian and editor at Gallimard, Pierre Nora, a few
months earlier in May 1980.[4] It was one of Gauchet's first publications in the
journal and in many ways served as a theoretical manifesto for the journal and
for much of Gauchet's future work. As he recounted in 2002, the critique of
human rights that he articulated in his articles for *Le Débat* and expanded in
several books, including *Le Désenchantement du monde* (1985), *La Révolution
des droits de l'homme* (1989) and *La Religion dans la démocratie* (1998), had
one ultimate purpose: to 'decipher and understand the disconcerting faces of
the new democracy that had arrived: triumphant, doctrinaire, and self-
destructive'.[5] Gauchet was not the only French intellectual of the time to
explore the social and political ramifications of human rights and democracy.
His writings were in conversation with those of François Furet, Pierre
Rosanvallon, Jacques Julliard, Philippe Raynaud, and others interested in the
legacy of the French Revolution and in the limits and contours of popular
sovereignty. Like Gauchet, many of these thinkers turned to the Revolution
and the nineteenth century to explore the problem of political embodiment
and analyse the tension between individual liberty and social cohesion.
Moreover, the connection between these thinkers was not only intellectual.
Many were affiliated with the Centre de recherches politiques Raymond Aron
founded in 1982 at the École des hautes études en sciences sociales (EHESS),
a research centre that Gauchet joined in 1989.

For some, this group of historians and philosophers inaugurated a much-
needed revival of liberalism in France.[6] For others, they contributed to the
development of a new republicanism.[7] Gauchet, however, refused both
labels. He was particularly explicit with regard to liberalism. If it consisted
in 'valorising the spontaneous dynamic of individual liberties within civil
society and consequently restricting the role of the state (*puissance publique*)',
then he was not a liberal. Rather, he thought of himself as a democrat and a
Socialist, albeit a Socialist deeply disillusioned by the history of socialism in
the twentieth century.[8] In this chapter, I follow Gauchet's own interpretation:
I read his essay on human rights as a strong critique of liberalism but also as
a plea for a new republicanism, which I define as a theory of the public, or
the *res publica*. Although the republicanism of the 1980s shared some of the
characteristics of previous historical and philosophical republicanisms –
particularly that of the Third Republic – most of its defining features were
specific to the French political, social, and intellectual landscape of the time.

My goal is thus neither to reinscribe this political philosophy within older republicanisms nor to evaluate its allegiance to a predetermined historical or theoretical framework. Instead, I want to highlight three of its defining features. First, the new republicanism that emerged in the 1980s was defined in opposition to the two dominant political models of the time: Marxism and 'human rights' understood as rights-based Anglo-Saxon liberalism. Second, it insisted on a specific division of private and public. According to Gauchet, the political failure of both Marxism and liberalism was due to their shared inability to balance individual rights and state power – in other words, their inability to imagine the public and the private simultaneously. For Gauchet, only the two most 'talented' theorists of liberalism – Benjamin Constant and Alexis de Tocqueville – had diagnosed the fundamental interdependence of private and public, but the consequences they had derived from this discovery were erroneous.[9]

Third and finally, Gauchet's republican articulation of private and public implied a particular organisation of race, gender and sexuality within society. Although he rarely addressed these topics directly, I want to show how other scholars adopted almost verbatim the chronology and typology underpinning Gauchet's critique of rights. This was the case, for instance, of Paul Yonnet who applied them to the study of race in his pamphlet against SOS Racisme, *Voyage au centre du malaise français* (published in 1993 in Gallimard's *Le Débat* series). Likewise, Mona Ozouf, Philippe Raynaud, and Claude Habib adapted them for their study of gender, and Irène Théry and Frédéric Martel referred to them in their analyses of sexuality.[10] Many of these conversations around private and public took place in *Le Débat* for which the scholars listed above frequently wrote, but also in other journals such as *Esprit* directed after 1988 by Olivier Mongin, and *Commentaire* founded by Raymond Aron in 1978. They also developed in institutions such as the Centre Raymond Aron and the Fondation Saint-Simon where much of this republican theory was, throughout the 1980s and 1990s, adapted into concrete legislation. Ideas that began as abstract debates within the confines of the intellectual left soon found a direct political application. More than simply a theory, republicanism functioned as a practice that guided many policy decisions during these two decades.

Gauchet's critique of rights

Gauchet's critique of rights takes shape within two parallel but intersecting chronologies: one more immediate and specific to the French left since May 68; and a *longue durée* narrative of the advent of democracy, from feudalism, through absolutism, to the age of revolutions. As Gauchet makes clear, his object of attack is not the defence of human rights in 'the East' where in their 'minimal expression', they served as an umbrella concept to gather a wide range of people fighting the 'dictatorships, despotisms, tyrannies, and

totalitarianisms of all sorts that have flourished on the planet'.[11] His concern
is the transformation of human rights from a specific mode of political action
into the single element holding together the entire social body: from *la
politique* to *le politique*.[12] According to Gauchet, in 'the West', and more
specifically in France, human rights has become the official *politique* of the
left in the post-totalitarianism era. One of the examples of this phenomenon
that Gauchet mentions is the *programme commun*, the alliance that the
French Socialist and the Communist parties signed in 1972. In this context,
human rights provided the consensus that various conflicting groups on the
French left needed to mask the flagrant contradiction between their
unconditional advocacy of freedom in 'the East' and their endorsement of
economic planning and nationalisation in 'the West' – or, in Gauchet's words,
the contradiction between the 'imperative of autonomy and the means of
political, administrative, and economic concentration that desperately
continue to figure in the programmatic horizon of the left's past (*antiquités*)'.[13]

Beyond the *programme commun*, however, Gauchet attributes the turn to
human rights to the larger intellectual failure on the part of the left to
understand power, except negatively:

> There is an intrinsic curse to power. One must above all not seek to take
> power because it will automatically reverse the project of emancipation
> and turn it into a project of oppression; no politics that stain, only
> moralisms that cleanse and save – all we can do is resist.[14]

Resistance, in other words, demands domination and requires the
demonisation of the state, 'an adversary imagined as substantially intangible
and always self-identical'.[15] This 'curse to power' was obvious even in the
workers' movement, which never recognised that it needed capitalism just
as much as capitalism needed workers. By refusing to grapple with the
complexities of power, the left has, according to Gauchet, trapped itself in a
political and theoretical deadlock. From this perspective, human rights no
longer signify 'the preservation and consolidation of the acquired democratic
guarantees'. Instead, they function as a 'lever of critique designed to shatter
the existing order'.[16] As an example of the latter, Gauchet lists the 'multiple
"dissidences"' of groups who, over the past decade, have affirmed their
'sexual, ethnic, and generational difference'.[17] Gauchet also pauses on the
environmental movement to illustrate the impasse facing the many leftist
groups born out of May 68 who, despite their ability to gather great support
and legitimacy, remain 'caught in apocalyptic fantasies and bucolic dreams'
and are thus unable to participate in the political process or the *res publica*.[18]

The return to human rights, then, is a product of the particular history of
the French left in the 1970s, caught between two legacies of May 68: anti-
totalitarianism and *droit à la différence*. But contemporary rights talk is also
the result of a longer history, one that has interested Gauchet throughout his
career: the emergence of democracy and the concurrent invention of the

individual. As Gauchet suggests, the 1970s may have been one of those 'great oscillations' in western civilisation, 'linked to the difficulty, if not the impossibility of imagining the individual and society together, of reconstituting a society from individuals'.[19] In the *longue durée*, the story of the relationship between the individual and the social is also a story of the construction of public and private. Gauchet argues that the eighteenth century brought about a fundamental shift in the organisation of the relations between individuals and society. Prior to this turning point, the foundation of the collectivity and the social came from above – from the king, and ultimately from God. In this context, the individual as such did not exist: he could only participate in society as a member of his various innate communities (familial, parochial, corporate . . .). With the democratic revolutions of the eighteenth century, the base of power shifted: the individual became the social unit, the bearer of sovereignty. From a world governed by *heteronomy*, we shifted to a world of *autonomy*. This shift brought about the fundamental problem of how to define and delimit society:

> if we admit that there are first and foremost individuals, that there are only individuals at the origins, how do we imagine their coexistence, their assemblage (*compossibilité*) within a given society? How do we reach a viable collective sum from the irreducible plurality of separate existences?[20]

Historically, Gauchet tells us, there have been two solutions to this political dilemma: the market and the social contract. But each one tends towards its extreme form. With the market model, this means a conception of the social body as a simple 'association of individual monads (of equal property holders)' and with the social contract, a 'radical and totalitarian negation of the individual' forced to blend into an undifferentiated collectivity.[21] Neither Marxism nor market-driven liberalism has been able, according to Gauchet, to imagine the individual and the social together, as they have emerged and as they will forever continue to exist. With the critique of totalitarianism in the late 1970s, the market and individualism re-emerged as the only viable *politique* for the West, and with it the assumption that

> if we were alone in our corner, everything would be better. Unfortunately, we are destined to live in a society, and constituting a society is necessarily harming the autonomy of each individual who is assembled to constitute it. It is necessarily inflicting an irreparable damage to personal sovereignty.

Here lies, Gauchet continues,

> the greatest peril concealed by this return to human rights: the possibility of falling back in the rut and the impasse of a theory of the individual against society. This would mean succumbing to the old illusion that we can build upon the individual and begin with the individual, with his

demands and his rights, to reach back up to society. As if we could
separate the search for individual autonomy from the push towards social
autonomy.[22]

For Gauchet, however, the problem with modern individualism is not just
social and political. It also has important psychic consequences – consequences
particularly pertinent given Gauchet's long-standing interest in psychoanalysis
and psychiatry.[23] 'The affirmation of individual autonomy', Gauchet writes,
'has invariably gone hand in hand with the increase of collective heteronomy'
and with the alienation of all.[24] This concept of alienation – in its basic
definition as a disjunction between individual and collective points of view,
or between private and public – is central to Gauchet's work.[25] As he sees it,
human rights and individualism have brought about three types of alienation:
the alienation of individuals from the state, from each other, and from their
own autonomy. Indeed, as his *longue durée* narrative makes clear, and as his
analysis of the French left corroborates, the rise of the individual is inextricably
linked to the rise of state power and the bureaucratic management of society.
It was only with absolutism and with the king imagined to represent popular
sovereignty that the individual could emerge. Autonomy, in other words, did
not arise spontaneously as an 'intimate conviction'. Rather, the idea that
individuals constituted 'independent, self-sufficient, equal entities' came from
the *outside*, from a power strong enough to transcend local, familial, religious,
and corporate bodies. 'There can be no free and active citizens', Gauchet
argues, 'without a separate power able to embody the social universe (*univers
social*)'.[26] This is the paradox of freedom in modernity that Constant – whose
political works Gauchet prefaced around the same time he wrote the human
rights article – had already observed in the nineteenth century.[27] The
development of freedom historically and theoretically entails the expansion
of administration, bureaucracy, control, and hence, dispossession: 'state
expropriation and consolidation of human rights have to this day gone hand
in hand.'[28]

The second form of alienation that Gauchet explores is produced by abstract
individualism. At the same time as the state recognises and caters to the
specificity of the individual, it constructs him as an anonymous and
interchangeable being, hence once again dispossessing him from his subjectivity.[29]
Finally, the third and perhaps most pernicious expression of this alienation is
the alienation of the individual from his own autonomy. The fact that society
grants rights to individuals does not in any way imply that it gives individuals
the means with which to exercise this freedom. Thus, in modernity, human
rights become 'the right to disinterest oneself from the consciousness of social
existence, to enclose oneself into one's private sphere'.[30] Privacy in this sense,
leads to two problems: one at the scale of the individual who becomes
narcissistically isolated, and another at the scale of society where the individual
seeks others exactly like him.[31] Although Gauchet does not give specific
examples of this kind of behaviour, we might think of fascism or the politics of

the far-right Front National, which had begun to gather steam in the early 1980s. Gauchet developed this thesis in later works, particularly in *La Religion dans la démocratie* in which he accounts for the emergence of 'radical communitarianism' (*communautarisme*) as an effect of democracy and human rights understood as privacy.[32] This is also Yonnet's argument in *Voyage au centre du malaise française*. Yonnet blames the rise of the Front National – which he interprets as populism – on the philosophy of the *droit à la différence* emerging out of May 68 and more specifically, on the antiracism movement epitomised by the organisation SOS Racisme.[33]

Gauchet concludes his 1980 essay by arguing that human rights should in no way constitute a *politique* because they have and always will entail 'the reinforcement of the role of the State, the deepening of social anonymity, the aggravation of the disinterest for the public good, and the anguished banalisation of behaviours'.[34] Human rights, in other words, can only function as vectors of depoliticisation. We might feel more free in modernity,

> but only within a society entirely taken care of by the State (*de part en part prise en charge par l'État*). We might feel like *ourselves*, we may live according to our particularities, but we are interchangeable (*n'importe qui*) from the point of view of the overall organisation in which we are inscribed. From the outside, we are independent social units, but from the inside we are incapable, on the one hand, of imagining ourselves amid others and in relation to the collectivity, and on the other hand, of acknowledging our difference in relation to others.[35]

For Gauchet, but also for many of the contributors to *Le Débat*, France was at a turning point in the early 1980s. It was caught between the crisis of the left and the rise of the extreme-right on the domestic front and the growth of the European Union, the progressive weakening of the Soviet Union, and the rise of the 'American model' abroad. Even so, as Gauchet and many other neo-republican thinkers made clear, human rights and liberalism were not the answer.

Privacy at the Fondation Saint-Simon

The critique of individual rights and of privacy that Gauchet so cogently articulated in *Le Débat* found echoes in many sectors of French political and intellectual life during the 1980s and 1990s. In particular, Gauchet's plea for a new *politique* beyond left and right concurred with the mission of an important think tank, the Fondation Saint-Simon. Founded in 1982, the Fondation Saint-Simon was named after the Comte de Saint-Simon who had wrestled with the social effects of industrialism at the beginning of the nineteenth century.[36] The Fondation was originally set up by Philippe Vianney (a resistance fighter who, after the war, had sought to promote a dialogue between Communists and priests, and between workers and the bourgeoisie), Roger Fauroux (the president of the glass factory Saint-Gobain), and his right-hand man, Alain Minc. Fauroux – a graduate of the the prestigious École normale supérieure – was weary of economic reductionism and his idea for the Fondation was that it would encourage industrialists and businessmen to engage more actively with intellectual culture. Fauroux convinced the historian of the French Revolution François Furet to join him, as well as the political scientist Pierre Rosanvallon, an economic advisor at the Confédération française démocratique du travail (CFDT) trade union and a professor at Sciences Po. During the two decades in which it was operational, the Fondation gathered some of the most prominent and influential intellectuals, business leaders, civil servants, elected officials, and journalists. The members of the Fondation met for monthly lunches that were followed by a talk by an invited speaker. Several of these were subsequently published as short essays (*notes*) ranging from 10 to 100 pages, of which a thousand or so copies were printed.

Many of the talks and *notes* at the Fondation developed the critique of privacy articulated by Gauchet in 1980. Those involved with the Fondation were by no means ideologically and politically uniform, but they did share the sense that France was at a point of transition, between the ongoing demise of Marxism on the one hand, and the growing influence of the United States on the other. As Alain Minc put it, the mission of the Fondation was to overcome the 'ideological and sociological cold war' that had paralyzed France at the end of the 1970s. In the words of Pierre Rosanvallon, the Fondation was born after the 1981 election of Mitterrand, 'at a time when the French left was still entangled with the intellectual and political archaisms of the *programme commun*'. Like Gauchet, Rosanvallon emphasised the need for the left to put an end to the 'demonisation of governmental culture'.[37] This meant the elaboration of a new form of republicanism, one of the central axes of which was the distinction between private and public, expressed as the difference between individual rights and the state. At the same time, the members of the Fondation were aware of the dangers of modern democracy: it was here that the powerful concept of *communautarisme* was developed and popularised. Soon, *communautarisme* came to be defined tautologically as what was not republican, what was not French, and what was symptomatic of human rights having become a *politique*.[38]

Two of the Fondation's *notes* from the mid-1990s were particularly important in establishing the limits of privacy in the context of sexuality. The first, written by the sociologist Frédéric Martel, was entitled 'The communitarian temptation: Homosexual liberation and the fight against AIDS'. The second, by the sociologist Irène Théry, focused on France's first domestic partnership bill – the Contrat d'union sociale (CUS).[39] Martel entered the debate around privacy by distinguishing good homosexual politics from communitarian 'temptation', which turned human rights, understood in Gauchet's sense of the term, into a *politique*. Théry, for her part, reframed public and private by assimilating heterosexuality to publicity and homosexuality to privacy.

Martel's talk at the Fondation Saint-Simon in April 1996 was an excerpt from his history of French homosexuality since 1968, *Le Rose et le noir*, which was released at the same time. Much has been written about Martel's controversial theses in this book, particularly his assertion that French gay circles were partly responsible for the spread of AIDS in the early 1980s because of their 'denial' of the virus.[40] What interests me here, however, is Martel's chronology of the homosexual movement, from the 'revolution of desire' (1968–79), through the 'era of socialisation' (1979–84) and the 'end of the carefree life' (1981–9), to the 'era of contradictions' (1989–96). If the 'era of socialisation' is characterised by the final decriminalisation of homosexuality under the auspices of the Socialist Party – in other words, the good kind of human rights – the 'era of contradictions' corresponds to the rise of homosexuality as a *politique*. To elucidate this distinction, Martel targets the group Act Up, 'a political movement' that he contrasts with Aides, the association founded by Michel Foucault's long-term partner Daniel Defert in 1984, which Martel describes as a 'social movement'.[41] Martel's interest in Aides lies primarily in the fact that it stressed the moral character of its mission; it emphasised the importance of cross-community solidarity and it refused to be considered a 'gay organisation' despite the fact that it was fighting AIDS. As he puts it, they were 'homosexual activists but not homosexuals engaged in identity politics (*luttes identitaires*)'.[42]

In contrast to Aides, Martel argues, Act Up was an organisation of complicated origins. On the one hand, it was imported from the United States, the country that had given birth to the most radical forms of *communautarisme* 'where it is possible to be promoted to a full professor because you are gay'.[43] On the other hand, it was in line with the philosophy and political tactics of the French extreme left during the 1970s from which it borrowed 'its contestatory sense, its general assemblies . . ., its appearance of direct democracy'.[44] In Martel's narrative, Act Up epitomised the type of minority group – a 'homosexual association' – that mobilised human rights at the expense of the social and of the state. 'Act Up', Martel writes, 'believes in the role of state, (only) by criticizing it permanently.'[45] Within this model, the state is necessary, both as the structure that constantly needs to be attacked *and* as the solution to the most pressing political problems.

Although Martel is unequivocal in his support for the decriminalisation laws of the 1980s, and even more for the domestic partnership legislation of the late 1990s – both of which were promoted by its advocates as 'human rights' – he is particularly sensitive to the limits of the discourse on rights. Martel pauses on two examples to illustrate its excesses (*dérapages*). The first is the defence of rape and paedophilia that certain gay activists, 'swept by the new logic of rights, almost intoxicated by it', staged in the 1970s.[46] The second is the phenomenon of 'Gay Pride', which Martel denounces as 'offensive communitarianism' and indicative of the 'gradual move towards the Americanisation of French society'.[47] Although Martel recognises that 'Gay Pride' 'reflects a legitimate concern about the place of homosexuals in tomorrow's society', he contends that

> these communitarian demands also reveal modes of disarticulation, the
> dissolution of the bonds of society in contemporary France. And every
> society must be able to rely on all its members, who must be able to
> communicate among themselves . . . Today, it seems that homosexuals are
> demanding not just equal rights but also, perhaps, collective recognition.[48]

Homosexuals, Martel argues, should not be assimilated to other minorities – ethnic or religious – and homophobia is neither eternal nor natural:

> Those who suggest that homosexuals of necessity face a hostile world are
> not quite in touch with reality, and they show an immoderate interest in
> being cast as victims. Or perhaps the repeated denunciation of
> homophobia is a strategy aimed at maintaining a semblance of unity in
> the 'homosexual community'. If so, then it is a very risky business, since
> the gays' salvation will not come from a logic of victimization or from the
> conviction that, as people, they are pariahs.[49]

Martel's analysis of homosexuality thus forecloses any analysis of structural violence. It suggests that if integration has been a problem for homosexuals – as the case of AIDS made especially evident – it is because of *their* own failure to integrate themselves into society. Martel ends his book, and his talk at the Fondation Saint-Simon, with a call to

> leave behind communitarianism and a reductive, 'homogenizing' identity
> . . ., to abandon a form of sexual kinship that cannot keep its promise of
> community . . ., to propose that the issue of homosexuality no longer has
> any meaning or reason for being.

As he concludes, 'homosexuality', in quotation marks, as an identity or a 'human right' mobilised to make a series of specific political claims, should no longer exist.[50]

One of the best mechanisms of integration according to Martel – and consequently, one of the best protections against communitarianism – is the domestic partnership law that France debated throughout the 1990s and that was eventually adopted in 1999. Irène Théry's *note* at the Fondation Saint-Simon addressed the first version of the bill – the CUS – that preceded the better-known Pacte civil de solidarité (PACS), and sought to grant a series of rights to all cohabiting couples, whether heterosexual, homosexual, roommates, siblings, or joined by any other bond. The promoters of the CUS strategically designed the bill to include unions of all sorts, thereby ensuring that it remained within a 'republican logic'. The influential philosopher and intellectual Elisabeth Badinter, for example, gave her support to the bill precisely because it was 'universalistic'. As she told the newspaper *Libération* in 1992:

> I am convinced that we are now within the right to 'indifference': leave us alone, we are like everyone else. The right to difference is what gives rise to the ghettoisation of minority communities, to the rejection of the majority community, and to oppression.[51]

The organisers of the Gay Pride parade took a similar view of the CUS. In 1996, more than 100,000 people marched in the streets of Paris demanding the 'right to indifference'. As one of the Pride coordinators explained:

> We are not within an Anglo-Saxon communitarian logic of 'ghettos'. It is exactly the opposite. This contract has a universal impact: it seeks to recognise the link between two persons who have a project of common life, whatever their sex may be.[52]

After a long and complex argument, Théry ended up opposing the CUS for three main reasons: because the CUS sought to encompass non-sexual relationships; because it refused to distinguish homosexual from heterosexual couples; and because it undermined the power of republican marriage. She proposed to replace the new law with a series of specific and limited reforms. She advocated more rights (housing rights, tax breaks, and health insurance) for all cohabiting couples, as she drafted a reform of marriage, divorce, and inheritance laws, to make marriage more accessible and attractive for heterosexual couples. Parallel to this, Théry suggested that the government create a 'contract of coupled life' restricted to same-sex couples, similar to the one that many Scandinavian nations had set up. 'The proposition of a true "contract of coupled life"', Théry argued, 'is a way to engage much more clearly in the legal recognition of the homosexual couple, in the name of equality, while saying no to assimilation, in the name of difference.'[53] This new contract, Théry specified, would grant same-sex couples exactly the same rights given by marriage but it would not give access to adoption or to reproductive technologies, two of the most controversial questions during these debates.[54]

Théry's talk at the Fondation was republished in the journal *Esprit* in October 1997. A few months later, Théry was solicited by the Socialist Minister of Justice, Elisabeth Guigou and by the Socialist Minister of Labour and Solidarity, Martine Aubry, to produce a report on the state of the family – including an assessment of same-sex partnerships. Her thoughts thus had a direct impact on legislation. In this sense, Théry provides a good case study of how the republican theory of private and public was applied to actual policy. Much of Théry's analysis of the CUS was premised on her previous work on the family, and especially her 1993 book, *Le Démariage: Justice et vie privée*, in which Théry conducted a vigorous critique of rights and privacy in the domain of sexuality and family law. Théry's book centres on the question of divorce, but it also offers a history of marriage in France, the chronology of which is remarkably similar to that of Gauchet. In fact, Théry explains that she chose to title her book *le démariage* (as opposed to *le divorce*), in reference to Gauchet's work, and more specifically to his *Désenchantement du monde*, in which Gauchet discusses secularism not as the opposite of religion but rather as an 'exit from religion'. Marriage therefore serves as the primary frame of reference for Théry, in the same way that religion does for Gauchet:

> When we say that marriage has become a private matter, we do not simply designate a change in the personal expectations vis-à-vis a union, but rather a cultural phenomenon analogous to . . . the 'disenchantment of the world' that Marcel Gauchet describes in relation to religion. Like religion, marriage is no longer consubstantial with the human universe of our societies. It has become a subjective experience. To embrace it or to break it is a question relegated to one's individual conscience.[55]

This sense of freedom deriving from the phenomenon of *démariage* has shattered the very definition of the private.

Théry's argument rests on a very specific history of marriage in France. It begins in 1792 with the secularisation of the sacrament and the establishment of civil marriage. The years that followed were marked, according to Théry, by a tension between two legal understandings of marriage and family. She calls the first a '*droit de principe*' (law of principles). According to this legal philosophy, 'human rights do not stop at the door of the private' and the family has no particular specificity. As a result, it is governed by the same principles that underlie all political rights. Théry opposes this *droit de principe* to what she calls a *droit du modèle* (law of models), 'founded on the idea that the family is an irreducibly specific society and that the role of the law is to preserve the particular nature of the relations between father, mother, children and spouses'.[56] If revolutionary family law ended up privileging the *droit de principe*, the 1804 Civil Code represented the consecration of the *droit du modèle*, and thus of a particular configuration of the public–private divide. The architects of the Civil Code were indeed adamant about the fact that the family was constitutive of the social. Writing in the aftermath of the Terror, they argued that the family controlled and framed men's natural instincts and passions, that it constituted a crucial normative structure, and that it provided the social and psychic stability necessary for a steady and secure political life.

For Théry, the 'turning point' – which is akin to the turning point of 1968 in Gauchet's history of secularisation – was the 'quiet revolution in family law' in the 1960s and 1970s, which modified several of the key clauses in the Civil Code concerning marriage, filiation, adoption, parental authority, and divorce. According to Théry, these reforms were inspired by a new legal philosophy of 'human rights' that privileged freedom and equality at the expense of the cohesion of the social body.[57] Family law, in other words, became exclusively governed by a *droit de principe* as opposed to a *droit de modèle*. The new laws were presented as the simple adaptation of law to the more 'liberal, pluralistic, and "neutral"' mores of the day. But they also implied a greater degree of involvement of the state. In short, they were increasingly 'managerial (*gestionnaire*)'.[58] In her narrative, Théry holds the left particularly responsible for abandoning 'a normative logic in favour of a social logic'.[59] The left, she writes, was characterised by a 'mistrust of the law as an instrument of domination. This is why it claimed for itself, not an alternative legal norm, but rather the pure and simple refusal of all legal limits on individual autonomy.'[60] The best example of this is the 1975 divorce law, which doubly illustrates Gauchet's critique of human rights. First, it reveals the left's inability to understand power positively and to work with the state, rather than against it. Second, it exemplifies the double-bind of modernity described by Gauchet whereby the liberalisation of the law and the increase of individual freedom actually bring about greater state surveillance and a tighter administrative control of the family and private sphere.

In Théry's view, private life since the 1970s has become 'a space in which the individual no longer wants to account to anyone but himself'.[61] This means that we are at once 'more free and more exposed, more responsible and more insecure, more autonomous and more fragile'.[62] The question of *démariage* is a collective one, Théry writes, because 'it explodes our normative universe. The real stake is not the withdrawal of the law but the problem of how to establish a new foundation for our common law'.[63] Théry, like Gauchet, attributes this new individualism to the history of France during the 1960s and 1970s. She also portrays it as an American import. In particular, Théry relies on an article by Philippe Raynaud, entitled 'From the tyranny of the majority to the tyranny of minorities' (published in 1992 in *Le Débat* and also presented at the Fondation Saint-Simon) and on François Furet's work on American 'democratic utopianism'. Both texts depict the United States as the land of political correctness, hyperindividualism, and the reigning 'ideology of minority rights'.[64] In Théry's analysis, the US serves as a case study to explore the social consequences of human rights having become a *politique*. In the American model, the state has merely 'one power and one duty: to protect the rights to self-determination and self-fulfillment'.[65] As for the individual, 'his only collective identity is that which his group of belonging – or his biological group – grants him'.[66] And like Gauchet, Théry pauses on the psychic effects of this new individualism, and particularly on the alienation of individuals absorbed with their insular concerns – their *petites affaires*, to use Tocqueville's term.[67] Like Martel, Théry concludes with an ominous warning about the dangers of this 'dubious communitarianism'. Thankfully, she writes, France has not yet reached the stage of the US but the 'recent debates concerning the rights of children, the veil and *laïcité*, medically assisted procreation, female circumcision, and the right to difference indicate the extent to which it is easy to feel disoriented by the idea of private freedom'.[68]

In her presentation at the Fondation Saint-Simon, Théry reiterated the need to establish new norms to regulate communal life in the face of this growing individualism, epitomised notably by the CUS. Despite the fact that supporters of the CUS presented it as universalistic and republican because it was open to all couples, Théry argued that this was a ruse, a 'republican mirage':

> This 'contract for all', which reveals itself as perfectly compatible with the harshest forms of separatism of culture and mores, has nothing particularly 'republican' about it. We will have to understand by what mystery such a watchword has become the emblem for the fight against the slippery slope of *communautarisme*, of the Americanization of mores, and of the politically correct.[69]

Théry opposed the CUS for misconstruing the relationship between private and public and for attempting to give public relevance to private lives – namely, homosexual lives – that in her opinion ought to remain private. Unlike cohabitation, marriage, which could only be heterosexual, was the best public expression of privacy. As Théry put it, republican marriage constituted the link between 'democratic debate, the values of citizenship, and private life'.[70] Rhetorically assimilated to *laïcité*, the Declaration of Human Rights, and the principle of equality of all citizens before the law, heterosexual marriage was the condition for the right kind of privacy and the right kind of *politique* for France.

Towards a new republican symbolic

According to Théry,

> one of the most profound paradoxes of this era of *démariage*, which began producing its full effects at the turning point of the 1970s–80s, is that it demands a reconstruction in other terms of symbolic and legal reference, at the very moment when we are turning away from the law.[71]

The critique of human rights and privacy was thus, in Théry's eyes, only the first step of the greater intellectual challenge of constructing a new theory of law, an alternative *droit de modèle* that would link private and public. This has been the impetus behind much of Théry's work since *Le Démariage*: a 'return to the law' to overcome both 'the impasses of utilitarianism and of liberalism . . . and the collapse of (a Marxist) vision of the law as the ultimate form of legitimation for class domination'.[72] One of the concepts that is most useful for Théry in this 'return to the law' is that of 'the symbolic'. Loosely derived from the works of Claude Lévi-Strauss and Jacques Lacan, 'the symbolic' allows Théry to establish a causal relationship between psychic, familial, and social structures, and to ground them in heterosexuality. Thus, her 'return to the law' is premised on the centrality of heterosexual marriage, the institution required to guarantee psychic well-being and social cohesion, which is the necessary condition for France's *politique*.

This concept of the symbolic is also crucial for Gauchet who has described his project as a 'transcendental anthroposociology' inspired by two great 'masters': Claude Lévi-Strauss and Jacques Lacan.[73] From anthropology, Gauchet derives a theory of the human, 'of what constitutes the humanity of man'. Sociology is the necessary counterpart to anthropology since man is intrinsically social. Furthermore, Gauchet's theory is transcendental in the sense that it aims to discern the conditions of possibility and the philosophical dimension of 'the whole'. In his words: 'I seek to understand the articulation of what makes man social by nature – that is to say, that which governs the architecture of our societies – and the psychic organisation that is ours'.[74] Gauchet's notion of a 'transcendental anthroposociology' offers us a model of private and public (the anthropological and the social) that is universal, structural, and solidly grounded in sexual difference. Within this paradigm, heterosexual exchange serves as the necessary condition for social and psychic development. Because Gauchet presents this model as structural, his construction of private and public appear normative, logical, and beyond all geographic and historical specificity. Gauchet's 'transcendental anthroposociology' – his symbolic – can be interpreted precisely as a republican *politique*. It is a political, social, and psychic model able to unify public and private in a universalist and transhistorical framework premised on heterosexual exchange.

More generally, Gauchet's critique of rights had important intellectual and political ramifications. It shaped the agenda of *Le Débat* for two decades and offered a template for other scholars interested in examining how Gauchet's articulation of private and public might be 'applied' to specific social groups. The talks delivered by Frédéric Martel and Irène Théry at the Fondation Saint-Simon were two examples of this 'application' in the context of sexuality. Because these talks were attended or read by some of the most prominent figures of the French political world, they also allow us to trace how republican ideas were translated into concrete legislation. The republican vision of sexuality, in other words, did not simply remain an object of theoretical speculation: it actually guided many of the laws concerning homosexuality throughout the 1990s, including the PACS. Most importantly, the interventions of Martel and Théry highlighted the significance of Gauchet's analysis: his discussion of private and public was not simply about rights and the domain of the law; it was also a battle over norms. The new theory of democracy devised by Gauchet and developed by Martel and Théry depended on a transcendental, universal, and ahistorical understanding of (sexual) norms. As a political theory, republicanism offered the possibility of resisting history and refusing the social diversity that was increasingly visible and vocal in late twentieth-century France.[75]

Notes

1 Marcel Gauchet, 'Les Droits de l'homme ne sont pas une politique', *Le Débat* 3 (July–August, 1980), republished in Marcel Gauchet, *La Démocratie contre elle-même* (Paris: Gallimard, 2002), 1–26.

2 Gauchet, 'Les Droits de l'homme', see Note 1, 5.

3 Gauchet, 'Les Droits de l'homme', see Note 1, 4.

4 For a history of these early years of *Le Débat*, see Marcel Gauchet, *La Condition historique* (Paris: Stock, 2003), 197–220.

5 Gauchet, *La Démocratie contre elle-même*, see Note 1, i.

6 Mark Lilla, *New French Thought: Political philosophy* (Princeton: Princeton University Press, 1994).

7 Serge Audier, *La Pensée anti-68: Essai sur les origines d'une restauration intellectuelle* (Paris: La Découverte, 2008).

8 Gauchet, *La Condition historique*, see Note 4, 342.

9 Gauchet, *La Condition historique*, see Note 4, 342–3. For an analysis of Gauchet's reading of Constant and Tocqueville, see Samuel Moyn, 'Savage and modern liberty: Marcel Gauchet and the origins of new French thought', *European Journal of Political Theory* 4, 2 (2005): 164–87. On the complicated relationship of French liberalism to individual rights, see Raf Geenens and Helena Rosenblatt, eds., *French Liberalism from Montesquieu to the Present Day* (Cambridge: Cambridge University Press, 2012) and Lucien Jaume, *L'Individu effacé ou Le paradoxe du libéralisme français* (Paris: Fayard, 1997).

10 For how the division of public and private operated in relation to gender, see 'French seduction theory' in Joan Wallach Scott, *The Fantasy of Feminist History* (Durham, NC: Duke University Press, 2011), 117–40.

11 Gauchet, *La Démocratie contre elle-même*, see Note 1, 2–3.

12 Gauchet shares Lefort's understanding of *le politique* as that which institutes society (*la forme de la société*) and which 'constitutes social space'. See Claude Lefort, *Essais sur le politique: XIXe–XXe siècles* (Paris: Seuil, 1986), 20.

13 Gauchet, *La Démocratie contre elle-même*, see Note 1, 9.

14 Gauchet, *La Démocratie contre elle-même*, see Note 1, 10.

15 Gauchet, *La Démocratie contre elle-même*, see Note 1, 11.

16 Gauchet, *La Démocratie contre elle-même*, see Note 1, 11.

17 Gauchet, *La Démocratie contre elle-même*, see Note 1, 12.

18 Gauchet, *La Démocratie contre elle-même*, see Note 1, 13.

19 Gauchet, *La Démocratie contre elle-même*, see Note 1, 15.

20 Gauchet, *La Démocratie contre elle-même*, see Note 1, 15.

21 Gauchet, *La Démocratie contre elle-même*, see Note 1, 16.

22 Gauchet, *La Démocratie contre elle-même*, see Note 1, 17–18.

23 See Gauchet, *La Condition historique*, see Note 4, Ch. VIII, and Samuel Moyn, 'The assumption by man of his original fracturing: Marcel Gauchet, Gladys Swain, and the history of the self', *Modern Intellectual History* 6, 2 (2009): 315–41.

24 Gauchet, *La Démocratie contre elle-même*, see Note 1, 18.

25 Gauchet, *La Démocratie contre elle-même*, see Note 1, 25.

26 Gauchet, *La Démocratie contre elle-même*, see Note 1, 19–20.

27 Marcel Gauchet, 'Benjamin Constant: L'Illusion lucide du libéralisme' in Benjamin Constant, *Écrits politiques*, ed. Marcel Gauchet (Paris: Gallimard, 1997), 10–110.

28 Gauchet, *La Démocratie contre elle-même*, see Note 1, 21.

29 Gauchet, *La Démocratie contre elle-même*, see Note 1, 22–3.

30 Gauchet, *La Démocratie contre elle-même*, see Note 1, 23.

31 Gauchet, *La Démocratie contre elle-même*, see Note 1, 23–4.

32 See Marcel Gauchet, *La Religion dans la démocratie: Parcours de la laïcité* (Paris: Gallimard, 1998).

33 Paul Yonnet, *Voyage au centre du malaise français: L'Antiracisme et le roman national* (Paris: Gallimard, 1993).

34 Gauchet, *La Démocratie contre elle-même*, see Note 1, 25.

35 Gauchet, *La Démocratie contre elle-même*, see Note 1, 25–6.

36 See Christophe Prochasson, *Saint-Simon, ou, L'anti-Marx: figures du saint-simonisme français, XIXe–XXe siècles* (Paris: Perrin, 2004).

37 Emile Favard, *Les Echos*, 4 April 1997; Pierre Rosanvallon, 'La Fondation Saint-Simon, une histoire accomplie', *Le Monde*, 23 June 1999. For more on the Fondation Saint-Simon, see Fondation Saint-Simon, *Les Notes de la Fondation Saint-Simon: Une Expérience intellectuelle (1983–1999)* (Paris: Calmann-Lévy, 1999); 'Suicide collectif au temple de la "pensée unique"', *Événement du Jeudi*, 1–7 July 1999; Vincent Laurent, 'Les architectes du social-libéralisme', *Le Monde diplomatique*, September 1998; Jean-Gabriel Freder, 'Le suicide de "Saint-Simon"', *Nouvel Observateur*, 1 July 1999.

38 For more on how the rhetoric of *communautarisme* developed during these years, see Clarisse Fabre and Eric Fassin, *Liberté, égalité, sexualité: Actualité politique des questions sexuelles: entretiens* (Paris: Belfond, 2003); Laurent Lévy, *Le Spectre du communautarisme* (Paris: Éditions Amsterdam, 2005); and Joan Wallach Scott, *Parité! Sexual equality and the crisis of French universalism* (Chicago, IL: University of Chicago Press, 2005).

39 Frédéric Martel, 'La tentation communautaire: Libération homosexuelle et lutte contre le sida', *Note de la Fondation Saint-Simon* (April 1996). Irène Théry, 'Le contrat d'union sociale en question', *Note de la Fondation Saint-Simon* (October 1997).

40 Frédéric Martel, *Le Rose et le noir: Les Homosexuels en France depuis 1968* (Paris: Seuil, 2000). See the postface to the second French edition for a summary of these debates.

41 Act Up-Paris was founded in 1989, two years after its American counterpart. Although it was originally formed to fight against AIDS, it was also involved in other causes apart from gay rights, immigration, social rights, intellectual property, and prison reform. See Christophe Broqua, *Agir pour ne pas mourir: Act Up, les homosexuels et le sida* (Paris: Les Presses de Sciences Po, 2006), and Didier Lestrade, *Act Up: Une Histoire* (Paris: Denoël, 2000).

42 Martel, *Le Rose et le noir*, see Note 40, 397.

43 Martel, *Le Rose et le noir*, see Note 40, 490.

44 Martel, *Le Rose et le noir*, see Note 40, 504.

45 Martel, *Le Rose et le noir*, see Note 40, 507.

46 Martel, *Le Rose et le noir*, see Note 40, 668.

47 Frédéric Martel, *The Pink and the Black: Homosexuals in France since 1968* (Stanford, CA: Stanford University Press, 1999), 355. The English translation of Martel's book republished the note de la Fondation Saint-Simon in an epilogue titled 'A Dubious Communitarianism'.

48 Martel, *The Pink and the Black*, see Note 47, 354.

49 Martel, *The Pink and the Black*, see Note 47, 355.

50 Martel, *The Pink and the Black*, see Note 47, 359.

51 Elisabeth Badinter, 'Union civile: Le Courage est payant', *Libération*, 23 April 1992.

52 Élisabeth Fleury, 'Interview with Laurent Queige', *L'Humanité*, 28 June 1997.

53 Irène Théry, 'Le contrat d'union sociale en question', *Esprit* 236 (1997): 185.

54 Théry, 'Le contrat d'union sociale en question', see Note 53. For an analysis of why reproduction was so central to these debates, see Camille Robcis, *The Law of Kinship: Anthropology, Psychoanalysis, and the Family in France* (Ithaca, NY: Cornell University Press, 2013).

55 Irène Théry, *Le Démariage: Justice et vie privée* (Paris: Odile Jacob, 1993), 15.

56 Théry, *Le Démariage*, see Note 55, 25.

57 Théry, *Le Démariage*, see Note 55, 79.

58 Théry, *Le Démariage*, see Note 55, 80.

59 Théry, *Le Démariage*, see Note 55, 91.

60 Théry, *Le Démariage*, see Note 55, 120.

61 Théry, *Le Démariage*, see Note 55, 444.

62 Théry, *Le Démariage*, scc Notc 55, 445.

63 Théry, *Le Démariage*, see Note 55, 445.

64 Théry, *Le Démariage*, see Note 55, 446–9. François Furet, 'L'utopie démocratique à l'américaine', *Le Débat* 69 (March–April 1992) and Philippe Raynaud, 'De la tyranie de la majorité à la tyranie des minorités', *Le Débat* 69 (March–April 1992).

65 Théry, *Le Démariage*, see Note 55, 447.

66 Théry, *Le Démariage*, see Note 55, 447.

67 Théry, *Le Démariage*, see Note 55, 462. For an analysis of this rhetorical use of the American social model during these years, see Éric Fassin, 'Good Cop, Bad Cop': Modèle et contre-modèle américains dans le discours libéral français depuis les années 1980', *Raisons politiques* 1 (2001): 77–87.

68 Théry, *Le Démariage*, see Note 55, 449.

69 Théry, 'Le contrat d'union sociale en question', see Note 53, 165.

70 Théry, 'Le contrat d'union sociale en question', see Note 53, 171.

71 Théry, *Le Démariage*, see Note 55, 125.

72 Irène Théry, 'Vie privée et monde commun: Réflexions sur l'enlisement gestionnaire du droit', *Le Débat* 85 (May–August 1995): 110.

73 Gauchet, *La Condition historique*, see Note 4, 18.

74 Gauchet, *La Condition historique*, see Note 4, 13.

75 In this context, it is interesting to compare Gauchet's attack on liberalism to that staged by many American academics who explicitly position themselves on the left. In their edited volume *Left Legalism/Left Critique* (Durham, NC: Duke University Press, 2002), for example, Wendy Brown and Janet Halley urge us to move beyond the liberal paradigm of human rights and to focus instead 'on the social powers producing and stratifying subjects that liberalism largely ignores' (6). For Brown, Halley and the other authors in the anthology (which include Lauren Berlant, Michael Warner, Katherine Franke and Judith Butler), rights function as vectors of power, discipline, and regulation that encode rather than emancipate subjects. Ultimately, rights, privacy, and 'wounded attachments' contribute to a dangerous depoliticisation of the public sphere. Thus, although Brown and Halley appear to share Gauchet's diagnosis, the solutions that they propose are radically different. While Gauchet and Théry turn to a transcendent articulation of private and public, Brown and Halley propose to embrace critique. By focusing on 'the workings of ideology and power in the production of existing political and legal possibilities' (27), critique can reveal how certain categories get constructed as natural or inevitable and how particular norms – such as heterosexuality – become mobilised in particular situations. Critique, in other words, reveals the historical construction of norms and thus offers us tools to change them, to imagine alternative norms. By contrast, Gauchet's 'transcendental anthroposociology' aims to dehistoricise norms and to present them as fixed, necessary and immutable.

12

Cultural Insecurity and Political Solidarity:

French Republicanism Reconsidered

Sophie Guérard de Latour

Translated from the French by Emile Chabal

Is multiculturalism 'un-French'?[1]

The nature of social movements and their political impact underwent a profound transformation in the 1960s and 1970s. Debates over minority identities and cultural domination led not only to new policy measures such as anti-discrimination laws and the promotion of diversity, but also to the elaboration of new paradigms of political justice.[2] The latter have often been grouped under the generic term 'multiculturalism'.[3] It is now widely acknowledged that, of the major Western democracies, France has been one of the most resistant to this normative change, whether at the level of policy-making or political theory.[4] This is often considered to be a consequence of France's republican public philosophy. In the past three decades, faced with the rise of identity politics and the *droit à la différence* (right to difference) movement, a new republican consensus has emerged in France. Its main aim has been to defend the specificity of a 'French model of integration', particularly with respect to immigrant and ethnic minority populations.[5] This republican revival has been led by a group of philosophers and public intellectuals that have come to be known as 'official republicans'.[6] They have emphasised the importance of the nation as a vital form of cultural mediation and a prerequisite to citizenship. They have also repeatedly argued that multiculturalism is a threat to civic harmony and that political mobilisation by minorities is dangerous.

One of the more recent examples of the mobilisation of France's republican public philosophy was in 2002 when the far-left (*la gauche populaire*) adopted it as part of a broader strategy of political reorientation.[7] In the presidential elections of that year, the leader of the far-right Front National party caused a political shock by reaching the second round at the expense of the Socialist candidate Lionel Jospin, and it was in this context that members of the *gauche populaire* reiterated their republican credentials. They argued that, not only had the Socialist Party 'lost touch with the people' because of its adherence to neo-liberalism, it had also been converted to political liberalism by supporting minority rights for women, asylum seekers, homosexuals and others, all of which had contributed to the left's growing detachment from the working class.[8] This attack on the moderate left renewed the republican critique of multiculturalism in a number of ways. First, it was explicitly anti-elitist. It was not the political identity and 'communitarianism' of minorities themselves that was called into question, but the negligence of the (Socialist) political élite. The latter were accused of 'betraying their social base', for instance by concerning themselves more with the rights of foreign rather than French workers.[9] Second, it stressed egalitarianism. The defence of minorities had contributed to the left's 'rightward drift' because it served to focus attention on cultural issues at the expense of apparently insoluble socio-economic problems.[10] Finally, it incorporated the idea of 'cultural insecurity' alongside egalitarianism. Critics from the *gauche populaire* claimed that the moderate left's acceptance of multicultural diversity meant that it was no longer committed to the common culture required to build civic and national identity. Worse still, the defence of minorities had contributed to a general stigmatisation of the working class who were perceived as racist, xenophobic, sexist and homophobic. Deprived of a common identity and confronted with an overwhelmingly negative image of themselves, the 'indigenous' French working class (*Français de souche*) had become a psychologically vulnerable and poorly-represented minority. Their cultural insecurity was reflected particularly in spatial segregation: cast out into distant neighbourhoods, they were being excluded from the dynamic and positive effects of globalisation that were transforming the modern metropolis.[11]

This left-wing critique of multiculturalism raises a number of difficult empirical questions. For instance, further research would be required to demonstrate a causal relationship between multicultural policies and the declining Socialist vote among the French working class. These, however, are questions that belong in the realm of the social sciences. My aim here will be of a more philosophical nature. I want to analyse the normative project that lies at the heart of this critique of multiculturalism. I intend to examine critically the claim that multiculturalism is essentially anti-republican because it does not take seriously enough the importance of a community of citizens to realise civic equality. For the partisans of the *gauche populaire*, multiculturalism has undermined the nation by making individual rights and cultural diversity into a new political horizon. Its ultimate goal is to detach citizenship from 'archaic' national particularism. But this does not constitute social progress; on the contrary, they argue that multiculturalism creates new kinds of insecurity. It damages the symbolic power of the nation; its emphasis on difference loosens the bonds of a common culture; and it excludes the most vulnerable social groups from a political space that is supposed to guarantee equality and justice within French society.

Seen from the perspective of contemporary philosophical debates surrounding citizenship and cultural diversity, such an interpretation is highly questionable. For a start, not all normative theories of multiculturalism endorse cosmopolitanism. Many stress the importance of national cultures over the rights of foreigners and thereby come close to adopting a position commonly known as 'liberal nationalism', in which the aim is not to transcend the nation but to create more equitable relations between different groups within a multinational nation.[12] Moreover, not all theories of multiculturalism are explicitly opposed to policies of integration directed at immigrant populations. Rather, they criticise these policies in their most 'assimilationist' form and seek to reformulate them so that they are more acceptable to foreigners and immigrants.[13] Finally, it is important to remember that diversity and equality are not mutually incompatible policies; the vast majority of scholars of multiculturalism see their theoretical insights as a way of combatting new forms of social injustice and inequality by exposing their cultural foundations.

If nothing else, these observations suggest that there is no intrinsic theoretical incompatibility between the defence of minority rights and republican ideals. It is not surprising, therefore, that a new generation of neo-republican philosophers have tried to introduce more liberal ideas into French political culture in an effort to curb its more dogmatic and sectarian tendencies.[14] In this chapter, I would like to extend this project by proposing a liberal neo-republican reading of the philosophy of Emile Durkheim, one of the founding fathers of French republicanism. Durkheim is especially relevant here since he was a major theorist of social integration, an issue which is at the heart of the left-wing critique of multiculturalism. One of Durkheim's main contributions to this question was the theory of social solidarity he developed in *The Division of Labour in Society* (1893) as a way of reconciling social unity and the rise of individualism in modern society. His analysis rests on the close connection he saw between 'social facts' and 'moral facts'.[15] In this interpretation, integration is intimately related to the way in which certain norms emerge among groups and the way in which they coalesce around strong collective representations. Of course, these insights also had a normative function for Durkheim: his scientific analysis was a way of legitimising the republican nation-building project of the Third Republic.[16] One might argue that, in the light of technological, economic, social and political change, this contextual specificity has rendered his insights obsolete. But Durkheim's sociology continues to influence contemporary debates, particularly with respect to the relationship between French republicanism and minorities. It thus provides a useful starting point for a liberal reinterpretation of republicanism, while still retaining the distinctive national and historical character of French republicanism. In what follows, I want to propose three ways in which the French 'model of integration' can be reworked using Durkheim. My aim is to identify a middle ground between a communitarian and an anti-communitarian interpretation of Durkheim's thought that takes the community of citizens seriously without undermining minority rights.

A Rousseauist account: National identity, transcendence and civic virtue

The insistence of republicans on the importance of integration and, more recently, 'cultural security' is not simply a French idiosyncrasy. It has deep roots in a classical republican tradition that views politics as a civic act. In this view, freedom is a public good rather than a private good since it is derived entirely from the responsibility that all citizens have in a republic to choose their collective destiny. Republican freedom is therefore closely tied to membership of a political community that guarantees a sense of 'security' through an egalitarian ethos based on mutual respect.[17] Classical thinkers were already aware of the importance of patriotism as a form of collective identification and the basis of political belonging.[18] Contemporary republicans have remained attached to this model, although they have adapted it to the context of the nation-state, which has become the foundation of popular sovereignty in the modern age.[19] One of the great achievements of the multicultural critique of the nation has been to question the extent to which citizenship should be inextricably tied to a dominant national culture. Using historical examples, it has highlighted the authoritarian practices that have underpinned national assimilation in modern Western democracies and the subsequent marginalisation or obliteration of minority cultures.[20] This, in turn, has undermined the widely-accepted distinction between a *civic nation* and an *ethnic nation*. National integration does not depend on universal political principles alone; it also relies on ethno-cultural characteristics such as language, customs and national symbols in order to create a sense of shared community among citizens.

For liberal philosophers of multiculturalism, the process of national assimilation in a multicultural society is problematic because it embodies a new and pernicious form of 'state communitarianism' and 'tyranny of the majority' that imposes the norms of a dominant ethno-cultural group in the name of civic universalism. But French 'official republicans' hold the opposite view. The work of well-known sociologist Dominique Schnapper, for instance, provides a good example of the ways in which the sociology of Durkheim has been deployed to defend republicanism against the claim that it necessarily leads to an overbearing 'state communitarianism'.[21] Schnapper accepts that the public sphere is ethnically-orientated, but she rejects the normative conclusions of multicultural theory:

> It is true that the state is never truly neutral and that a common culture, elaborated and guaranteed by public institutions, dominates particularistic cultures. But is this not the price to pay so that all citizens can participate fully in national society (*la société nationale*)?[22]

From a normative point of view, the argument of a 'price to pay' provides an instrumental justification for national integration policies. A majority culture is imposed on minority cultures as a condition for the realisation of a civic project, apparently without the need for any reference to the intrinsic value of a specific national culture (such as the 'genius' (*génie*) of the French language). And yet, Schnapper also recognises that, because of the sociological characteristics of the modern nation-state, no civic project can exist without 'a link, that can only be 'communitarian' or 'ethnic' in nature'.[23] It is at this point that Schnapper invokes Durkheim: she uses his theory of social solidarity in order to defend the positive and non-exclusive character of her proposed republican 'community of citizens'.

In *The Division of Labour*, Durkheim presented an original reading of the modernisation of social relations that ran contrary to the widely-accepted idea that community had disappeared.[24] In opposition to Ferdinand Tönnies' model of the movement from *Gemeinschaft* (community) to *Gesellschaft* (society), Durkheim argued that the shift from rural and agricultural society to urban and industrial society did not automatically entail the atomisation of social relations, nor did it imply the dissolution of social bonds. Solidarity had not disappeared from modern society; it had simply changed from a 'mechanical' solidarity based on similarity to an 'organic' solidarity based on difference. Whereas traditional communities were held together by imitation, shared ancestry, a respect for common values and the reproduction of similar modes of life, modern society was marked by a division of labour that had created ever-closer relations of interdependence. For Schnapper, the originality of Durkheim's communitarian conception of modern society lies in the pivotal role played by politics. This was, according to her, neglected by previous theorists of nationalism who had emphasised the role of technological, economic and ideological factors.[25] For Durkheim, on the other hand, the state was the 'social brain' (*cerveau social*) of a society governed by the division of labour.[26] In his analysis, the

state is the unified expression of new collective norms and ensures that
citizens have the possibility of developing their individual personalities with
a view to integrating themselves more effectively into society.[27] Durkheim
thus imagines the nation-state as a privileged means by which citizens can
break away from their cultures of origin and their traditional lifestyles: even
if national integration imposes a majority culture on all citizens, it remains
fundamentally liberating.

Schnapper uses Durkheim's model of social modernisation in order to
demonstrate that there is a qualitative conceptual difference between a nation
and an ethnicity. She argues that the former is founded on organic solidarity.
It embodies a 'principle of potential inclusion' that seeks to 'transcend
particularistic, biological, historical, economic, social, religious or cultural
forms of citizenship' and 'define the citizen as an abstract individual, above
and beyond his context (*déterminations concrètes*)'.[28] By contrast, ethnicity is
founded on mechanical solidarity. Its tendency is to exclude difference –
above all, ethnic difference – in an effort to preserve its specificity. This
distinction allows Schnapper to maintain that, 'unlike ethnic identity', the
nation is not founded on a 'cultural identity'.[29] Even if the cultural heritage of
a nation plays an important role in unifying citizens, it is not the nation's sole
raison d'être but simply a condition for the elaboration of a common civic
project. National cultures, then, are communitarian but not exclusive.

But, while Schnapper's distinction between two different forms of
solidarity makes it possible for her to defend an open and plural vision of
the nation-state, she nevertheless believes political claims by minorities to be
illegitimate. This is because they represent a regression towards a more
mechanical form of solidarity that Durkheim could not have predicted:

> Durkheim did not analyse the relationship between the two types of
> solidarity in dialectical terms, nor did he imagine that there could be
> a return to particularistic solidarities and identities; he did not foresee
> that 'mechanical' integration could emerge at the expense of 'organic'
> integration, or that ethnic passions could once again get the better of civic
> principles.[30]

The danger of minority claims is clearly stated in this passage: they will
rekindle 'ethnic passions' and undermine the 'civic reason (*la raison civique*)'
that lies at the heart of Schnapper's sociological conception of the nation. It
is for this reason that Schnapper criticises proponents of multicultural
politics such as the philosophers Charles Taylor and Will Kymlicka. In their
attempts to combat the assimilationist and exclusionary effects of national
integration, they 'risk contributing to social fragmentation by juxtaposing
closed communities without any mutual interaction'.[31] For Schnapper, the
republican state should not 'organise and subsidise particularism', but
instead work towards 'the unity of a common political space governed by
abstraction and the formal equality of citizens, whatever their social,

religious, regional or national origins'.[32] Moreover, ethno-cultural diversity should be handled in the same way as religious diversity – through a single principle of neutrality in the public sphere and the 'flexible application of republican citizenship'.[33]

The limits of Schnapper's reading of Durkheim's theory of solidarity lie in her conception of republicanism, which is strongly marked by a Rousseauist sensibility that seems ill-adapted to the exigencies of modern democracy. In Schnapper's view, integration into a national culture can be justified on the grounds that it allows citizens to 'transcend particularism'. Even if the 'transcendental' reality of the nation is still contaminated by residual ethno-cultural traits, the nation itself does not institutionalise particularism as long as it creates a political space that facilitates the movement from simple socialised subject to fully-fledged citizen. To put it in Rousseauist terms, it is necessary first to belong to a nation in order to gain access to the civic rationality that underpins the general interest. This, in turn, subdues 'ethno-religious passions' created by particularistic allegiances and factionalism. Hence why Schnapper sees the demand for cultural or minority rights as regressive: as citizens become ever more concerned with their individual rights, they turn away from the shared civic project that conferred citizenship on them in the first place.[34] Multicultural policies actively contribute to this fracturing of the community of citizens and the attrition of civic responsibility:

> Civic responsibility can transcend particularism, but, the more it weakens, the greater the possibility of a resurgence of ethno-religious passions. Believing in the rationality of man requires a good deal of will and optimism.[35]

Schnapper's response to multiculturalism is, therefore, to recreate a community of citizens founded on moral republicanism.[36] The implication is that national integration depends on the virtue of individual citizens – in other words, their personal ability to steer clear of private interests and rise to the level of the general will. But there are two major objections to this kind of moral republicanism. First, it relies on an unusually demanding conception of freedom that seems more appropriate to the classical than the modern age insofar as it emphasises moral self-control and the promotion of civic virtue. Second, it is clear that the burden of virtue falls disproportionately on minorities. The duty to integrate into a shared national culture is more easily fulfilled by the majority – who have defined the contours of the nation – than by minorities. These two objections suggest that mobilisation by minorities is not, in fact, a sign of 'archaic' forms of solidarity. Rather, such mobilisation is the expression of a desire for justice and equality in modern society. This is the interpretation that forms the basis of Jean-Fabien Spitz's neo-republican reading of Durkheim, to which we will now turn.

A neo-republican account: Non-discrimination and non-domination

Spitz's book, *Le Moment républicain en France* (2005), is an attempt to incorporate into French political theory the insights of Quentin Skinner, Philip Pettit and other Anglo-American theorists of neo-republicanism who have defended the relevance of a republican idea of freedom against the dominant doctrine of political liberalism. These thinkers do not endorse the classical republican ideal of freedom since they feel it demands too much self-control and self-abnegation for citizens in modern democracies and conflicts with the sociological realities of pluralism. However, respecting the diversity of values and ways of life people are likely to endorse in modern democracies does not mean that their freedom can be limited to 'non-interference' alone, as many traditional liberal thinkers have claimed. Instead, neo-republicans argue that freedom can be framed in terms of 'non-domination', or the absence of vulnerability to the arbitrary actions of others. In contrast to the marked scepticism of classical liberalism towards authority, Anglo-American neo-republicans maintain that the state and collective norms are essential in order to protect citizens from hidden forms of domination. Spitz adapts this analysis to a French context. His aim is to show how a republicanism of non-domination has long existed in French political culture. To this end, his reading of the texts of the founding fathers of the Third Republic stresses their conception of civic solidarity, which he sees as well-suited to modern society and yet capable of protecting civil society from intrusion by the republican state. Given his historical approach, it is not surprising that he is also drawn to Durkheim, who plays a central role in Spitz's liberal reinterpretation of French republicanism.

It is interesting that, even though Spitz and Schnapper both discuss Durkheim, they diverge sharply in the way they address the problem of difference and pluralism. Spitz does not associate the theory of 'organic solidarity' with a model of integration that can transcend particularism; instead, he stresses the strong relationship between the emergence of minority demands and the legitimisation of solidarities founded on the principle of difference. In his words:

> Durkheim was convinced that the desire to be recognised for our differences and specificities – and the desire for rights to protect the expression of these differences – cannot exist except in a society in which the differences between individuals have become very clear as a result of the division of labour.[37]

This argument is incompatible with the view that mobilisation by minorities represents a step backwards towards communitarian and conservative forms of solidarity. On the contrary, it suggests that any such mobilisation is a natural part of the evolution of society and the individual norms implicit in the division of labour. The clearest expression of this evolution is a desire for justice and an unprecedented demand for equality. It is worth clarifying here that, for Durkheim, organic solidarity does not simply refer to a functional process; it embodies a new form of solidarity characterised by a new relationship to the individual. As he puts it: 'as all other beliefs and practices take on less and less of a religious character, the individual becomes the object of a sort of religion.'[38] In other words, it is justice – defined as the imperative to respect humans in the abstract – that becomes the overriding 'common faith' of modern man. Spitz interprets this to mean that 'in the absence of collective beliefs and a strong collective conscience, solidarity can only be built on a feeling of not being discriminated against and of being treated according to our merit'.[39] Equality of opportunity is therefore an extension of Durkheim's religion of the individual, and opens society to all individuals, regardless of their social and ethnic origins.

For Spitz, the originality of Durkheim's approach lies in its republican inflection. In contrast to utilitarian economists of the late nineteenth century – especially Herbert Spencer – Durkheim believed that the liberalisation of social relations was not an entirely spontaneous process since it could take pathological forms such as the 'anomic (*anomique*) division of labour' or the 'constrained division of labour'. Spitz blurs the boundaries between the two pathological forms in his analysis, but it is the latter that is most relevant to a discussion of minorities. For Durkheim, the division of labour is 'constrained' when the allocation of social tasks no longer takes place spontaneously according to the capacities and talents of the individual, but instead falls back on preconceptions inherited from earlier forms of solidarity. In these circumstances, individuals are assessed on the basis of their similarity to their group of origin and thereby excluded from tasks that might correspond to their skills.[40] Although Durkheim does not deal specifically with the case of ethnic discrimination, there is a clear parallel and Spitz uses it to reinforce his argument about non-domination. More generally, this reading of Durkheim strongly suggests that mobilisation by minorities does not automatically mean a worrying return to 'ethnic passions' that might undermine civic life; rather, the problem lies in the social conditions that limit equality of opportunity. What unifies members of ethnic minority groups is not a straightforward mechanical solidarity, but 'a class of vulnerability'.[41] Whether or not specific individuals have been the target of discrimination, their membership of a minority group makes them vulnerable to domination. This naturally leads to a stronger collective identity and greater bonds of solidarity among minorities. The result is that individual demands for non-discrimination are expressed through a collective attack on domination and a rapid politicisation of identities that were hitherto consigned to the private sphere.

Spitz argues that, for Durkheim, the role of the republican state is precisely to combat social pathologies that give rise to forms of domination. It does this by creating rules and norms that protect citizens from the arbitrary exercise of power:

> The pathologies of a society of individuals arise simply because the implicit rules of society are inadequately formulated and insufficiently implemented. The Republic is the solution [to this problem].[42]

Durkheim did indeed see the Republic as a 'solution' to the pathologies of modern society. He saw the state as a regulatory body that does not impose rules from outside but merely codifies norms that emerge naturally from the division of labour. In the same way that the brain depends on other organs, the modern state depends on unconscious and spontaneous processes of social regulation. The only difference is that the complexity of modern society requires superior forms of social integration. These can only be guaranteed by the state, the purpose of which is to strengthen existing patterns of liberalisation within society. Not surprisingly, Spitz concludes that the metaphor of the state as 'social brain' is a sign that Durkheim's republicanism is fundamentally modern. The state does not exist to counteract the atomising tendencies of modern individualism and recreate a collective civic virtue. Its role is to reinforce and rationalise the rules that will ensure equality of opportunity and allow individuals to pursue their greatest happiness:

> The state is not a power which constrains, controls, and represses individual differences since, on the contrary, its function is to articulate the constitutive rules which allow for their true fulfilment. [. . .] The state's first function, then, is to create the conditions of maximal mobility and differentiation and to remove any obstacle which goes against a genuine or spontaneous specialisation of functions.[43]

Thus, where Schnapper invokes Durkheim to condemn minority and identity politics, Spitz deploys the work of the French sociologist to rather different ends. He maintains that Durkheim's argument about the pathologies of the division of labour is a sociological critique of the processes of discrimination that have undermined equality of opportunity in modern societies. Because discrimination has weakened the sense of justice that binds together the citizens of a republic, it has also weakened social solidarity. The state must therefore intervene in order to correct this tendency, specifically through anti-discriminatory policies, to which the majority of French official republicans are hostile.

One of the great benefits of reading Durkheim's republicanism in this way is that it gets away from a tired opposition between diversity and equality. Spitz shows clearly how minority rights are entirely consistent with the normative structures that gave rise to citizens' rights in general. In both cases, the aim is to protect individuals against the arbitrary exercise of power and domination – whether in the form of socio-economic exclusion or racism, xenophobia, sexism or homophobia. There is no need to set 'whites (*petits blancs*)' against minorities, as left-wing critics of multiculturalism have tried to do. When correctly understood, multicultural policies do not sacrifice the security of the former in order to defend the latter since non-domination is a common rather than competitive good.[44] If the republican state supports ethnic minorities by accepting the validity of their collective mobilisations and by giving them a place in the public sphere, it is to reinforce civic bonds. The state has a duty to integrate citizens, but this cannot be achieved merely by the imposition of a unified national culture in the name of civic virtue. The state should instead elaborate rules that reduce forms of domination within society, especially where this domination relates to cultural preconceptions inherited from older forms of solidarity. Ultimately, Spitz's reading of Durkheim's theory of solidarity opens the possibility of a convergence between different struggles for minority rights: as long as solidarity among minority groups is founded on non-domination, it is by definition moving towards integration with a national culture. In time, all citizens will perceive themselves as equally vulnerable and they will all work together to demand just laws that can protect them from domination.[45]

A liberal-communitarian account: Towards an inclusive national imaginary

Spitz's reading of Durkheim is, to my mind, an improvement on that of Schnapper. It expands the concept of republican political emancipation to encompass minority politics, not as a symptom of a backward-looking insularity, but as a legitimate form of expression within a modern democracy. This means that the republican state can only promote integration and emancipation by encouraging the mobilisation of minorities. Above all, Spitz's reading avoids casting minority politics as an irreconcilable clash between a majority culture and minority cultures. Instead, it suggests that we should analyse multiculturalism in much the same way that Durkheim analysed socio-economic inequality in his day, not as a problem of competition over 'salaries' but as the sign of a common experience of 'alarming moral misery (*alarmante misère morale*)'.[46] Durkheim was as concerned with the mobilisation of workers as he was with socialist doctrine, and he saw them as the embodiment of new collective representations that had emerged from the social relations of the modern age. The workers' movement was, in his view, a form of moral indignation at the collapse of old networks of solidarity. Its demands reflected the need to replace these old networks with modern social norms fully adapted to the complexity of modern society, a task undertaken by the diverse formulation of socialist reforms.[47] In the same way, we can see contemporary minority politics as the answer to the moral indignation created by social exclusion and ethnic discrimination, to which new social policies – such as anti-discrimination programmes – are the only adequate response.[48]

Spitz's account nonetheless remains reductive in that it never acknowledges the communitarian dimensions of Durkheim's republicanism. In opposition to the philosopher Mark Cladis – who sees in Durkheim's thought 'a communitarian defence of liberalism' – Spitz insists that 'Durkheim rejects . . . anything that might appear to resemble an embryonic communitarianism (*communautarisme*)'.[49] This argument rests on Durkheim's distance from his positivist contemporaries in the late nineteenth century who suggested that it might be necessary to reactivate collective consciousness in order to combat the nefarious effects of individualism. By contrast, as Spitz recalls, Durkheim was convinced of the morally positive nature of individualism and developed a theory of social integration based on this conviction. From the point of view of inter-cultural relations, the anti-communitarian interpretation of Durkheim's theory of solidarity implies that republican policies towards minorities should limit themselves to anti-discrimination measures that can liberate individuals from their respective communities. But this means that state support for minorities remains instrumental and provisional: there is no attempt to give identity-difference a positive value in society, merely an attempt to reduce discrimination on the grounds of identity. The main aim is to make difference visible and predictable so that it does not compromise equality of opportunity. Yet this strategy is still underpinned by a concept of equality that is blind to difference, insofar as it guarantees the same opportunities to all, regardless of their cultural specificity.

If we want to go further in elaborating an effective form of republican multiculturalism, we need to take into account the fundamentally communitarian nature of modern society. This requires an examination of an aspect of Durkheim's thought that Spitz neglects. We have already seen how the originality of Durkheim lies in his argument that the individualisation of modern society does not result in greater atomisation, but rather in the reconstruction of new forms of solidarity. In his reading, Spitz discusses organic solidarity and the resulting interdependence that is a consequence of the division of labour. But he minimises the importance of mechanical solidarity that continues to unite members of a modern society. Spitz recognises that there still exists 'a common belief in justice' but goes no further than Durkheim who, in *Division of Labour*, maintained that 'the religion of the individual' remained individualistic and had no significant potential for solidarity:

> If this religion is common to all, in that it is shared by the community, its object is individual. If it turns all minds towards the same end, this end is not social . . . It is from society that it derives its force, yet it does not attach us to society but to ourselves. As a result, it does not constitute a veritable social bond.[50]

Durkheim, however, returned to this question in later years alongside his growing interest in religion. In his work on suicide, and above all in the article he wrote during the Dreyfus Affair – 'L'individualisme et les intellectuels' (1898) – he reiterated the importance of the 'cult of the individual' as a way of preserving social bonds in modern society.[51] Durkheim subsequently referred not to 'religion', but to the 'cult of the individual', which allowed him to bring out the cultural and symbolic dimensions of moral individualism. As with all religions, individualism draws its authority, not only from a belief system, but also from the practices that unite believers around common rituals and symbols. These practices make it possible for individuals to recreate their sense of attachment to the community, which then expresses itself as an unconditional respect for all things sacred. This is the concept of 'social symbolism' that Durkheim developed at length in his *Elementary forms of religious life* (1912).[52]

The consequence of this argument is that mechanical solidarity, which corresponds in modern society to the sense of justice, can only operate within a specific culture. Or, to put it another way, the respect for man in the abstract presupposes the sharing of concrete and historically-situated symbols. As Cladis has shown, this sociological reformulation of republican patriotism lies at the heart of Durkheim's defence of those who supported Dreyfus (*dreyfusards*).[53] Where conservatives attacked the *dreyfusards* for putting individual rights above the nation (in this case, embodied in the French army), Durkheim responded that they were actually the true defenders of the nation:

> The individualist who defends the rights of the individual simultaneously defends the vital interests of society; for he prevents the criminal impoverishment of the last remaining reserve of ideas and collective sentiments that are the very soul of the nation.[54]

The key point here is that the *dreyfusard* ideal of justice is not simply an abstract ideal; it is derived from a historical reality, namely the political traditions inherited from the French Revolution. And, since the latter is a national political cult with its symbols, saints and martyrs, it provides a focal point for the renewal of civic solidarity.

If we take seriously this communitarian defence of individual rights, we can look at the issue of difference in a new way. Let us assume that civic solidarity is dependent on a certain cultural context and national symbolism; the question, then, is whether the symbols on which this solidarity is based are inclusive or exclusive. Seen this way, the repeated references by ethnic minorities to memory and historical injustice are not simply ways of 'distracting' attention away from socio-economic exclusion. On the contrary, they suggest that solidarity has two sides – mechanical and organic – which Durkheim refuses to separate. While it is certainly the case that individualism constitutes the foundation of differentiated solidarity, this does not negate the fact that citizens are morally bound together by a common belief in justice, which is coterminous with their membership of the nation. But, in the absence of a shared history – for instance, a shared history of immigration – this membership can only be partial. The historian Gérard Noiriel has demonstrated how, despite a long history of immigration in the nineteenth and twentieth centuries, there are very few traces of immigration in French national memory.[55] As a result, immigration has never been considered an integral part of national identity, even though it is a vital component of contemporary French society.[56] This symbolic exclusion explains why a good number of French citizens of foreign origin have struggled to find a 'legitimate' place in the economic, social and cultural life of their own country.[57]

A republican defence of minorities cannot, then, be limited to the principle of non-discrimination alone. It also requires a positive recognition of ethno-cultural difference, with a view to pluralising national cultures and acknowledging the diversity of the civic community. This form of pluralism still remains within a republican logic since it emphasises political freedom and maintains that the rights of the individual are inseparable from membership of a political community and its networks of solidarity. It nevertheless allows us to work towards 'an intersubjective understanding of citizenship', as well as recognise existing processes of social exclusion. In the words of the political theorist Cécile Laborde:

> one may enjoy the formal rights of citizenship and yet, by virtue of one's perceived or assigned cultural or religious identity, be arbitrarily excluded from the imaginary construction of the *patrie*. Thus, in a republican view, people's civic standing can be affected by discursive constructions of collective identity. They can be denied citizenship by being denied symbolic membership in the nation.[58]

The benefit of reading Durkheim alongside a neo-republican ideal of non-domination is that it allows us to bring together the fight against discrimination and a radical revision of the concept of national identity. This, again, highlights the limitations of the critique of multiculturalism by the *gauche populaire*. Multicultural policies do not undermine the nation and neglect the interests of the working classes; rather, they make it possible to redefine the contours of the national imaginary so that all citizens, regardless of their origins, can belong to and participate in the nation.

Great thinkers are those whose work resists easy interpretation. In this chapter, I have evaluated three different readings of Durkheim's theory of social solidarity. I have tried to show how the theoretical insights of one of the founding fathers of French republicanism can be used to prevent republicanism from becoming a dogmatic and exclusive form of state communitarianism. In the first instance, the concept of organic solidarity, understood as non-domination, suggests that political claims by ethnic minorities do not represent a regression back to mechanical solidarity, but a legitimate pattern of mobilisation in modern society, motivated by nothing more than a desire for justice. But we must also accept that the latter is deeply anchored in a nationally-determined 'cult of the individual'. This cult needs to be enriched by the cultural diversity of the community of citizens: this is the only way we can ensure that it does not become exclusive and discriminatory. Reconsidering Durkheim in the light of neo-republican theories thus allows us to capture more precisely the intimate connections between freedom as non-domination, civic equality and collective identity. In so doing, we can see that French republicanism, far from being intrinsically hostile to multiculturalism, has the potential to take seriously both the community of citizens and competing minority claims.

Notes

1 Jeremy Jennings, 'Citizenship, republicanism and multiculturalism in France', *British Journal of Political Science* 30, 4 (2000): 589.

2 The term minority refers to a wide variety of groups (women, disabled persons, lesbians, gays, transexuals, bisexuals etc.), as well as racial, ethnic, religious or linguistic minorities. In this chapter, I focus my attention primarily on ethnic minorities, even if I have chosen to retain the term 'minority' in order not to exclude other forms of difference.

3 Iris Marion Young, *Justice and the Politics of Difference* (Princeton, NJ: Princeton University Press, 1990); Amy Gutman, ed., *Multiculturalism: Examining the politics of recognition* (Princeton, NJ: Princeton University Press, 1994); Will Kymlicka, *Multicultural Citizenship: A liberal theory of minority rights* (Oxford: Oxford University Press, 1995); Bhikhu Parekh, *Rethinking Multiculturalism: cultural diversity and political theory* (London: Harvard University Press, 2002).

4 The Multiculturalism Policy Index (http://www.queensu.ca/mcp) places France near the bottom of the list of those countries that have adopted multicultural policies. See also Pierre-André Taguieff, *La République enlisée. Pluralisme, communautarisme et citoyenneté* (Paris: Éditions des Syrtes, 2005).

5 Cécile Laborde, *Critical Republicanism: The hijab controversy and political philosophy* (Oxford: Oxford University Press, 2008), 187–92.

6 The term 'official republicans' does not refer to a specific group or school of thought. Rather, it is used by the political theorist Cécile Laborde to describe a specifically French political philosophy of republicanism which is the subject of her book *Critical Republicanism*, see Note 5.

7 Laurent Baumel and François Kalfon, eds., *Plaidoyer pour une gauche populaire: La Gauche face à ses électeurs* (Paris: Éditions Le bord de l'eau, 2011). It includes contributions by Laurent Bouvet, Christophe Guilluy, Rémi Lefebvre, Alain Mergier, Camille Peugny.

8 Laurent Bouvet, 'Le sens du peuple', *Le Débat* 2, 164 (2011): 136–43.

9 Bouvet, 'Le sens du peuple', see Note 89, 139.

10 On this point, the critique of the *gauche populaire* is in accordance with the argument in Walter Benn Michaels, *The Trouble with Diversity: how we learned to love identity and ignore inequality* (New York: Henry Holt and Company, 2006).

11 Christophe Guilluy, *Fractures françaises: Pour une nouvelle géographie sociale* (Paris: François Bourin Editeur, 2010).

12 Yael Tamir, *Liberal Nationalism: Studies in moral, political and legal philosophy* (Princeton, NJ: Princeton University Press, 1995).

13 Peter Balint and Sophie Guérard de Latour, eds., *Liberal Multiculturalism and the Fair Terms of Integration* (Basingstoke: Palgrave, 2013).

14 Jean-Fabien Spitz, *Le Moment républicain en France* (Paris: Gallimard, 2005); Laborde, *Critical Republicanism*, see Note 5.

15 Emile Durkheim, 'Détermination du fait moral', in Emile Durkheim, *Sociologie et philosophie* (Paris: Presses universitaires de France, 2004).

16 For the historian Claude Nicolet, Emile Durkheim 'is one of the rare – perhaps the only – thinker to have elaborated a science of and for the Republic' (Claude Nicolet, *L'Idée républicaine en France (1789–1924)* (Paris: Gallimard, 1982), 312). The normative dimensions of Durkheim's sociology explain its recent rehabilitation in the fields of political and moral philosophy. See for instance Mark Cladis, *A Communitarian Defense of Liberalism. Emile Durkheim and contemporary social theory* (Stanford, CA: Stanford University Press, 1992); Will Watts Miller, *Durkheim, Morals and Modernity* (London: UCL Press Ltd., 1996).

17 See Montesquieu, *De l'Esprit des Lois*, XII, 2 (Paris: Garnier-Flammarion, 1979), 328; and Philip Pettit, 'Civility and trust' in Philip Pettit, *Republicanism: A theory of freedom and government* (Oxford: Oxford University Press, 1997), 261–70.

18 'If we cherish our own citizenship and our own freedom, we have to cherish at the same time the social body in the membership of which that status consists' (Pettit, *Republicanism*, see Note 17, 260). See also Maurizio Viroli, *For the Love of Country: An essay on patriotism and nationalism* (Oxford: Oxford University Press, 1995).

19 Sophie Guérard de Latour, 'Reworking the neo-republican sense of belonging', *Diacrítica* 24, 2 (2010): 85–105.

20 Will Kymlicka, 'Human rights and ethnocultural justice', in *Politics in the Vernacular* (Oxford: Oxford University Press, 2001), Ch. 4.

21 Dominique Schnapper, *La communauté des citoyens: Sur l'idée moderne de nation* (Paris: Gallimard, 1994); *La relation à l'autre. Au cœur de la pensée sociologique* (Paris: Gallimard, 1998).

22 Schnapper, *La relation à l'autre*, see Note 21, 445.

23 Schnapper, *La relation à l'autre*, see Note 21, 445.

24 Emile Durkheim, *De la division du travail social* (Paris: Presses universitaires de France, 1998).

25 Schnapper, *La relation à l'autre*, see Note 21, 388.

26 Emile Durkheim, *Leçons de sociologie* (Paris: Presses universitaires de France, 2003), 89.

27 Schnapper summarises Durkheim's position in Schnapper, *La relation à l'autre*, see Note 21, 445.

28 Schnapper, *La relation à l'autre*, see Note 21,449.

29 Schnapper, *La communauté des citoyens*, see Note 21, 140.

30 Schnapper, *La relation à l'autre*, see Note 21, 398.

31 Dominique Schnapper, 'La République face aux communautarismes', *Études*, 2 (February 2004): 184.

32 Schnapper, 'La République face aux communautarismes', see Note 31, 184.

33 Schnapper, 'La République face aux communautarismes', see Note 31, 188.

34 Dominique Schnapper, *La démocratie providentielle: Essai sur l'égalité contemporaine* (Paris: Gallimard, 2002).

35 Schnapper, *La relation à l'autre*, see Note 21, 492.

36 Alain Renaut and Sylvie Mesure, *Alter ego. Les paradoxes de l'identité démocratique* (Paris: Aubier, 1999), 162.

37 Spitz, *Le moment républicain*, see Note 14, 265–6.

38 Durkheim, *De la division*, see Note 24, 147.

39 Spitz, *Le moment républicain*, see Note 14, 297.

40 Durkheim, *De la division*, see Note 24, 370.

41 Pettit, *Republicanism*, see Note 17, 122.

42 Spitz, *Le moment républicain*, see Note 14, 283.

43 Spitz, *Le moment républicain*, see Note 14, 284–5.

44 Pettit, *Republicanism*, see Note 17, 125. See also 'freedom as non-domination . . . is a common good to the extent that no member of a vulnerable group – no woman or black and, ultimately, no member of the society as a whole – can hope to achieve it fully for themselves without its being achieved for all members: no member can hope to achieve it fully for themselves except so far as membership of the group ceases to be a badge of vulnerability' (Pettit, *Republicanism*, see Note 17, 259).

45 Pettit, *Republicanism*, see Note 17, 125.

46 Emile Durkheim, *Le suicide* (Paris: Presses universitaires de France, 1995), 445.

47 Emile Durkheim, 'Sur la définition du socialisme', in Emile Durkheim, *La science sociale et l'action* (Paris: Presses universitaires de France, 1987), 226–35.

48 Sophie Guérard de Latour, *Vers la république des différences* (Toulouse: Presses universitaires du Mirail, 2009), Ch. 3.

49 Spitz, *Le moment républicain*, see Note 14, 241.

50 Durkheim, *De la division*, see Note 24, 147.

51 Emile Durkheim, 'L'individualisme et les intellectuels' in Durkheim, *La Science sociale et l'action*.

52 Emile Durkheim, *Les formes élémentaires de la vie religieuse* (Paris: Presses universitaires de France, 2003), 330.

53 Cladis, *A Communitarian Defense of Liberalism*, see Note 16, 24, 61.

54 Durkheim, 'L'individualisme et les intellectuels', see Note 51, 274.

55 As Noiriel points out, one way of preserving the memory of migration might
    have been to transform the selection centre in Toul that recruited the majority
    of migrants in inter-war France into a museum celebrating the contribution of
    European migrants to the construction of the French nation (rather like Ellis
    Island in New York). Instead, the building has been destroyed.

56 Gérard Noiriel, *Le creuset français. Histoire de l'immigration XIX–XXe siècles*
    (Paris: Seuil, 1988).

57 Gérard Noiriel, *État, nation et immigration. Vers une histoire du pouvoir* (Paris:
    Belin, 2001), 11.

58 Laborde, *Critical Republicanism*, see Note 5, 247.

Conclusion

France – The Eternal Crisis?

Sudhir Hazareesingh

It is almost three years since the election of François Hollande to the presidency and, as if to confirm the uncertainty theme that has run through this book, France now seems less confident than ever about its sense of direction. The new president's ambition to change the terms of European policy-making by pushing for a more growth-oriented and socially progressive agenda have faltered in the face of German opposition, thereby quashing the (fanciful) dream of renewed French leadership in Europe. And domestic disenchantment has rapidly set in as Hollande's approval ratings fell dramatically within months of his installation at the Elysée, with the Ayrault administration's standing following suit. Even the slight fall in unemployment in September 2013 did little to revive French public confidence in its governing élites.

A weak executive is normally a boon for the opposition, but the centre-right UMP is in a parlous state after years of brutal infighting over Nicolas Sarkozy's succession. The toxic atmosphere on the right has been further poisoned by the Sisyphean question of how the UMP should position itself in relation to the Front National (FN). It is a problem to which there is no obvious solution: institutional cooperation is impossible, and neither outright rejection nor ideological collusion has proved effective in the past. Fortified by a general disaffection with national political élites, and riding on a wave of economic and cultural populism, the FN is the only political movement currently enjoying some momentum. Yet its xenophobic nationalism further underscores the extent to which French political culture has lost its bearings. Little wonder, then, that the country seems seized by a pervasive sense of gloom. A poll published in *Le Monde* in the summer of 2013, measuring public attitudes in major European countries (including Britain) showed that the French were the most pessimistic on all issues – from the state of their economy to national and European governance. An overwhelming majority believed that things would get worse in the coming years, both for themselves and for their country.

There is, of course, nothing particularly new about such collective feelings of despondency. The nightmare of decadence is deeply ingrained in the French psyche to such an extent that, in the famous Astérix stories, the Gauls fear only one thing: that the sky will fall on their heads. But such sentiments were historically kept in check by the optimistic intuition – shared by all the dominant political traditions of the modern era, from Revolutionaries, Bonapartists, and Republicans to Communists and Gaullists – that France was capable of the *grand sursaut* which would lead to regeneration. Such signs of hope are hard to come by in contemporary French political culture. In August 2013, a cover story in one of France's biggest-selling weekly magazines, *L'Express*, was entitled 'Le génie français: pourquoi il ne faut jamais désespérer de la France' but in the series of self-congratulatory articles about the nation's successes, there were no references to French intellectuals or political thinking. In a more serious vein, political commentators such as Pierre Rosanvallon have argued that the emergence of a 'negative democracy' in France may be evidence of a potentially creative trend: an evolution in which the State is confronted by an invigorated civil society, and where demands for wider institutional accountability are matched with greater civic mobilisations. In themselves, these movements may not be powerful enough to generate viable political and intellectual realignments, but (this is the glimmer of hope) they carry the potential for a move towards a more robust and participatory democracy. It is certainly true that political actors are now subjected to a greater degree of scrutiny than ever before, notably from judges, courts, and their own activists and voters. This process has been reinforced by the creation of a primary system of candidate selection, which has now been adopted by the main parties for the presidential elections, and has been extended to municipal contests in towns such as Paris and Marseille.

This forward movement is reflected in the issues and controversies examined in the different chapters of this book. There have been spirited and often captivating debates about the transcendence of the division between left and right, the meaning of republican citizenship in a post-colonial (and European) age, and the intellectual alternatives to Marxism, although no new syntheses have emerged which can attract a durable consensus. Thus, liberalism's precipitous and none-too-dignified retreat after the 2008 financial crisis was preceded by a moment in the sun in the late twentieth century; in the same vein, despite the failure of multiculturalism to make any significant headway in France, the Jacobin state has shown some willingness to devolve power to localities and regions, and even to recognise that regional languages belong to the nation's heritage. We have come a long way since the early twentieth century, when the great republican politician Emile Combes claimed that the Bretons would be part of the nation only when they spoke French. And while French *laïcité* has sometimes manifested itself in exclusive formulations, such as the veil and burqa bans, it has also shown itself in a more open and pragmatic light, notably with the construction of mosques and Islamic prayer rooms, and the *de facto* public recognition of Islam in the creation of the Conseil Français du Culte Musulman.

Yet there is a more pessimistic reading, namely that this French negativity reflects a political culture that has become increasingly inward-looking, defensive, and mired in petty quarrels and idealised representations of the past. It is no accident that mayors, the incarnations of the politics of parochialism, are the only elected figures whose image remains overwhelmingly positive in France. National political institutions have come to be seen as increasingly remote, not only because of their inability to deliver on major issues but because the system's central pivot (the presidency) tends to force political actors into polarising postures, even when they are known not to correspond to any ideological reality (at least with respect to the mainstream parties). There is, in this respect, a real contradiction between the left–right division maintained by the presidency and the electoral system, and the increasing social and intellectual homogeneity of the dominant political class, which is largely recruited from and trained in the country's technocratic *grandes écoles*. François Hollande's election in 2012 marked a return of this élite, which has dominated French politics since the Chirac presidency and has come to be known as the *énarchie* after France's most prestigious civil service training school, the École nationale d'administration (ENA). Seen in this light, French resistance to liberalism and multiculturalism can be read as manifestations of an anti-pluralist tradition, and of a collective imaginary that continues to be framed by such Jacobin ideals as the priority of the general interest, the illegitimacy of any ethnic or religious conception of the nation, an interpretation of equality as uniformity, and the potentially threatening nature of any movement operating outside the realm of the state.

Ideas in France are the products of political imagination and mythology, and it is in these contexts that the deadening weight of the past remains the heaviest. There is, for instance, more than a touch of nostalgia in the widespread attachment to a so-called 'republican model'. This frequently manifests itself in the celebration of the Third Republic as a golden age, the most recent example of which was Hollande's symbolic post-election homage to Jules Ferry, the father of the modern republican education system (the fact that Ferry was the champion of French colonial expansion was quietly glossed over). A backward-looking mentality also shines through in the cult of memory entertained by public authorities through the celebration of historical anniversaries, and rituals as the Journées du Patrimoine, which bring more than 12 million visitors to the country's heritage sites each year. Perhaps the most telling sign of nostalgia is the iconic status of Charles de Gaulle, widely revered as the incarnation of French heroism, the founding father, the unifier of the nation, the sage, and the saviour. Indeed, with the emptying of all ideological content from the mainstream right, this tradition of messianism has arguably become the defining feature of the UMP. Sarkozy's entire career, from his decisive leadership as Minister of the Interior to his 'hyperpresidency', was placed under the sign of conservative providentialism – notably in his strong attack on the values of May 68, equated with corruption and immoralism, and in his repeated attempts to trade on the fears and anxieties of the French people. Even when he campaigned for re-election in 2012, the incumbent repeatedly donned the mantle of the 'protector', arguing that his robust handling of the Euro crisis had averted a national catastrophe. Since his defeat and withdrawal from front-line politics, Sarkozy has continued to hint at a possible return to save the nation (and his party) from disaster.

In the case of the Front National, the resort to negative mythology is even more pervasive. Despite claims that she has 'normalised' her party since taking over its leadership from her father, Marine Le Pen's imagery remains wedded to the traditional demonology of French conservative nationalism. Hence the barrage of conspiracy theories about the alienation of French national interests by technocrats, bankers, and European federalists, and the warnings of the dispossession of the nation by immigrants, Islamists, and Gulf sheiks. Amid this cacophony, what has become of the left? Even though the mainstream parties of the left have quietly buried the revolutionaries' ambition of creating a new type of social order, their instincts remain rooted in the negative myths of the progressive tradition, notably anti-capitalism and hostility to the market. Hence, the important contribution of the left to the victory of the 'no' camp in the 2005 referendum on the European constitution and Jean-Luc Mélenchon's populist denunciation of financial oligarchies during the 2012 presidential election. It is a measure of the negativity sweeping across the left that the most popular Socialist in the first two years of the Hollande administration was the hard-line Interior Minister Manuel Valls, whose profile bears a troubling resemblance to that of Nicolas Sarkozy – right down to the stigmatisation of the Roma community. At times like these – and with the recent elevation of Valls to Prime Minister – Marx's famous observation comes to mind: when history repeats itself, it is first as a tragedy, then as a farce.

INDEX